Greek Folktales and Psychoanalysis

Greek Folktales and Psychoanalysis presents a dialogue between psychoanalysis and folktales from the Greek oral tradition, many of which have never before been published in English.

Each folktale or group of related tales is presented in full, followed by an analytic text that explores the central themes. The wealth of tales includes versions of oral stories that have been passed down through generations and that will provide professionals in the psychoanalytic field with a vast, unexpected panoply of strong images and metaphors on which to draw in their clinical work.

Greek Folktales and Psychoanalysis will be of great interest to psychoanalysts in practice and in training. It will also be relevant reading for academics and students of psychoanalytic literary criticism, folklore and oral tradition, Greek history and culture, mythology and anthropology.

Anna Angelopoulos is a psychoanalyst and anthropologist based in Paris, France. She has worked on and continues to oversee the *Catalogue of Magic Greek Folktales*, and she conducts a seminar entitled The Folktale and Psychoanalysis in collaboration with Sylvette Gendre-Dusuzeau. Anna Angelopoulos is a member of the Fédération des Ateliers de Psychanalyse and was its president from 2010 to 2014.

"This book follows the road of oral folktales and their enigmas to take us back to the dawn of humanity. Dreams, stories, descriptions of analyses are interwoven to convey the substance of life, while enigmas introduce alternatives and metamorphoses. But interpreters in quest of meaning are needed to decipher these enigmas without fear, at the 'crossroads in the labyrinth' where we might meet the minotaur, if we have lost Ariadne's thread, offered us by the authors of the book. The metamorphoses we speak of sometimes spark jubilation and prompt a paradoxical insight into the encrypted truth of the patient, who until then had lost his way in his own life."

Patrick Chemla, *Psychiatrist, Psychoanalyst,*
Bezannes, France

"This remarkable work reminds us of the fundamental ties between folktales and psychoanalysis; its chapters re-examine one by one the great concerns of human life: love, death, envy, rivalry, power and failure. The work draws on folktales derived from famous myths, to help us understand the paradoxical and contradictory objectives of human beings, by placing human nature in an easy-to-understand psychopathological perspective. This is not just one more book of psychoanalytic theory applied to folktales, but an essential *vade mecum* inviting each of us to live, to love and to die accompanied by echoes of oral tales as ancient as human existence on Earth. The book reinstates dialogue in its role as a means of creating cohesion, pulling us back from the edge of a possible chasm of barbarity."

Pierre Delion, *Child Psychiatrist and*
Psychoanalyst, Lille, France

Greek Folktales and Psychoanalysis

A Dialogue

Anna Angelopoulos

With contributions by
Sylvette Gendre-Dusuzeau

Translated by Agnès Jacob

Routledge
Taylor & Francis Group
LONDON AND NEW YORK

Designed cover image: Cover image from Paramythokores by Anna
Angelopoulos. Copyright Hestia Publishers and Alecos LEVIDIS.

First English edition published 2025
by Routledge
4 Park Square, Milton Park, Abingdon, Oxon, OX14 4RN

and by Routledge
605 Third Avenue, New York, NY 10158

*Routledge is an imprint of the Taylor & Francis Group, an informa
business*

First French edition published by Éditions Corti
Contes de la nuit grecque, Anna Angelopoulos (sélection)
© Éditions Corti, 2013

Library of Congress Cataloging-in-Publication Data
Names: Angelopoulos, Anna, author.
Title: Greek folktales and psychoanalysis : a dialogue /
    Anna Angelopoulos ; with contributions by Sylvette
    Gendre-Dusuzeau ; translated by Agnes Jacob.
Other titles: Contes de la nuit grecque. English
Description: New York, NY : Routledge, 2025. | Includes
    bibliographical references and index.
Identifiers: LCCN 2024032608 (print) | LCCN 2024032609 (ebook) |
    ISBN 9781032674216 (hardback) | ISBN 9781032674179 (paperback) |
    ISBN 9781032674230 (ebook)
Subjects: LCSH: Tales—Greece—History and criticism. | Folklore—
    Greece. | Psychoanalysis and literature.
Classification: LCC GR170 .A54613 2025 (print) | LCC GR170 (ebook) |
    DDC 398.201/9—dc23/eng/20240913
LC record available at https://lccn.loc.gov/2024032608
LC ebook record available at https://lccn.loc.gov/2024032609

ISBN: 978-1-032-67421-6 (hbk)
ISBN: 978-1-032-67417-9 (pbk)
ISBN: 978-1-032-67423-0 (ebk)

DOI: 10.4324/9781032674230

Typeset in Times New Roman
by Apex CoVantage, LLC

Contents

Acknowledgements

We would like to express our warmest thanks to all participants and speakers in The Folktale and Psychoanalysis seminar, whose faithful presence – despite the necessary travel in some cases – sustained our passionate debates, and whose invitations to their own seminars have stimulated our reflection over the years, in the spirit of friendship. We also thank the founders of the Fédération des Ateliers de Psychanalyse, who accompanied us in the early stages of the seminar. Special thanks to our friends at the Artaud Centre in Reims and at La Criée, patients and colleagues in the GEM group (Groupe d'entraide mutuelle), as well as to Éditions D'Une who published the story *The Normal Man*, and Hestia Publishers in Athens, who published *Paramythokores* by Anna Angelopoulos in 1991, and is granting us use of the mythical bird image created by Alecos Levidis for the cover of the present book. We are grateful to our Greek friends and colleagues, especially those who contributed, year after year, to creating and expanding the *Catalogue du Conte Grec.* Last but not least, our thanks go to our patients, our friends, and our families.

Abbreviations

AT   A. Aarne and S. Thompson, 1961. *The Types of Folktales: A Classification and Bibliography*, 2nd edition, revised, FF Communications, No. 184. Academia Scientiarum Fennica.

ATU   H. J. Uther, 2004. *The Types of International Folktales*, 3 volumes, FF Communications, Nos. 284–285–286. Academia Scientiarum Fennica.

CGMF   G. A. Megas, A. Angelopoulos, A. Brouskou, M. Kaplanoglou and E. Katrinaki, 2012. *Catalogue of Greek Magic Folktales*, FF Communications, No. 303. Academia Scientiarum Fennica.

CPF   P. Delarue and M. L. Tenèze, 2002. *Le conte populaire français*. Maisonneuve & Larose, 4 volumes: 1957, 1976, 1985 and 2000.

FS   Folklore Studies, Hellenic Folklore Research Centre, Academy of Athens.

GFT   Jacob and Wilhelm Grimm, *Grimm's Fairy Tales*, Calla Editions, 2010.

KEEL   Kentro Erevnis tis Ellinikis Laographias tis Akadimias Athinon [Folklore Archive of the Hellenic Folklore Research Centre, Academy of Athens].

SE   S. Freud, *The Standard Edition of the Complete Psychological Works of Sigmund Freud*, Hogarth, 1953–1974.

SM   *Syllogi Mathiton* (Collected from schoolchildren, archived at the KEEL).

Foreword

A. Angelopoulos and S. Gendre-Dusuzeau

This book is the outcome of a research seminar entitled The Folktale and Psychoanalysis conducted by two psychoanalysts in Paris since 2006. At first, the seminar focused on researching Greek oral literature, particularly mythical tales contained in a number of previously unknown ethnographic archives compiled between 1881 and 2002. They were the subject of various anthropological studies, and generated several published works in Greek and in French. As the seminar developed, it turned its attention to the use of these materials as a source of psychoanalytic reflection, both at the clinical and the theoretical level.

The questions examined give the English-speaking reader the opportunity to become acquainted with a great wealth of unknown mythical material, and with about 30 transcribed folktales, each one followed by an analysis of the latent content presented in its images. These stories illustrate fully the folktale's recognised attributes when it comes to entertaining, fabulating, consoling and healing.

The book also discusses the correspondences between oral folktales and certain events in our psychoanalytic practice that resonate with them. But how did this connection between the folktale and psychoanalysis come about?

The oral folktale, most often called folkloric, differs greatly from the fairy tales written by great literary figures such as Charles Perrault or Madame d'Aulnoy in the seventeenth century. The oral folktale has been transmitted by word of mouth since time immemorial. This universally accepted fact refers back to the origins of speech and language, if we accept that human beings "told their story" as soon as they acquired language. The oral folktale is endlessly re-created across generations, languages and countries, in a constant dialectic relation between the storyteller and their audience, who listen to them and incite them to reshape the stories to their liking. The oral folktale is a travelling companion and a go-between.

In the time-space of a psychoanalytic session, orality, or stories, are enacted differently. In the context of Freud's novel idea that two speaking beings who are together communicate through transference in search of the patient's unconscious desires, orality holds an essential place, although words are never enough.

Regarding psychoanalysis, let us note that it is the only field of knowledge whose practice is legitimately transmitted orally (that is, by undertaking a personal analysis) and that this oral transmission is unique in the Western world. One does not become a psychoanalyst through university learning or simply by reading books.

This is how, from one orality to another, at their boundaries, certain psychical events in the session can cause our thoughts as psychoanalysts to turn more specifically to the folktale, which stimulates the capacity for reverie in our listening.

In addition to orality, another shared aspect of folktales and psychoanalysis, but one with different implications, is "figurability", that is, metaphorical expression through symbols. In a psychoanalysis, dream images are the personal production of the dreamer. The articulation of their manifest content is what makes it possible to share them. The interpretation of their latent content only acquires its particular meaning in the transferential address to the psychoanalyst.

In the folktale, on the other hand, the images in the manifest narration of the hero's adventures are a collectively produced fiction. This fiction holds within it phantasmatic material relating to vital turning points in human life: birth, death, love – as well as important moments of transition and transformation.

Nevertheless, folktale images are a coded language carrying a latent meaning that is revealed in metaphors to each listener. Thus, this collective fiction speaks about that which cannot find words, the unspeakable, the unthinkable. It provides the deepest fears with a representation. This is what makes the collective story useful in therapeutic groups; the story acts like a shared dream, setting in motion the process of phantasmatisation, which creates psychic scenes to take the place of absent inscriptions.

The specific approach psychoanalysis takes to the psyche has always drawn on the rich sources of various forms of art. Since Freud, psychoanalysts have attested to this abundantly. The encounter with the oral folktale, which preserves the traces of the human voice since the dawn of prehistory, contributes to enrich the potential sphere of the listener's acceptance of himself and of the other.

Introduction

Anna Angelopoulos

And if I talk to you in tales and parables
it's because it's more gentle for you that way;
and horror really cannot be talked about
because it's alive,
because it's mute and goes on growing:
*   drips by day, drips in sleep,*
memory-wounding pain.[1]

> George Seferis, "Last Stop", October 5, 1944 (Translated by E. Keeley and P. Sherrard), *Collected Poems*, Princeton University Press, 1967

Stories of the Night

One summer night, an old woman who lived in the village stopped before the house of her neighbour, an ethnologist. She needed help to remember a tale from her childhood. She remembered that some small animals had to save a poisoned princess. But she had forgotten the rest. When she had been a child, people told stories, but "real stories which had something to say, not like the stories you hear today!". She remembered that on the night her mother died her father had gathered the twelve children at her bedside to watch over her together. They were filled with apprehension. Throughout the night, by the bedside of the dying woman, the father told them stories. Her mother left them at dawn.

The old woman understood the essential nature of tales. Since they had been part of her childhood and part of her family's life, she knew that they were travelling companions, ferrymen. She remembered that when facing the unimaginable – death –, her father had counted on stories to get him through. She testified to a situation where the figurability of the story opposed the unthinkable. The story acted as a metaphor to help pass the time – in this case, the final hours of a life –, and brought consolation.

For centuries, stories have been told at nightfall. It is when all the birds stop singing at the end of the day and settle on a tree branch to sleep that the voice of the storyteller rises. It is the evening hour when men and women come together. In the houses and barns of yore when nights were spent working, or during evening gatherings, stories were told to pass the time.

DOI: 10.4324/9781032674230-1

Reading stories to children at night is commonplace. Didn't Plato[2] say that myths only serve to entertain old nursemaids and put children to sleep? And yet something awakens us, rouses us from this apparent death. Stories ask us to believe this, when they portray sleeping beauties like Snow White or the Sleeping Beauty in the Wood, awakened from the curse of unending sleep by Love.

We are all familiar with the famous imaginary scene where the kiss of a Prince Charming brings the unconscious princess back to life; or the scene where Eros, the handsome god with golden curls, is awakened by Psyche, who sees him in the light of a candle. Folktales originating in the oral tradition provide images that are less well known but just as memorable.

They are recurrent and punctuate the narrative. And although the stories are made up of words, words are never enough for the storyteller or for the audience. To reach the heart of the story, one must follow the path shown by images and hear the voice of metaphors, which lead into the space of the latent content of the tale, where its psychical substance lies.

Is it not the case that the role of myths and stories has always been to reinvent, in a timeless sphere, a word-space we need to fall asleep, as well as to awaken, in this world or in some other imaginary world?

Why should folktales be told, translated and interpreted? And what is this human recollection transmitted by word of mouth, which lets us lie in the arms of Morpheus each night and awaken to Eros at dawn?

The stories for which we offer psychoanalytic interpretations in this volume are taken from the French collection entitled *Contes de la nuit grecque*, which contains 61 folktales translated from the Greek by Anna Angelopoulos, and are followed by ethnographic comments.

These stories originate in various folkloric sources (books, journals and archives), from several regions in Greece – where different dialects are spoken –, and from regions of Turkey where Greek was spoken at one time. The folktales were collected over more than a century, between 1881 and 2002. Material concerning these stories is dispersed and can be found in both public and private archives.[3] Some portions of these archives have been published in journals and books in Greece and in other countries.

Thus, the French collection reconstitutes, as it were, the history of the oral transmission of folktales from Greece, whose ancient myths have become a major founding element of European culture. Given this formidable competitor, stories from the oral tradition have difficulty emerging as objects of reflection and research. Compared to the ancient Greek myth, the folktale remains a minor genre, belonging to everyday life and considered part of paraliterature. And yet, it endures, it makes people dream, it consoles.

It is important to note that the Greek language has preserved a specific meaning for the word "myth" in the Ionian Islands, where the expression "to tell a myth", in the sense of "to tell a story", or even "to speak a word", is still in use.[4] "Myth", used to mean "word", was already present in Homer's texts.

While in modern Greek the word "myth" has come to refer to myth, story or word, "para-myth", which means story,[5] has remained more or less unchanged. It indicates a smaller myth next to a major one, a parallel myth, as well as an untrue tale. In everyday language, the word used for "story" also means "lie". It is noteworthy that the word "para-myth" contains the idea of consolation, "*paramythia*", which means consolation in classical Greek. This usage comes from academic texts, so that local storytellers were undoubtedly unaware of it. However, the idea that a story consoles is widespread and enduring.

Stories construct a narrative of the unthinkable and the indescribable, a function which is consoling in itself. The storyteller transmits the overt content of the tale through metaphor, with its store of unspeakable feelings and archaic phantasies emerging at times of crucial transition in human life, such as birth, death and encounters with love.

For instance, in his *Poetics*,[6] Aristotle speaks of the "voice of the shuttle".[7] He borrows this expression from a lost play by Sophocles, *Tereus*. It is the story of a young woman raped by her brother-in-law, King Tereus, and reduced to silence by having her tongue cut out. By moving the shuttle of her loom between warp and weft, the heroine weaves the images of her unspeakable tragedy. She sends the tapestry to her sister, who understands the violation the weaver suffered. This example can be seen as a metaphor showing what a story often hides at its roots – the dark and cut-out aspects of the human psyche, figuratively portrayed by the images employed in the story.

In Aristotle's time, every young girl was taught to weave and to spin, so they could provide for their own needs and those of the community; therefore, the loom could easily be used as a means of communication.

Moreover, the "voice of the shuttle" can also produce images in words – it can be a metaphor for the language of the story. Thus, the "voice of the shuttle" is a means of keeping memory alive, of preventing forgetting. It is also a metaphor for the unspeakable, used to reach a destroyed, ignored or lost memory. It functions like a poetic act emerging from under the words of the story.

Nocturnal Humanisation

Tales told at night are often love stories. Doesn't love transform people? Let us look at "Eros and Psyche". In one of its versions (Vryssivoulos), a young girl marries an animal that changes into a handsome young man every night. The representation of the transformed animal spouse can be seen as a metaphor for initiation to sexuality. The animal-husband alludes to a distant past when wild men belonged to two worlds at once. In his nocturnal form, the animal becomes a man in love. Thus, the humanisation of the hero takes place at night. He takes off his animal skin during the amorous encounter, and dons it again during the day, when he is seen in public. This theme constitutes a surprising inversion of the usual pattern of nocturnal metamorphoses found in wolf tales or stories about vampires, which set diurnal and nocturnal forces against each other, oppose man to animal, and the natural world to the supernatural.

It is at night that ghosts, goblins and vampires appear, and that Mr. Hyde takes possession of Dr. Jekyll. At dawn, the first rays of sunshine make the wild and supernatural side of these characters disappear. But in our story the image is reversed. The hero recovers his human form during the night and loses it during the day. Here, the focus is on the humanising role of love in human life. The hero of the story, who came into the world in animal form and has not known the socialising company of other children, meets another person in his adolescence. Initiation to love, through the secret of the night, leads to definitive abandonment of the animal skin, and to complete humanisation. Thus, this story is about human animality. Animality tends to bring to mind bestiality, and therefore extreme degradation. But in myths, the hero's animal form symbolises the state of every human at birth. The child-creature can be considered a psyche held captive in a maternal matrix, a child yet to be individualised and socialised; this psyche will emerge later, thanks to a love relationship. Caught up in phantasmatic incestuous relations, the young boy stays hidden in his first skin, with which he came into the world. Indeed, this was the curse that had been put on him: "You shall remain an earthworm, a serpent, except if a woman loves you as you are." This is also the ambivalent wish of the barren mother who desires a child without thinking of his future: "Let me have a child, even if it be a frog!" Here, the tiny human animal is the object of maternal hatred even before he is born. He can only achieve complete humanisation through the miracle of the love of a third person. The sexual initiation of the hero and the heroine takes place by way of the strangeness of human animality and of the magic of transformation, illustrated by the hero's alternating human and non-human form.

The prohibition to see her lover during the night could be a necessary first stage for the heroine of the story, in view of our knowledge of sexuality. Indeed, a certain amount of time must be allowed for physical contact before the young girl becomes used to seeing the beloved's body, without diminishing her feelings. Thus, in the story, Eros endows the lover with the strangeness of another species through the metaphor of the animal skin he takes off at night and dons again at dawn.

Greek Stories?

Stories change and are reshaped as they travel from one country to another. This raises the question of borrowing: the borrowing of particular motifs or of whole passages or episodes from other stories. Entirely separate stories are sometimes blended together or contaminate each other.

These changes bring about specific developments in various regional areas. This produces very different versions of "ordinary tales" as defined by international specialists: unique structures sometimes difficult to connect to the same plot or the same mythical pattern. In these versions, we encounter the very limits of the folktale type. Let us take "Tom Thumb", for instance. In certain versions found in Greece and Cyprus, he grows up and marries the princess or Little Red Riding

Hood, who is a boy in certain regions. We can see that the narrative space of the story, including its deepest meaning, can be entirely reshaped and even reinvented within the parameters of a single cultural zone.

The borrowing of themes, episodes or entire stories often takes place within a zone of shared popular tradition, in a space delineated by geographic or historical boundaries. We have the example of the Alps, a mountain range which has always acted as a barrier to the oral transmission of Oriental and Balkan tales. A geographic and historical boundary of regional collective memory, these mountains constitute the main cultural frontier of Western Europe. On the other side of the Alps, the folktale landscape changes: many Oriental mythical themes are reshaped and story sequences, and even entire stories, disappear.

In the introduction to his *Catalogue of French folktales, Le Conte populaire français*,[8] Paul Delarue confirms this barrier function of the Alps, saying:

> Indeed, it is quite surprising that a number of Mediterranean themes, widespread throughout Italy and the Iberian Peninsula, have not made their way into France, as if the Pyrenees and the Alps had barred their entrance (among these are themes well-known in Spain, Catalonia, Italy, Greece, Turkey, North Africa, such as "The Girl with the Pot of Basil", "The Sleeping Prince", "The Ghoulish Schoolmaster" and 20 others).

It is interesting to note that this collective amnesia most often applies to some particular regional motifs, motifs that serve to introduce the story, that have a mnemonic function in the narrative, so that their presence (or absence) changes the latent content of the tale or sheds a different light on the hero's origins. Let us look, for example, at the Greek Cinderella story, whose versions in the oral tradition explain how she became an orphan and why her stepmother mistreats her. The motifs of matricide and of the cannibalistic meal where the sisters eat their mother after a spinning contest are presented. Cinderella is then seen as being responsible for her fate, for being an orphan, since she set in motion the cycle of misfortunes that haunt her.

"Folktales merit the old, now discarded, name of mythical tales," says Vladimir Propp,[9] who considered that "a similar construction is displayed by a number of very ancient myths [. . .]. Evidently, this is the realm back to which the tale may be traced." Propp studied ancient societies whose religious beliefs have long since disappeared, and whose ancient myths have been discarded. He therefore concluded that what was left produced the folktale.

Our first impression is that the Greek folktale is, before all else, an Oriental tale in Europe. Many Greek tales are shared with neighbouring countries, Turkey and the Near East. They follow the narrative pattern of Oriental variants of folktales well known in the West. The study of Greek folktales reveals a surprising number of local variants, as well as the similarities of the Greek tales with Albanian, Bulgarian, Romanian, Serbian, Turkish, Sicilian and Maghrebi-Arabic tales (from Kabylia, for instance).

Today, we are seeing renewed interest in folktales everywhere in Europe. New storytellers have come on the scene, collections of popular stories are being published, studies are conducted, and tales are exchanged. The oral folktale is seen as a powerful traditional form with distant origins in time and in space, using Greek or another language to transmit its message.

As for elements originating in ancient Greek myths (motifs, episodes or entire narrative patterns), they exist but are covered over, inverted or barely suggested in the folktales of modern Greece. For centuries, pagan stories were repressed, prohibited and opposed by the Christian Church. Thus, Greek myths were subject to massive censure, which interrupted their transmission. They survived thanks to the subterfuge of being transformed into seemingly inoffensive narratives such as folktales serving to pass the time. To recognise in these tales the mythical themes of Antiquity, one must decipher them, because they often appear inverted "in the mirror of the fairytale", to use Nicole Belmont's poetic expression.[10]

As an example, let us look at the story "Muskamber". This folktale belongs to a group of tales elaborated from the myth of Adonis, son of Myrrha, born of her incestuous relationship with her father, King Theias. During a period of nocturnal festivities, she crept into her father's bed for twelve nights. On the last night he uncovered her identity and wanted to kill her. To save her from paternal wrath, Zeus turned her into a myrrh tree. Adonis is the child born of the tree with the lovely fragrance. As for Muskamber, he is a young man made of fragrant spices by a young princess unable to find a husband to her liking. It is the king who brings his daughter the spices she needs to create the perfect mate. In some versions, she creates a child instead of a man.

It is easy to recognise the child of incest, conceived with the father in the imagination. The myth and the folktale appear to differ. Myrrha gives birth to a child in an actual incestuous situation, in shame. The princess in the story, on the other hand, actively fashions a husband/child – phantasmatically incestuous –, whose arrival is triumphantly hailed as a happy event. In the myth, the mother disappears after the birth, while the fairy-tale princess marries her creation, who is her son and her lover at once, only to lose him and be reunited with him in another world.

These two instances of magical birth – the baking of Muskamber by the princess, and the transformation of Adonis' mother Myrrha into a fragrant myrrh tree – show that the crucial attribute of the hero, his scent, has been carefully preserved in the oral tradition of the Eastern Mediterranean region. The name of the sacred perfume, myrrh – from Myrrha – has been replaced by musk-amber, the name of the artificial son Muskamber, which maintains a relation with rare and precious aromatic plants. The storyteller has been able to preserve Muskamber's major mythical qualities, masking his incestuous origins throughout the extraordinary story of his being brought into existence by a beautiful princess in search of love.

But as far as these circumstances are concerned, the storyteller repeatedly warns us against his own lies, saying: "But I wasn't there, and neither were you, to believe it", as we see at the end of "Muskamber", a variant on the fairy tale of the baked figure of a bridegroom brought to life. This closing formula illustrates a type of discourse that remains deliberately ambiguous about its deeper meaning, and that sometimes openly tells the listener lies: "Once upon a time there was – or, rather, there was not – a king [. . .]." In most cases, this opening formula is followed, as the narrative advances, by other interjections coming from the storyteller. They are intended to warn the listener of the false character of his narration. He must certainly not be believed, it must be clear that he is a liar, and the listener must attribute an enigmatic character to the story, especially given that the portion of truth in the story could threaten the religious or moral values of the audience.

Thus, the storyteller must be able to make use of the representations always present in myths, while concealing the irrational elements – the marvellous – that are contrary to the Christian morality of his listeners. His audience must not believe in the incestuous desires of young girls, in matriphagy, in the existence of gods of the Underworld, or in parental curses condemning adolescents to take animal shapes. The storyteller must skilfully handle a symbolic language most often impossible to decipher, and use all the means at their disposal to transmit a number of mythical themes preserved in the collective memory, in a concealed or inverted form.

In the folktales collected here, most often a single motif or sequence from a recognisable ancient myth has remained. For instance, we know that Cronos ate his children and that, when Zeus was born, Rhea made Cronos swallow a stone, to save her youngest child. In the story entitled "The Brothers and the Ogre", a version of the Greek folktale "Tom Thumb", the hero has to fight the ogre, a devouring paternal figure, and gives him a stone to swallow, to kill him:

> Thirteen was very crafty. He told the ogre: "I know that I can't get away and that you will eat me. So why go to all this trouble? Open your mouth and close your eyes and I will jump into your throat to satisfy you." The ogre did as he was told, and Thirteen threw a stone into his mouth. And that was the end of him.

Sometimes, mythical beings such as the Cyclopes reappear in folktales. The Cyclopes came on the scene as the first beings created at the Origin, sons of Uranus (the sky) and Gaea (the Earth). They were thrown into Tartarus, below Hades, by their father, who feared that they would dethrone him. At the third generation, Zeus freed the Cyclopes. To thank him, they made the thunderbolt and gave it to him together with sacred fire and lightening.

The Cyclopes and their sacred fire reappear in the folktale "Is It a Boy? Is It a Girl?". Here, the heroine, dressed in men's clothing, fought and won a war, because her father was too old to do battle. As a reward, she was given a princess to marry, but the marriage could not be consummated. Therefore, to be rid of such a useless son-in-law, the king sent him off to accomplish impossible tasks. The last of these consisted of stealing the sacred fire from the Cyclopes. The heroine was able to accomplish this task with the help of her mare. Seeing her return victorious, holding the fire in her hand, the Cyclopes put a curse on the thief: that she become a boy if she was a girl, and a girl if he was a boy. The story has a happy ending thanks to the introduction of this particularly rare mythical motif.

Isolated mythical motifs can also emerge in folktales. A tale called "The Promised Child", the story of a much-desired baby born from the leg of his father – pregnant unbeknownst to him –, brings to mind Dionysus' birth from the thigh of Zeus.

These unusual mythical motifs produce strong dreamlike images, undoubtedly shaped by collective secular oral transmission, but also by the individual imagination. Among them, we have the young spinner who eats cotton and whose mother turns into a cow; the son born of tears drunk from a glass; and Misokolakis, the infant who takes off his slippers before jumping into a boiling pot.

Folktales don't spare our feelings; cruelty and violence abound in them: stepmothers persecute young girls, fathers whose daughters refused to marry them kill their grandchildren in revenge, daughters and mothers fight each other to the death . . .

At the end of the story, the listener exposed to its violence feels relief, no doubt due to a cathartic effect. At the same time, this imaginary violence brings to mind the most archaic human instincts. The images in the story embody the phantasies representing these instincts in the subject's prehistory. For example, in the folktale belonging to ATU type 327C, "The ogress carries the child home in a sack", the tiny hero expresses an oral instinct frustration, illustrated in the story by the ogress's threat to eat him. Through this inversion, the hero manifests his own oral instinct.

The hatred seen in the maternal attitude when the child is sent into the forest where he will be lost or will die is a radical manner of expressing ambivalent feelings. In the folktale, the mother's desire for a child is often accompanied by hatred of the baby. In some stories, the unborn child or the baby is detested as much as he is desired. The archaic mother in Southern European folktales prays for a child at any cost, "were he to be a serpent or a frog". The human being born in animal form as a result of such a request carries a curse that can only be broken by love. Through various figures of hate turned into love, stories conceal and reveal the phantasies of primary mental states.

When we read these stories today, we still have the impression that at the end of a passage we might glimpse something that will provide the answer to a question, the key to an enigma, offered by the collective oral fiction of these craftsmen of the past to each individual listener. The folktale always brings the audience an unexpected and mysterious message to be deciphered across the centuries.

The Greek mythical tale is a rebellious child. Despite attempts to censure them, folktales have remained incorrigible children unwilling to abandon the search for their origins.

Notes

1 Aeschylus, *Agamemnon*, line 179: "while we sleep, slowly drips the painful memory"; μνησιπήμων πόνος: literally, "memory's pain".
2 Plato, *Theaetetus*, The Liberal Arts Press, 1955.

3 Hellenic Folklore Society, Hellenic Folklore Research Centre of the Academy of Athens; the Historical Dictionary of Modern Greek of the Academy of Athens; Centre for Asia Minor Studies, etc.

4 D. Loukatos, *Aetiological Tales of Modern Greek Proverbs*, Ermis, 1972.

5 *Paramythi*.

6 Aristotle, *Poetics*, Book XVI. This is the second of the four means of recognition (through an event, an incident in the plot – such as the work of the shuttle, in this case).

7 The voice of the shuttle: *Kerkidos phonè*.

8 P. Delarue, *Le conte populaire français*, PU MIDI, 2017.

9 V. Propp, *Morphology of the Folktale*, University of Texas Press, 1968, p. 100.

10 N. Belmont, "Orphée dans le miroir du conte merveilleux" (Orpheus through the Looking Glass of the Fairy Tale), *L'Homme*, 25 (93), 1985, pp. 59–82.

Chapter I

The Folktale as Therapeutic Tool, Narrative, Creation and Healing*

Folktales can constitute a therapeutic tool not only for patients, but for caregivers as well. We are going to look at what makes the folktale conducive to reverie, to playfulness, to thinking – in short, what makes it a therapeutic tool.

I shall start by asking a simple question: why the folktale instead of another form of discourse? Aside from the pleasure it gives us, how can it contribute to our therapeutic work? How does it bring us comfort in difficult moments? To answer these questions, we need to look at the oral folktale more closely.

One important fact has to be mentioned first: what most people call a "tale" is a literary, written story belonging to the scholarly tradition. It is a text set in writing and signed by an author like Perrault, Andersen or others.

By contrast, the oral tale is a collective creation transmitted by word of mouth since time immemorial. In communities and various other groups, these tales were told at nightfall, at gatherings where a collective task had to be accomplished: weaving, building, alcohol distillation . . . Stories were told to keep the participants awake, but also just for pleasure. Similarly, in military barracks and on ships, seafarers' stories helped to pass the time.

Ever since humans acquired speech, they have felt the need to relate their experiences, expressed through their dreams, their thoughts, their suffering.

The folktale is addressed to everyone and is always passed on orally in traditional societies. Its strength lies in the human experiences it reflects: birth, death, love, wealth, poverty, envy, rivalry, the apprenticeship of life, the mystery of origins.

The language of the folktale still has the familiar quality of oral tales, despite the influence of very widespread literary versions, like those written by the Brothers Grimm, Charles Perrault and Madame d'Aulnoy. The folktale was intended to be *told*, not read. Yet, in therapeutic workshops, we are in the habit of reading folktales, which sometimes limits the possibility of play between the internal reality of the subject and external reality. This play, which can be established between patients and therapists in a folktale workshop, is important because it creates a transitional space in which the tale is inscribed, a life-giving space.

---

* Presentation by Anna Angelopoulos at Nant Hospital, Switzerland: theoretical discussion followed by a workshop held June 6 and 7, 2019.

DOI: 10.4324/9781032674230-2

The folktale can act as a mediator in the psychic life of children in distress, as well as adults whose internal world lacks sufficient structure, and who have considerable difficulty with symbolisation. For them, the folktale can serve as a mediator, allowing them to replenish their imagination. Moreover, the folktale facilitates representability, guiding a child's disorganised experiences – hard for them to link up with their real objects – towards the enchanted universe of representation. It has been our experience that fundamental distress, caused by non-representation, can be thoroughly defeated by the art of storytelling.

The story provides the child with the possibility of thinking and dreaming about what is happening to them, and with images that answer their questions about their origins and their future. The folktale speaks not only to children in distress, but to all children, including the eternal child in the adult. We shall illustrate our discussion by giving clinical examples that could be useful to healthcare professionals working with storytelling in group settings, be they children, adults, or groups of geriatric patients.

The Folktale as Transitional Object

In a storytelling workshop, the oral folktale creates what Winnicott described as a "transitional space", an intermediary space between internal reality and an external reality perceived by two people. The folktale – play on words, play with meaning – is inscribed in this space, creating a form of "life-giving" play. From this point of view, the folktale can be considered an attempt to deal with anxieties inherent to the functioning of human thought.

As you well know, many psychotic children – not only those who are autistic – do not speak; speech is a problem for them. But in a storytelling workshop a narrative pact is made with the patients, and we have observed that sometimes this leads to an awakening. Some children who have difficulty speaking start to say a few words in the group – they want to participate.

We could say that children in therapy – like all of us – have a hidden story, a personal story they cannot or do not want to share with others. They carry an encapsulated internal object. If the person with this difficulty feels they can trust the therapists in the storytelling workshop, they will certainly come there to hear the stories or to create stories in the group.

Children find it easier to tell stories than to recount dreams, and they are very willing to be part of a storytelling group. There, they can phantasise, better still, phantasise together, among themselves, with the caregivers and sometimes with the parents.

You don't have to have suffered repeated trauma to be familiar with the "abhorrence of a vacuum". For instance, on Greek vases from the Geometric Period, the entire space is filled with decorative motifs surrounding mythical scenes; there is not a centimetre of empty space left. The history of art calls this phenomenon "*horror vacui*".

Sharing the folktale makes it possible to weave a whole world in images, a world that counteracts the void and the impasse in thinking. We might say that, in therapeutic groups, the folktale acts as the narrative of a common dream. Images lead to metaphors, and the metaphoric use of language opens onto another scene, a psychic scene at the place where an as yet unspoken trauma occurred. Through the intermediary of the metaphor, a depressed child can sometimes express the unspeakable.

Screen Memories

This raises a question for us. When we use the folktale in therapeutic workshops for children, are we not creating what Freud called screen memories? That is, childhood memories that are particularly clear and, at the same time, seem to have rather insignificant content. In *Psychopathology of Everyday Life*,[1] Freud asserts that some people replace their own childhood memories with the memory of their favourite stories. He adds that details and situations present in fairy tales are often found in dreams as well.

Unlike therapeutic work, storytelling, or drawing the content of a story and talking about it, makes symbolic grafting of screen memories possible; it makes it possible to graft what is unconscious, providing a psychic foundation. Rooting human existential questions in the structure of the oral folktale produces the same effect as rooting meaning and achieving symbolic fullness in storytelling workshops. Each tale asks an existential question that it answers precisely each time it is told, each time it is seen in a dream.

In storytelling workshops, fairy tales and dreams prove to have three points in common:

- the representability of images;
- the displacement of fears;
- secondary psychic elaboration used as a reconstructive narrative to transmit a comprehensible content to the audience.

Thus, the folktale can be considered a narrative rendering the most deeply buried fears representable.

Based on Freud's screen theory, a symbolic screen of *positive screen memories* can be created, to be used as a safeguard to prevent the sudden emergence of delusional behaviour. This has a healing effect on the psyche. Of course, psychotic children react differently to tales from the way that neurotic children do. They tend to take the content literally, not seeing it as a metaphor. This is why it is important to preserve the opening and closing formulas of the tales, which help psychotic children face their fears through play and through pretend games.

After an inevitable opening phrase such as "Here is a story. Let me tell it!", the story continues: "Once upon a time, when men and animals spoke the same language"; this leads into a space-time dimension from which it is not so easy to emerge. Finally, the tale ends with a closing formula such as: "They lived happily ever after" or "They lived well and we even better." This can be followed by interjections like: "*Snipp, snapp, snute*" (Norwegian). These rituals bring the story full circle, creating a closed world which cuts off the child's fears (greater in psychotic children, as we said).

To create this fictional space-time, a space is needed in the hospital (always the same space), as well as a schedule that never varies. This place must be easily accessible and easy to leave at the end of the storytelling activity. It is important for seriously disturbed children to be able to situate the scene of the fairy tale in concrete space-time.

Thus, without being therapy, the narration of the folktale performs the psychic function of reconstructing grounding, of grafting an unconscious element, creating psychic fabric, as well as bringing order to chaos. In order for collective symbolic points of reference to be passed down by mythical ancestors into the unconscious, a group practice is necessary: the use of the folktale is a collective task.

The group allows the children to experience thinking together and sharing something thanks to their collective involvement in the story, as well as to each one's particular contribution. The folktale only exerts its power in the sharing.

Interpreting the Therapeutic Tale

While I worked with patients in a day hospital in Reims, I reread the best-known folktale interpretations by psychiatrists and other health professionals. First, Bruno Bettelheim's *The Uses of Enchantment*,[2] a famous work translated into numerous languages. After being imprisoned in a Nazi concentration camp, Bettelheim wrote a study entitled "Individual and Mass Behavior in Extreme Situations".[3] To summarise his thinking, I would say that Bettelheim perceives and transmits the importance of representing horror and violence in the folktale, thus transforming them and bringing them into the light. He says: "The hero is an exceptional being who travels his solitary road and comes into his own by facing horror."

A great literary poet, intimately familiar with West Indian oral folktales, Patrick Chamoiseau,[4] who gave us the pleasure of coming to our seminar to speak, has written essays in which he discusses these questions of the unspeakable and the unthinkable, which the folktale has always made possible to apprehend. The context of these folktales is slave trade and slavery in Martinique. "The old storytellers spoke face to face with the night", he says, adding that "the night stood face to face with death".[5] These tales were called on to overpower the unspeakable; they were told during funeral vigils. The storyteller's task is to say: "Come over to the side of life! Become warriors of the imaginary!", Patrick Chamoiseau writes, drawing attention to the importance of the function of images that can be shared in extreme situations.

I have also recently reread the great Russian formalist thinker Vladimir Propp, the first to speak of the representation of lack and of departure as two functions of the fairy tale. At the age of 28, living in a totalitarian regime, Propp wrote an astonishing book, *Morphology of the Folk Tale*,[6] bringing order to all previous written accounts on the subject. He defined 31 functions of the fairy tale, among which "departure" and "lack" are absolutely indispensable. He declares from the start: "There is no fairy tale without a departure." The hero must set out on a quest, for he suffers from a lack. If he doesn't suffer from one, the storyteller must create a lack for him, to cause him to depart. Often, he will fall into an abyss, or into the bottomless pit of another realm, from which he will have to return alive. He will have to encounter symbolised death as an initiation rite. Without this, there can be no story, Propp maintains. It is interesting to note that Bettelheim and Propp completely agreed about the fundamental place of "lack", although they did not know each other's work. The lack in the fairy tale or folktale is obviously a *founding lack* – founding existence and creativity.

For instance, the fairy tale teaches us that human beings always have to come through the darkness of the night to reach daylight. Passing through death is the road to life, the way to become fully human, to be able to love others, to understand them. The hero of the tale goes through all possible forms of initiation: religious, ritualistic, traditional – to achieve inner maturity.

These elements of the folktale are what we use in therapeutic storytelling workshops. The patients who attend them in day hospitals need narratives that can repair the fundamental lack that causes the hero of the tale to depart for another world. Children always want him to return triumphant. This is what makes the folktale a means to fight depression and renders it a counterphobic object, as said earlier.

I have recently reread *Contes et divans* (*Folktales on the Couch*) by René Kaës,[7] which brings together texts on this subject by different psychoanalysts. Kaës himself contributes a text on the mediating function of the tale in psychic life.

Kaës considers the oral folktale to be *training for the imagination*, and uses it "to re-establish the conditions needed to overcome a psychic disruption or discontinuity". Fairy tales perform this remarkable function. Kaës speaks of their speech-bearing and *symptom-bearing function.* In his own words: "The important thing is . . . its position as an intermediary, specifically the fact that it moves between myth and phantasy, between cultural and psychic reality; the story provides the *transition, playing the role of a transitional object*, through successive overturnings of the forces at play in myth and phantasy."

In my view, to *entertain*, to *lie* and to *heal* are the three functions that endow the folktale with a great force of survival, which it transmits to us when we encounter it.

Of all forms of fiction, the tale is the closest to the content, the scenes and the unfolding of dreams, as well as to their intersubjective transmission. Hence, the tale should perhaps be seen as the waking dream of a sleeping collectivity, acting as the intermediary, through speech, between the individual body and the social body.

Géza Roheim, a psychoanalyst and anthropologist who was a contemporary Freud contemporary, was particularly interested in folktales. He is the author of an important work entitled *The Gates of the Dream*.[8] In it, he draws a parallel between the folktale and the dream – as others have done –, but he offers a different interpretation. He speaks of the "maternal well of sleep" and its central role in connecting sleep with the tale. When the child is about to slip all alone into sleep – brother of death – he asks to be rocked, consoled. He is afraid of separation, of falling into the bottomless abyss of the unknown. But we know that dreams are encountered in the same sphere. Here, the fairy tale and the lullaby both serve to allay fears. The author sees this as the junction between the dream and the tale, which are both woven on the edge of this well, as sleep draws near.

Roheim suggests that the first folktales were individual dreams, recounted and transmitted collectively, thus becoming a common good. Although their origins differ, the dream and the tale share the enigmatic images they draw from the same raw material of the psychic sphere. They are nocturnal creations.

As we can see, night plays a crucial role in the creation and transmission of the oral tale. In our work with patients in therapeutic workshops, we often use the motif of a passage through the night to reach daylight; this passage has never lost its effectiveness as a symbol.

When the folktale is connected with life, it acquires its full therapeutic value, finding both its concrete and latent meaning, as I had occasion to see, once again, when working with patients and caregivers as part of the GEM (*Groupe d'entrade mutuelle*) association[9] at the Artaud Centre, Reims Day Hospital.

A Collective Story: In Search of the Normal Man

Anna Angelopoulos

I was asked to work with a group of adult patients and caregivers to create a collective tale whose theme had already been chosen by the patients: "In Search of the Normal Man".[10] But let us go back to the beginning. I must admit that, to start with, I found it hard to go along with the notion of the "normal man", but I told myself that the GEM patients probably had a particular relation to what is called "normality". So we went ahead.

Overall, these meetings were happy occasions and I was accepted quickly. There were four caregivers: psychologists, educators and me. We worked in a free-flowing fashion, so that those who had been absent could join in at any stage when they returned. We trusted that the fiction-creating process would provide opportunities to step in. As was done during evenings of storytelling in traditional societies, where entering a fictional space was ritualistically designated by the use of opening and closing formulas, we first created a narrative space. In the beginning, we would spend time drinking tea and talking about this and that, avoiding the main subject almost entirely. Then someone would bring up the subject of the story. I stayed on the sidelines, doing no more than asking how we were going to write the story of the normal man. Interestingly, at one point all of us fell into the same routine. The first time, someone said: "Each of us could write a bit of the story if we all sit down at the table." After that, the same thing happened each time: after we talked for a while, someone led the way to the table and the writing continued. Of course, the agreement to create the story was flexible and depended on everyone's inner disposition. There were days when some people were not well enough to write.

There were times when we all wrote in silence; afterwards, each person read the passage they had written. A transferential link was gradually coming into being. We were surprised to find that our story fragments completed each other, resembled those of the others, and together created a meaning that was shared by us all. It was not difficult to put these fragments together into one common narrative.

After some experimentation, we had our first session of collective writing. A character had to be invented, preferably a man – the hero of the story –, although there was a slight attempt to create a heroine. The hero had to set off in search of the normal man. The patients all spoke at the same time, each one tried to impose his idea of the hero. "He kills himself because there is no normal man, he doesn't know where to look!" They all seemed to agree. I tried to apply the rules governing a folktale: "The hero cannot be killed from the start. It's not possible! He must be made to depart, that's all!" Busy focusing on Vladimir Propp's ideas,[11] I had over-looked the effects of psychosis. They answered at once: "All right, he leaves, the Earth opens up before him, swallows him up and that's the end of him!"

It was a slap in the face, I admit, but I had acted thoughtlessly. This unexpected, terrifying opening up of the Earth seemed to constitute an initial psychic event. But afterwards the patients romanticised this terrifying image to make it easier to bear (no doubt reacting to my horrified expression). The plot thickened, it acquired an opening sequence in which the hero, on his way to the casino, bought a newspaper called *The Normal Man*. Once inside the casino, the man threw the dice; it was then that the Earth split open and he was swallowed up.

Opening the Earth, Opening the Narrative

Thus, the Earth splits in two and we all find ourselves at the bottom of the abyss. How will we escape? Can we come up again? Can we find our way out? I am not the only one who worries. From that point on, ideas, images, colours and sounds are brought forth frantically by the group. There are about twelve of us working to build the story, with renewed fervour, completely forgetting the normal man. It was the least of our worries. It was then, when we had to find a solution, that someone invented the storeys. In the bowels of the Earth, there were storeys, so that one could go up and down stairs. These were parallel worlds with sliding windows. Some people fell accidentally, while others let themselves fall into the chasm. When faced with the horror of the void, we became creative, we invented a fictional device. Was this a way to resist being engulfed in the chasm of death?

This brilliant invention allowed each participant to choose one of the storeys as his own and write a personal narrative within the collective story: an episode taking place on his storey, which he could make up as he wished. Each person had his own storey, his own transitional space in the transition. One storey was soundless; on another, language had to be invented. In the end, we kept three stories. Here I must mention that several people dropped out during the ascent from the abyss. Only four or five patients wanted to go all the way to the end of the story. But we agreed in principle that if anyone wanted to come back, he or she could take a storey and continue his journey with the group.

The Mountain Goat, A Travelling Companion

At our next meeting, for the first time, someone introduced an animal into the narrative. It was a mountain goat – we were in the mountainous Vosges region. This endearing animal that everyone is fond of was to take us up, storey by storey, to the top. It would bring us back into the world. But first, we must make it appear; it can't always be seen, so the conditions that let it be visible must be created. When it approaches, Tyrolean music is heard. The goat speaks, as animals always do in fairy tales, and it shows the way towards daylight, that is, towards the lights of the casino, in most participants' opinion. Very soon, the goat became the mascot of the story, the travelling companion, the animal in the refrain of the song. But what song? Suddenly, we were talking about music, about singing, and the patients said they would like music to be played and sung in the story. Among us, there were musicians who promised to take care of this. The patients composed a song for each storey and a refrain of the normal man for everyone.

I reflected on folktales and their collective construction in the oral tradition. How is it done? For instance, every time the hero is thrown into a well, or falls in, he finds himself in the netherworld. And, believe it or not, every time an animal, such as a ram, appears, to lead him back to the light of day. But the patients don't know these traditional folktales. It seems that they invented this scenario unconsciously, since they are the ones who created the story in our group. They invented the animal needed for the passage based on unconscious transgenerational representations; they chose the mountain goat, introduced by a refrain of Tyrolian music.[12]

Next Session: The Hero

At that point, we all decided at long last to keep only one character for the journey in the bowels of the Earth. There would be only one hero, shared by all. A man or a woman? I did not comment. The next question was addressed to me directly: "Anna, would you rather have one hero or several?" I answered: "Whatever you want; I would prefer for the story to be about one hero at a time." And that is what we did. The next question concerned our identifications with the heroes of the story, as is the case with any fiction. Our tale about the normal man unfolded in a comprehensible way, no longer tucked away in the inner folds of the narrative. This hero was placed on three different storeys. The first was soundless and lacked language. The second was the storey of computers, where he was taken captive by the Master of Screens and had to regain his freedom. He succeeded, jumped down and landed on a horse on the third storey; this horse kept running and could never stop. But the hero tamed him and took care of him. Contrasting characters saying very different things were invented; they were entirely fictional, yet familiar.

Once again, it is as if our story was a traditional tale where the hero and his horse are one, the horse being the double of the hero. In our story, the hero tamed a wild horse and came to love him. We sung together during each of the hero's adventures to the tune of *J'ai rêvé d'un autre monde* (by the group Téléphone). I had the impression that on each invented storey a hidden personal story unfolded, one that was not shared with the rest of the group. My friends in the team of caregivers, who looked after these patients, confirmed my impression: "Yes, the scenario he made up for his storey is really his personal story." We were stuck in the obvious contradiction of constructing the tale, caught between sharing everything and not sharing anything about oneself.

Next Session: Dulcinea

Our work continued. We agreed that there would be encounters in the bowels of the Earth. We hesitated. I said: "With loved ones, and why not an encounter with love?" They hold up immediately the "fear of that kind of meeting". Again, I feel that I really lack intuition. I was unable to foresee the impossibility of romantic meetings in our communal fairy tale. The patients do not want them. No one really wants them. Instead, they propose that the hero be replaced in various ways: by the newspaper vendor at the casino, on the soundless storey, by the pixelated villain, or by an animal elsewhere. Finally, somebody says: "In the newspaper *The Normal Man*, there could be an article entitled 'Dulcinea' and the hero could read it. But he puts the paper in his pocket because he is in a hurry to leave with the mountain goat which soon appears . . ." So it was all settled . . . So much for amorous fiction! I had been told off soundly once again.

> *I Dreamed of a Normal Man*[13]
>
> Yes, I know it's very strange,
> Where could it have disappeared?
> I don't even see my feet,
> Now the Earth has split in two
> And I fall into the chasm,
> Yes, it had to happen to me,
> It was meant to be my fate.

We were finally seeing the light of day. The patients were saying: "The normal man doesn't exist, we can see that! The hero never meets him because he finally comes back to normal life, meaning that he doesn't care about these things anymore. Once he returns to the surface of the Earth, he forgets them completely and goes back to the casino to gamble. In the meantime, the goat eats the newspaper

The Normal Man that he had in his back pocket, and then disappears!" Our story ends with brass band music, the casino and the goat, which disappears. With it, we have travelled to the surface of the Earth and can now take our first steps.

To Create the Human

Once our hero has been freed, he goes up on the stage and addresses the public at the casino. For now, as one patient put it: "The hero has a public to speak to, other people, and he can say 'my fellow men'! He asks them: 'Have you seen the play *The Normal Man*? It's original! I'm here with you – the public – once again! I hope that the experience has been as enjoyable for you as it was for me. I bid you good night!'"

We have come to the end of the journey, we arrived at the human, just when the phantasy of the normal man disappears with the newspaper eaten by the goat. The normal man was but a dream.

To Conclude

What happened during this journey to the bowels of the Earth and back? I see it as a fictional rendition of the process of humanisation, as shown in the final scene where the hero faces his fellow men at the casino. The imaginary character of the "normal man", which was created and then vanished like a dream, made it possible to go through the persecutory reality of a breakdown, and gradually make room for creative imagination, in the warm and containing transferential context provided by the caregivers. The presence of an animal needing care, to whom one can speak, offers mutual support. It is essential for the creation of a fictional hero. To put the unbearable experience of the abyss into words became possible for those who carried on until the end with the construction of this radical artistic endeavour, made up of words and music. We all experienced the power of fiction, which took us beyond reality in the collective narrative which I had the opportunity to carry through successfully, producing an incredible story.[14]

Notes

1 S. Freud (1901), *Psychopathology of Everyday Life*, SE 6, Hogarth.
2 B. Bettelheim, *The Uses of Enchantment: The Meaning and Importance of Fairy Tales*, Vintage, 2010.
3 B. Bettelheim, "Individual and Mass Behavior in Extreme Situations", *The Journal of Abnormal and Social Psychology*, 38 (4), 417–452, 1943.
4 Of Chamoiseau's numerous works, let us mention the three most recent: *La matière de l'absence*, Paris: Seuil, 2016; *Le conteur, la nuit et le panier*, Seuil: 2021; *Le vent du nord dans les fougères glacées*, Seuil, 2022.
5 P. Chamoiseau, *La matière de l'absence*, Seuil, 2016.
6 V. Propp, *Morphology of the Folk Tale*, Martino Fine Books, 2015.
7 R. Kaës, *Contes et divans*, Dunod, 2022.
8 G. Roheim, *The Gates of the Dream*, International Universities Press, 1969.

9 GEMs: self-help groups created in 2005 in hospitals, following the reduction of hospital beds and of human resources allotted to healthcare. Each GEM (there are 600 in France) has association status (Law of 1901 regarding associations) and receives an annual operational grant from the ARS (Regional Health Association). GEMs help individuals with psychic or physical difficulties to be reintegrated in society through employment whenever possible. These self-help and self-managed groups base their functioning on the sharing of experiences related to illness.

10 The process of creating the tale "In Search of the Normal Man" was presented at the Study Days of the Fédération des Ateliers de Psychanalyse (January, 2018), under the title "Health and Life" then published in *Le Coq Héron*, 2018/3, No. 234, Erès, pp. 11–16. My thanks go to all those who made this project possible: Patrick Chemla, Laure Thiéron, Guillaume Allemany and Corinne Chemin, as well as all the patients in the GEM group who created the tale.

11 Propp considers, as mentioned earlier, that the hero's departure is a necessary condition for building a story.

12 The antelope belongs to the goat family, like the ram, who is a magical helper in folktales; the ram is well known in the Vosges region, and so in the vicinity of the Reims Day Hospital.

13 Lyrics composed to the tune of *J'ai rêvé d'un autre monde* (by the group Téléphone).

14 This story was published in a book: GEM La Locomotive, *À la recherche de l'homme normal*, Éditions D'une, 2021. The book includes the text and etchings produced by all the participants.

Chapter II

Feminine Rivalry

"Snow White" and "Cinderella" Stories

The story of Snow White explores various psychic aspects of the relation between mother and daughter in a context where the father is absent. It also portrays the mythical birth of a girl desired by her mother to be beautiful, "white as snow and red as blood". The mirror, or its equivalent, is the focal point of the rivalry between mother and daughter, where persecution and envy originate. The stories about sisters, which follow, depict this rivalry from a different angle. The Mediterranean versions of "Snow White" below will be followed by different versions of "Cinderella". These two fairy-tale types are closely related in that they share the motif of a heroine with jealous sisters.

LITTLE SNOW WHITE[1]

A king had a wife and she did not bear children. One day when his wife was sewing, the needle went into her hand, and the blood flowed. And she said, "Would that God had given me a daughter, and that she had cheeks like this!" A year later his wife gave birth to a daughter, and she had cheeks like blood.

The queen died, and the king took another wife. This wife had no liking for the daughter. One day she spoke to two executioners and ordered them to take her to a mountain, and then bring back her eyes. They led her away, and when they arrived there, they put her into a cave. And they were grieved to take out her eyes. They had a dog by them and they took out his eyes, and brought them to the king's wife.

This woman was wearing her fine clothes, was dressed beautifully and was gazing into the looking-glass. In the looking-glass she saw the girl, and did not believe that she had been killed.

The girl, when she had gone into the cave, had found seven plates there. And she ate from the smallest, and drank wine from the smallest cup, and went to sleep on the smallest bed. Late in the evening the seven men came, and they saw that their food was missing. When they went to bed, they

---

DOI: 10.4324/9781032674230-3

looked, and there was a girl asleep. They asked her: "Where did you come from?" and the girl told them. Afterwards they decided to take care of the girl, as if she were their mother.

The girl's stepmother was wearing her fine clothes, was dressed beautifully and was gazing into the looking-glass. Again, she did not believe the executioners had killed her.

One day she took belts and went off to sell them. She went to the cave and saw the girl at the window, and cried, "I sell belts." When the girl heard her, she bought a belt from her and put it on. When she put it on, she fainted. Late in the evening, when the young lads came home, they saw the girl in a faint. They gave her medicines with the intent that she should awaken.

Afterwards, the eldest brother saw that at her waist she was wearing a belt. When he took it off, the girl woke up. Afterwards they ordered her not to go out of the house.

The mother wears her fine clothes, is dressed beautifully and gazes into the looking-glass. Again, she sees the girl. And she does not believe that they have killed her. She takes rings, goes off, and is selling them. Again she goes to the cave. "I sell rings!" she cries. Again the girl buys a ring. She puts it on. Again she faints. Late in the evening the seven youths come. They look and find the door closed. They climb up the walls and see the girl in a swoon again. They look all around but don't find anyone. The youngest sees that on her hand she is wearing a ring. He takes off the ring and the girl wakes up. Afterwards they order her never to open the door, no matter who should come. When day came, the youths went off to work.

The mother wears her fine clothes, is dressed beautifully and gazes into the looking-glass. Again, she sees the girl. Afterwards she takes apples, smears them with poison, goes to sell them. Again, she goes to the cave." I sell apples!" she cries. When the girl sees her, she does not open the door. She lets down a string and takes an apple. When she eats it, it stays stuck in her throat. Late in the evening, when the seven youths came, they found the door locked again. When they opened it, they found the girl in a swoon. They searched up and down. They did not find anything. Afterwards they opened her mouth: "Let us see what is the matter," they said. They saw that she has a piece of apple in her throat. When they took it out, the girl woke up. They were afraid to leave the girl in the house by day. They took her to their work.

Then, a year afterwards the girl died. They put her into a golden box. This they kept in the place where they worked. One time a king's son saw it. He said to them: "I will buy it." And they sold it. When he had taken it home, he brought it into his room. He wanted to learn what was inside the box. He opened it and found the girl. She woke up. When he had seen her, he showed her to his father. Afterwards they were married and they invited the girl's father to the wedding.

Dimitrios Lazaru Exarakos

SNOW WHITE AND THE SUN

Once upon a time there lived three orphaned sisters. One day they decided to find out which one was the most beautiful. At the hour when the sun goes down, they went out on the terrace, stood side by side facing the Sun and asked him: "Sun, handsome Sun, which of us is the fairest?"

– The first is beautiful, the second too, but the youngest is the fairest of all three.

Hearing these words, the two older sisters were mortified. They went back into the house tormented by jealousy. The next day they donned all their finery and dressed the youngest sister, Myrsina,[2] in old, dirty rags. Once again, they asked the Sun: "Sun, handsome Sun, which of us is the fairest?"

– The first is beautiful, the second too, but the youngest is the fairest of all three, he replied again.

Hearing these words, the two older sisters were even more offended; unable to win the Sun's favour, they went to their room with a heavy heart. The third day they asked the question again, but the Sun's answer remained the same. Now, devoured by the fire of their jealousy, they planned to rid themselves of poor Myrsina.

– It has been many years since our mother died. We shall rise early tomorrow morning to go to the cemetery and rebury her. But we must prepare everything tonight because her tomb is high up in the mountains and we must leave at dawn.

Myrsina believed her sisters. The next day they all left to exhume their mother, taking with them a *prosforo* [round bread blessed by the priest] and a plateful of *kolyva* [boiled wheat with sugar and nuts]. They walked a long way and finally reached the forest. They stopped before a poplar. The eldest said: "This is where our mother is buried; give me the shovel so I can start to dig!"

– Oh, said the other sister, we forgot to bring the shovel! How are we going to dig? We have no spade, we have no pickaxe. What should we do?
– One of us has to go back to fetch the shovel, said the eldest.

– I am afraid, said the second sister.

– Me too, said Myrsina. The sight of a small bird soaring in the sky might make me faint.

– Well, then, Myrsina, you will stay here while we both go to get the spade, because neither one of us wants to go alone. You can watch the kolyva and the blessed bread while you wait for us.

– All right, but come back quickly because I am scared!

– Just the time it takes to get there and back.

And the two sisters left, laughing. Poor Myrsina waited for them until sunset. At nightfall, when she realised that she had been left alone on the mountain, she started to cry. She cried so much that the trees took pity on her. An oak tree told her: "Don't cry, fair maiden; just let your blessed bread roll down the hill. Where it stops, you can stop for the night. And don't be afraid!"

Myrsina tossed her round bread as far as she could and ran after it for a long time. The bread would stop for a moment, then continue to roll. She followed close behind until, she knew not how, she found herself in a ravine. There, she saw a little house; she went in. The house belonged to twelve brothers, the months of the year. During the day, they were away travelling the world; at night, they came home. When Myrsina happened upon their house, there was no one there.

She rolled up her sleeves, found a broom and cleaned the whole house. After that, she cooked a good meal. She set the table, tasted the food and hid in the attic in a safe place. Just then, the twelve months came home, went into the house and . . . what a surprise! They saw that everything was in order, the table was set, and the meal was ready! What could have happened? They cried out: "Who made us this gift? Let him show himself without fear. If it is a young man, he shall be our brother; if it is a young woman, she shall be our sister!" But no reply came. They sat down, dined and went to bed with their questions unanswered.

The next day they were gone early. Myrsina came out of hiding, swept the whole house and made a delicious *pita* [pie in puff pastry]. In the evening, she set the table and put out the dish she had prepared. She ate a small piece of *pita* and returned to her hiding place. Soon, the twelve months came home and saw that everything was ready again; they did not know what to think. "Who is making us this gift? Let him show himself! He has nothing to fear!" But Myrsina did not show herself. They sat down, ate their dinner and were ready to go to bed. That's when the youngest brother said: "Tomorrow I will not come with you. I will stay here and hide, to see who is taking such good care of us." The next day, they all rose and left the house, except the youngest, who stayed hidden behind the door.

Myrsina came down into the parlour to do her work as usual. The young-est brother grabbed her dress and said: "So it's you who makes us this gift! And you stay hidden from us? You have nothing to fear; you shall be our sis-ter. What you do for us is priceless." The young girl was reassured and told him how her sisters abandoned her and how she had come upon this house. After that, she did her work as usual. She cleaned, cooked and took care of everything, like the best of housekeepers.

In the evening, when the other brothers came home, they met Myrsina and were very pleased. They were eager to show their gratitude. They dined and went to bed. But the next day, when they came home, they brought her a pro-fusion of presents: golden earrings, sumptuous dresses with the colours of all the flowers in the fields and all the fish in the sea – beautiful, fairy-tale dresses. So Myrsina continued to live happily with the twelve months. But one day her two older sisters learned that she was living a wonderful life and became very envious. They decided to poison her. They baked a poisoned cake and set out on the journey to Myrsina's new home. They knocked on the door.

– Who is there?
– Your sisters whom you so quickly forgot!

Myrsina took them in her arms, deeply moved. "But where have you been, little sister? We came back to the cemetery with the shovel, but you were not there! We thought you might have gone off with a stranger. We are so happy to have found you!" They gave their sister the poisoned cake and left. But before tasting the cake, Myrsina gave a little piece to her dog and the poor animal died. Realising her sisters had wanted to kill her, she threw the cake into the fire.

Sometime later, the two older sisters learned that Myrsina was still alive and went to visit her with a poisoned ring. They knocked, but Myrsina didn't let them in. So they said: "Open the door, little sister, we have something to tell you. We brought you the ring that belonged to our mother, whom you barely knew because you were so young when she died, and you hardly remember her. Our mother asked on her deathbed that this ring be given to you, so we brought it for you."

Myrsina opened the window, took the ring, placed it on her finger and fell to the ground lifeless. That night, when the twelve months came home, they found Myrsina's inanimate body. They lamented, wept and wailed so loudly that their cries echoed through mountains and valleys. Three days later, they dressed her in magnificent garments and placed her in a golden chest that they kept with them in the house.

Soon afterwards, a prince was passing through the region. He saw the golden chest and admired it greatly. He asked the twelve months to sell it to him. At first, they refused; but when he repeated his request several times, they finally agreed to sell it to him, but warned him never to open it. The prince took the golden chest to his palace. A little later, he fell ill and almost died. He told his mother: "I am dying without knowing what is in this chest. Bring it to me, I want to open it. And I want everyone to leave this room!"

When he was alone, he opened the chest and saw Myrsina asleep, dressed in precious garments, so beautiful that even lifeless she looked like an angel! The prince was speechless. He noticed the ring she was wearing and thought: "Maybe the ring has a name engraved on it so I might find out who this poor creature is." When he removed the ring from her finger, Myrsina came to life at once. She started to speak: "Where am I? Who brought me here? This is not my home. Where are you, little brothers?"

The prince said: "I am your brother now. You are in the royal palace." He told her that he had bought the chest from the twelve months, that he had found her lifeless inside, and that she came to life as soon as he took off her ring. Myrsina remembered her sisters and said: "Ah, my King, this ring is bewitched and poisoned; you must throw it in the sea. It's the ring my sisters brought me; I fell down lifeless as soon as I put it on, and that is how you found me!"

The prince asked Myrsina to tell him her whole story. He was enraged and wanted to kill the nasty sisters, but the young girl stopped him. When he recovered from his illness, he married Myrsina and they lived happily together.

But the two sisters learned that Myrsina was alive and happy, living with the prince. Infuriated, plagued by jealousy, they went to the palace to poison her again. They told the guard: "We are Queen Myrsina's sisters; we want to see her, where is she?" – "I must first ask the king's permission", the guard answered, "no one can see the queen without his consent." He told the king that his wife's sisters were there. Without further ado, the king gave his soldiers the following orders: "Take both of them and do with them what you know how to do so well. For they are here to poison the queen."

So the guards took the two sisters away; I know not what they did with them. I only know that they were never seen or heard from again. And so, the royal couple reigned in peace and lived happily ever after. People everywhere still speak of Myrsina's great beauty and enormous kindness. One day, I too went to the palace and saw Queen Myrsina. When I was leaving, she gave me a handful of gold coins. On my way home, when I went by my friend Melachro's house, her dog attacked me. He chased me and I had to throw him the gold coins; I saw him run off with them.

If you hurry and bring Melachro's dog a round bread tomorrow at daybreak, maybe he will give you the gold coins.

Sources and comments

"Myrsina", KEEL 1268 (SM 98), Edessa, Macedonia.
CGMF 709: *Snow White* (*Chionati*).
ATU 709: *Snow White.*
GFT 53: *Little Snow-White.*

Myrsina is one of the names of Snow White in Greece; two others are Chionati
and Rodia). There are 188 versions of "Snow White" in Greece, with different variants. As we know, the German version of "Snow White" was
made famous by the Brothers Grimm (GFT I, No. 53), and then by Walt
Disney. This folktale belongs to the cycle of the persecuted princess. The
central theme of the stories in this cycle is feminine rivalry.

Alba and the Question of the Father

Sylvette Gendre-Dusuzeau

"Snow White" is not generally associated with the sun. The "Snow White" we
know best is the one portrayed by the Grimm brothers, or the one in Walt Disney's
movie, in which the mother, disguised as a wicked witch, has terrorised generations
of children.

In Grimm's fairy tale, Snow White is a little girl whose mother, the queen,
pricks her finger with her sewing needle when she is distracted by falling snow, and
wishes her child to be white as snow, red like drops of blood, with hair as black
as her ebony window frame. It would be a winter's child. When she is born, the
queen dies and the king remarries.

The story continues with the stepmother, usually described as "wicked", whose
terrible, murderous actions symbolise feelings of unconscious, hateful rivalry, jealousy and envy a mother may unknowingly harbour towards an adolescent daughter.
The story portrays the psychic separations at work in the ambivalent mother-daughter
relationship, producing the metamorphoses that will lead Snow White, when she
awakens, to her encounter with the prince.

For Snow White, the entire question of becoming a woman is concentrated
in the pivotal element of the story represented by the maternal mirror, a mirror
for two, an enchanted mirror reflecting side by side the season of ageing, for the
queen, and the threshold of adult life for Snow White. In other words, the mirror,
the unmerciful gaze of Time, clearly shows that the moment has come for each
of them to have her own mirror. To make this possible, the story leads us down
a perilous path of psychic transformations involving a whole range of affects,
representations, identifications and symbolisations associated with the advent of
adolescence.

"Snow White and the Sun" brings us into the universe of the oral folktale. The narration is no longer set down in writing, like the Grimm brothers' story. The folktale is a living form that changes with each telling, occasioning many variants whose common theme is feminine rivalry. Particularities appear at once: the snow is replaced by the sun, like in the African variants, for instance.[3] The strong link between mother and daughter is replaced by an equally ferocious link between sisters. In the story, three orphaned sisters ask the Sun which of them is the fairest.

Three times in a row he answers: "It is the youngest, Myrsina." Here, it is no longer the gaze in the mirror that gives rise to envy of beauty and youth, but rather the gaze of the Sun, an inevitable celestial presence. His judgement creates ferocious jealousy on the part of the two older sisters against the youngest, like the jealousy that might be sparked by a father who chooses a favourite among his children.

Just as the written tale reveals the jealous mother's unconscious hate-filled and sadistic impulses, the oral folktale portrays similar feelings between sisters. They are illustrated by the two older sisters who decide to get rid of the youngest by leaving her to her fate in the far-off cemetery where their mother is buried, after taking her there supposedly to exhume the mother's body, as is the custom in Greece three years after burial.

Later, when the sisters learn that the youngest is alive and living happily in a small house in the forest with the twelve months – who replace the Grimm brothers' dwarves –, madly jealous, they bring her a poisoned ring that causes her to fall down, lifeless, and be placed in a chest until the arrival of the prince. When her sisters hear about her wonderful life at the palace, their jealous rage sends them there at once to attack her again.

Envy and jealousy are destructive forces. They are often spoken of interchangeably, but they are in fact different from the standpoint of the psychical functioning underlying them, relative to archaic and primary elements. Jealousy describes someone's feelings towards another person, or several other persons, and involves the wish to be included in a sought-after relation. Envy, on the other hand, is related to "seeing" and its emergence affects internal objects. Folktales about feminine rivalry allow us to re-examine these two phenomena often encountered in psychoanalytic practice.

These questions surfaced in my practice with a young girl I shall call Alba, since her story resonates with the fairy tale. Early in our work, Alba spoke of a white apparition she had seen, and which remained an uncanny mystery for her. When she was about eleven years, at the garden gate, she saw a woman in a brilliant white wedding dress. She had called her sister, who saw the apparition as well; but their brother didn't see anything. Troubled, Alba wondered if it had been a hallucination or the Virgin Mary. What did I think? No, I didn't know, I told her; we would have to take the time to understand.

Later, this feminine apparition found its masculine equivalent in the form of a ghost who appeared in one of Alba's dreams at the start of our work: a ghost was walking in the room across from hers. Then, Alba was in a forest with a very tall man; the man was strange, and she realised he was the ghost she had seen in the room. Alba turns into a fragile dragonfly that cannot take flight because she is carrying the man on her shoulders. Then, she finds herself confronting her father's gaze: his eyes are staring at her and she is afraid, although she likes expressive eyes. I remember having had the impression of entering the universe of Alba's fairy tale, with the luminous apparition and the dream showing her struggling with her brother, her sister, a ghost and a paternal figure heavy to carry.

I told myself that she was coming to see me to lighten the weighty family burden that prevented her from spreading her wings. In the course of our work, the white vision became clearer. It had appeared one night when Alba opened the shutters to see if her mother was returning home. The apparition was like a Blessed Virgin dressed in flowing robes, bathed in light that seemed to emanate from within. She had seen it in profile, but her sister saw it face to face.

Alba had been afraid to see it face to face, because of the eyes. When she recounted all this to her mother, Alba noticed that she had a piercing gaze like the apparition. When Alba wanted to know what her mother thought about the vision, she answered that it must have been a play of light.

I was slowly coming to understand the confusion related to persecutory eyes in the family, eyes with an almost hallucinated gaze belonging to faces of the past, faces of dead women – particularly the face of a little sister of Alba's mother, the youngest and the father's favourite. As a child, Alba's mother was made to suffer by this preference, because she adored her father, although he was cold and distant towards her. When she recounted these things later, she never spoke of jealousy, but she told Alba that she had opted for a marriage of convenience to keep all her love for this adored father. But her marriage quickly deteriorated after her father died, and the spouses slept in separate rooms from then on. Alba was born at that period, in that setting of the mother's impossible mourning.

Alba was very fond of her mother, who was her confidante and her adviser. She was the only parent who counted, for she had always presented the children's father to them as being dangerous and nasty, forbidding them to have contact with him, although he lived in the house with them. As a child, Alba, who was hearing these things from her mother, secretly wished to resemble one of her sisters whom the father loved, for then he might want to marry her. But she never saw feelings like her own reflected in her father's eyes, which she had to avoid without knowing why.

Alba's mother, who believed in psychoanalysis, had strongly encouraged her daughter to undertake analysis. She wanted Alba to understand that she had been right to keep the children away from their father. She demanded that Alba recount our sessions to her, and I sensed that she was suspicious of me. She criticised my work severely and several times she asked Alba to stop the analysis. Of course, our work took an unforeseen path. Alba's father, forced to be absent, became more and more a substantial presence in our sessions. Gradually, he took shape, with his family problems, his depression, but also his kindness and great generosity to the children. In the analysis, Alba realised that she had no unpleasant memories associated with him.

As these things were worked through, the story of the apparition changed. Alba remembered that the white lady appeared on the evening when, in most unusual fashion, her mother and father had gone off in a car together, and she was afraid there would be an accident. What question about a bride, about marriage, was coming through in this vision of Virgin Mary in flowing robes?

An evil spirit came back in one of Alba's dreams, dressed in black this time, in the form of a witch who threw children off the top of a tower, while I took Alba in my arms to console her. Later, when she spoke of the woman in white, she described the hard, authoritative gaze of her manipulative mother. She was discovering that her mother was far from being all white.

The day of Alba's engagement party, the families of both her parents came together, including her father, whom she had insisted on inviting. She was relieved to find that she had a family after all – a family with problems, of course, but an ordinary family all things considered. She could go ahead and get married.

At our seminar, I presented Alba's story, so similar to that of "Snow White" in my perception, with the white vision of a Blessed Virgin mother idealised in a bridal dress. This image, a site of condensation and displacement of psychic movements, led to the downfall of the ideality of the white mother, who took on the dark aspect of the witch in Walt Disney's film, this internal black and white mother, a concentrate of the Kleinian mother who, previously loving and nursing, is suddenly experienced as rejecting. As for Alba's father, he was slowly assuming the role of a father.

Time passed, and I was wondering how Alba was doing in her life now, when I found a message from her on my telephone. I was awestruck for a moment thinking of the power of unconscious communications or the surprise of coincidences. Alba had just had a third child, and she was panicked because her mother, who claimed to influence people from a distance, was making persecutory pronouncements about third children in the family being doomed to repeated misfortune and abandonment. The fact was that Alba's baby had a minor health problem. She did not really believe that influence from a distance was possible, but she had doubts, and she needed to hear from me what she herself thought: that it was not true. She was relying on our past work together.

A renewed look at maternal history reassured her that her child was not in danger. She went on with her life.

This twist in Alba's psychic life reminded me of a class of folktales that reveal unconscious feelings of envy and jealousy on the part of the mother towards her daughter's children. These folktales are classified under the "Substituted Bride or Wife" motif in the *Catalogue of Greek Magic Folktales*[4] and other sources. The heroine is killed by her evil stepmother, who also kills her children.

These types of tales are, in fact, found at the end of fairy tales with a heroine, when the heroine gives birth, and the mother seeks vengeance for being forced to let the daughter take her place. We have a famous example of this type of tale: Perrault's "Sleeping Beauty". Once the heroine is married, the stepmother, a disguised mother figure, comes back to persecute her daughter by attacking her most precious possession: her child. What is enacted in the story is the aggressive phantasy related to the mother's feelings of envy towards her daughter, and her frustration when she is forced into the position of grandmother.

Thus, the story of the "substitute bride or wife" is a new tale in the folktale. The *Catalogue* lists hundreds of versions of "Snow White"[5] that mention the different beginnings and endings of the fairy tale.

Reflections in the Mirror of Envy

Anna Angelopoulos

Taking up the theme of malevolent envy, despite a nagging a feeling of reiterating an already well-known topic, can be a daunting and perilous enterprise. This is why, in our seminar,[6] the prevailing concept of envy was closely tied to mythical materials transmitted by folktales or ancient myths. Our presentations paid close attention to the manifest images in these materials, before arriving at their latent content.

When it came to the theme of envy, we always considered it to be associated with hatred and primary maternal ambivalence. Melany Klein defined envy as the main manifestation of innate aggression, while Donald Winnicott saw it as a spontaneous gesture found by the child to express a budding *self*.[7] In any case, our task remains to deal with the essential question raised by envy in psychoanalytic treatment. How can we accomplish this with patients who want to free themselves of the tyranny of envy? Can transference deliver them from this rift, which sometimes emerges in the course of an analysis and can be irreparable, making transference irrelevant?

If we think of envy[8] as related to the witnessing of a desired scene by a witness who is excluded from the intimacy in the scene, we know that this envy can wreak dehumanising havoc,[9] can destroy all life. Envy illustrates the persecutory aspect of living beings. The place where I found a metaphor suggestive of this devastation is in the folktale "Snow White": mother and daughter, two faces reflected in the mirror of envy. First, the face of the mother, which Winnicott considers the mirror where psychic life originates, a mirror for the newborn to "contemplate in order to create".[10] The mother's wish is to have a daughter who will be white, red and black, and beautiful like her. It is as if she wants to reproduce symbolically, as a mirror image, her narcissistic ego ideal in her daughter. But the mother will hate her at puberty when the image in the mirror shows the daughter to be the more beautiful of the two.

For a long time, I used the story of "Snow White" as the paradigm of envy existing between mother and daughter, unfolding in several stages. It illustrates the devastation seen in the mirror, whose envious eye destroys the other's life. In this vivid and cruel folktale known the world over, the persecuted heroine's death is caused by the repeated attacks of her mother (euphemistically presented as a stepmother in some versions). But Snow White is also famous for being awakened by Prince Charming with a kiss.

I had to gather hundreds of versions of this folktale to understand that the story does not end there, nor does it begin there.[11] In Mediterranean countries like my own, the story does not end with Snow White's marriage to Prince Charming. In fact, Snow White has a child and after giving birth she is killed once again by her own mother (stepmother) who has come to take Snow White's child and to take Snow White's place in the Prince's bed. And the murderous attacks continue. First, the young woman is transformed into a bird, then into a fish and finally into a tree. Thus, the oral transmission of the story gradually makes the heroine leave the human species once and for all.

To escape being totally possessed by death,[12] she takes refuge in life cycles anterior to the human: first animal, then plant. Will she ever live in human form again? Yes, but not thanks to Prince Charming. An old woman, childless and therefore lacking a protective matrix, will adopt her symbolically in her lowly state, so that she may acquire human form again.

Freud said that "instincts are mythical entities", and we tend to forget that we are in the realm of mythical creation when we speculate on the origins of psychic life and of thought. At best, we create myths, or we borrow from the mythical that which helps us to develop our ideas.

We can say that, in the mythical realm, inherent maternal feelings are not perceived as being unequivocal. The mother is often portrayed as having a double nature, somewhat like the moon with its hidden face. Witches, ogresses, Baba Yagas and lamias are often portrayed as compassionate, coming to the aid of the hero who has befriended them[13] and offering him protection, while beautiful young mothers abandon their children in the forest, demand that their daughter's bloody heart be brought to them in a box, and so on. Thus, young mothers are often cruel stepmothers in their very nature.

Therefore, I conclude that all these mythical beings can be seen as conceptual characters. The craftsmen of the past have passed down to us in their folktales veritable tools for reflection based on the observation of mothers and all double-sided feminine figures,[14] especially in their scopic impulse; they are ambivalent figures belonging to the "mother species".[15]

To better illustrate the essential points of my discussion, I shall use the example of Medea's infanticide, an act which has come to symbolise ravaging maternal envy since Euripides wrote his tragedy in the fifth century BC. I think it useful to keep this metaphor in mind, for it can serve as a point of departure in our reflection. In the Hellenistic period, several centuries after Euripides' tragedy, the artist Timomachus painted a *Medea* with "crossed eyes", in a moment of agonising indecision as she is dragging her children to their fate, one eye lifted in anger, the other softened with pity. The commentator adds: "Timomachus' art mingled Medea's love with her jealousy." Medea's face expresses two contradictory feelings as she raises her sword.[16] This disjunction between Medea's eyes brings to mind talk of the "evil eye" in popular culture. According to Muriel Djéribi-Valentin's research on this subject, "the woman's own mother accuses her of being the one whose gaze threatens her newborn with physical harm".[17] Thus, the mother is seen as a potential danger to her child. Interestingly, the "evil eye" is always singular, an eye one might have and that produces the evil – without implying that the other eye is missing. This formulation exists in most languages in popular lore, for instance, in French, Greek, Arabic, Hebrew, English, Spanish and so on. It always expresses fear of "the eye", although a person normally has two eyes. It is as if disjunction is required to concentrate the destructive force in one eye. This disjunction reinforces the psychic cohesion indispensable to the destructive act.

Let us take "Snow White" as an example. In this story, it is the eye of the looking-glass that observes the young girl as she grows more and more beautiful. She grows up despite her mother, whose image always catches up with her in the mirror. The heroine has a disastrous fate and suffers the ravages caused by the discontinuity between violent episodes of *fusion and separation* in her relationship with her mother. The latter is often presented as a stepmother, when the storyteller wants to introduce the conflict between mother and daughter while protecting the original, pre-Oedipal mother who died in childbirth. The young princess is caused to die six times as a result of the queen's attacks on her. But she resuscitates each time and always starts over.

Here I must introduce a second element to consider in our discussion of envy, in addition to the gaze. This element is the relation to weaning. The heroine is often described as being "as white as milk", since in southern countries the whiteness of milk has precedence over that of snow when speaking of the lustre of a young girl's skin. Consequently, weaning constitutes the first separation from the mother; after this, the heroine grows up between milk and blood, "*entre late y sangre*" or "*mishiada sangue e latte*"(mix of blood and milk), as they say in Corsica. This striking motif associates the female body with the emotion called forth by the opposition of these two primary colours. This poetic image sets out the path of feminine maturation, from birth to puberty, or from maternal milk to the blood of the menses. The little girl must make her way from the maternal body to which she is attached to a woman's body that will become her own.

But let us look more closely at the mythical mother-daughter relation. In the folktale, the murderous maternal attacks always occur at crucial turning points in the daughter's life: puberty, the discovery of love, and childbirth. It is when the young girl passes from one stage of development to another that the maternal attack is launched, without, however, bringing about psychic separation, as evidenced by the fact that the heroine is always saved, only to fall prey to her stepmother again.

As we mentioned earlier, in its Southern European and particularly its Oriental variants, "Snow White" does not end with the heroine's marriage to Prince Charming. At the most decisive moment of the mother-daughter separation, that is, when the young woman marries the man who resuscitated her with the kiss of love – at the point where the tale usually ends –, another story begins. The motif of this second story in the international classification is "The Substituted Bride (or Wife)".[18]

The narrative is stereotyped, almost identical in all its versions and variants. All storytellers repeat it almost word for word. As we said, Snow White is about to become a mother. And it is when she is giving birth that her mother returns, kills her and takes her place in the prince's bed. The envious mother-witch has now taken hold of the whole feminine and maternal sphere by stealing the heroine's husband and child. This attack could be seen as the enactment of the young girl's phantasy of preventing psychic separation from her mother, something she equally desires and fears. It may not be amiss to ask which of the two women dreams of being free of the other.

But let us come back to the story itself. The storyteller says: "She gave birth; the queen arrived and stuck a pin in her skull, transforming her into a bird. Then the queen lay down in the prince's bed." This is the sequence in "The Substituted Wife", which alters childbirth in identical fashion in Snow White, Cinderella, The Girl Without Hands, Sleeping Beauty, The Three Oranges and The Three Golden Children, to name just a few tales. Despite being oral, this episode is always identical, fixed in its verbal expression in every story, to the point of resembling a recitation. We are stunned to see this "repetition compulsion" of malevolent envy which cuts short the lives of fairy-tale characters at this particular time of transition. I have to ask what the stereotyping might be covering over, in the language of the folktale. Indeed, this invariably identical episode strikes me as an assumption of universality. It seems to play out a common phantasy about the young girl who must die, as exactly this, when she becomes a mother– a phantasy applying to the whole mother species. Here, the transmission of the feminine is accomplished through the death of the girl, killed by her own mother. The mother kills when she sees her daughter become a mother – a prerogative hitherto reserved for her alone. The extreme violence portrayed in the story indicates that great pain is unavoidable for both women at the time of this transition.

I am reminded of how frightened certain patients are to think that their mothers could be present when they give birth. In fact, one of them even asked: "Could I have given birth to my child if my mother had been there? I avoided a great danger by keeping her away." I must point out that, day after day, her mother's arrival for the birth was becoming an obsession for my patient, like the threat of encountering a maternal ghost.[19]

In popular lore, the heroine's attachment to an archaic and deadly maternal element predominates. We could say that when a young woman is with a man, experiences desire and pleasure, and has a child, she enters a psychical sphere that excludes her mother. But for how long? In analytic treatment, the transferential response varies greatly, of course. But in the fairy tales we mentioned, these crucial events do not alter the relationship with the mother once and for all, since she is portrayed as being non-displaceable. In folktales, marital happiness does not seem to last, despite the famous closing formula: "And they lived happily ever after."

What can the analyst do to make this psychic autonomy last? Keeping in mind what folktales so vividly portray in the scene where the heroine gives birth, I was able to identify, in such instances of maternal resurgence, the phantasy that becomes an obsession for certain patients: *my mother will come and take everything away from me*, or else *I will ask my mother to come, and I will give her everything*. Thus, the event of childbirth endangers the freedom wrested from the mother, since the maternal invades the whole space of the feminine once again.

In the folktale, this temporary "killing" of the feminine is represented by a return to previous life forms (bird, fish, tree), caused by malevolent maternal envy. It is by means of this hatred that the storyteller will bring about a separation between mother and daughter. This emotion is hard to handle, because hatred, although most often destructive, also has a symbol-generating dimension that acts as a divider.[20] Indeed, in "Snow White", it is when the eye of the looking-glass creates malevolent envy that the initial dyad formed by the two women can be divided, after long-lasting persecution and six deadly attacks.

These increasingly violent maternal attacks illustrate the process of wearing out the trauma through repetition, something Ferenczi called "cathartic submergence".[21]

When Snow White appears again in a tree trunk, the folktale tells us that an old woman well past reproductive age is cutting wood and hears a little voice crying out: "Hit at the top, hit at the bottom, but don't hit in the middle because there is a little girl there whose head hurts." The old woman does as she is told, and cuts the wood around Snow White's body, letting her come out. Thus, she resuscitates far from the mother species, far from the womb and from actual birth, after having come through human phylogenetic history, brought back by the hands of a woman well past procreation, from another symbolic container, the hollow of a tree, to live whole at last, recomposed from all her fragments.

What does the folktale reveal about the psychopathology of the ordinary mother? It focuses on a process that exists *a minima* in the psyche, to make separation possible. The ambivalence love-hate takes on the aspect of a structuring element in the psyche, built around hate, which involves separating impulses; thus, the psyche must be able to tolerate inclinations towards hate in love, without acting destructively. The expected ambivalence does not necessarily lead to separation and murder; rather, it can act as a regulator in the best case. In our clinical practice, all these psychical readjustments take place within the container provided by transference.

But let us look at the newborn. I think we have all seen patients who experience bouts of hate towards their babies, when, in the worst moments, they are ready to throw them out the window, only to feel guilty afterwards. When we assure them that such feelings are common and to be expected, they are very relieved and often speak of the pleasure they feel to be with their child after such episodes. We can also say that it is possible to stamp out these archaic impulses that produce ambivalence by recognising them in the transference. We might even ask if Winnicott's "good enough mother" might not be an ambivalent mother who recognises herself as such, so that her ambivalence acts as a regulator.

Clinical Illustration: Elise

This young woman came to see me in a state of generalised despondency. She had been abandoned by her mother when she was one year old and her brother was five years old. She strove to be loved by her stepmother, but she couldn't succeed because the latter preferred her own children, the girl's half-brothers and half-sisters. Elise was separated from her older brother abruptly when he was sent to boarding school very early; after this, she lived in constant fear of being sent away from her father's home as well.

Elise's mother had gone back to her far-away country and never gave the family any news. She had other children. After undergoing an initial analysis, my patient had been prompted to renew her relationship with her real mother; she now went to see her once a year. While I felt it was very probably a good thing that Elise had re-established contact with her mother, I was aghast every time the gaping wound of the abandonment resurfaced in the sessions.

A few years later, when Elise was settling down with the man she loved, she wanted to invite her mother and eldest sister to Paris, to spend Christmas with them. Finally, she would be with family during the holidays. It was then, when Elise's relationship with her mother was being reinforced, that everything blew up.

When her mother was about to approach the territory Elise had so painstakingly carved out for herself, Elise suddenly started to scream in the session that this woman was a selfish monster, that she didn't want to see her, that her mother was incapable of love, and that her father had been right to complain about her. It was a complete about-face. I was shaken by the intensity of the hatred suddenly directed at this mother, who had been idealised in her absence until then.

In truth, the gaping wound of abandonment existing between the two of them had been negated up to that point. The analytic work my patient was pursuing with me was intended to allow her to internalise the fact that henceforth she should and could live without a mother.

A few years later, Elise gave birth to a little girl. I do not intend to expose here all the details of this analysis. But I want to speak of an exceptional aspect of it related to breastfeeding. My patient wanted to breastfeed her child. She contacted an association which was "spreading the word" about this fundamental practice. She tried to nurse her baby for a few days, and then she panicked. She did not want to give the breast, she envied her baby for having it, she didn't want the baby any-more, she hated her. Why? Because she, Elise, had to spend all her time with her baby, her husband didn't love her like he had before; he spent all his free time with the baby, and so on. A new crisis arose.

I let Elise know that this kind of resentment was completely normal, that if she asked her friends who had babies, she would find out that they often had negative feelings towards their children, who had transformed them into mothers. It was a healthy reaction to this sudden change made to their lives, to their identity, to their desire; they all confirmed this and Elise was reassured.

I suggested that Elise should go ahead and let her husband give a bottle to the baby during the night; this would not make her a bad mother but would let her get some sleep and be in a better mood the next day.

In the transference, I supported Elise by bolstering her psychic survival after the baby's birth, so that she would not be fixated on an idealised maternal image or terrorised by the fear of being a bad mother. She was not going to repeat the abandonment her mother had inflicted on her; she would just let her husband's mother babysit the child for two hours in the afternoon, so that she could get out of the house and have some free time. A pause was not abandonment; she would come home happy and ready to take the baby in her arms. She went ahead and put this plan into action. We freed bottle feeding from guilt, and we discussed her anxiety about breastfeeding, which overwhelmed her because, given her traumatic history with her mother, she could become both phobic and envious in relation to the breast, including her own. We spoke of her aggressiveness towards the baby, who forced her to be there for her all the time, and to modify the initial narcissistic position she had had as a young girl. So that she wanted to be able to *imagine putting an end to the whole thing* and resuming her previous life.

Just as her mother had done! The thought stayed with me. She both wanted and feared the repetition of the deadly act of abandonment; she was always ready to support and defend this mother, to find a thousand excuses for the fact that she had abandoned her as a baby. My patient had returned to a previous state, despite all the work of psychic separation done in the transference.

I then suggested to her that it was possible to set a limit, and that it was, indeed, very important if their relationship was to continue. To think that it is possible to stop everything sets necessary psychical limits – necessary among other things for her ability to love her child. This allowed her to breathe more easily and to navigate in her imagination between her child, herself, and her mother. She was able to feel less conflicted in her daily life, and to experience only the ordinary level of ambivalence needed to prevent disconnection.

A few times, I saw the two of them together in a session: Elise the mother and her baby; we talked, we played and then my patient thanked me, saying she could now come to the sessions alone, like before. After a time, we separated with cordial feelings. I must add that she had not informed her mother directly that she was about to have a child. She did not want to tell her, letting her find out by chance.

In the course of this analysis, I observed directly how necessary a limit to maternal jouissance is, and it was clear that negative feelings like hate help to set this limit. I acted as the transferential maternal grandmother. This experience taught me that it is the ambivalent structure of the mother that counts as a tool for reflection, rather than simply her ambivalent feelings.

In fact, I found it very important in the transferential process that the mother's ambivalent structure, which I had identified in folktales of the oral tradition, should become a tool for me at such decisive moments of extreme psychical transformation.

This allows me to work through, with my patients, the contradictory passions triggered by childbirth, without being overwhelmed by their intensity.

THE TWO SISTERS

Once upon a time there were two sisters, one poor and the other rich. The poor sister went to the rich sister's house every day, to work for her. She prepared the meals and kneaded dough for her bread and, when she finished, she left without washing her hands. When she arrived home, she made porridge from the bits of dough stuck to her fingers, to feed her little girl. Yet, strangely, the rich sister's daughter was pale and sickly although she was well fed, while the poor sister's daughter was beautiful and strong even though she ate only porridge.

One day, the rich sister asked the other sister: "Tell me, what does your daughter eat that makes her so beautiful and healthy?"

— "Oh, nothing much. I don't wash my hands when I leave your house, and I make porridge from the dough that sticks to my fingers."

—"In that case, from now on you will wash your hands well before you leave," her sister told her.

And the poor mother went home without bringing anything for her child, who started to cry because there was no porridge. She sat outside on the doorstep and continued crying inconsolably. Just then, an old woman came by.

— "Why are you crying, little girl?" she asked.

— "I was waiting for my mother to come home as usual, with her hands full of dough, but my aunt forced her to wash her hands today! She couldn't make me any porridge and I am hungry."

— "Oh, my poor child! How can I help you when I am poor myself! Come and delouse me if you want, sit down here beside me."

The girl sat down and started to delouse her.

— "What do you see, my child?"

— "I see golden lice and silver nits."

— "May you also possess gold and silver, my child! When you laugh, roses shall fall from your mouth; when you cry, your tears shall be of gold!"

With these words, the old woman disappeared.

The young girl was hungry and started to cry again. Gold coins fell all around her. Her mother arrived and could not believe her eyes. They bought all kinds of delicious food. The young girl laughed with delight, and she was soon surrounded by roses. The news spread all over town. The mean sister heard it too. The king's son came to see the young girl; he saw roses falling from her mouth and gold coins from her eyes. He fell in love with her and asked for her hand in marriage.

On the day of the wedding, the evil aunt arrived, furious at seeing the prince marry her niece. She paid some ruffians to tear out the bride's eyes, shut her up in a chest and throw her in the sea. She then sent her own daughter to the palace to replace the fiancée. But the prince suspected that he had been tricked, for he saw the young woman laughing but no roses falling from her mouth; she cried and no gold coins fell around her. The prince became dejected.

In the meantime, the chest with the young girl in it, carried off by the waves, was swept ashore near a pasture. The shepherds opened it and saw that it was full of gold coins, because the blind girl had not stopped crying. She told them her story. They took her to the cave that was their home. Happy to be there, the young girl started to laugh and roses fell all around her. She gave a rose to the youngest shepherd, asking him to go to the palace and exchange it for a human eye. "Don't accept anything else," she told him. The shepherd stood under the palace windows and cried out: "I will exchange a rose for a human eye!" The evil mother and her daughter wanted to buy the rose to give it to the prince, who already suspected them of trickery. So they gave the shepherd an eye in exchange for the rose. The young king pretended to believe that the rose had fallen from his wife's mouth.

A few days later, the shepherd came back to stand under the palace windows, and cried out: "I will exchange a rose for a human eye!" The king was observing all this. He heard the two women go out and offer money for the rose. But the shepherd refused, and they had to give him the other eye to get the rose. The king followed the shepherd and asked him: "Where did you get these roses?" At first, the shepherd didn't say anything, but in the end he consented to take the king to the cave where the young woman was living. The king recognised her at once and took her back with him to the palace.

They tied the two evil women to the tails of four horses, and they were drawn and quartered.

Sources

"I kakia aderfi" [The Evil Sister], FS 1321, pp. 8–11.
    Origin: Lira, Monemvasia.
CGMF 403A, *The Black and White Bride.*
ATU 403, *The Black and White Bride* [combines types AT403A and 403B]
CPF, *The Substituted Bride/Wife.*

The Poisoned Pearl of Envy

Sylvette Gendre-Dusuzeau[22]

Introduction

Envy[23] is one of the seven mortal sins prohibited by the ten commandments, because the desire to possess what God has given to another is opposed to the will of the Creator: "Thou shalt not covet thy neighbour's house; thou shalt not covet thy neighbour's wife, nor his manservant, nor his maidservant, nor his ox, nor his ass, nor anything that is thy neighbour's."[24]

Divested of its religious significance, envy means "a mixture of desire, irritation and hate felt by an individual towards a person who has something he does not have."[25] This feeling is expressed by the Latin verb *invideo*: "to look askance at, to cast an evil and sinister eye upon."[26] Thus, envy is directly related to the eye and to the gaze, to a coveted object one may wish to attack and destroy if one cannot have it.

Awareness of this painful feeling, which makes life unbearable, can emerge in psychoanalysis. Jacques Lacan presents this paradigm of envy in the now famous scene where Saint Augustine, as a child, is watching his baby brother suckling at his mother's breast with *amare conspectu*, a bitter look, which "seems to tear him to pieces and has on himself the effect of a poison".[27] Thus, envy is connected with "seeing which hurts",[28] seeing which dispossesses, seeing which confronts one with a completeness one is unwilling to lose. Of course, envy reaches its destructive peak in the inescapable biblical example of fratricide perpetrated by Cain, who envied his brother, whose offering received God's favour; but the example of Saint Augustine and his belated wish to return to the maternal breast is just as eloquent. In fact, each of us is inevitably confronted with the envy present in the first relationship in which the process of psychical structuring is shaped, in part, by rivalry and the experience of incompleteness.[29] In most cases, envy is overcome in childhood, and the experiencing of it helps to establish the psychic relation to the object, so that the latter can keep desire alive.

Folktales depict envy as a sin leading to misfortune and punishment.

Literary Folklore and the Oral Folktale

To better understand envy, let us look at the folktale, an imaginary narration, the expression of unconscious collective thought, revealing psychical and phantasmatic forms of functioning in which every person recognises an aspect of himself, and in which psychoanalysts hear echoes of their clinical practice.

Although folktales are not unconscious formations like nocturnal dreams, they are subject to the same processes of condensation and displacement, which make it possible to hide things left to be discovered. Like speech, which can constantly change, tales of the oral tradition are told and retold in different versions, revealing omissions and significant concealments.

The notion of envy brings to mind sisters or brothers who feel its sting, who have the feeling of being dispossessed of a place to which they had previously felt entitled; or who find other people's possessions better and more desirable; or find it painful to witness another person's happiness. Envy differs from jealousy, which involves three people and the desire to eliminate the person who has stolen one's love object. But, of course, jealousy can be tinged with envy.[30]

Fairies

Charles Perrault's story "The Fairy", familiar to every child, is a good illustration of this paradigm of envy. It is the story of a widowed mother and her two daughters. The elder is her mother's favourite, because she is just like her in every way. The younger is rejected because she looks just like her father. An old beggar woman, to whom she gives water at the fountain, endows the younger sister with the gift of having flowers and diamonds drop out of her mouth when she speaks. The older sister is subjected to the curse of spitting out serpents and toads as soon as she opens her mouth, because she refused a drink of water to a well-dressed woman when her mother had told her to expect to meet an old beggar woman. The younger sister married the prince, while the older one, chased away by maternal hatred, died in the forest.

The story is followed by two morals:

1 Money and diamonds make a strong impression on the mind; but sweet words yield even greater power.
2 Honesty asks us to go to some pain, it requires some indulgence. But sooner or later it brings its rewards, most often when we least expect it.

Presented as a morality tale about the kindness and honesty of young girls, this folktale conjures up the poisoned pearl of envy, not directly that of a sister towards the other sister, but rather that of a terrible mother who directs her envy towards her favourite daughter, whom she has drawn into a fusional relationship to alleviate the frustration of widowhood. When this daughter fails to satisfy her, the girl falls prey to deadly maternal hatred.

"The Two Sisters"

The Greek folktale that most closely resembles this Perrault fairy tale is "The Two Sisters",[31] which immerses us at once in another world, that of vital necessities, of survival.

In fact, this popular tale describes a custom associated with poverty. Servants working in households used to take away food surreptitiously on their hands – things like bread or pastry dough.[32]

"The Two Sisters", a less euphemistic folktale than "The Fairy", portrays two adult sisters; the one who has everything envies the other, who has nothing. The central elements in the narration are related to nourishment, to the eyes and to a marvellous coveted object. The object possessed by another becomes the unbearable element that drives the narration towards the hate-filled, murderous madness that ends in the attempt to kill the daughter of the poor sister and tear her eyes out. Indeed, hatred is the reaction to the extraordinary gift received by another, which remains unattainable and, for this reason, can only be rejected. The cruelty of this folktale conveys the destructive, hateful forces at work in the evil sister's envy, who, in an attempt to take control by force, attacks and destroys the coveted object. The repercussions are immediate.

In "The Fairy", the mother loses her own daughter and, in "The Two Sisters", the mother and her daughter die together.

The envy at the heart of this tale involves two adult sisters and their daughters. But, as in Perrault's version, it is not the sister or the cousin who envies the gift received by the other, which makes her speak roses and cry gold coins. It is the mother – a sister who is also a mother –, who is envious of her sister and keeps her in a state of submission and dependency, to better deprive her of her only enviable possession, as she has undoubtedly always done. Aside from depicting the envy directed by one sister towards the other, the story also reveals the dangers of pathological envy in a mother whose daughter is only a replica of herself.

The "moral" of the oral folktale could be a warning: beware of envy and its destructive effects.

In the story, another element illustrating deadly cruelty provoked by the coveted object concerns the eyes of the heroine. They are torn out, traded, recovered, one by one. Indeed, in traditional folklore envy has always been related to the eye: the "evil eye" and the "envious eye", which come into play particularly at times of transition such as breastfeeding, weaning, puberty or marriage.[33]

This tale of envy, in its written and oral versions, reveals that the psychical mechanisms of envy and its deadly effects are related to oral frustration and to attacks on the object through the eye.

Invidia at work

What role do envy and its effects play in clinical practice? What effects does envy have on transference?

At the end of our first session, Laureen (as I shall call her) asked me directly if there were mutual feelings between us. This question regarding affection remained present throughout the treatment in the form of regret that we could not become friends in reality. Moreover, she had warned me from the start that she was in the habit of ending relationships that she started, and she specified that she would find it hard to undertake long-term work because she knew that one day I would end the sessions. I remember feeling that the psychic space of the sessions was going to have a "last-minute", incidental feel, like a door slamming in my face. Very soon, I noticed that when I took a one-week vacation, she went away for a week when I returned. This occurred repeatedly. In addition, she did not choose to interrupt her periods of leave from work to attend sessions, even if she stayed in Paris.

I sensed that it never crossed her mind to pay for these missed sessions. She used to say that she could not bear to be compelled to do anything. I felt manipulated. I asked myself whether we would have the necessary time for a true encounter to take place, and what was at the bottom of her will to decide in my place. Yet she continued to come, as an office friend advised her to do, to consult "someone who didn't know her" about an important matter in her life. Should she keep or send away a man she had recently met, with whom she was not in love, but to whom she had already assigned the task of setting limits for her eight-year-old daughter and keeping her company at mealtimes. She had introduced him to her family, who found him likeable, especially since he was handy when it came to fixing things around the house. Laureen did not trust men. Her father, whom she adored, left the house after a turbulent divorce. For a long time, Laureen dreamed and waited for him to come and get her in one of the beautiful cars he prepared for car shows. But he never came. As for the father of her own daughter, she had sent him away on a variety of pretexts before the child was born, realising that all she had wanted was a genitor.

Laureen's family was composed exclusively of women: sisters, aunts, a fatherless cousin. When her daughter was born, family ties were reinforced so that the child might "have roots". Everyone came to live on two adjacent streets, creating a sort of family village. It was helpful, of course, for Laureen, who had a job, to have her mother look after her daughter and prepare the evening meal to take home at the end of the day for the two of them. Laureen thought this to be good, believing that she did not know how to bring up her daughter. Laureen described her mother as being authoritative, sure of herself, and imposing her will on her granddaughter. I realised that Laureen herself was very submissive, but was subjecting me to this maternal authority that gave me a feeling of confinement and paralysed me in the sessions. She described the persecution to which her mother had subjected her as a child to get her to tell the truth. Laureen's mother kept looking for lies by asking endless questions about school and about Laureen's friends. In the sessions, Laureen would discover that she was doing the same thing with her daughter, subjecting the daughter to an outright interrogation every evening. She remembered that as a child she always felt that things were being hidden from her, and that "everyone had already said everything before her turn came". Since she was the youngest, there was no other child to whom she could say anything. Therefore, there was no room for the little secrets that constitute one's own psychic space. On the other hand, the important things concerning her father and his whereabouts were kept secret.

One day, she arrived at the session completely shaken up. She was still shaking when she described the scene. She had dropped in to see an aunt on her way back from shopping with her daughter. She found her aunts, her mother and her recent friend together, amusing themselves while they sipped a drink after her friend had done some repairs. She felt stunned, evicted from her rightful place, for she had been dreaming of the day when she would introduce her family to a man of her own. And although this relationship was not satisfactory, she was still the one who had created it and they were taking away from her something she did not even possess. No one had told her about the gathering, and the man himself had not invited her to join them. It was terrible. Of course, they all felt that she was taking things the wrong way and told her so. Once again, no one understood her.

I took the liberty to point out that the world is full of men who can do repairs, and that at her age she might want something different from a man. She did not answer. I realised that in this recomposed family each person wanted to tell the others what to do, and in this circulation of power between superegos not one of them was in her proper place. Sometimes there were spats between these women, but they were quickly patched up because the family's watchword was "no one is to be excluded".

I saw how this phrase was tied to her repeated absences after my own, and how she excluded herself from our analytic relationship. She was no doubt attacking our linking in advance, caught up in the fear that we might grow close, become friends – something she desired and dreaded at the same time, and about which she occasionally inquired. She was also in the habit of interrupting the session when she was enjoying it, as a way to show me that it was she who was in control, not I. I kept in mind that the departure of her beloved father had been a cruel disillusionment which left her defensive and fearful of any relationship. I also asked myself whether there was not a deeper wound. I was thinking of the first relationship, that with the mother, involving envy, frustration, sadistic attacks on the maternal breast.[34] How had this mother – all-powerful today – welcomed her baby? Laureen's fear of establishing ties and her aggressive and frustrating absences reminded me of what Melanie Klein had said about the effects of envy in the transference, when the analyst is subjected to attacks intended for the mother. Was I now seen as a potential persecutor?[35]

During the same period, Laureen had to deal with her daughter's pathological attachment: "I don't want you to die, I will go to the grave with you." I asked her if it was necessary to envision death, before people can say that they love each other. This love she was unable to express was at the core of her relationship with her friend: "If I leave this man who eats at our table, my daughter will conclude that I, her mother, can also leave her." I was realising that she was on very slippery ground and there was nothing to anchor her, since men had no consistency in her family. At this point she decided to break off her relationship with her friend, who nevertheless continued to do repairs for the rest of the family.

One day, Laureen noticed that her daughter, whom she found unbearable, was, in truth, full of life and very pleasant. I ventured to tell her that it was because the young girl did not have the same mother she herself had. My comment made her laugh wholeheartedly, because she would not have had the courage to say so herself. She enjoyed coming to the sessions more and more; in any case, she did not systematically respond to my vacations by periods of absence, and she was less dissatisfied with herself.

Two events provided an occasion for us to advance our work.

The first was her daughter's stay at a summer camp – a decision Laureen had agonised over. When she came to see me the following week, she was very upset. She had been unable to bear the separation from her daughter and had driven to see her. But when she arrived, her daughter had become angry. Laureen had felt hated and excluded yet again. We tried to talk about what happened, about how she had felt. Seeing her bewilderment, I suggested that her daughter had no doubt prepared for this separation, which she both desired and dreaded. At the camp, she was trying to be all right on her own, without her mother. When Laureen came to see her daughter unexpectedly, she interfered with her daughter's efforts to do well while away from her mother. This was probably the real reason for her anger. My comment gave Laureen a new perspective and she admitted: "I want to be everything my daughter loves, but I am always afraid that I endanger this love." I pointed out that her daughter wanted a summer camp of her own, because in their family everything belonged to everyone. Everything had to be shared, one could not keep anything for oneself. But every person needs their secrets, a space where others cannot enter; all human beings need this. We continued to speak about secrets, lies, the need to have an inner door to close or to open at will. It became clearer and clearer to me that, to Laureen closing a door and keeping certain things to herself meant risking losing them by arousing envy in others, who might want to take them away from her.

Our work was going well – too well. When I returned from vacation, I had to face an attack: she announced that she wanted to stop the analysis, saying that she was happy that I had a vacation, but she did not want the sessions to become everything for her. I offered no interpretation. I simply said: "I want you to stay", and she stayed. Her mother had instilled in her that "a fault confessed is half redressed", so I talked about creating a necessary secret space in oneself, even if one has to lie to preserve it. I was, in a sense, praising the virtues of lying. She was very surprised, and she made the following association: "Did her mother truly love her father?" The following week it was I who was astonished when she announced that she had enrolled in a theatre course with her friend from the office. Later, while memorising a text, she made an important discovery: in her family, there was no place for men.

A second important event took place on a Sunday. She was at home relaxing when her mother called to remind her that she was supposed to bring her a board and some tools. Laureen did not feel like moving but was afraid to say so. I remembered that at the start of our work together she would say that her mother's requests were like a cockroach on her arm, and she would make a gesture as if to chase it away. I asked Laureen why she had been afraid to say "no" to her mother. Her answer went straight to the heart of the matter, bringing to light her mother's omnipotence. Laureen said that she realised at that moment that she could not "satisfy her mother's desire". I pointed out the sexual overtones of this expression, adding that she could never satisfy her mother sexually, and that for her mother she could never replace a man. For the first time, she opposed her mother firmly and effectively, refusing the hold her mother exerted on her.

Afterwards, she remembered having slept for a long time in her mother's bed after the divorce, and she talked at the same time about her daughter's affectionate declarations on her birthday: "You have beautiful eyes, Mommy." We had now embarked on a discussion about love, sexual desire and satisfaction. I felt that a separation was finally being created unhesitatingly within her. Suddenly things seemed to happen as if by magic, as is sometimes the case when the psyche is free to breathe. Laureen was able to tell her daughter, who did not want her to go out: "I am going to the theatre, it's what I enjoy doing." And, unexpectedly in this changing psychical context, for the first time, Laureen's mother gave her a birthday gift chosen uniquely for her, as a sign of the love for which she had always waited in vain.

She followed up an idea that had come to her in a session, concerning the love between her parents. She questioned an aunt and discovered a secret from the past. Her mother had been in love with a young man whom her parents forbade her to marry because of his social status. Humiliated, disappointed and deeply wounded, she got to know Laureen's father out of spite and married him quickly, before he could change his mind. He was a good man, but unfortunately she did not love him.

So many things left unspoken, so much repressed hate, which get in the way of living.

Finally, it occurred to me that, in the absence of a relationship that could confer cohesion to this family, what held it together was stifled hatred. If this hate could have been felt and expressed, it would have constituted a structuring and differentiating element that would have allowed each person, especially Laureen, to construct a separate psychic space. Exerting control over others is a form of hatred.[36] Hatred is frightening because it is associated with guilt about feeling it. This is clear to see in folktales, which emphasise the separating power of hate by depicting a struggle unto death between envious mother-sisters or between mothers and daughters.

But what stood out most clearly for me was that Laureen, caught in a fusional relationship with her mother, had excluded men from her life as a way of protecting herself from the hate-filled and destructive envy she, Laureen, would have provoked in her mother if she had exposed her mother to the sight of a loving and happy couple she herself might have formed with a man.

When Invidia Has a Change of Heart:
A Clinical Illustration

Sylvette Gendre-Dusuzeau

The following clinical case about sisters is enlightening.

Often it is the mothers, or sometimes the fathers of our young patients who tell us, when they bring a child to see us, that the child was very upset about the arrival of a baby brother or sister. I noticed that often the decisive moment is when the door of the maternity ward is opened and the child is confronted with the shocking and unexpected sight of the mother holding out her hand to her older child, while cradling a tiny infant who is crying or sleeping or looking at the world with a serious gaze. It is the visual shock of *invidia*, as in the original example given by Saint Augustine. The reactions described to me are varied: the child might close the door and take refuge in the corridor, hide under the bed, or eat all the chocolates someone brought, so that they are sick. We have all heard about or experienced for ourselves the shock of encountering this child-of-betrayal that the parents produced in secret, who knows how. Other stories told by parents as amusing family legends include hearing the older child ask when the new baby would leave or attempting to make him disappear by some dangerous means. What becomes of this aggressiveness, and even hate, caused by the loss of his place effected by the younger sibling, in a child's Oedipal development?

I remember the story of a patient who, as an adult, still had a very vivid memory of this radical change, although she was only three at the time. First, she was left with a woman she disliked. Then, her father used to take her to the maternity ward to see her little sister. On the way there each day, they saw a large poster for a circus, showing a lion. She remembered that when they would come to the poster, her father played a game, saying: "Oh, the big lion, hurry, hurry", and he ran quickly to pass the poster, as if they really had to be afraid. It was unusual for her to be out with him. She remembered that she did not find the game as amusing as he did, and that she had thought that what he did was silly. She did not remember seeing her mother at the hospital, but she recalled being attracted to a tiny cot, and intrigued by a little red head with a yellow spot on the forehead, as bright as an egg yolk. In the midst of all the strangeness, there was this familiar food on the baby. She tried to rub the spot away with her fingers, but she didn't succeed. Someone probably made her stop.

The next day, when she was home in her room, she remembered that, when she woke up in the morning, she saw the floor become tilted, as if it was rising on one side and going down on the other. In the session, she connected this with one of her favourite games, when she was about seven years old: she would take down one of the mirrors hanging on the wall and look in it as she walked about the room. She would soon become dizzy and fall. It was a strange sensation she liked to feel, all the while worrying that she would hurt herself when she fell.

One day, we disagreed about a missed session. It was after a short vacation. I had planned to set up my office in the building where I lived, close to my apartment. I had advised my patients and had even shown them the door where they were to ring at their next session in April. The day of the opening of my new office – a special event for me –, she was there on time, but in the café downstairs, where she usually waited before the sessions. She was a very responsible person, always on time, except that on this first Monday after spring vacation she made a mistake and rang the doorbell one hour late. She had come and she made sure she was on time, so it was not her fault that she wasn't at the session. She understood that I had waited for her, but she felt bewildered by what had happened. She thought it was completely irrational. She minimised the fact that the place was new and that this could have been disturbing for her, since she herself had moved many times throughout her life.

After some time, a dream involving her sister brought back a very moving memory. The memory made her cry, so that she was unable to tell me about it. It was only in her next session that she tried to talk about it, with great emotion. She was almost four years old and she remembered her nine-months-old sister sitting up straight in her pram. She remembered that when they were alone, she said nasty things to the baby. That day, by some strange chance, the baby was playing with a small blue pen belonging to their mother, which was not to be touched. Finally, the pen came apart as the baby twisted and pulled. She remembered that she scolded the baby, who started to cry. Seeing her distress, her sister felt a very strange emotion. She felt it was ridiculous for her to take her mother's side against the baby; after all, what could a baby know about a pen? A surge of love swept up in her. Suddenly, she changed allegiance and the detested baby became her sister that day. This new phenomenon was internalised. It resurfaced on the occasion of the great change that moving my office constituted for her.

The frame in which we conduct an analysis leaves room for unconscious mistakes which are often very successful in showing us what we do not want to know or remember. Through transference, through unknown shared emotions, my patient's internal journey allowing her to accept and even love her sister re-emerged on that occasion.

* * *

In the story of "Cinderella", presented in a number of variants, we see not only the stepmother's persecutory antagonism, but also the rivalry between sisters in various forms. Let us note that the three Greek versions presented here – "Cinder-Spindle", "Cinderella" and "Ash-Maiden" – differ from the well-known versions of the Brothers Grimm and Charles Perrault due to the introduction of the theme of matriphagy, in the scene where the mother is eaten by her daughters during a weaving contest. These folklore stories set up a conflict leading to the liberation of the heroine, free to pursue her path to womanhood.

CINDER-SPINDLE

Once upon a time there were three sisters. Two of them lost their mother and the third was born to their father's second wife. The two older sisters hated the youngest and called her Mary of the Cinders, chanting: "Stir the ashes, Cinder-Spindle, spin the spindle." Every day, the three sisters went to sit on a cliff to spin their wool. They said that the one who could not finish her skein would cause her mother to change into a cow. But in truth, only Mary of the Cinders had a mother; the other two had lost theirs.

The poor girl was always the first to finish her skeins of wool, and her half-sisters had nothing to blame her for. But to trip her up, they would always put more wool in the pile beside her, when she wasn't looking. And the greater the pile of skeins grew, the faster she endeavoured to spin them. But one day, Mary of the Cinders was not able to finish spinning all the skeins of wool and her mother turned into a cow.

In the evening, when they were returning home, they heard mooing. They opened the door and saw the cow in the middle of the room. When their father came home from work and saw what had happened, he was very troubled and said: "What can we do now, my girls? You, Mary of the Cinders, you will take the cow to the pasture every day, and bring her back in the evening." After she had done this for a few days, her father said: "Now go and rest, Mary of the Cinders; it's your sisters' turn to take the cow to pasture."

In the morning, the sisters wanted to lead the cow to pasture, but it refused to move. They kept trying until their father told them: "My girls, we shall kill this cow and eat it." When she heard this, Mary of the Cinders stood up suddenly and started to weep and protest very loudly. But her father did not listen and decided to kill the cow.

They roasted the cow in the oven and sat down to eat the meat by the hearth. Mary of the Cinders was sitting behind the hearth, watching them. "Come here and eat with us, Mary," her half-sisters said. But she only stared in silence and picked up the bones her sisters were tossing aside.

She gathered all the bones into a pile and went to bury them in a secret place. But she had kept the cow's tail and when she wanted to go somewhere, she would burn one of its hairs. Then, a leaping armoured horse would appear before her, as well as a golden dress. Mary's sisters never invited her to go with them when they went off to amuse themselves. But on one occasion the three sisters were invited to a baptism that would be followed by great revelry. As they were leaving, the two sumptuously bedecked sisters asked Mary of the Cinders to come with them. But the poor girl answered as she always did: "Since I have nothing to wear, how can I come with you?"

As soon as her half-sisters were gone, she ran to the place where she had buried the cow bones. She burned one of the hairs of the tail and an armoured horse appeared before her, as well as a golden dress. She mounted the horse at once and arrived before her sisters at the place where the revelry was held. When the guests saw this woman whose dress sparkled with gold coins, they naturally asked her to be the baby's godmother. She agreed and, after the baptism, she gave gold coins to all the guests. Her sisters had not recognised her. Happy with the gold coins they received, they returned home.

As for Mary, on her way home she stopped at a well to let her horse drink. But she accidentally let one of her shoes fall into the well. She tried to get it out, but the task proved impossible. She continued on her way. At the place where she had buried the cow bones, she burned a tail hair again and everything that had magically appeared now disappeared. Cinder-Spindle returned home and sat in the hearth. Soon, her two sisters arrived and recounted their evening merrily.

— You didn't come, Cinder-Spindle, Stir the ashes, Spin the spindle, and didn't see what an amazing evening it was! A beautiful woman arrived, dressed in gold, on a saddled horse. She was the godmother. At the end of the evening, she gave out fistfuls of gold coins.
— Show me your gold coins then, Mary of the Cinders said.

Laughing happily, the sisters opened the box in which they had put the coins. They looked inside and what did they see? The box was full of coal! Surprised, they went to see their neighbours who had been at the baptism as well. But the other guests all had their gold coins. The sisters realised that something strange was happening.

One day, the prince went to the well to drink water. He looked into the well and saw a shoe shining at the bottom. He let the pail down and was able to bring up the shoe. Losing no time, he went to all the houses in the village asking who the shoe belonged to. Every woman said the shoe was hers. But the prince made each one try it on and, seeing that it did not fit perfectly, he went on to the next house. At last, after having been to every house in the village in vain, he knocked on Cinder-Spindle's door. But the two half-sisters, who suspected something out of the ordinary when their gold coins turned to coal, and when they heard that the prince was going through the village looking for the woman whose gold shoe was in the well, took hold of Mary of the Cinders and pushed her into a large basket that they covered with a piece of cloth.

When the prince entered their house, the sisters offered him a chair to sit down, but he sat on the basket instead. When the two sisters saw the shoe, they cried out and claimed that it was theirs, thanking the prince for the joy he caused them by bringing it back. But in vain! The shoe was too small for them when they tried it on. Cinder-Spindle, who sensed what was going to happen, had taken a large needle with her before being closed up in the basket. She pricked the prince with it.

— What have you put into this basket, that is pricking me? the prince asked the two sisters.
— Nothing, Your Highness, the only thing we have is a hen.

Right away, Cinder-Spindle pricked the prince again, and he asked once more what was in the basket. The young girls answered: "Nothing, Your Majesty, it's only a hen." But the third time, the prince had had enough and he uncovered the basket. He saw Mary of the Cinders with the needle in her hand. He asked her to try on the shoe, to see if it was hers; the shoe fit her perfectly!

The prince hastened to return to the palace. He found his father and said: "Father, I must tell you that I have decided to marry Mary of the Cinders."

– What? You, my son, with all the riches you possess, you want to marry Cinder-Spindle, Stir the ashes, Spin the spindle? the king exclaimed.

But when he saw, to his regret, that he could not make the prince change his mind, he gave him his blessing and told him to bring the young girl to the palace.

The next morning, the prince donned his gilded garb and rode to Cinder-Spindle's house. She was expecting him and had made preparations. At dawn, she had gone to the place where she had buried her mother's bones, after she was changed into a cow and slaughtered. She burned a hair of the cow tail, which she had kept. The armoured horse and the dress covered with gold coins appeared at once. She rode the horse to her dwelling. The prince had just arrived there and the two of them rode to the palace together.

A year later, Mary of the Cinders gave birth to a child. Her sisters were very jealous of her and wished to see her dead. One morning, they disguised themselves to look like old women and went to the palace. They knocked and a servant appeared.

– We want to see the queen.
– That won't be possible. She has just given birth.
– That is the reason we want to see her.

The servant opened the door and led them into the room where the queen lay resting with her baby. The servant left the room. Losing no time, the witches took a pin and pricked the queen's head with it. She was transformed into a bird at once.

One of the sisters lay down in the bed and pretended to be the new mother. The king knew nothing of this. But the baby, who did not have his mother's breast to suckle, cried all day long and could not be appeased. The king came into the room and asked: "Why does this child cry all day and never quiets down?"

– Because I don't have milk to feed him, that's why he cries, said his "wife".
– And why don't you have milk?
– Because I have just given birth, she answered.

The child cried and cried all the time, and no one knew what to do. Milk was brought for him, but he would not calm down. Before the palace stood a tree, and a bird perched on one of its branches; the bird was really the baby's mother. Every morning the bird would sing and the child would stop crying. The fake queen noticed this and gave orders for the bird to be killed. The king disagreed, but since his wife kept insisting, he gave his consent.

The hunter who killed the bird took it in his hands and looked at it carefully. He saw a pin and removed it from the bird's head. As soon as he did this, three drops of blood fell on the ground. And on that spot, before the palace, a beautiful apple tree sprung up. It grew tall and every time the child passed by, it bent its branches so he could take hold of them. It only bent like this for the king and the little boy, so they could reap its apples. When her sister, the witch, came close, the apple tree lifted its branches.

The evil sister understood what was happening and ordered the tree to be cut down. The king did not want to see the tree cut down, but he finally consented. A lumberjack was called and told to cut down the tree. From the place where the axe struck the tree, a voice was heard crying out: "Oh, my loins!" The lumberjack ran to see the king and told him what happened. The king said: "You have to split it in two, at least." The lumberjack struck the apple tree even harder, to slice it into slivers. But the voice hid in one of the pieces of wood; by chance, the lumberjack took that very piece and placed it on a rock.

One day, an old woman happened to pass by the place with the rock. She saw the piece of wood and took it to her abode. The next morning, she rose and went to the mountain to look for firewood. When she came home in the evening, she saw that someone had brought water, had cooked and had fed the cats. She asked: "Who fed you, my little cats?" But there was no answer. The next day, she pretended to leave but she hid in a barrel instead. From her hiding place, she saw Mary of the Cinders clean the house. The old woman asked: "Is it you, little lady, who does all the chores when I am not here?"

– Yes, it's me, Grandmother, Mary told her.
– Why haven't you shown yourself since you have been here?

So the young woman told her story, from the beginning: "I am Mary of the Cinders, Cinder-Spindle, Stir the ashes, Spin the spindle . . ."

In the meantime, the prince, who had realised one day that his "wife" was not his real wife, fell gravely ill and was in danger of dying. All sorts of people came to the palace and prescribed the most miraculous remedies, but in vain. The illness got worse and worse, and the prince refused all the remedies brought to him. The old woman, who heard of this, told Mary of the Cinders: "We are going to visit your husband too. We will boil cabbages, we will put your wedding ring in them and give them to your husband."

Mary agreed and they set off. When they arrived at the palace, her half-sisters came to meet them and asked what they wanted, and where they were taking the cabbages. They said the cabbages were a remedy for the sick prince. The fake queen answered: "The most miraculous remedies were brought to him and he refused them. You think he will eat these cabbages?"

— At least, let us see him, the two strangers said.

They were allowed in and taken to the king's room. They found him at death's door, ready to take his last breath. They begged him: "Your Majesty, if you eat a forkful of cabbage, you will see that you will recover at once." The king was about to eat the cabbage, but his fork struck the ring. He was cured at once, and rose from his bed. He took hold of Mary's half-sister and burned her in the oven. He gave the old woman a carriage filled with gold coins, and she returned home.

The king recognised his true wife and they lived happily ever after, but not as happily as we did.

Sources

"Stachtadrachto" [Cinder-Spindle], SF 1420, 5–7.
   Version transcribed by Dimitris Rendifis in 1964, in Tsoukalades, Livadia.
   Ioannis Martios, stockbreeder, age 50.
CGMF 510A, *Cinderella.*
ATU 510A, *Cinderella.*

CINDERELLA

Once upon a time, a man and his wife had a daughter. The girl liked to eat cotton and people would tell her: "Don't eat the cotton because if you do, your mother will turn into a cow." But she didn't listen and in the end her mother turned into a cow. Soon, her father married a woman who had a daughter as well.

The first girl, the one who was orphaned, would take the cow to pasture. One day, when they went there, her mother told her: "On Saturday your father will have me killed. You will gather up my bones and bury them behind the door. You will burn incense for forty days and forty nights. Then, whenever you wish, you will push the earth aside and, among the bones you will find a beautiful dress, red slippers and a white horse." On Saturday, the father killed the cow and the daughter did what her mother told her. Forty days passed.

One day, a travelling show came to their town. The stepmother and the stepsister got ready to go to the fair. "What about you, Cinderella, aren't you coming with us?" They called her Cinderella and laughed at her because, since her father had remarried, she was always sitting in the ashes. She only came out to take her mother, the cow, to pasture. "No, no, I am not coming. Go without me," she answered. But as soon as they were gone, Cinderella got up, pushed the earth aside and, among her mother's ashes, found the dress, the slippers and the horse. She put on the dress, mounted the horse and rode to the church.

When the priest had almost finished mass, she rose quickly, went home, hid her beautiful attire and went back to sit in the ashes of the hearth. When the two women came home, they said: "You didn't come to the church, so you didn't see the foreign princess, so beautiful in her marvellous clothes." How could they have known that she was the princess? "It doesn't really matter," she replied. The next Sunday the same thing happened, the two women left first and Cinderella followed them later. She left the church before mass ended and no one noticed anything.

But the third time Cinderella went to the church, she left a little later than the other times, and she stopped at the well to let her horse drink. Suddenly, she saw the prince far-off, coming towards the well. She spurred her horse and, as she rode away, one of her slippers fell off. When she got home, she sat in the ashes again. The prince also stopped at the well to let his horse drink. But the horse would not drink. Surprised, the prince thought: "What could be troubling my horse like this?" He dismounted and, looking in the well, saw the slipper that frightened the horse.

He held it in his hands and exclaimed: "What a beautiful slipper! I want to marry the woman who wore this slipper." He mounted his horse and rode from house to house in the village. When young girls lived in a house, he made them try on the slipper. But the slipper did not fit any of them. Then the prince came to the house where Cinderella lived. Her stepmother had heard that the prince was making the rounds in the village, and had made sure to hide her stepdaughter in a chicken crate. As soon as the prince entered their house, the stepmother's daughter tried on the slipper.

– Look, it fits her perfectly! exclaimed her mother.
– No, her foot is too big, the prince replied. And he sat down on the chicken crate. Cinderella pricked him with a pin. The stepmother told the prince: "Be careful, there is a hen in the crate."
– Let's see just what kind of hen it is, the prince said.

He opened the crate and saw Cinderella.

– My God! he exclaimed. What a beautiful young girl! Please try on this slipper, he told her.

Cinderella tried on the slipper and it fitted her perfectly. The prince married her. When his father died, the prince became king and Cinderella became the queen. Her stepmother and half-sister were crazed with envy. One day, the stepmother disguised herself as a gypsy selling spools, thread, needles and other things of this sort. In her basket, there was an enchanted needle. She went to the palace. "Come look at my wares, my ladies!" she called. "Come and buy whatever you need." Cinderella went out to see her. As she bent down to look inside the basket, the stepmother stuck the enchanted needle in her skull. Cinderella was instantly changed into a bird and flew away into the garden. The king was overwhelmed with sorrow. He stayed inside the palace all day with the baby. One day, while the gardener was watering the garden, he heard a bird calling him: "Gardener, my gardener, is the king sleeping?"

- He is sleeping, the gardener answered.
- And the baby? Is he sleeping?
- He is sleeping, the gardener said again.
- May the king sleep peacefully, the bird said. And may the baby sleep peacefully too. And may the bitches who poisoned me sleep on thorns! Go and tell the king what they did, or else may the tree on which I sit wither and fall!

But the gardener said nothing to the king and the tree started to wither. Then, one day, the gardener decided to tell the king what the bird had said. So the king went into the garden and heard the talking bird himself. He called out: "Where are you hiding, lovely bird? Fly a little lower!" The bird sat on a lower branch. Little by little, it came down from branch to branch, and finally came to perch on the king's knees. When he caressed the head of the little bird, the king found the poisoned needle. He took it out and the bird changed back into the queen. The king took her in his arms. As soon as she told him that the gypsy was her stepmother, he took hold of her and had her tied to two horses that pulled her to pieces. And the queen could live in peace at last.

They lived happily ever after, and so did we.

Sources

"Stachtopipiliarou" [Cinder-Sucker], No. 49, pp. 322–324, in Giorgos Ioannou, *Contes de notre peuple*, Hermès, 1975.
  Collected in Kassandra, Halkidiki.
CGMF 510A, *Cinderella*.
ATU 510A, *Cinderella*.

ASH-MAIDEN

Once upon a time there was an old woman who had three daughters. It happened that in their kingdom lights were banished from all dwellings by order of the king. So the old woman took her three daughters to a dry well. They went down into the well, settled in as best they could and started to spin wool. Some time passed and they were left without food; they could not even feed the animals. The three girls said: "The first one who drops her spindle will be eaten by the others." Soon, their mother tipped her spindle over; the girls said: "We will spare your life this time, because you are our mother, but if the spindle falls again we won't spare you." But she knocked over the spindle again, and the daughters said: "We will spare your life again, because you are our mother and you brought us into the world, but if your spindle should fall again, we won't spare you."

The old woman dropped her spindle again. The daughters killed her and roasted her in the little dry well. The two older sisters ate her and threw the bones aside. They told the youngest: "Come and eat with us." But she answered: "No, I don't want to; how can I eat my own mother?"

She sat in a corner and picked up all the little bones. She had hidden beans in her bosom – the clever girl – and she was munching them to pretend that she was biting the little bones. But instead, she gathered up the bones, made a little pile and buried them in a pit she had dug behind the door. Then she burned incense for forty days. On the forty-first day, she thought: "Let me see what has become of my mother's bones!" She opened the pit and, to her amazement, what she saw there were dresses, shoes, jewels. For every small bone, there was one of these marvellous things.

On Sunday, her sisters put on their finest garments to go to church. They said: "Come with us, Ash-Maiden." But she answered: "Go ahead, I'm going to stay home." And she sat down in the ashes. As soon as they left, she washed off the ashes, put on the beautiful clothes she found in her mother's grave, and she went to the church. The king saw her and admired her beauty. "Who is she?" he thought. "She is not a queen, but who is she?"

As soon as mass was over, she quickly left. She went to the dry well, took off her clothes and sat in the ashes. Later, her sisters told her: "It's too bad you were not there, Ash-Maiden, because you would have seen the beautiful young woman who came to church dressed in gold."

– I don't want to go there, she said. You ate my mother, I don't want to see anything.

But she went to church secretly three Sundays in a row. The third Sunday the king forbade anyone to leave the church before mass was over. Honey was poured on the doorstep. When mass was over, Ash-Maiden was the first to leave and her shoe was left behind, glued to the honey. The king took the shoe and ordered all the women of the kingdom to stay home because he would make the rounds in search of the woman who had worn the shoe. He went to every house and finally he came to the house where Ash-Maiden lived.

The king went in and had one of the sisters try on the shoe; but it did not fit her. The second sister tried on the shoe, but it did not fit her either. The king looked for the third sister, but the other two had hidden her under a basket. The king sat down on the basket. They told him: "For Heaven's sake, Your Highness, we have a hen in the basket and her chicks just hatched. We don't want them to get away."

But the king sat on the basket just the same, and Ash-Maiden pricked him with a big needle. The king exclaimed: "The Devil take this hen, she bit me!" He turned the basket over and saw Ash-Maiden. He told her: "Put on this shoe." The shoe fitted her perfectly and the king ordered that she be taken to the palace. Before going there, Ash-Maiden asked the king to send a cart to her house. When it arrived, one of the palace servants started to empty the mother's pit, which was filled to overflowing. Then Ash-Maiden and all her possessions were taken to the palace.

A long time passed and one day the oldest sister said: "Let us go to the palace to see how she is doing." They went there and saw that Ash-Maiden was expecting a baby. The king was about to go off to war. He told the oldest sister: "You must watch over my wife."

– Have no fear, she said. We are here now, so you mustn't worry.

When the time came, Ash-Maiden gave birth to a baby boy who looked like the sun and the moon. The sisters plotted with the midwife not to show the baby to the king. They put it in a chest which they threw in the sea.

Not far from there lived a dervish who found a date on a date palm every morning. But one morning he found two dates and a chest with a child in it. The second date was the child's luck. From then on, the dervish found two dates every morning, one for each of them. It was enough to feed the child and feed himself too. The child kept growing.

Time passed and Ash-Maiden gave birth to a little girl; but she was thrown into the sea too. The same dervish found her. In the meantime, the king was told that his wife was giving birth to kittens. She became pregnant for the third time and gave birth to a baby boy, who was thrown into the sea like the others. All three children were living with the dervish. They played outside, in the countryside.

One day, the king was out hunting. He met the children and asked the dervish: "Where did you find these children?" The dervish said: "Your Majesty, each day I went to this date palm tree and found a date to eat. One day, I found a child there; that day, there were two dates on the tree, to feed both of us. When I found the second child, there were three dates. When I found a third child, there were four dates. This is how I was able to feed them."

We must also say that many years before, the king had ordered that his wife be shut away under a drain and that all those who pass by spit on her to punish her for giving the king kittens instead of children. When he heard what the dervish had to say, the king invited him to the palace with the children, for dinner. That is when the little boy saw his mother under the drain and told his sister:

"Look, there is our mother." Beginning to suspect something, the king asked them: "How can it be – your mother?" So the children told him their story from the beginning, exactly as it happened. And they said: "Now she has to be taken out of there, bathed and dressed."

The king ordered that she be dressed in royal garb. She was brought into the palace. The king gave orders for the midwife and Ash-Maiden's sisters to be brought before him. He asked them why they had done these terrible deeds. Then, he ordered that they be drawn and quartered by horses pulling a bagful of stale nuts in one direction and the three women in another direction. This was done just as he wished.

Tonight, my child, I happened to be there, I swear it, and I asked for a bread, but the black dog took it away from me and ate it.

Sources

"Athokatsoulo" [Cinder-Pussy], Anna Angelopoulos, *Paramythocores*, Hestia, 1991, pp. 56–59.
  Version collected in Rethymno, Crete, in1962.
CGMF 510A, *Cinderella*.
ATU 510A, *Cinderella*, and ATU 707, *The Three Golden Children.*

Comments on the Three Foregoing Cinderella Stories[37]

Anna Angelopoulos

The archaic theme of devouring the mother, made more palatable by transforming her into a cow, is startling to say the least. To take the mother into oneself by swallowing her flesh, like the two elder daughters do, certainly does not encourage separating from her psychically. By contrast, Cinderella, who refuses this consumption, undertakes a process of separation by observing the rituals of mourning.

The heroine keeps her mother's bones, in a jar or somewhere else, an act which alludes to the rite of double burial practised in Greece and in other Greek Orthodox countries. Then she continues to sit in the hearth, where she is covered in ashes, as her name indicates, for the entire time needed for mourning. Living through this mourning period is what allows a psychical separation from the mother, favouring individuation.

Spinning and weaving are ever present in these stories, presented as the traditional activities that mothers teach their daughters. In the folktale, they are part of the tendencies of fusion and separation at work. Transmission of the feminine is achieved through the metamorphosis brought about by the splendid dresses Cinderella finds beside her mother's buried bones. The Greek and Balkanic versions presented here give us a glimpse of the difference between the distant origins of the Cinderella story and the tale now famous all over the world.

Notes

1 R. M. Dawkins, *Modern Greek in Asia Minor*, Cambridge University Press, 1916.
2 Myrsina is a genus of plants brought to church on Palm Sunday, for Epiphany on Good Friday, as well as on All Saints' Day.
3 G. Calame-Griaule, *Contes cruels, contes tendres du Sahel nigérien. Le langage du conte*, Gallimard, 2002.
4 G. A. Megas, A. Angelopoulos, A. Brouskou, M. Kaplanoglou and E. Katrinaki. *Catalogue of Greek Magic Folktales*, FF Communications No. 303, Academia Scientiarum Fennica, 2012.
5 G. A. Megas, A. Angelopoulos, A. Brouskou, M. Kaplanoglou and E. Katrinaki. *Catalogue of Greek Magic Folktales*, FF Communications No. 303, Academia Scientiarum Fennica, "Types and Versions", AT, pp. 700–749.
6 The Folktale and Psychoanalysis seminar, conducted by Anna Angelopoulos and Sylvette Gendre-Dusuzeau at the Fédération des Ateliers de Psychanalyse since 2006.
7 These concepts were set forth and developed by Jacques Lacan, Alain Didier-Weill and Pascale Hassoun, in a special issue of *Autrement*, under the direction of P. Hassoun (issue 24), "Envy and Desire, a False Alliance", 1998.
8 Most authors published in the series *Autrement* ("Envy and Desire, a False Alliance", No. 24, 1998) refer to Lacan, who speaks of *invidia* in the 1938 text "Family Complexes in the Formation of the Individual. The Complex: A Concrete Factor in the Psychology of the Family", a text most often quoted to refer to a phrase from St. Augustine on the *invidia* felt by the small child who sees his baby brother suckling at the mother's breast. Etymologically, *invidia* comes from *in-vedere*, meaning to see inside, as has often been pointed out.
9 Lacan was also the first to speak of the "havoc" wreaked by the mother-daughter relationship, in *L'étourdit*. See also M. M. Lessana, *Entre mère et fille: un ravage*, Hachette, Pluriel Psychanalyse, 2009.
10 To use Pierre Delaunay's poetic phrase in *Les quatres transferts*, Fédération des Ateliers de Psychanalyse, 2012.
11 Aside from the written version of *Snow White* by the Grimm brothers, made famous by Walt Disney, in the oral tradition of numerous countries, there are hundreds of versions of this story, collected by scholars mostly in the nineteenth century. These stories are variations on the central theme of this folktale.
12 See Gisela Pankow, *L'Homme et sa psychose* (*Man and His Psychosis*), Aubier Montaigne, 1977. Pankow presents the phenomenon of the lost body and the dynamic structuration work leading to regaining the body; she describes patients who regain the limits of their bodies lost in extreme experiences, such as that of her patient Jean Cayrol, a concentration camp survivor, persecuted and tortured as an inmate, who left his body to take refuge in an old apple tree in his garden (another form of being) in order to survive psychically during torture.

13 For instance, the hero gains their favour by sucking at their sagging breasts tied behind their back, in order to be "adopted" by them.
14 I would say that this classification includes the dichotomy of feminine clichés, such as "madonna" and "whore". We know, moreover, that since ancient times there have been two Aphrodites: the heavenly and the pandemian, the one belonging to the entire *demos*, the public one.
15 I made up the term "mother species", modelled on "human species". Τέχνη Τιμομάχου στοργήν και ζῆλον ἔμιξε Μηδείης. A. S. F. Gow and D. L. Page, *The Greek Anthology: Hellenistic Epigraphs, The Garland of Philip*, Vol. II, Cambridge University Press, 1968, pp. 43–44. Caesar bought this painting for 80 talents, along with a painting of Ajax about to commit suicide.
16 I owe this image of the cross-eyed Medea to Adrienne Dimakopoulou, author of *Pâle Rossignol*, Apolis, 2009.
17 M. Djéribi, "Oeil d'amour, oeil d'envie" ("Eye of Love, Eye of Envy"), *Nouvelle Revue de Psychanalyse*, 38, Gallimard, 1988.
18 Aarne-Thompson-Uther, *The Types of International Folktales*, Academia Scientiarum Fennica, 2004.
19 N. Abraham and M. Torok, *The Shell and the Kernel*, University of Chicago Press, 1994.
20 H. De Macedo, *De l'amour à la pensée*, L'Harmattan, 1994.
21 S. Ferenczi, "The Principle of Relaxation and Neocatharsis" (1929) in *Final Contributions to the Problems and Methods of Psycho-Analysis*, Routledge, 2018.
22 S. Gendre-Dusuzeau, "Le miroir de l'envie" in *Le Coq-Héron*, No. 228 (under the direction of C. Guy), Érès, March 2017.
23 The question of envy was examined between 2013 and 2015 in the seminar Fairy Tales and Psychoanalysis given by Anna Angelopoulos and Sylvette Gendre-Dusuzeau. This followed upon a year devoted to the subject of deadly transgression.
24 King James Bible.
25 *Le petit Robert* dictionary.
26 Latin etymology.
27 J. Lacan, *The Seminar of Jacques Lacan: Four Fundamental Concepts of Psychoanalysis*, Book XI, W. W. Norton, 1998.
28 Pascale Hassoun discussed this question in 1998 in the journal *Autrement*, in which she published "L'envie et le désir: les faux frères"; see her article "Maladie d'envie" (Envy Sickness), p. 19.
29 J. Lacan, *The Seminar of Jacques Lacan: Four Fundamental Concepts of Psychoanalysis*, Book XI, W. W. Norton, 1998.
30 M. Klein, *Envy and Gratitude*, M. R. Khan (Ed.), Random House, 1997.
31 A. Angelopoulos, *Contes de la nuit grecque*, José Corti, 2013, pp. 89–92.
32 The vital element of food introduces the question of feeding, and therefore of orality. Eating the dough sticking to the mother's fingers brings to mind the oral stage and the frustration of the *infans*, around which Melanie Klein developed her theory of envy. See M. Klein, *Envy and Gratitude*, in M. R. Khan (Ed.), Random House, 1997.
33 See Muriel Djéribi's fascinating research on "the evil eye", especially the article "Oeil d'amour, oeil d'envie" (Eye of Love, Eye of Envy), in *Nouvelle Revue de Psychanalyse*, 38, Gallimard, 1988, pp. 99–110.
34 M. Klein, *Envy and Gratitude*, M. R. Khan (Ed.), Random House, 1997.
35 M. Klein, *Envy and Gratitude*, M. R. Khan (Ed.), Random House, 1997.
36 H. O'Dwyer De Macedo, *Letters to a Young Psychoanalyst*, Routledge, 2017.
37 A. Angelopoulos, "Fuseau des cendres" (Ash Spindle), in "Cendrillons" (Cinderellas), *Cahiers de Littérature Orale*, No. 25, 1989, pp. 71–95.

Chapter III

Creating the Male Hero

The folktales in this chapter offer representations of the masculine hero, depicted from his origin in the desire of his parents – who can be young or old –, a desire that leads to his being born or not, and to follow the course of his life until he reaches the age of maturity in adolescence. This is the case of Yannakis, in "Born of His Mother's Tears", who is born of the tears of a distressed, orphaned woman who, in some versions of the tale, mourns for the children she lost when they confronted the ogre and were killed by him. Born of her tears, Yannakis is destined to immortality. This is also the case for another Yannakis, born of the wish granted to his barren mother, and of "Tom Thumb", who experiences several symbolic births. Sometimes, when boys are abandoned, they are saved by helpful animals or ogres acting as protectors. Their subjective experiences at puberty and in adolescence – a time of physical and psychical metamorphoses –, impossible to put into words, are represented through powerful images everyone can recognise.

BORN OF HIS MOTHER'S TEARS

Once upon a time there was an orphan girl; she had neither mother, father or brother. Her only remaining family was a godfather. She often cried from loneliness and desolation. One day, she cried so much that her tears filled a whole glass. She drank them and found herself pregnant. Her belly grew and grew, and nine months later she gave birth to a little boy. Her godfather was very upset and wanted to know who the father was.

The girl screamed, pulling out her hair: "I didn't sleep with anyone!" But he insisted: "I want you to tell me the truth, I want you to confess!" Finally, she told him how one day she had drunk her tears. Hearing this, her godfather forgave her. They named the baby Yannakis and baptised him.

On the third day, the Fates came to decide the child's future. The first one said: "Since he is the son of an orphan, he will have no fortune; I give him my strength. May he always be brave and victorious in battle!" The second

DOI: 10.4324/9781032674230-4

said: "I give him my wisdom and intelligence. May he become wise and intelligent, so that no one can ever mislead him!" The third Fate bestowed her beauty on him, wishing him to become handsome and kind, and loved by all.

Yannakis became stronger, wiser and more handsome as he grew. At school, he was always in first place. He was his mother's consolation. The teacher was very fond of him, and preferred him to the other children, who were jealous of him. One day, three of them decided to wait for him at the end of the school day, jumped on him and began to beat him. They hit him so hard that the poor boy almost fainted!

That is when Yannakis hit back: he punched the first on the head, the second on the back and the third in the belly; he knocked them all out. Blood was flowing from all their wounds. The children ran off to complain to their mothers, who ran to school to tell the teacher.

The teacher asked him why he hit his schoolmates. The orphan's son answered: "Master, it was not my fault. They are the ones who beat me, they hit me and wouldn't stop. What was I to do?"

— Very well, the schoolmaster said, I forgive you since it's the first time, but don't do it again.

When the other children saw that the teacher had not punished him, they were enraged. The children in all the classes got together and attacked him. They beat him and hit him over and over. He hit back in his turn and crushed them all. This caused great outrage. Once again, the mothers complained to the teacher. This time, the teacher got angry, threatened Yannakis and started to beat him. It must be said that when this teacher started to hit someone, he could not stop; someone else had to stop him. So he hit Yannakis over and over, until the boy, unable to take it anymore, slapped him so hard that he found himself on the ground.

The boy stood still, terrorised. He thought he had killed his teacher. He went to see his mother and told her: "Mother, I am leaving!" She cried, she tried to make him stay. But he kept saying: "I can't take it anymore. I have to leave Skyros!" So she put his things in a bundle for the road, and wrapped some bread, some olives and a few coins in a handkerchief – it was all she had. She gave him her blessing, saying: "Write to me, my child and be well!"

And he set out. He walked and walked towards Marmaro, then went down to Pefko to look for a vessel on which to leave the island. When he reached the mountain, he stopped to rest and took out a piece of bread and some olives, for he was hungry. While he ate, he saw a man approaching; the stranger was very tall, a giant, with a whip hanging from his belt. He saw the boy's bundle and bent down to open it.

— Eh, oh! Yannakis said, that's my bundle, with my clothes in it. My mother gave it to me.

— Shut your mouth! the thief said. If you come near it, you'll see what happens to you!

— The bundle is mine, the boy repeated, put it down and leave it alone!

The thief kept trying to open it. Getting angry, Yannakis approached him, lifted his fist, hit him and watched him keel over, unconscious. The thief was not expecting this, he could not imagine being beaten by a child. When he opened his eyes, he reached for his whip to strike the boy. Yannakis jumped on him and said: "This whip is sure to strike better than my hand!"

He took it and struck the thief. This whip was, in truth, magical: it killed as soon as it struck. So that was the end of the thief. Yannakis took the bundle, tied the whip to his belt and went down to Pefko. In the distance, he saw a vessel offshore. He heard voices and the sound of people running in all directions. What a hubbub! He approached a small group of people and asked what was going on. They said that a pirate vessel had been seen far off and the captain of the trawler wanted to set sail quickly to get away from it.

The boy went to see the captain and begged him to let him embark on his ship. But the captain didn't want to take a child along, because there was great danger. Yannakis said: "Why worry about me? What happens to you will happen to me. I want to come with you no matter what!" When the captain saw that the boy really wanted to leave, he said: "If you are not afraid, come."

The ship sailed away. When they were on the open sea, they saw forty pirate ships coming towards them. What a fright! All of them, from the captain to the lowliest sailor, hid away to save their lives. The boy stayed where he was, on the mast, waiting for them to come back. The captain called to him, they all called him, but he didn't want to come down. They all cried – the captain and the sailors alike –, thinking that the pirates would make him a slave or kill him.

The pirates came near, dropped anchor and jumped on the trawler. Yannakis said to them: "What are you doing here? Go away!" One of them tried to come near him. A single blow of the whip and he lay dead on the ground. Yannakis kept swinging his whip, which hissed like a serpent over his head. He jumped even higher to reach them all. He reaped their heads like a field of wheat. In the end, he killed all the pirates from the forty ships. He took a rope and hung the forty captains from the mast.

From their hiding places, the sailors and the captain heard all kinds of noises, and the cries and moans of the massacred men. But the crew didn't know what was going on. When the uproar died down at last, the captain sent a sailor to see if Yannakis was still alive. The sailor sneaked up on the deck quietly. He looked around and went down again. He told the captain: "He killed them all!" They didn't believe him. Yannakis shouted: "Come up and see what I did!" They went up and saw all the dead pirates lying on the ground, and their captains hanging from the masts. What jubilation! They all kissed and hugged Yannakis, shouting: "Well done!" and crying tears of joy.

When they sailed into the capital, where the king lived, they decorated the ship with flags and flowers. The captain was standing at the helm steering the ship and Yannakis stood at the stern with his whip. They left some of the bodies hanging from the masts to impress the crowd and sailed into the port very slowly to let everyone admire them. When they disembarked, all of them – captain and sailors – described how Yannakis killed all the pirates by himself and declared that he was never afraid.

This is how the king came to hear the story; he asked to see the young hero and asked him: "What would you like me to give you? My fleet can use you. Do you want to be captain of one of my ships?" This caused the commander of the fleet to become jealous; he was afraid that Yannakis would take his place. Therefore, he told the king: "My venerable sovereign, since he is so brave, why not give him a few ships and send him to fight the Gorgon, the terrible monster holding sway over the sea of no return? He may defeat her and be able to kill her, just as he was able to destroy an army of pirates."

The king, who had grown fond of the handsome young man, did not wish to send him into the seas of the Gorgon, from which no one ever came back. The Gorgon was a monster, the dread of the sea. She had emptied all the seas around her of all life. No ship could sail there. She stood before them, seized them by the hull and sunk them to the bottom of the ocean. There was no escaping her!

The king said: "No, I don't want him to go, for he would never return." But Yannakis declared: "And who says I would not come back? Those who did not return probably did not want to. I will go and I will return. I only ask you, Your Majesty, that you have a golden axe made for me, strong and unyielding, for I will surely need it."

The axe was made as he asked. The ships sailed away. The king had told Yannakis that if he defeated the monster and came back, all the vessels of the fleet would be his, along with a thousand other gifts.

All the men aboard the ships, be they captains or sailors, were sad, for they expected to die. They continued on their way, but they were disheartened. Yannakis was the only one who was not afraid, he had no worries. Come what may, they were sailing towards their appointed destination.

One morning at dawn they arrived in the waters where the Gorgon was known to appear. They embraced and asked forgiveness for their sins, for their final hour was near. Yannakis was sleeping. He heard their cries and lamentations. He rose and asked them what was troubling them. They told him. He answered: "I am going back to sleep. Wake me when the Gorgon appears. I will manoeuvre my ship to place it in front of the others."

Suddenly, the sea became agitated and stormy. They thought of waking Yannakis, but decided to let him sleep because they loved him and didn't want him to die. They thought: "Let the other ships be in front. The Gorgon will exhaust herself while she fights them. Yannakis will be saved or, if he is to die, he will be asleep and won't feel the difference." But the young man heard the commotion and the shouting. He jumped up, seized his golden axe and went up on deck. When he saw all the other ships aligned in front of his, he ran to them and shouted: "Stay back, all of you! My ship must be the first in line." He placed his ship in front of the others and steered it towards the foaming waves. They saw the bubbling, swollen sea. The waves rose very high and in their midst the Gorgon suddenly appeared. She grabbed the hull, pulled on the ship and turned it around. The whole crew thought: "We are lost!"

Yannakis came running, struck the Gorgon's hand with his axe, cut it off and threw it in the sea. The Gorgon flew into a rage; she leaped up and grabbed the hull with her other hand. Yannakis struck again and cut off her other hand. She then held on with her teeth, howled and foamed at the mouth, and she pulled on the ship again to sink it beneath the waves. Yannakis lifted his axe and cut off the monster's head, which sunk into the sea. He bent forward to see where the head had fallen, but the storm had erased all traces – of the head, the body, everything. He only saw a dove flying away. He wondered: "What is this dove doing here, in the middle of the ocean?"

All the men came running to him. They kissed his hands and feet, they hoisted him on their shoulders, not knowing what else to do for him. They decided to sail home. Yannakis said: "I am not going back. You are going to leave me here. I will stay on those mountains we see in the distance. You can return home. I am entrusting the ships to the oldest man among you, so he can distribute them as he sees fit. Do what you want with them!" They begged him to leave with them, take command of the whole fleet and set off for new adventures. But he refused. He gave them a letter to give to the king. They left him on an inhospitable shore lined with cliffs and steep ravines, and they returned to the port from which they had set sail.

Yannakis walked and walked; he climbed and descended mountainsides; he crossed deep valleys. He saw no one, not even a bird in the sky. He became sad. He kept walking on and on, until finally he saw a castle. He went nearer; the walls were very high, there were neither windows nor doors. Nothing. He looked. Might he not see someone? He knocked on the wall, he called out, but there was no answer. Suddenly, he saw a ball bouncing on the other side of the wall. It bounced very high, hitting the sun, and then came down again.

"Oh, he thought, there is someone inside who is playing with a ball." He took hold of the branches before him, climbed up on the wall, leaped down and entered the castle through a round hole, through which the ball had bounced out.

He saw a beautiful naked woman playing with the ball. He went nearer and spoke to her, but she made no response. She was playing with the ball and did not bother to look at him or answer. Suddenly, he caught the ball the young woman had just thrown in the air, and he threw it up, taking her place. The ball went beyond the sun. Defeated, the beautiful maiden turned into a dove and flew up towards the clouds.

Once again, Yannakis found himself alone. He went inside the castle, found a table set with food, cutlery, a slice of bread, a glass of water, a warm dish. It was as if everything had been prepared for a man to dine at that precise moment. He was very hungry, and he ate. He lay down, rested, then rose again and looked for the door. Finding no way out, he dug a tunnel and went on his way.

He walked and walked and after much time had passed he came to another castle even taller than the first. He tried to go in, but there were no doors or windows. He hung onto a tree branch and jumped on the balcony. He saw a tall, robust and beautiful girl. She said: "How did you dare come in? Were you not afraid?"

– And you, why are you not afraid?
– I am not a human being, she answered. Anyone who comes here must fight against me; he has no choice.

Yannakis said: "Why fight against you? I haven't come here to fight!"

– We will fight and the one who defeats me will become king. My mother told me this a long time ago.

The fight began. Yannakis lifted her up and threw her on the ground. She sunk into the ground to her ankles. Yannakis became excited, grabbed her, struck her violently against the ground, and made her sink in to her knees. She tried to free herself, she struggled, but to no avail. "You beat me," she said. He went to her and helped her free herself. But she turned into a dove and flew out of his hands. He entered the castle. Again, he found a table set for one person. He ate, he lay down and rested, then dug a tunnel and left. He walked and walked, but found not a soul, not a village, not a single city. He couldn't bear never to see a bird in the sky!

He came upon another castle, which did not look like the others. It had a door and some windows. He went in but saw no one. He opened a door and then another, but the rooms were empty. In a dining hall, he found a table set with three warm dishes, three knives, three forks, three slices of bread and three glasses of water. He was hungry. He ate a mouthful of each dish, drank a sip out of each glass and broke off a piece of each slice of bread. Finally, he felt sated. He asked himself: "Who is this meal for?" He hid in a closet and waited. He saw three doves fly in through the window; they changed into young girls, one more beautiful than the other. They greeted each other warmly.

– Good day, my sister!
– How are you, my sister?
– Come and eat, my sister!

They sat down at the table. The first one said: "Who touched my plate?" The second said: "Who broke off a piece of my bread?" The third said: "Someone drank from my glass."

The first sister said: "Someone came all the way here. But who could it be? We are so unprotected here that anyone can make his way to us. Oh, if only we had Yannakis with us! We would not be afraid and he would keep us company."

– Oh, if only he was here, he could be a brother to us. He is so brave, so intelligent and wise! We would need no one else, said the second sister.
– May he be well wherever he is! Let us drink to his health, said the third sister.

Hearing this, Yannakis came out of his hiding place and said: "I am here too. But who are you, and where do you know me from?" What joy! They wanted to know how he had come to be there. The first sister told him: "I am the Gorgon and you cut off my head and my hands." The second sister said: "I am the girl who played with the ball; but you threw it up higher than I did, and you defeated me." The third sister said: "I am the eldest, but you defeated me too; you sunk me into the ground up to my knees."

Then, Yannakis told them how he had found his way there, and how sad he had been while he was alone in the mountains. So he stayed at the castle with the three sisters. They treated him like a brother, and they all lived together contented and happy.

But Yannakis became restless; this idle life did not suit him. He told the sisters: "My sisters, I can't stay closed up here any longer. I have to be out in the world, I have to hunt, I have to do battle. Give me a weapon. I will leave, but I will be back." They gave him a weapon and advised him to hike in the woods without going into villages or making contact with other men, for then he would forget them and would not come back. Their mother had told them what to expect when she talked about the stranger who would come from far away and defeat them.

So Yannakis went off into the mountains. He saw deer and lions and hunted them. Time passed. One day, as he walked in the wilderness, he saw a marble slab with forty rings. He wondered what it was hiding and lifted it up. He saw some stairs, went down forty steps and entered a narrow corridor. Forty rooms were aligned on both sides of the corridor.

In the last room, he saw a chimney and an old man who had a pot on the fire and was stirring its contents with a huge ladle. Nearby, on a table, he saw forty plates, forty place settings, forty slices of bread. The old demon was surprised to see him.

- How did you find this place? he asked.
- I found the marble slab, I lifted it up and I walked down the stairs, Yannakis answered.

The demon said nothing, although he was impressed that Yannakis had moved the slab by himself, because it usually took forty demons to lift it.

- What are you doing here? Yannakis asked.
- I live with my sons, forty strong demons. They are out hunting and I am making their midday meal. They will be back soon.
- Give me something to eat, Yannakis said. I am hungry and I can't wait.
- Until my sons take the big pot off the fire together, you won't be able to eat.
- Is that the only reason? asked the young man.

He took hold of the pot, lifted it as if it were an apple and took it off the fire. "Now serve me the food!" The old demon was afraid, and gave him food and something to drink. He prepared a bed with embroidered sheets for him, and insisted that he retire for the night. He was afraid of his sons' reaction to the visitor and wanted to avoid a fight, for he could see that Yannakis could kill them all with the strength he had. He wanted a chance to tell his sons about Yannakis first, and explain what he could do, although he was just a man.

Yannakis was very tired and fell asleep. When the demons came back, they said: "It smells of human flesh here." And they looked for the human visitor, to eat him. The old man told them: 'Shhh! Don't wake him up, don't make noise, he is a very strong man. He lifted the slab by himself, and he was able to take the pot off the fire alone!'" That is when Yannakis woke up and came out of his room. The demons welcomed him warmly, they got along well and soon the brothers treated him like one of them.

He stayed with them for a while. Then he left to see his sisters again. They were overjoyed. They thought that he had forgotten them and would never return.

Yannakis said: "I intend to stay with you from now on. I only want to leave once to go to Skyros, to see my mother." They answered: "After all these years, your mother is dead. You can't defeat death. Don't go, for you will not find her there."

– No, said Yannakis, I want to go even if I won't see her.

When they saw that he had made his decision and would leave in any case, the Gorgon clapped her hands and a djinn appeared.

– How fast can you take our brother to Skyros? she asked.
– In five minutes, Madam, he replied.
– Take him then, said the Gorgon, but be careful with him.

The djinn took him and five minutes later set him down at the market in Skyros, in front of the cafés. Yannakis looked around, to the right, to the left; he didn't see any familiar faces. All those he had known were dead. Charon had done his work. He went to his house, hoping to find his mother there; but she had died years earlier. He remembered that his sisters spoke of death, saying that it would come for him too one day. They told him that if he sees an old man with a sack on his shoulder who asks him to carry it for a while to give him a reprieve, he must not touch the bag because the old man is Death himself, trying to exhaust him by making him carry a heavy burden. He remembered all this and was afraid.

He didn't want Death to catch up with him; he walked very fast. At Stavros, near Antoniou, he saw an old man carrying a sack walking on the road. Yannakis broke out in cold sweat. He started to run, to try to get ahead of him and escape him. The old man was following him. Yannakis started to tire. He slowed down, and so did the old man. Yannakis could not get away from him no matter what he did.

When the old man caught up with him, he said: "My child, could you carry my sack for a while, for I am old and tired?" Yannakis refused. Night fell. The old man said: "Whatever you do, you are mine! Take the sack willingly, if not I will catch you and we will fight!" Yannakis would not consent. The old man threw the sack on the ground; they fought. They delivered blows and received blows. Yannakis grew tired, and so did Charon. "If I don't take you today, it will be tomorrow!" Death told him, sitting down to rest. Yannakis collapsed; he couldn't move and had almost stopped breathing.

His sisters had a magic mirror and each night they looked to see where he was. When they saw him so exhausted, pitiful, in such a terrible state, they were overwhelmed with grief. The middle sister clapped her hands. A djinn appeared before her and asked: "What is your wish? What is your command, Mistress?" She said: "How long will it take you to go to Skyros and bring back our brother?" He thought for a moment and said: "Three minutes."

– Impossible! Death will be quicker. Go, I don't want you!

Then, the youngest sister clapped her hands and a djinn stronger than the others appeared. She asked him how long it would take him to go and come back. He thought for a moment and said: "Right this minute!" They told him: "Go, run, before Death wakes up!"

He disappeared at once, took Yannakis and brought him back to the castle tower. He had become a shadow of himself, he didn't have the strength to speak or even lift his arm. His sisters prepared medicines and tonic lotions for him. They healed him and saved his life.

Death woke up and looked for Yannakis. He looked everywhere but didn't find him. He thought: "He couldn't have gone far. Anyhow, he can't get away from me." Death changed into a cold wind, scattering and killing everyone on its path. But this icy wind could not reach Yannakis where he was, where his sisters had given him shelter. He was safe and had time to heal; he regained his strength and lived with his sisters, always healthy and in good spirits, always laughing and joyful.

Sources

"O Yannakis, o gios tis orphanis", Niki Perdika, *Skyros*, II, pp. 233–245.
CGMF 301B, *Born of His Mother's Tears*.
ATU 301 (including type 301B), *The Three Stolen Princesses*.

THE LITTLE RED OX

Once upon a time there was a young boy named Yannis. He was an orphan and very poor. He had to survive with almost nothing. Since he didn't have any way to earn his living in his village, he decided to travel far away, to a foreign land, to see what fate had in store for him. He set out and walked for a long time. One day, he met a priest on the road and greeted him.

– Where are you going? the man asked.
– I am looking for work, the boy answered. I have to find a way to make a living.
– Then stay with me and I will give you work.

Indeed, the priest hired him to be his servant; it was his job to take the animals to pasture. One of the animals, the red ox Roussos was different from all the others. He stood out because of his size, his strength and his intelligence. He had a man's judgement; there was no other like him in the world.

Yannis was a handsome boy, strong and well built. The priest's wife was resentful because he was more handsome than her son. So she wished for Yannis to fall ill, for his radiant skin to turn pale. She kneaded bread made of ashes for him to eat. One day, when Yannis was hungry, he opened his bag and found ashy bread in it. He got angry and beat the little red ox.

– Why are you hitting me like this, Yannis? Roussos asked.
– Because my mistress is giving me bread kneaded from ashes, he answered.
– And that's why you beat me? You better throw that bread in the bushes and come drink from my horns; one is full of milk and the other is full of honey.

So instead of becoming thin and pale, Yannis grew stronger and more handsome each day. The priest's wife was vexed and resentful to see him like this. She did not understand what was happening. She decided to spy on him and follow him to find out what he did with the bread when he was out in the field with the animals. So she saw the boy throw the bread into a thorn thicket and drink from the horns of the ox. That night, she demanded that her husband give orders for Roussos to be slaughtered. The priest protested: "What are you asking, woman! Have Roussos killed, the most magnificent, the most intelligent ox there ever was?"

But his wife insisted so much that her husband gave in to her wishes. Fortunately, Yannis, who slept in the next room, was awake and heard everything. The next day he told the red ox everything. "Don't worry, the ox said. When the priest will try to catch me, I won't let him. And when he will get tired and discouraged, you will ask him to give you the rope to catch me. Then, you will climb on my back and I will start to run. And we will run away together." No sooner said than done.

At nightfall, the two companions were still fleeing at a run. Then they wanted to rest for a while and went into a cave they found along the way. Inside, there was a gigantic bed, so big that they were sure it belonged to an ogre. So they dug a hole in the ground for Yannis to hide in. The boy went down into the hole so the ogre would not eat him. Roussos covered the hole with a big stone slab and went to sleep in the ogre's bed. A little later, the ogre came home.

– Mmmh, he said when he saw Roussos in his bed, it's been a long time since I feasted on an ox!
– And it's been a long time since I had a chance to eat an ogre, the red ox replied. Let us fight and let the winner eat the loser.

They agreed and the fight began. Roussos pinned the ogre to the ground. But when he was about to deliver the fatal blow, the ogre begged him: "Don't kill me, make me your servant instead."

– Very well, Roussos agreed. But only if you consent to be my plough mate and for us to be yoked together.
– But how will we be plough mates if we have no ploughman to work for?
– I have the ploughman we need with me, Roussos answered. If I show him to you, will you eat him?
– No, but who is he?

Roussos lifted the slab and Yannis came out of the hole. The ogre befriended him at once. The ogre had heard that the king had proclaimed he would give his beautiful daughter's hand in marriage to anyone who could plough all his fields in one day; he offered to take up the challenge so that Yannis could marry the princess. But they had neither plough nor yoke. So, Roussos asked the ogre to go into the priest's house during the night to take away his saddle, his whip, his yoke and his plough. No sooner said than done. Roussos told the ogre where he could find each of these things and the ogre left. He came back with everything except the whip. "How will I drive you forward without a whip?" Yannis fretted. "Don't worry," the ogre said. "Use this whistle instead of the whip. Instead of whipping us, blow the whistle. This way, we will know when to run and when to make a turn."

After they agreed, the three companions went to the palace. Yannis went in and spoke to the king. He explained what he and his companions were going to do. He said: "I shall plough all your fields and in return I will only ask for a little meat and a little grass." The meat was for the ogre and the grass for Roussos. The king agreed and the next day the three companions went into the fields with their farm tools.

There, they saw two valleys, each of which was to be ploughed by its own team. They went to work and at noon Yannis and his friends had already ploughed half the valley given to them. When they felt hungry, they stopped to eat. Yannis was exhausted and fell asleep. After some time, the other team was about to finish its work. Roussos was feasting on his grass and didn't notice that the other team was about to win the competition. But as soon as he realised what was happening, he woke Yannis and they quickly went to work.

Yannis kept blowing the whistle. Roussos and the ogre, yoked together, ran as fast as they could, and finished before the other team. Then they all went back to the palace to claim the princess's hand for Yannis. She did not find him very much to her taste, but what could she do? She had to obey her father's will. So she married Yannis. After the wedding, the ogre said: "Now that you are married to the princess, you don't need me anymore. Let me go back to my cave." Yannis agreed and the ogre returned to his cave.

But after his marriage Yannis continued to drink milk and honey from the horns of the ox. And he never even tasted the dishes his wife made for him. At first, she was surprised. Then she became angry at the way her husband scorned her by refusing the meals she prepared for him. She thought: "He can't go without eating, so he must be eating something else." She spied on him and discovered that he sucked milk and honey from the horns of the ox. So one night when they were going to bed she told him: "My dear husband, we don't need all these animals anymore; we are part of the royal family and having cattle is not suited to our position. We have to slaughter Roussos." Yannis refused, but in time his wife wore him down.

As he had done once before, with a heavy heart Yannis went to tell Roussos: "My wife wants me to kill you." And the red ox who loved Yannis dearly told him: "Since it is your wife's will, kill me. But you must give my flesh to the common people, and you must ask that all the small bones be brought to you. Bury them in a hole that you will dig secretly outside the palace. On that very spot, a very tall tree will grow, and it will be 'the tree of the ox'. Be careful, afterwards some young men will come to take away this woman who is your wife but doesn't love you. Challenge them to a contest: let them make bets to guess the name of the tree, and the one who guesses right shall have the woman."

Everything was done as the red ox had instructed. Yannis killed Roussos and followed his advice. Then, young men who wanted to take his wife away arrived. All of them tried to guess what kind of tree grew before the palace, but none of them won the contest. Yannis' wife, who did not love him and wanted to leave with her lover, tried desperately to give him a hint so that he would guess right. One night when she was asking the same question and he stood before the palace, she was able to make Yannis whisper to her: "It's called the tree of the ox." Acting surprised, she repeated very loudly: "The tree of the ox!" so that her lover would hear.

He heard and left quietly so Yannis would not notice anything. The next day, he came back to the place and gave Yannis the answer: "tree of the ox". He won the contest and the woman. And Yannis, foolish and sad, regretting that he had killed Roussos, his loyal friend, for a disloyal woman, became revolted by the world of humans and went to live with the ogre in his cave.

From then on, he lived with the ogre in greater harmony than with his fellow men.

Sources

"Roussos", DH, 847, 121–126, (KEEL 2777), pp. 363–367.
CGMF 511A, *The Little Red Ox*.
ATU 511A. Included in type 511, *One Eye, Two Eyes, Three Eyes*.

THE SERPENT TREE

Once upon a time there was a mother with a simple-minded and unlucky son. Each day, she took her son – whom people ironically called "Well-born" – and went begging with him; it was her way of making a living. One day, they came to a cave. They sat down beside it to rest. They didn't know that thieves used this cave to store and to count their money. They divided it up and stored it in bags guarded by an enormous serpent.

"Well-born" sat down with his mother in front of the cave; he took out his flute and started to play and dance. Hearing the music, the serpent started to dance gaily. He invited Well-born to come inside the cave and gave him a handful of gold coins. "For the joy you gave me with your song, take these gold coins. I want you to come here every day at the same time and sing for me; each time, I will give you a handful of gold coins. If you do not come, I will die; but you will take my body and bury it in your garden. You will plant me there and I will become a huge tree whose name no one will know. You will challenge the merchants passing through here to guess the name of the tree. They will bet on it and lose the bet, and you will take all their merchandise; soon, you will be rich." So Well-born went to the cave every day at noon; he played the flute, and the serpent gave him gold coins.

But when he was about to be married, he forgot to go and see the serpent because of the wedding preparations. When everyone was coming together around the table, he remembered. He took his flute and went to the cave. When he got there, he found the serpent dead. He took the body and planted it in his garden. Three years later, a beautiful tree stood on that spot and kept growing and growing. But no one knew its name. One day, a rich merchant was passing through town. He saw the beautiful tree, wanted to have one like it and asked Well-born what it was called. The young man answered: "Try to guess its name by yourself. If you guess right, I will lose my house, but if you are wrong, you will lose your merchandise."

The merchant could not guess the name of the tree and lost his merchandise. So he was left alone and destitute. But he had hidden in his pocket his most valuable possession: a gold cross. He wanted to rebuild his merchandising business no matter what. So he went to see Well-born's wife and said: "If you can hide me under your bed tonight, I will give you this cross. I will be under the bed and you will sweet-talk your husband into telling you the name of the tree in your garden. He must say it out loud." Well-born's wife was impressed with the cross and accepted the bargain.

That night, after trying a few times, she was able to make her husband say the name of the tree, which was "serpent tree". As soon as he heard it, the merchant left through the door that the woman had left open. The next day, he went to see Well-born and asked to make another bet. If he was going to be wrong this time, he would lose his life! Well-born agreed, thinking that he could not possibly guess. But the merchant gave the right answer and Well-born lost the bet and all his fortune.

Destitute, he went back to begging with his mother. One day, they found themselves in front of the thieves' cave again; the thieves had deserted the cave and were hiding their money somewhere else. Now, the Sun and his mother lived there. The Sun burned and ate anyone who came near his home, but he was away just then. So Well-born's mother had a chance to ask the Sun's mother not to burn them, but to let Well-born ask the Sun for advice about the best way to recover his goods. So the Sun's mother did not let her son eat Well-born, but asked him to reveal the young man's fate to him. The Sun told him: "To recover your goods, you must make another bet with your rival. Tell him that you are sure that tomorrow the sun will rise in the west. He will not believe you, but I will rise in the west and the merchant will lose the bet."

And this is what they did. The next day the sun rose in the west and Well-born recovered his fortune. And they all lived happily ever after.

Sources

"I tychitou Kalogennimenou" [Well-born's Fortune].
    Collected by Ekaterini Houtou in Tripoli of Arkadia, Peloponnese.
    Told by Maria Paraskevopoulou, age 70.
CGF 3B, pp. 867–868.

CGMF* 460B, *The Serpent Tree*.
ATU 507, *The Monster's Bride* (including AT types 507A, B and, 506–506B, 506**B and 508).
ATU 460B, *The Journey in Search of Fortune*.

THE BROTHERS AND THE OGRE

Once upon a time there was a man who had thirteen children. The youngest was called Thirteen. The parents were so poor that they could not feed their children. They decided to lose them in the forest, where the wolves would eat them. But Thirteen overheard the parent's conversation. The next day, they took all their children into the forest, saying that they were going to chop wood. But Thirteen had been careful to fill his pockets with corn kernels, which he strewed upon the path.

When they were deep in the heart of the forest, the parents asked the children to separate and go off to gather wood, each on his own. They were all to meet later at the place from which they left, with the wood they had gathered, and they would return home together. But the parents ran away as soon as the children were out of sight. When the children came back and saw that their parents had disappeared, they understood that they had been abandoned. But Thirteen started to pick up the corn kernels he had spread along the way that morning, and in the evening they arrived home. When the parents saw that they were back and understood that it was thanks to the corn kernels, they decided to take them to another forest, farther away. Thirteen heard their parents' conversation again. Since they had hidden the corn kernels, he filled his pockets with wheat. As soon as they all set out for the forest, he strewed the wheat grains upon the path.

When they reached the heart of this distant forest, the parents asked the children again to go and gather wood. They would come together afterwards to return home. But when Thirteen and his brothers returned, their parents were gone. Thirteen started to look for the grains of wheat he had spread on their way to the forest, but the parents had taken some away and the birds had eaten the rest, so that they could not find their way home.

The thirteen brothers wandered aimlessly in the forest for a long time before taking a path without knowing where it would lead. Night fell. In the distance they saw a light and walked towards it. They came to a hut; they knocked, to ask for shelter for the night. The hut was the home of an ogre. His wife opened the door and said: "For tonight, go and sleep on the terrace beside my children. But be careful! If the ogre wakes up in the night ravenous, he could very well eat you. Be very quiet!"

When the ogre came home at midnight, he was hungry. The ogress had told him that some children had knocked on their door and were now sleeping next to their children. The ogre decided to eat them.

– Be careful not to eat our own children, who are wearing night caps.

Thirteen, who heard what the ogress said, quickly took off the night caps of their host's children and put them on the heads of his brothers. Now, the heads of the ogre's children were bare. The ogre ate his own children while Thirteen and his brothers were running off across the terrace.

They had walked a long time when they encountered a king on horseback, near his palace.

– What do you think of me? the king asked the children. Am I not very handsome?
– Yes, very handsome, they answered. But if you had the ogre's horse, you would be more magnificent still.
– And who could bring it to me?
– Thirteen could, said the brothers, who did not like him because he was much more intelligent than they were.

So Thirteen went back to where the ogre lived. When he arrived before his hut, the horse he had come to take away started to neigh, as he always did when a stranger came near. Hearing the horse neighing, the ogre came out to feed him. Thirteen jumped behind a pile of wood to hide. When the ogre left, the boy tried once again to catch the horse, who began to neigh like before. The ogre came out again and started to beat his horse: "I just fed you," he said. "Why are you howling like this?" This scene was repeated a few minutes later and when the ogre came out of the hut, Thirteen barely had time to hide. Then he caressed and cajoled the horse until he was able to mount it. The animal seemed relieved to be carrying a lighter horseman and took the boy all the way to the king's palace without protest.

– How do you find me now, the king asked again. Am I not very dashing?

The children answered:

– You are certainly very dashing, but if you had the ogre's horse blanket you would be even more magnificent.
– And who can bring it to me?
– Thirteen can.

And Thirteen returned to the ogre's home. The horse blanket was spread out over the balcony railing; it was enormous and embroidered with gold thread. But the bells attached to it started to jingle when Thirteen pulled on it. The sound of the bells brought the ogre out of the house. Thirteen hid. But he pulled on the blanket again and this time the ogre, who was quicker to rush out, caught him. He saw that this was the boy who tricked him into eating his own children. He grabbed Thirteen, tied him up, hung him over a huge pot and asked his wife to chop wood and boil water. Then she was to cut the cord so the child would fall into the pot. And he would eat him when he returned from hunting. While the ogress was chopping wood as she was told, Thirteen said: "This is not how you should chop wood, you're going to a lot of trouble for nothing."

— And how should I do it? the woman asked.
— I'll tell you. Let me come down, untie me and let me show you, and then you can tie me up again.

When the ogress freed him, Thirteen took hold of the axe: "Be careful, he said, don't bend your head or the axe could hit you!" He hit her on the head so hard that she died. He put her in the pot to boil, took the horse blanket and returned to the royal court.
The king asked:

— What do you think of me now?
— We think you are very handsome, the children answered. But if we brought the ogre here alive, you would be even more impressive.
— And who could bring him here?
— Thirteen can!

Thirteen went back to the ogre's home. He was almost there when he met an old man. Thirteen asked him: "Where are you going?"

— I am going to see my friend the ogre, the old man answered.
— I am going there too, the boy said. And he told the old man what he planned to do. The old man replied: "If you want to succeed, you need an old man like me. Kill him, cut him up and put on his skin to trick the ogre.
— And where can I find a better old man than you, Thirteen answered. Anyway, you are coming to the end of your road."

He killed the old man, put on his skin and went to the ogre's hut. The ogre greeted him: "Good day, my friend. It's been a long time since I saw you. To what do I owe the pleasure of your visit?" He invited the old man to eat with him; they shared a big pot of curd and Thirteen said in a shaky voice like that of the old man he had killed. "You know, my friend, one of my kinsmen has just died. I must prepare a coffin for him. He was as tall as you are, so it would help me if you tried out the coffin I am making. "Why not?" The ogre agreed and when he was lying in the coffin Thirteen put a wooden board over him and nailed it shut. He told the trapped ogre who he really was: the boy he thought he had eaten. Then he hoisted the coffin on his shoulders and took it to the king.

While Thirteen and his brothers were sitting in a circle around the king, the ogre was able to break the coffin and climb out. He threw himself upon the king and the children, and devoured them. Only Thirteen was able to get away. He climbed up a tall tree, and took two big stones with him. The ogre quickly got to the tree and started to bite the trunk furiously, foaming at the mouth. He wanted Thirteen, who had caused him to eat his wife and his children, to fall out of the tree. But Thirteen was very clever. He said: "I know that I can't escape and you are going to eat me. You don't have to go to all this trouble. Open your mouth and close your eyes and I will jump into your mouth so you can devour me." The ogre did as he asked and Thirteen threw the stones into his open mouth. The ogre was killed. Thirteen came down from the tree; he took the horse and the blanket to give them as gifts to his parents, as soon as he found out where they lived. He recounted all his adventures and the common people, impressed with his intelligence and his courageous deeds, made him their king.

Sources

"Dekatreis" [Thirteen].
    Version collected in Evrytania by Dimitrios Koutroumpas.
    Told by Maria Paraskevopoulou, age 70.
CGF 3A, pp. 365–368.
CGMF 327B, *The Brothers and the Ogre*.
ATU 327B, *The Brothers and the Ogre* (AT, *The Dwarf and the Giant*).

MISOKOLAKIS

Once upon a time there was a child called Misokolakis ("Half-a-Behind"). One day, he went into the forest and climbed an apple tree to pick apples. While he was busy picking them, a fox shouted: "Misokolakis, throw me a little apple!" The boy threw the fox an apple, but the old fox pretended not to see it and shouted: "I don't see it. Come down, Misokolakis, and show me where it fell."

The child came down from the tree to show the fox the apple. The fox caught him and put him in her sack. Happy with her catch, the sly old fox started on her way home to bake Misokolakis in the oven and eat him. But, along the way, she remembered that she had some other things to do; she tied the sack with a rope and went off.

But Misokolakis was smart. He ripped open the sack with the knife he had in his pocket and came out. Then he filled the sack with stones, tied it shut and ran off as quickly as he could. When the fox came back to take her sack, she found that it was much heavier than before. She thought: "Misokolakis has put on weight", and continued on her way.

She stood before the oven and emptied the sack. The stones made a loud noise when they fell in. The fox, wild with rage, ran into the forest to catch clever Misokolakis. She found him in the apple tree picking apples." "Oh, Misokolakis, tell me how you climbed into the tree," she said (but in truth she wanted to eat him).

— I took glasses, put them one above the other, and I climbed up.

So the fox brought many, many glasses and put them one on top of the other. But when she tried to climb, the glasses broke and the fox (who thought she was smart) fell, cut herself all over and died.

Misokolakis lived his life happily and we even better.

Sources

"Misokolakis" ["Half-a-Behind"].
    Origin: Western Asia Minor.
CGMF 327C, *The Ogress Carries the Hero Home in a Sack.*
ATU 327C, *The Ogress Carries the Hero Home in a Sack.*

TOM THUMB

Once upon a time an old woman and an old man lived together. They loved each other but were sad that they did not have children. One morning, when the old woman had no bread to give the man who was going off to work in the field, she promised to bring him some food later. The old man left. The old woman kneaded the dough well, put a pancake in the oven – *for a pancake is put in first to test the temperature of the oven* –,[1] then she baked the bread. When the bread was ready, she took up her complaining: "Woe is me, if only I had a child, he would take the bread to his father, instead of me." She looked at the jar full of beans near the oven. "If only all these beans could be children!" she mused with a sigh. And God heard her wish; all at once, as many children as there were beans came out of the jar.

– Mother, I am hungry, mother, I am hungry . . ., all the little ones cried together.

She cut pieces of bread to give to them. They ate them all, until there was no bread left. They even ate the raw dough. The old woman was upset and started to cry. What was she going to take to the old man who was working in the field? She lifted the jar full of children and threw it in the torrent to kill them all and be left in peace. They all drowned. Then she lit the oven for the second time and when the dough was baked again, she lamented: "If I would have kept just one, he would have taken the bread to his father." One little bean which had escaped by hiding behind the broom came out and shouted: "Mother, I am hungry." She kissed the child, very glad to see him, and gave him all the food he wanted. Then she told him: "Now go and take your father his meal in the field." The child set off at a run. "Father, I am bringing you bread." The old man was surprised, and asked him who he was. Tom Thumb – for that was his name – told him his story. The old man was happy to hear it. They shared the bread sitting by the roadside.

Then Tom Thumb said: "Father, help me to make a little hollow in the plough so that I can sit in it and plough the earth for you." This is what they did. The little child steered the oxen from his hiding place; the old man sat eating bread a little way off. Two rich merchants passing by were surprised to see the plough advancing by itself, with the oxen. They wanted to know how this could be. The old man explained that his son was in the plough steering the oxen. But they didn't believe him. So they made a bet: if they found someone in a hollow in the plough, they would give the old man all their horses and merchandise; if not, they would take his oxen and his plough. The old man called out to his son: "Tom Thumb!" And the child appeared at once. The merchants had lost the bet; they gave all their horses and merchandise to the old man and they left.

In the meantime, Tom Thumb went back into the plough and went on with his work. Just then, a cow went by very close to him, saw him and swallowed him in one gulp, before he could cry for help. Only when he was in the cow's stomach did he call out for help to his father, who didn't know where he was. "Father, father! Help!" But the old man could not understand where he was calling from. He looked all through the plough but found nothing. He looked all around, but Tom Thumb was nowhere to be seen. The poor old man went home alone.

The cow went on grazing. In the evening, she went back to the barn. Saturday morning, she was sold at the fair. Her new owner slaughtered her to sell the meat. But the old woman who bought the cow entrails went to wash them in the river. Poor Tom Thumb, hidden in the cow's innards! He was afraid he would drown in the river. He started to shout loudly: "Help! Mother, help!". Terrified to hear a human voice coming from the entrails, the old woman tossed them away and started to run.

Tom Thumb was walking away from the river looking for his father, but he couldn't see him anywhere. Because he was so small, he climbed up on an ear of wheat to see better all around him. Just then, a raven that was flying by took the child in his beak and flew far off to eat him. But he dropped Tom Thumb on the roof of one of the first houses in the village. Frightened, the child started to climb down from the roof. When he came to the kitchen window, he was caught by the owner of the house, a voracious man who put him in his mouth and swallowed him.

Tom Thumb found himself in the man's stomach. He shouted, he screamed, he tapped on the walls of this enormous stomach, but in vain. How could he get out? Enraged, he started to leap up and stomp down without stopping, to dance and to spin. The fat man became nauseous; he rubbed his stomach to stop Tom Thumb's blows, but the child stomped even harder. The man vomited and the child fell into the river. But this was not the end of his adventures; in the river, he was swallowed by a big fish, which was caught by a fisherman who took the fish to the king.

The king was very surprised to find a tiny child inside the fish. He talked to the child and Tom Thumb answered in a human voice. Curious, the king asked him: "How did you come to be in here?" Tom Thumb told him his story. "Once upon a time there was an old woman and an old man who had no children . . ." The king took him in his arms, told him that he would live with him at the palace from then on, and would always be like his own son.

One day, the king sent his adoptive son to war. Tom Thumb fought at the front, where he was killed by a spider.

The king was sad and distressed when he heard the news. He gave the little man a royal burial with full honours. The cross on his tomb bore the inscription: "Here lies Tom Thumb".

Sources

"Misokolakis" KEEL, 1281, SM 11, pp. 37–40.
    Version transcribed in Kyparissia, Peloponnese.
CGMF 700, *Thumbling*.
ATU 700, *Thumbling* (previously *Tom Thumb* in the AT classification).

The Filthy Boy Character in Mediterranean Folktales[2]

Anna Angelopoulos

My discussion concerns the imaginary sphere of folktales that focus on young heroes going through the transitional phase of puberty.

I am referring to folktales of the oral tradition, which travel unimpeded and anonymous from country to country, presenting the same theme in a number of variants and versions.

This is in complete contrast with the literary tale we all know, which has an author and a set form. We shall base our discussion on transcripts of the oral form compiled for the most part in the nineteenth century. Several of these folktales are centred on the question of "growing up" – they are about adolescence. The term "adolescent" only emerged in the nineteenth century, but these stories, with their strong images, are much older than that.

We shall examine together, by means of the folktale, a series of representations relating to puberty, this mysterious period of life when unavoidable changes affect the body and the psyche of a young person. Indeed, at puberty the child we know disappears, a new person takes his place, and we must learn how to treat him. Most of us have experienced this more or less directly: the child changes dramatically and a total stranger appears before us. His behaviour is subversive; its violence matches the internal violence to which the adolescent is subjected by his extremely radical vital metamorphosis.

The first definitions of the word "adolescent" sheds light on our investigation. The Latin verb *adolescere* means to grow up. In Greek, the word for adolescent is *ephebe*. Its literal meaning is "on the pubis". This image underscores the importance of sexual initiation, one of the major physiological changes characterising this period. As is to be expected, sexual maturity translates into great and sudden burgeoning, and the emergence of genital sexuality.

These two major events often lead to the abandonment of infantile psychic characteristics abruptly and for a long time (these infantile traits return in old age). Growing up and becoming an adult inscribes one in the social fabric. This transformation constitutes the theme of the folktale we will discuss today. I chose as an example the "Lazy Boy" stories, as they are called in international classifications.

In its literary form, this fairy tale has existed for four-and-a-half centuries. The version known in Italy is that written by Straparola in 1551, in his *Le piacevoli notti* (*The Facetious Nights*).[3] It is the oldest written version of the tale. The same story is found in Italy 80 years later in Basile's *Pentamerone*.[4] Many attested versions exist in France, Greece and other countries in the Southern Mediterranean, the region where the tale originated, according to specialists. The hero of this folktale is a young boy, an adolescent of the seventeenth century. The story reveals striking similarities between him and the young men of our times.

Depending on the version of the tale, the youth is described as lazy, filthy, messy, silent, secretive, given to dreaming, violent or scornful. He sits in the chimney (the fireplace) and is totally dependent on his mother. No father or other paternal figure is present. The story describes the difficulty the boy has in leaving his childhood behind, through a series of incidents that provoke laughter without erasing unease.

In the Greek versions, the boy always has his feet in the ashes. Even when he mounts his donkey to go and cut wood, he has two big bags of ashes tied to his feet, as a way of taking his house with him wherever he goes. People call him "Ashy Bottom" or "Ashy Boy", sometimes even Cinderella in a masculine form. Interestingly, Perrault calls the heroine of his Cinderella story "Ashy Bottom". She too has her bottom – the region of her sexual organs, in any case – in the ashes.

In the narrative, the "ashy" boy undergoes a transformation. Foolish and filthy at first, he eventually becomes smart and clean. He becomes a handsome, intelligent, educated and wealthy young man. Instead of laughing at him or pitying him, the reader admires his transformation. The anti-hero changes into a true mythical tale hero. At the same time, the story of his adventures shifts from being a facetious tale to being a fairy tale.

In the vocabulary of folktales, what we call facetious stories are satirical tales intended to provoke laughter. They are made up of a series of episodes which can be told together or separately. However, these incidents involving a young hero unable to start living his own life also make the reader uncomfortable. In contrast, the fairy tale (also called a "mythical tale" by Vladimir Propp), is a story of initiation in which the protagonist comes into his own. In the tale we are discussing, the tale of the filthy boy, the adolescent gradually becomes an adult. Generally, in folktales this transformation can take different forms depending on the story: sometimes a young girl becomes a woman, or a young boy becomes a man, and there are even stories where there is a shift of sex. In adolescence, anything is possible.

Now I will tell you the story, to illustrate all this more clearly. The version I chose is from France.

Once upon a time there was a fellow so foolish that everyone called him Foolish John, a name that suited him perfectly. One day, his mother said: "I am going to bake a bread, you have to go and gather wood and bring me a bundle." Foolish John went off to look for branches in the forest. Feeling tired, he sat down on the riverbank. Suddenly, he saw a large eel in the water and caught it. They looked at each other and the eel said: "Don't kill me.

Spare my life and I will give you a gift. You shall have anything you want simply by calling out my name.

— *Very well, John said, I agree! And he threw the eel back in the river.*

Then he continued on his way. He arrived in the forest but did not feel like cutting wood or carrying it home on his back.

He thought for a while and decided to ask the eel to grant him a wish. He said: "Let it be the will of my eel that I fly in the sky with my twigs!"

All at once, the branches are cut up and tied into bundles; John is sitting on them and soaring above the village. The villagers see him and laugh. John flies before the palace, the princess sees him and she too starts to laugh. The young man is very hurt, so he says:

"Let it be the will of my eel
For the princess to carry my heir!"

Then he continues his flight and forgets all about the princess. He arrives home and is scolded for being late. "What will we eat?" his mother asks. My savoury bread is not baked." But Foolish John answers: "No need to worry.

"Let it be the will of my eel
A good jug of wine
And of potatoes our fill!"

All at once the table is set, they eat and drink; the mother has no reason to complain.

A few months later, the princess finds herself pregnant. Her parents want to know who the father of her baby is. She swears that she never spent the night with anyone, but her belly continues to grow. After nine months, she gives birth to a beautiful baby boy. The king is so enraged that he wants to kill both of them by throwing them into the sea. But his wife, the queen, says: "No, you will not kill your daughter and your grandson. We had better find the father and force him to marry her." So the town crier calls all the men in the village, regardless of their colour, religion or social class, as we would say today, to come to the palace. They are to file past the child, who is now one year old. The man to whom the child gives a flower will be recognised as his father. The child is entrusted with recognising his father.

All the men in the village file past the child to no avail. Finally, Foolish John's turn comes. Seeing him with his rough clogs, the guards want to keep him out, but the king intervenes. Foolish John stands before the child, who gives him a rose. The king is shocked. He can't believe it: "You had this child with Foolish John?" he asks his daughter.

— No, father. I swear that I don't know him.

No matter, the marriage is held. Then the king takes a barrel, punches holes in it and puts his daughter, Foolish John and their baby inside. He places the barrel on a raft with some bread and water, and sets the raft off onto the sea. Very soon, the raft disappears from view.

Conditions on the raft are difficult to say the least. After a few days, all the bread and water are gone. The waves shake the raft and they are barely holding on. The princess doesn't speak to Foolish John and he doesn't know what to do. When there is nothing left to eat, he says:

"Let it be the will of my eel
A good jug of wine
And of potatoes our fill!"

Suddenly, all this appears and they eat. The princess is astonished and asks: "How did you do that?" Foolish John answers: "I can fulfill all my wishes through the power of my eel."

The next day, when it was time to eat and the princess saw that Foolish John was about to express the same wish as the previous day, she said: "Maybe you could ask for something else? A good roast, white bread and white wine?" And his wish was granted. After that, the feasts kept getting better and better. Then, one day, the princess suggested that Foolish John stop being foolish: "Can't you ask your eel to make you smarter?" John voiced that wish and indeed, he became smarter. He cried out at once: "My God! We are not going to live here forever! We will go ashore and we will build a house." He asked his eel for all this and he had it instantly.

Time passed, the child grew. They had everything they needed. But there came a time when they wanted to go home. Foolish John made this wish, asking for a greater and more beautiful palace than the king. He wanted the palace to appear during the night across from the royal palace. It would be the place where he would live with the princess and their child.

The next morning, when the king and queen awoke, they were amazed to see the new palace that had sprung up overnight. The king said: "I think it is my daughter, but the man who is with her is refined, he is a gentleman, he wears a white shirt, he looks educated – I don't understand. We will go visit them." So they went to see the couple and their son, who had grown up.

> *The princess and Foolish John welcome the royal couple and invite them to have dinner with them. At the end of the meal, when the king is about to leave, Foolish John whispers:*
>
> *"Let it be the will of my eel*
> *That in the king's pocket*
> *The gold spoon lies concealed."*
>
> *As the king and queen are leaving, Foolish John points out that a spoon is missing. They all look for it and finally find it in the king's pocket. Foolish John says: "We welcome you in our home and you steal a spoon from us?"*
>
> *— I don't know how this spoon landed in my pocket, the king said.*
> *— Just as your daughter didn't know how she found herself pregnant.*
>
> *Then the king understands and kisses his daughter. They all reconcile and live happily ever after.*

This is the end of the beautiful tale where two young people leave their parents' home, and where a young boy comes into his own in the world of adults.

In most versions of the story, the fish is not an eel but a tuna fish, with whom the boy exchanges a meaningful look. Indeed, regressive identification takes place with this phallic fish, that John will call his "little eel" from then on. This illustrates the boy's phantasy of sexual omnipotence, the phantasy of fulfilling all desires through male strength. The fact that the boy does not eat the fish symbolises his liberation from orality. His refusal to eat his "little eel" allows him to leave the family nest and enter the realm of phallicity and later that of genitality.

Another decisive scene in the story is that where Foolish John provides food for his mother. After doing this, he is able to leave her: she no longer feeds him, he is the one who provides her with food thanks to his "little eel".

Then comes the stage of sexual transformation. Indeed, unwittingly the boy gains access one day, suddenly and without warning, to the sexual power of his penis. To his surprise, he discovers that he can assert this strength by using the magic power of language, previously unknown to him. This allows him to take revenge on the princess for laughing at him. According to Ruth Bottingheimer,[5] an American researcher who wrote about this folktale, what the princess is laughing at is the enormous bundle of twigs on which Foolish John is sitting. In some versions, the bundle of sticks is replaced with a huge fish, and sometimes, in bawdy versions of the tale, by Foolish John's huge penis. So the princess laughs because she sees him sitting on an enormous penis, and this is what offends Foolish John.

In Foolish John, we can easily recognise a modern-day adolescent at the stage of sexual awakening, tormented by uncontrollable erections that embarrass him and make him feel ashamed, particularly in front of girls. Thus, we can understand the hero's anger and his wishing that she had become pregnant by him. But it will only be much later, after a number of trials, that the young man will succeed in integrating these physical changes at the psychic level.

For the fairy-tale hero, sexual initiation is most often symbolised by marriage at the end of the story. In contrast, in the folktale we just discussed, the story starts with a marriage, with access to uncontrolled and uncontrollable genitality.

The magic word is what sets the hero on the path to initiation. His experience of puberty starts with verbal reference to his penis in the phallic representation of the enormous fish he frees and which will always stay with him from then on. In fact, he acquires a wife and a child without sexual relations.

But all these physiological changes cannot be inscribed in his psyche. For a very long time, John remains subject to the impatient and capricious drive that dominates him. It will take him much longer to become an adult.

The story paints an image of exile at sea. It introduces an intermediary space-time of internalisation through the metaphor of gestation in a barrel thrown into the sea. John is portrayed as being in exile during the period of genital transformation and internalisation.

Finally, after a long detour, he can imagine and integrate the spectacular changes occurring in his body and in the bodies of others around him. In this story, this allows him to become a father, a husband and the king's son-in-law at the same time.

His Oedipal relation to his father-in-law will serve as a model for his physical and psychic development. He compares himself to the king: he wants a bigger palace facing the king's palace. This is how he acquires his identity and becomes ready for social relations, once he has definitely separated from his mother, his previous incestuous love object. The young hero can now move away from the marginal position he has always held.

This fairy tale about the lazy and filthy boy is the equivalent of the facetious tale Silly Billy (Jean le Sot in French). I would like to mention Virginie Chardenet's beautiful book[6] in which she analyses several variants of this folktale. She provides us with many elements I use in my discussion.

First, I will recount two episodes of the tale "Jean le Sot", to illustrate what I will be discussing.

"Jean le Sot wants to go and see the girls. His mother asks:

- Have they kissed you?
- No, Jean answers, they don't want to see me.
- You have to give them the eye.

The next day, when Jean takes his flock of sheep to pasture, he gouges their eyes out and puts them in his pocket. When he sees the girls, he throws the sheep eyes at them, aiming them at the one he likes the most. You can imagine the disaster!"

Later in the story, he takes a gosling to give to Jeannette as a present. He puts it inside his trousers. When he sees Jeannette, he tells her: "I have something for you in my trousers."

This makes us laugh, of course. But after several similar episodes, we don't feel like laughing anymore. We understand the hero's difficulty in extricating himself from his childhood. In fact, the tale ends tragically when the hero drowns in a lake while trying to fly with wings of his own making. In contrast, in fairy tales, although the characters can be ridiculous and provoke laughter, there is optimism in the plot.

Why is this young boy just entering adolescence described as filthy? What is this layer of dirt he wears like a second skin during latency? The hero's filth represents his psychic envelope during the long period of his mutation. The adolescent is trapped in this cocoon, while he tries to hide the external signs of puberty. This brings to mind Françoise Dolto's book *Paroles pour adolescents* (*Conversation with Teenagers*), which describes the lobster complex.[7] Dolto explains that when lobsters change their shells, first they shed the old one, and are left defenceless while the new one grows. In the meantime, they are exposed to great danger. A conger eel can always be lurking, ready to devour them. "For lobsters," she writes, "adolescence is a catastrophe. For us, the conger is everything that threatens us from the inside and the outside, things we usually don't think of."

The distress of young people during this moulting period can be compared to the distress of the newborn infant, relatively speaking. The newborn is in fact separating from the foetus he was, he has lost the placenta and the umbilical cord, and has left the uterus. This makes us wonder if the ashes of the hearth covering the hero like a second skin might not represent the mourning for his child self, which disappears before it can be replaced by his adult self. Growing up and becoming an adult by moving away from the margin and into the symbolic realm are the two major themes of this folktale. Dolto has commented, in fact, that adolescents often dress in black, a sign of mourning for their childhood. Thus, filth is a substance that envelops and contains the pubescent hero, a boy needing a new identity. The preponderant place of the body at this age, the smells, the body hair, the clothes, the shoes, the messiness – all these indicate a person in transition, who is "building his new shell", as Dolto says. She draws attention to the new secretions generated by nocturnal emissions. The filthy adolescent is temporarily covered with these new productions of his budding genitality.

There are many folktales in which the hero is born in animal form or lives as an animal, until he becomes human when he falls in love.

To conclude, I will discuss a second tale focusing on the same elements as Silly Billy. This tale is about Strong John (*Jean le fort* in French). In Greece, this is a folktale type – that is, it names a number of different tales about a hero with great strength. Strong John draws his strength from very unusual sources, even magical. For instance, he could be a "child of tears" (see "Born of His Mother's Tears"[8]); the countless tears his mother shed render him invincible. Sometimes, he is presented as the son of a bear; in Greece, he is the son of a female bear who raped a priest.

Just like "Lazy John", "Strong John" can be portrayed as sitting in the ashes of the hearth; they have this in common. In some versions he is covered in ashes and draws his strength from the smouldering fire, from the embers under the flames.

Strong John is helped by collective transgression. He meets a gang of boys who engage in what we would call delinquent activities: they eat all the baker's bread, drink all the milk of the cows and kill the villagers with a club. It is a phantasy of collective male omnipotence. Strong John's companions have extraordinary qualities. For instance, one of them joins two mountains together with his penis; another one has a mouth so wide that it can devour everything.

In the story, they all go down into the realm of the dead. They have trouble getting back but succeed in doing it. Then they wage war and dethrone a very powerful king. In the end, Strong John, conqueror and gang leader, marries the princess and accedes to the throne. This is how the story ends.

By joining the gang of boys in which he finds his masculine identity, Strong John embarks on his destiny as an adult man. He takes his place as the hero of a mythic tale by becoming king and marrying the princess. Here, we are no longer in the facetious sphere, which confines the hero to an infantile world of attachment to his mother. These types of stories are about adolescent transgression, which opens onto rites of passage. This passage occurs through exertion of male strength, the development of muscles, and rivalry about penile attributes. In time, all this allows the young boy to become a full-grown man. As for the form of the folktale, these plot developments also transform the narrative, as was the case for the "Lazy Boy" tale. Instead of being facetious, the story is now mythical.

The Grateful Dead

The two folktales that follow have occasioned numerous anthropological research studies, since they describe different types of religious rituals. They concern the rite of passage applying to a boy who, contrary to his older brothers, is unable to respond to the paternal injunction, accompanied by a death threat, to enter the working world by choosing an occupation, so as to acquire wealth and avoid reducing the fortune of the kingdom. The particularities of his journey are discussed in the remarks given after the second story.

THE GRATEFUL DEAD

In ancient times, a king summoned his three sons and told them: "We are living in peace now, but have you ever thought what would happen if one day a more powerful king attacked us with his army, took over our kingdom and all our wealth?" The king's sons were silent and fell to thinking.

After a little while, the king added: "My children, every day I think of what we should do so that we don't end up trying to save a sinking ship when it's too late. You are young now, in full possession of your power and your wealth. But you must learn a profession you can rely on later if the need arises. No work is dishonourable; no matter what it is, it must let you earn enough to cover everyone's expenses, so that you are not subjected or indebted to anyone. Tomorrow morning you shall wake early and come to see me; I will give each of you the money he needs to find the occupation that suits him. You will receive God's blessing as well as mine, for God never lets a working man starve!"

When he finished speaking, his sons told him what they wished to do: the first wanted to become a wheat merchant, and the second an oil merchant. But the youngest was ashamed to say what he wanted to do. His father and brothers insisted until he finally said that he wanted to be a butcher; he wanted to buy cattle and resell them, or else raise cattle for slaughter and sell the meat.

Finally, the father said: "My sons, have you thought of all the difficulties you will face in your occupations? Have you thought of crooked people who will see that you are novices with money to spend, and who will do everything to steal it from you? They will try to devour you like beasts of prey. So this is what you will do. Each of you will make one of his servants an associate, so that one of the partners will bring the money and the other the professional skill." All the sons agreed and went off to choose their associates.

A few days later, the two older sons had found their partners, had been to see their father and received the money they needed. They went off to see to their affairs. As for the youngest, he had tried but could not find a partner. He asked people who were poor, people who were rich, and he offered to pay in advance. But to no avail: no one wanted to become his associate!

Hearing this, his father was sad and angry at the same time. He was sad to see that his youngest was so courteous to people who did not like him; and he was angry because this son had never been able to make a single friend. He summoned him and said: "Listen to me carefully. If you don't find a partner before Saturday, I will have your head cut off!"

Poor child! Hearing these words, he almost lost consciousness, certain that his father was not joking. He went off with tears in his eyes, his heart broken. He went down the stairs and walked away, not knowing what to do. One last time, he gathered his courage and went to see all the butchers, telling them what his father had decided, crying and hoping that one of them would have pity on him and become his partner. But it was all in vain! No one even turned around to glance at him. The young man was already dying on the inside. A needle prick would have caused pus to burst through his skin.

As the royal deadline was drawing near, the young man decided to go to a village some distance away, where there were several butchers, hoping to find a partner at last. When he arrived, he went into the inn, sat down, ordered coffee and invited all those present, whether he knew them or not, to drink with him, while he explained why he had come. All the butchers in the environs were called to see him and he told them his story. But in vain; no one accepted his offer. Some said they were tired of this occupation, others said they needed no partners. In short, he did not find an associate. Put yourself in his place! He had only two days left. When he thought that his head would be cut off in two days, he wanted to run away and go frolic on the mountaintop.

To ease his grief, he asked the innkeeper for a glass of raki. "Come, you all, let us drink together! To the devil with associates!" Those present asked for nothing better; they gathered around him to drink and raised glass after glass.

In the midst of their revelry, they heard cries outside the inn. They saw a crowd walking by, and four people carrying a corpse wrapped in a carpet. Babies were screaming, adding to the commotion. Seeing this spectacle through the tavern window, the young man went out and asked what was going on. The men carrying the body told him that a destitute stranger who had been living of late in the village had been found dead. They were going to throw him on a dung heap, for no one knew what kind of man he had been.

- And why not bury him? the king's son asked. Is it not a shame to throw him on a dung heap?
- Yes, sire, but we found not a penny in his pockets.
- What does that matter? Put the body down on the ground and go get the metropolitan bishop and the priests of all the nearby villages, so that we can give this man a decent burial.

People listened to him in amazement. They thought that the king's son must have lost his reason, since he insisted on burying a beggar with such pomp and ceremony! But when they saw the prince throw a fistful of gold coins on the tavern table and tell the innkeeper to pay the costs of the burial with the money and then tell him if he needs to add more, they hurried off to carry out his orders.

No more than 68 hours later, everything was ready: the metropolitan, the priests, the altar boys and the dead man's casket. The kolliva[9] was prepared at once; this is what money can do! Finally, when everything was ready, the whole village came together and a funeral mass unlike any other even seen in Skamnia was held.

When the dead man was buried and everyone returned to their affairs, the prince returned to the inn and ordered raki in memory of the deceased. While they drank, those present said: "May God forgive his sins!" And they added, to toast the prince: "May you live long!" At that moment, a naked man holding a knife suddenly entered the inn. His face was coarse and dark-skinned. His eyes were black and in the gloom only their whites could be seen, as if his pupils were surrounded by pus. He wore no clothes, he was completely naked. He was not laughing, and when he opened his mouth to speak, his huge, horrifying teeth could be seen.

So the Naked Man came into the inn, greeted the guests and went to sit next to the prince, who was afraid at first but then offered him a drink. Someone asked him who he was. The Naked Man answered that he was poor and unlucky, for in his country his occupation was badly paid. He had been forced to go away, to another village, to find someone who would agree to become his associate; together, they could earn enough to make a living.

– And what is your occupation? the people asked.
– You can guess by looking at my knife, the Naked Man answered. I am a butcher. But alas, I have no money! Before, I had savings but people took everything I had. I found myself on the street, naked, like the day I was born.

Hearing this, the king's son was filled with hope.

– You are a butcher? he asked the Naked Man. And you want to work but you have no money? Then why don't you become my partner? I will contribute the money and you the know-how.
– How can I refuse? I am ready whenever you say, the Naked Man replied.

Everyone was delighted! They drank and sung. At last, the prince had found a partner and he was no longer in danger of losing his head.

The prince and the Naked Man set off at once to return to his home town. When they arrived, the prince went to see his father to tell him the good news: that he had found a partner. The king was very relieved to hear this. He had also worried while he counted the days his son had left to find an associate. He was sick with fear, for everyone knew about his decision to cut off his son's head if he did not succeed. Therefore, he would have been forced to carry out his threat, to keep his word and to set an example.

– Where is your partner? Bring him here quickly so I can see him.

The prince replied mournfully: "My sire, I have found a partner, it's true, but he is a little strange. I am afraid you will dislike him."

– What is he like?
– He has a strange habit – an eccentricity, we might say –, he walks around naked with a knife in his hand.
– It doesn't matter, said the king. Bring him to me to conclude the agreement and tomorrow morning you will rise early and start your work.

A servant went to get the Naked Man in the palace courtyard. The man, silent as Lazarus, as we have come to know him, dim-witted and brooding, went in and squatted at the king's feet. They discussed everything together and decided that the prince would invest all the money required, and the Naked Man would contribute his skill. All the money earned would be split equally between them. They also prepared the papers that had to be signed. The king stamped them with his personal seal and the seal of the kingdom. The Naked Man, who could not write, signed with his thumbprint. Then the king counted the money required in front of him, before indicating that he could take leave.

But as soon as they rose to leave, the Naked Man turned to them again and insisted: "Dear friends, we drew up papers and signed them, so we're sure that we won't have a dispute later. But I repeat, so there won't be any misunderstanding: everything we earn will be divided in two, do you agree?"

"Of course, we agree," both the king and the prince replied.

They went down the stairs and continued on their way. Early next morning, everyone who had come out to see the hanging of the prince, saw him instead go off with the Naked Man, each of them riding a horse. They rode to the port to find a skiff and sail across the sea to Anatolia, to buy cattle.

But let us leave for the moment all those who ask questions (who is this man the prince made his partner?) and all those who have answers of all kinds. Let us stay with the prince and the Naked Man. They found a skiff and crossed to the Anatolian shore. The kingdom where they wanted to buy cattle was inland; it took four days to reach it, and the road was rough. Once they landed, they continued on horseback on desert-like terrain. At no point through the day did they find a peaceful place to rest, a fountain from which to drink and next to which they could stop to eat. It was only at the hour of evening prayers that they came upon a beautiful green prairie. Two or three plane trees grew there, and beneath them there was a spring of sparkling, cool water. Seeing this lovely landscape, the prince wanted to stop there and spend the night. But the Naked Man wanted to keep advancing towards their destination. In the end, they did as the prince wished. They dismounted, rested and at sunset ate their dinner. Then, at nightfall, they lay down under the plane trees.

The prince fell asleep at once, for he was not used to such an arduous life. The long day had exhausted him and he had to sleep. The Naked Man lay down and pretended to snore, but he stayed awake. At midnight, a great din was heard and suddenly a beast with seven heads appeared. Seeing the Naked Man, the prince and the horses, he sprang on them to devour them. But the Naked Man, who was only pretending to sleep, leaped up with his knife and started to slice off one head of the monster after another. My listeners, I tell you that on that night he cut off all the monster's heads in the time it takes to count to three. When the monster was dead, he dragged him a little farther and dug a hole. He hid the beast's tongues in the hole, after having salted them so they would not rot. He washed his knife at the fountain, then lay down next to the prince. The prince had not heard anything. In the morning, when he rose, he saw that the Naked Man was still sleeping. He taunted him, saying: "You see, you didn't want to sleep here and now you don't want to wake up!"

The Naked Man rose a little later. They washed, mounted their horses and rode off. A quarter of an hour later they found themselves in a desert. All day, they rode through this terrain full of thorns and wild plants; they were overwhelmed by the heat. But in the evening, they were lucky to find a cool, green space like the day before. Seeing this place, the prince asked the Naked Man once again to agree to sleep there. They dismounted, washed and cut some clover for the animals. Then they prepared their evening meal and ate. It was still daylight and the prince could see that the Naked Man was sad. He wanted to question him about his past, but the man wasn't talking. The prince saw that he would not break his silence. So he lay down and went to sleep.

The Naked Man lay down a little farther but only pretended to sleep. Suddenly, a beast resembling the one from the night before appeared. The Naked Man rose and did the same thing to this monster as he had done to the previous one; again, the prince didn't see anything. The next morning when the prince rose, he teased the Naked Man once more, saying that he was not tough enough to wake up early in the morning. How could he have known that during the past two nights he had fought fierce battles! The Naked Man finally rose and they continued on their way.

At sunset, they found another beautiful prairie and the same thing happened. The prince wanted to stay there and the Naked Man wanted to leave. But the prince won out like before. I know that this can seem rather boring to my listeners, but I am held to the promise not to leave out any part of the story.

At midnight, there was a great din. But his time it was not the beast with seven heads. It was an ogress making all the noise, a mother whose sons were ogres.

This ogress was riding a hare and was carrying a pitcher on her shoulder, to fill it at the fountain. When she saw the men and the horses under the plane tree, she said nothing; she filled her pitcher and went back to the cave where her forty sons were hiding. She wanted to tell them that there was an unexpected treat in the prairie and that they should come quickly to devour it.

But the Naked Man, who was not sleeping, followed the ogress and stayed outside the cave when she went in. The ogres started to come out one by one, while he stood there with his knife. As soon as an ogre came out, one blow threw him to the ground. All forty of them were killed this way. When their mother came out to see what they were doing, he killed her too, then went down into the cave. And what he saw, what he found there, I could never describe! There were many rooms in this cave, all in a row: he counted forty. He opened the doors one by one and in each room found treasures he never could have imagined. In one room there was a mountain of gold coins and diamonds. In another, there were golden books that were priceless, hematite stones and objects worthy of a prince. In another room, he found a dead man who had been strangled, as well as dead animals, that the ogres had kept there intending to eat them. In another place, he found what they harvested, their dry biscuits, their ritselia,[10] their Basma tobacco,[11] their trahana[12] – everything they needed in their daily life.

He opened the door to another room at the back of the cave. And what did he see? He found three young girls, all of them princesses, hanging by their hair. The ogres had abducted them and had asked their parents to pay ransom for their freedom. When the girls saw the Naked Man, they started to shout, begging him to save them. He untied them and asked them who they were. Each one told him her story and what had happened to her. By chance, one of them happened to be the daughter of the king they were going to see, to buy cattle from. The Naked Man did not reveal any of this, he spoke to them gently, told them to wait inside the cave and not to worry, for he would do everything in his power to free them. He showed them where to find the reserves of food and he left the cave. He pulled out the teeth of the dead ogres and those of their mother, and hid them. Then he lay down next to the prince to sleep.

The first rays of sun from the mountain top woke them at dawn. The Naked Man said nothing about the feats he accomplished during the night. They mounted their horses and rode away.

At twilight, when shepherds come back from pasture, they saw the city they wanted to reach. They arrived when it was time to light the lanterns. They dismounted before the inn. After they tied up their horses and drank their coffee, they told some people why they had come. They asked them if they knew who had cattle to sell, so that they could meet them at dawn the next day. In the meantime, they heard the clamour of the town crier and everyone stopped to listen. "Listen well, people of this village and those nearby! Tonight you must close very early, you must cover all the openings in your houses, close your doors and windows and go to bed early, because the king's daughter will come out for a stroll. Don't wait and regret it later, and above all, don't say you didn't hear this announcement.

When the town crier finished, the people at the inn continued their discussion, but the prince and the Naked Man were astounded by what they heard.

– I can't believe my ears, what can this mean? the prince mumbled to the Naked Man. Because the princess goes for a stroll everyone has to stay home? Is it necessary to close all the windows and doors and cover all openings?

For the first time, the prince saw the Naked Man smile. But he said not a word. Who could tell what he was thinking?

The prince stayed where he was but his thoughts kept going back to the words of the town crier, which made no sense to him. Finally, he turned to the people at the inn: "Tell me friends, why is it that when the king's daughter goes for a stroll the whole village has to be disturbed?" At first, the people laughed at his question, but then they answered: "It's because you are a stranger that you don't know. You see, the princess is so beautiful that anyone who sees her loses his reason. It's so that no one will suffer that she warns us in advance, so that everyone can hide and be unharmed."

– Oh, is she that beautiful then?
– Oh, my poor gentleman, she is a real feast for the eyes! answered a broken-hearted man at the back of the room.

The prince fell silent, but he thought that he wanted to see the beautiful princess no matter what the cost. The Naked Man, on the other hand, did not seem interested in this kind of thing. In the meantime, the gendarmes were going through the village to close the stores and the houses, and people were quickly going back home, one after the other. The prince and the Naked Man stayed at the inn with the innkeeper, who busied himself covering all the openings. He filled up the cracks as best he could. He brought two mattresses and two pillows and put them on top of trunks on either side of the tavern. He wished the two strangers "good night", telling them to go to sleep.

It must have been around three o'clock. As soon as they lay down, the prince kept turning over restlessly. He thought only of what he could do to see this princess. He had an idea: with a small knife he had in his pocket, he started to make a hole in the wood big enough to see who went by outside. When he was finishing his work, he heard a sound and saw some light. He placed his eye over the opening and lo and behold! He saw about a hundred young girls, all very lovely, coming down the road. In their midst was the princess. Her beauty was so dazzling that the poor young man fainted at the sight.

When he recovered, she was already gone. He lay on his bed thinking. He thought of the princess until dawn, as if she had bewitched him! In the morning, the Naked Man asked the prince to go and find people with cattle to sell, so they could see to their affairs. But now the young man had other things on his mind. Indeed, the poor man had fallen madly in love with the princess. When the Naked Man finished speaking, the prince thought for a moment, then said: "Listen to me, my friend. I have something to tell you because there is no one else here to hear my confession. Last night I did a foolish thing. While you were sleeping, I made a hole in the wood and I saw the princess on her walk.

— What of it? asked the Naked Man.
— What do you mean: "What of it?" She is so beautiful that I fell in love at once. I must marry her or else I can't go on living. I shall stab myself or bury myself alive. You can't imagine what a magnificent, ravishing woman she is. Such a beauty can be found nowhere else in the world. What am I to do? Tell me what to do!

But the Naked Man seemed not to care.

— I don't know, he said. We came here to work, not to fall in love. Forget about all this and do what I tell you: let us take care of buying cattle.

You, my listeners, can imagine how sad the prince was when he heard these harsh words. His eyes filled with tears, and he cried like a baby! As the song says, love is a cruel thing: "Cursed be love and the one who puts his faith in it. Woe betide the one who trusts the untrue dog."

When the Naked Man saw the prince in such a pitiful state, he felt sorry for him and said: "Don't cry like this, my child, for you are breaking my heart! What's done is done. It would have been better had you not seen her. Yes, you were foolish, but what can we do now? I will do everything I can to help you."

This was all the young man wanted to hear. He asked the Naked Man at once to go and see the king and ask for his daughter's hand in marriage. After some hesitation, his associate consented. And so it was that our handsome Naked Man went off to the palace. The king's sentries, seeing such a wild, naked man holding a knife, refused to let him pass. But the king, who happened to be on his balcony and to hear the commotion, ordered the guards to let him in.

Once inside the palace, the Naked Man stood before the king and said: "Long life to Your Majesty! Last night while your youngest daughter was taking a stroll, the youngest son of the king of my land happened to see her. He fell in love and has decided to marry her. He sent me here to ask you for her hand in marriage. Do you accept or not?" These were the plain and simple words used by the Naked Man to make the marriage proposal. The king replied: "Very well, but I cannot give my daughter's hand to whoever

I want, because I vowed to give it to the man who can accomplish three tasks first, no matter who he is. Listen carefully and tell the suitor what I am telling you now. If he accomplishes these three tasks, he can come to the palace to be my son-in-law. First, in a certain place there is a seven-headed beast; in a second place there is another seven-headed beast; and in a third place there are forty ogres living with their mother. All these beasts and ogres are on the lookout for strangers who come to our country to buy cattle. They eat anyone who comes here. You can guess how damaging this is to the country. No one comes anymore to buy cows or bulls. And as if this was not enough, they kidnapped my oldest daughter and are asking for a huge ransom to free her. Now you know. So the man who will kill these monsters and ogres, who will free our country from this plague and bring back my oldest daughter, that man shall be my son-in-law, the husband of my youngest daughter."

Thus spoke the king. And the Naked Man was happy as he listened, for he realised that the king was speaking of the beasts and ogres he had already killed. But he said nothing. He took leave of the king, went down the stairs and walked away.

He returned to see the prince, who was waiting for him impatiently. He sat down beside him and recounted everything in detail. The poor prince listened, filled with dread. He did not know what to do. Instead of reassuring him by saying: "Don't worry, for I already slayed these monsters," the Naked Man asked him bluntly: "What do you think? Can you accomplish the tasks required to marry the princess?" The prince started to cry again and begged his partner: "I beg of you, dear associate, you will be the one who will accomplish these tasks, it will be you once again." His face was bathed in tears. In short, the Naked Man took pity on him again. He rose and pretended to go off to kill the beasts – the ones he had already killed, of course!

He went and dug up the tongues of the first monster he had killed. When he returned in the evening he took the young prince to the palace. But first they stopped in a dark corner; he showed the prince the tongues of the seven-headed beast and asked the young man to tell the king that he was the one who killed it.

The young man showed the king the tongues, taking them out of his shirt. He described the fight with the beast in detail, the pain he endured, how he had almost died, and many other lies to make the king believe him. The king believed him and asked him to kill the second monster.

The next day, the Naked Man dug up the tongues of the second beast; he went to the palace with the prince, to see the king. Again, the king believed that the prince had killed the second beast; so he sent him to kill the ogres too and if he accomplished this task, he would become his son-in-law.

Early next morning our handsome Naked Man went to get the teeth of the ogres, and took them to the king when he and the prince went to the palace together. When he gave the king the teeth, the young man told him that his oldest daughter was waiting, hidden in the cave, and that they needed to go there with many soldiers and mules, to carry the gold coins and diamonds away and to bring the princess back to her father, together with two other young girls.

The poor king cried tears of joy when he learned that his daughter had been freed and that his country was rid of monsters and ogres. He didn't know how to show his gratitude. He took the prince in his arms, kissed him and called him "my son" and "my son-in-law". Then he summoned his youngest daughter, the one who was dazzling. He asked her to bow and kiss the prince's hand. He told her that the prince would be her husband, and that he had been chosen because he freed her sister from the ogres and delivered the country of monsters.

The beautiful, smiling and joyous princess sat down next to the prince. Soon she rose again, went to get a silver try and crystal glasses and offered him something to drink. After that, she gathered basil and other herbs, added carnations and made a scented bouquet that she tied with a ribbon of gold and red silk, and gave it to him. The princess's attendants covered tables with striped tablecloths of fine damask linen and embroidered napkins. They placed all kinds of dishes and delicacies on the tables. There was even bird's milk cake! Then the king made it known that all the people should come, eat, drink and make merry, for his oldest daughter was free and their country was rid of monsters.

Next morning, the prince and the Naked Man left, with many soldiers and animals, to bring back the captive princesses, and the gold coins and diamonds. At nightfall, everyone was waiting for them at the city gates. The crowd saw the Naked Man first, followed by the three princesses and the young prince; then came a long line of a hundred animals loaded with gold coins and diamonds, with the soldiers behind them. The crowd was wild with joy. Everyone gathered before the palace and they all spent the night eating and drinking.

The king's son was happy. He stayed near the princess all night, dancing with her and looking at her the whole time. At dawn, the king summoned them to tell them to get ready for the voyage, for the wedding would take place in the king's country. When everything was ready, the princess' father wrote a letter to the prince's father, and prepared many gifts to take to him. Finally, the Naked Man and the prince, with the dazzling princess whose beauty caused those who saw her to lose their reason, followed by two hundred animals loaded with gold coins honestly earned, took leave of the king and with his blessing they all went to the fiancé's village for the wedding celebrations.

One morning, when the fiancé's parents had just woken and were drinking their coffee, a large fly landed on the king's jacket.

– Oh, said the queen, we will soon receive congratulations! I know which of our children will give us the good news, and whoever the girl is, she will be welcome.

She had barely finished speaking when a man, barefoot and dirty, appeared before them to announce that their youngest son was arriving, bringing with him two hundred animals loaded with gold coins and diamonds that he had earned, and that he was accompanied by a young girl, his future wife, whose great beauty had no equal.

Hearing this, the king and the queen rubbed their eyes. How could it be? Their youngest son, the lazy one, the unlucky one, the one who had had so much trouble finding an associate to work with – he was the one who was bringing all this back?

When the messenger left, the king said to his wife: "If all this is true, the saying my father liked is true: "Poor little ship sails into the great port!" – We must go and welcome him then.

Just then, another man arrived; he gave the king the letters and gifts from the princess's father, as well as a letter from the prince. Now, there could be no more doubt. The king hurried off to meet his son, with musicians and soldiers. They all went down to the port to welcome this son so badly treated by his father in the past, who had even threatened him with death. But now this son had shown himself to be the most talented and hard-working of his children. The crowd reached the ship and saw the gold coins and the beautiful princess the king's son had brought back to marry. Everyone rejoiced.

With great ceremony, to the sound of music, they slowly made their way back to the palace. The marriage was celebrated soon after. And what a wedding celebration it was! I can't describe it, any more than I can describe the bride's dowry or the ornaments, or the songs sung to the bride while she was being dressed in her wedding gown. What pageantry! Words fail me, I leave it to your imagination.

After three days of feasting, the guests began to disperse. That night, the newlyweds would finally be alone for the first time. But it was almost dawn and soon the call of the rooster was heard. The last guests were leaving, only a few cousins and aunts were left. The maids of honour started to put out the light, to signal the end of the celebrations.

Just then, heavy footsteps were heard on the stairs and the Naked Man appeared, holding his knife. He was a frightful sight. "Holy Mary, have pity on us!" He was so furious, so full of rage that his eyes seemed bloodshot. He burst into the room like a storm cloud and, after throwing a murderous look at all present, he planted himself in front of the groom and stood there like a post. He was so angry that he couldn't speak. He could only gulp loudly. People were looking at him dumbfounded, not knowing what to expect. He looked at them spitefully and threw a terrible gaze to the groom, saying in a shaky voice: "We have been here for all these many days. I see that you, the lucky one, are spending them feasting and enjoying yourself. But tell me, when will we work out our accounts, the two of us? I need to know! You have plenty to eat, but have you asked yourself how I am getting along? I want to see the accounts right away.

Having said this, the Naked Man stomped his foot on the ground; he was playing with his knife, he was foaming at the mouth. The prince told him: "Look here, partner, is this the right time to take care of the accounts? Come tomorrow, we will sit down, take our time and work out all our problems."

– Oh, tomorrow you say, the Naked Man answered. That's very nice! Put it off 'til later again. I'm telling you that we are going to do it right now. No more waiting!

Now the prince too got angry. "Very well, we'll do it now if that's what you want. Our accounts are very simple. We have brought back two hundred cartfuls of gold and diamonds. All you have to do is take a hundred from the cellar and be on your way."

– Have we brought only money from our journey?
– What else? the prince asked.
– What about her? the Naked man asked, pointing to the bride.

The people around them smiled at these words, thinking that the Naked Man had lost his reason.

– Yes, the Naked Man continued angrily. Our agreement was that we would divide between us everything we earned on our journey. Have we not brought back this woman from our last expedition? Half of her is mine and I will not give up my share. Do you think that it was from the goodness of my heart that I worked so hard to help you have her hand in marriage?
– God, Almighty, said the prince, what you're asking is impossible! Since when can a woman be shared? It's unthinkable! This is all a joke or else you have lost your mind.
– It doesn't matter, the Naked Man said. Half of her is mine and I want it!

The prince could no longer contain himself.

– What do you take me for, a cuckold? he asked. You want to have my wife for five days and I am to have her for the next five? Is that it? Go, get out of my sight!

He signalled to his servant to take hold of the Naked Man and throw him out. But he had no time to finish what he was saying.

– No, I think we can only share her like this!

And before anyone could stop him, he threw himself on the bride, seized her by one foot and turned her over on her back. Then he lifted his knife to cut her in two. The young woman barely had time for a sigh before she fainted. Suddenly, coiled serpents came out of her mouth. The Naked Man attacked the serpents, turning away from the young woman. He killed them all one by one with his knife.

When they were all dead, he turned to the people who were watching petrified with fear, and said in a sweet voice that touched their hearts and gave them the impression that he was no longer a naked savage: "Listen, all of you . . . Listen, you first, son of the king. We have shared bread and salt, and we shared great adventures, like brothers. This young girl you married has been bewitched by her mother, who put a spell on her so she would take no pleasure with her husband. The first night she would sleep with him, these serpents were to come out of her mouth and bite him so that he would die. If we would not have killed these serpents, and if you and your bride would have spent the night together, tomorrow morning you would not have been alive! Now you know why I acted like I did tonight, and why I performed the other good deeds that only the two of us know about. I did it all to prove that I am not ungrateful. And to prove that good deeds, even if they are done for a dead man, are never in vain. For I am the man you found when he was about to be thrown on a dung heap, the man for whom you interrupted your voyage and to whom you gave a decent burial. Farewell!"

And the Naked Man disappeared in an instant.

He has never been seen or heard from again.

Sources

"O gymnos me timachaira" [The naked man with a knife], S. Anagnostou, *Lesviaka*, III, 1903, pp. 161–183.

CGMF 505, *The Grateful Dead.*

CGMF 507C, *The Serpent Maiden.*

ATU 505, *The Grateful Dead* (including AT types 506–506B, 506**B and 508).

ATU 507, *The Monster's Bride* (including AT types 507A, B and C).

THE MONSTER'S BRIDE

Once upon a time there was a fisherman who had a wife and a son. The boy was about fifteen years. His father went fishing every day, it was his occupation. He had a little canoe and nets. One day, his son said: "Father, take me with you."

– No, you have to go to school.
– Today is Saturday. School will be over at noon. Take me with you.

So they went to the sea together. For hours and hours the fisherman threw his nets in one spot and then another, but to no avail. At nightfall the nets were still empty. The fisherman was sad, for he needed to make a living.

– Father, the boy said, throw your net one more time, I want to test my luck! The old man threw the net to please his son, and he caught a little golden fish.
– Very well, he said, watch him now. You will dig a hole in the sand and put him there until I get a jar, so that we can give him to the queen as a present.

But the child, who saw the fish opening and closing his mouth, took pity on him. He swung his arm to toss him back in the sea.

No sooner had he done this than he became afraid. He thought: "My father will be back soon." And he started to run. On the road, he met a young shepherd and greeted him:

– Good day, he said.
– I am glad to see you, the shepherd answered. Where are you going?
– I don't know, the boy answered. And he told his story.

The shepherd said: "A terrible thing happened to me too. I went to sleep and during the night my sheep invaded a field and ate all the young shoots. I was afraid of the owner so I left and took this road.

Together, they walked towards Smyrne. They had become like brothers who loved each other. The young shepherd said: "What work will we do to earn a living?" For they were strangers and knew no one.

– Wait, the fisherman's son said. I had two gold books in my pack; if they're still there, we will be able to work.
– As for me, I learned to be a butcher.
– Then don't worry, we are saved.

They bought a goat carcass and sold the meat which was very tasty. After that, everyone came to buy meat from them. They started to sell beef; their business was doing well. At the end of the first year, they had become very rich. The fisherman's son told the shepherd "Go and visit other places and when you come back, I will leave for a while and do the same thing." Now they had employees and considerable wealth.

The shepherd left and travelled for a month. When he returned, he said: "This is a good place, but I saw other places that are even better." But he had spent much money. Now, it was the fisherman's son's turn. He wrapped up his bundle and started off on foot, not embarking on any vessel. When he was hungry, he went into an inn. After his meal, he rose to pay.

But they told him: "Here no one pays. Your money is of no use to us." He came back that evening and the same thing happened.

– But how do they do it? he wondered. They must have enormous expenses, with these thousands of people coming to eat here. Where do they get the money? He asked them whether they never ran out of funds.

They answered: "Go and see at this address, this street, this number, where there is a cobbler. He has forty employees. Each day, each of them makes a pair of shoes with a silver ornament. Each night, the cobbler puts all the shoes in a bag, breaks them into a thousand pieces and throws them into the Tsai River. If you discover why he does this, we will tell you why the inn can spend so much money."

The next day, the young man went to the cobbler's shop. He waited for the employees to finish their work and saw that everything took place just as he had been told. The cobbler took all the shoes, broke them to pieces with a pickaxe and went to throw them in the torrent.

– My brother, he said to the cobbler, where do you get all the money that you throw away like this? Why do you waste your money like this?

The cobbler answered:

– Go to this place, where there is a *hodja* (scholar) who always laughs as he goes up to the minaret to make the call to prayer, but cries when he comes down. Find out why this is, and I will tell you why I do the things you saw.

The next day, without wasting any time, he went to see the hodja. He sat down at the foot of the minaret to observe what would happen. He saw the hodja laugh as he was going up to sound the call to prayer. But on the way down he was weeping and wiping his eyes with a handkerchief. That night, he knocked on the hodja's door.

– I am a stranger, he said, can you take me in for a night?

In those times, men were kind. The hodja took him in, took care of him and offered him food.

– I saw you laughing while you went up in the minaret and crying when you came down. What happened to you? Why do you do this?
– Oh, my son, when I was young I used to go up to sound the call to prayer and the angels surrounded me. I was innocent! I was without sin! Now, it seems that I have sinned, for I don't see anything anymore. I laugh because I hope to see something. But I see nothing, and I am in despair. That is why I cry.

The next day, the fisherman's son went to see the cobbler.

– Did you find out why the hodja laughs and cries?
– Yes, I did.
– Then tell me why.

The young man told him what he knew (and what we already know).
Then the cobbler said: "Some years ago, I was a street cobbler. At that time, the king proclaimed that the man who would make a pair of shoes for his daughter without taking measurements, without thread or stitching, would become his son-in-law. Many men tried, but they all failed and were decapitated. As for me, I had nothing to lose. "I will try; either I am decapitated, or I succeed and become the king's son-in-law." I succeeded. But one day, I thought: "Who was I and who have I become?" I asked myself. At that moment, I lost my wife! She disappeared. Where did she go? What became of her? I don't know."
Then he took the young man into a small room separate from the others and he showed him, in a corner, a pile of gold louis; in another corner, a pile of gold sovereigns. "All this is my wife's dowry. What good is it to me? Since I lost her, I spend as much as I can, hoping the money will run out and I will be able to go far, far away, to see where my fate takes me."
The fisherman's son returned to the innkeeper.

– What did you do all this time?
– You sent me to the cobbler, and he sent me to see someone else.

He told the story of the hodja and that of the cobbler who spent so much money.

– Come here, said the innkeeper. He took him inside, into a room where there were two lions. The first spewed out gold and the second was minting coins.
– Can this ever run out? he asked. You understand now how we can spend as much as we want.

The young fisherman set out on his way home, for he wanted to return on foot. Along the way, he met two men on horseback. He followed them and heard what they were saying: "That poor man who died! He was unable to make the princess speak and he was killed like the others!" Without saying a word, the fisherman's son followed them; they arrived in the kingdom about which the men were speaking. The next day, he asked where the king went to drink his morning coffee. He was told to go to a certain inn. There, he introduced himself to the king.

– What do you want?
– I heard about the contest and I want to try my luck.

Seeing how young he was, the king pitied him, for he was going to die needlessly.

– I don't pity myself, why would you pity me?
– In that case, let us go and see.

The princess seemed to fall in love with the young man and started to speak. The king wanted them to be married at once, but the young fisherman refused.

– I have parents, I have to return so they can give me their blessing. Give me your blessing before we leave.

How could the king refuse his blessing and his daughter's dowry: nine mules loaded with gold? So the young man took the nine stubborn mules and the young woman, and they left. When he arrived where his brother lived, he said: "You left and you saw many strange lands. I left and I brought back this woman and riches! Now it's time for us to go home.
They sold all their possessions to pay for the voyage. When they reached the place where they had met, the fisherman and the shepherd separated, for each of them had come from a different place.

– My brother, the shepherd said, we will divide everything equally. You will take five bags of gold coins, for you are the one who brought them, and you will take the woman.

They said their farewells and were about to continue on, when the shepherd called the fisherman back.

– Come here, we didn't divide well. I will take three bags and leave you six, since you brought them.

The fisherman's son always agreed to everything the other suggested. They said their farewells again. But the shepherd called his friend back again.

– Come here. Let's share really equally; each of us will take half, and we will each take half of the woman too!
– All right, we can do that too, the fisherman answered.

So each of them started to pull on one of the woman's legs. The shepherd, who was also a butcher, took out his knife to cut the woman in two. He lifted the knife, she was terrified, cried "Aaahh" and spat out a snake. Snakes just kept spilling out of her mouth.

– You see, he told her, these snakes are the souls you destroyed, all the young men whose head your father cut off. One day, these snakes were going to come out and kill both of you. Now, the shepherd said, you can keep the woman and all the money. For I am the little fish you caught and spared! He leaped up and suddenly fell into the sea.

And the fisherman's son married the woman. They lived happily ever after, and we lived even better.

Sources

Untitled, M. X. Papadopoulou-Demertzi, "Oriental Songs and Tales" [Asia Minor Annals], IV, 1948, pp. 239–243.
CGMF 507C, *The Serpent Maiden*.
CGMF 505, *The Grateful Dead*.
ATU 507, *The Monster's Bride* (including AT types 507A, B and C) 506–506B, 506**B and 508).
ATU 505, *The Grateful Dead* (including AT types 506, 506B, 506**B and 508).

Remarks on The Grateful Dead[13]

Anna Angelopoulos

The representations of the travelling companion in Greek folktales are quite diverse, ranging from the grateful dead to the faithful servant. There are also Christianised figures such as Saint Nicholas, Christ or even God, and more enigmatic figures such as in "The Grateful Dead", the savage in the cave, the king of fish, and the little golden fish. All of them become the hero's friends for a time and accompany him during his passage from boyhood to manhood. All of them are older than him and are representations of ancestors. Only the faithful servant[14] is presented as a double, of the same age as the hero. This character originates from the transformation of a grateful fish – a primordial ancestor – who returns to the sea for good at the end of the story.

The versions of "The Grateful Dead", collected mainly in the Aegean Islands, form four groups of folktales:

A. The hero saves a fish which was to be used to make an ointment to heal his father's eyes. The fish comes back in the form of a faithful servant who helps the hero to survive the trials he encounters, in his turn saving him from mortal danger.
B. The hero is sold or promised (by his mother or father) to Saint Nicholas, the patron saint of sailors. Thus, the saint becomes the boy's protector, without revealing his identity until the end of the story.
C. The hero is helped by his father's "blessing" (the father is often embodied by a well-meaning character or by a magic box hidden in his pocket) which brings him luck.
D. The hero is helped by a companion who turns out to be dead and had been left unburied until the hero paid his debts and gave him a proper funeral.

A Liberating Action

For the hero, paying to have the dead man buried represents the unconscious adoption of a new father, a sort of godfather to replace his real father. Surprisingly, the adoption of this symbolic father coincides with his burial. The fostering ethnologists hold so dear takes no time at all! The initiator is buried as soon as he is found. This seems clear to the guests at the inn, who make the traditional wish for someone who has just buried his father: "I wish you long life!" The young prince is now a free adult who has fulfilled his filial obligations and can follow his own path. As an initiation trial, our hero has taken it upon himself to repay the debt of the dead man. Of course, the real father who supplied the money might have some objections.

The question of the dead man's debt returns insistently in the different versions of the tale.

It appears that here the buying back, as it were, of the body is part of the rationalisation of motives in the tale. According to Vladimir Propp,[15] what matters most is to bury the dead man, turning him into an ally. The idea of "buying back" must have emerged in a later era, when the circulation of money became an important element in the life of a society. Becoming wealthy became part of the values a hero had to adopt. Let us note that his father's money is treated almost like a burden by the young hero, although it was theoretically intended to help him explore the world. Instead, he rids himself of the money by paying the dead man's debt, thus acquiring a servant.

The hero's father considers his spending extravagant. But by treating the dead man like a symbolic relative (a noble gesture of filial love, made in the most disinterested way), the hero acquires his future gratitude. One day, the prince himself may have debts, and the dead man's debts create a common ground between them. This allows a process of acquisition to begin at once. As we remember, the dead man's pockets were empty when he was found. Without the symbolic fare, he could not have crossed the Acheron into the realm of the dead. But despite his irritation at the buying back of the body of a stranger, the king does not fly into a rage. His son's unconscious gesture of disguised filial love remains acceptable because it ensures the continuation of intergenerational tradition: funeral rites are the guarantee that the enduring duty of burial has been passed down.

Our hero becomes prosperous by civilising people in foreign lands, by bringing them a kind of know-how that may be the equivalent of cooking, in the context of the tale. Is it a mythical equivalence? Aside from being a butcher, the young man is also a cook, one who introduces the use of salt in cooking. Knowing how to prepare meat, raw or cooked, comes from ancient religious traditions involving animal sacrifices. For instance, in the Bible,[16] God commands that all animals sacrificed to Him be seasoned with salt. Finally, the use of salt in a tale about a dead body deprived of a burial could refer to a means of preventing putrefaction.

The Sacred Office of Butchering

Today, being a butcher means sectioning and selling meat. But the first butchers were mystery worship officiants; they performed the sacrifices, they were killers. According to Marcel Détienne,[17] their function was to exert an effect on "the demoniacal powers which rejoice in the vapours and emanations produced by the blood and flesh defiling the altars".

Butchering starts with killing. We will remember that slaughtering is a blood crime for the Hebrews as well as the Greeks. Among the former, it could only be performed in the sacred space;[18] as for the latter, they consider it impure. The butchering ritual has its own gestures, its specific times and its technical vocabulary.

First slaughtering, then skinning, then cutting up, and then hindquartering. The one who first slaughtered can later become a chef. As a chef, he has the skill needed to cut up and to divide the meal into equal portions. He slices off choice morsels like shank, sirloin, chuck or the head of the animal. This masculine occupation, highly valued by the mysterious Vlachs, has preserved all of its ritualistic mystery in the Balkans. It is a sensuous occupation, whose charm is celebrated in certain popular songs[19] of the urban subculture through the figure of the handsome, tender-hearted young butcher whose knife strikes the butcher's block harder when a pretty girl goes by. Let us remember the prince who was ashamed to tell his father what trade he had chosen. An occupation of touch and flesh. Yielders of the knife and attendants to the oven, butcher's boys are consigned to the back kitchen.

The time has come, I think, to weave all these elements together into a story about the trade of human or animal flesh: fresh meat, canned meat, living flesh, raw meat, cooked meat, spoiled meat, salted meat. In modern Greek, the word *kreas* accompanied by an adjective can convey all these different types of meat. In ancient Greek, the word *sarx*, which still exists, was used to mean "flesh"; but today the word *kreas* is often used to mean both meat and flesh.

This is also a story in which the ancestor who protects plays a crucial role. For, from whom does the young man learn the carving of meat? From the fish, of course, his most distant ancestor. In the different versions of this folktale, the grateful fish often teaches the hero the butcher's trade, making him immensely rich, since his meat is always the best. He is a skilled butcher who can tell by sight what the weight of each cut of meat is.

Finally, in the versions where the young man does not have a trade but is looking for a travelling companion, he must choose him carefully because he needs someone who will share fairly. Sometimes it is his mother or a cook who gives him advice about the choice he must make for his future. He must never choose someone who wants to eat out of his plate. He should opt for someone who divides the bread equally, or gives him the bigger half when he has cut an apple in two.

If tasting is a manner of touching, sexual consumption is only a step away. In truth, this folktale can be seen as a story of mentoring the hero during adolescence, a sort of sexual initiation. The episode where the hero meets the dangerous woman is present in all versions where a woman is not bought out of slavery, which would amount to the same thing, as indicated by the hero's behaviour towards the woman he wishes to marry. Before making her his, he must let her become accustomed to him, free her of the spirits that possess her or of the demon who loves her; he must liberate her.

Freud presents the same ideas in "The Taboo of Virginity"[20] where he describes "the custom of primitive peoples who entrust defloration to an old man, a priest, a saintly man, in other words to a father substitute". Thus, the *droit du seigneur* could be one of the ramifications of this custom, related to the image of paternal figure transmission. "It is therefore not surprising to find among the father substitutes charged with defloration images of the gods themselves."

The hero is impelled by fear to confront the woman who kills her suitors on their wedding night; he is embarrassed by this fear of the beloved, for whom he will, nevertheless, risk his life. Fear of death and fear of the woman: these are his two reasons for being triumphant, bringing together the ancestral and marriage. "A husband is, so to speak, never anything but a proxy, never the right man; the first claim upon the feeling of love in a woman belongs to someone else, in typical cases to be father; the husband is at best a second."[21]

We have come to the point where the folktale asks us to look more closely at the young man's actions when he faces this mysterious and unattainable being of the opposite sex whom he loves enough to put his life at risk. Now, the time has come for him to ask for the help of the ancestor, knowing that he can count on it.[22] Together, they will fight the demon, without knowing who he is.

It is well known that there are many women who have a strong attachment to their father; [. . .]. I was struck, above all, by two facts. The first was that where the woman's attachment to her father was particularly intense, analysis showed that it had been preceded by a phase of exclusive attachment to her mother which had been equally intense and passionate. Except for the change of her love-object, the second phase had scarcely added any new feature to her erotic life."[23]

Notes

1 Storyteller's aside to the audience.
2 Text presented at the DERPAD Conference (for professionals specialising in childhood and adolescence), March 14 and 15, 2006, Espace Reuilly, Paris: "The Folktale and Adolescent Grime." Conference theme: "Proper Regard for the Body".
3 G. F. Straparola, *Le piacevoli notti* (*The Facetious Nights*), Salerno, 2000.
4 G. Basile, *The Pentamerone*, Franklin Classics, 2018.
5 R. Bottingheimer, "Luckless, Witless and Filthy-Foote: A Sociological Study and Publishing History Analysis of the Lazy Boy", *Journal of American Folklore*, 106 (421), 1993, pp. 259–284.
6 V. Chardenet, *Destins de garçons en marge du symbolique: Jean Le Sot et ses avatars*, José Corti, 2010.
7 F. Dolto, *Paroles pour adolescents ou Le complexe du homard*, Gallimard Folio, 2007.
8 CGMF 301B, *Born of His Mother's Tears*, p. 268.
9 Boiled wheat kernels served at funerals.
10 Preparation made of apples, quince or apricots cooked and preserved in molasses made of grapes.
11 Sun-cured tobacco leaves.
12 Fermented wheat grain resembling grains of rice.
13 A. Angelopoulos, "Un Homme nu le couteau à la main", in *Cahiers de littérature orale*, 46, *Le mort reconnaissant*, INALCO, 2000.
14 The figure of the faithful servant also belongs to another folktale type, AT516 (*Iron John*). Iron John is conceived and born at the same time as the hero, through the same magical process; he is almost a twin of the hero.
15 V. Propp, *Historical Roots of the Fairy Tale*, Western Washington University, 1997.
16 Leviticus, 2: 13.
17 M. Détienne, *Apollon, le couteau à la main. Une approche expérimentale du polythéisme grec*, Gallimard, 1998, p. 65.
18 Leviticus, 17: 3 seq.: "If any one of the house of Israel kills an ox or a lamb or a goat in the camp, or kills it outside the camp, when he should have brought the animal to the entrance of the Meeting Tent as a gift to the LORD in front of the LORD's Holy Tent, he is guilty of killing."
19 These songs are called *rembetika*. See Holst Gail, *The Road to Rembetika*, Denise Harvey, 1973.

20 S. Freud (1918), *The Taboo of Virginity*, SE 11, Hogarth.
21 S. Freud (1918), *The Taboo of Virginity*, SE 11, Hogarth.
22 The question arises whether in this folktale the search for the woman is connected with the search for the ancestor. In another study (A. Angélopoulos, "Blanche-Neige ou l'enfant-ancêtre", *Revue des études néo-hélléniques*, 2, Daedalus, 1992, pp. 170–188) we observed that mythical heroes in search of origins travel to the Underworld to look for a woman (Orpheus) or an ancestor (Ulysses). The same is true in folktales such as "L'Enfant voué à la Sirène" ("The Child Promised to the Siren") (AT316), where the hero, promised or sold to a demon, must leave to save himself.
23 S. Freud (1931), *Female Sexuality*, SE 21, Hogarth.

Chapter IV

"Cupid and Psyche" or "The Search for the Lost Husband"

The five folktales that follow are five Greek versions of the oral folktale type "Cupid and Psyche", also called "The Search for the Lost Husband". Hundreds of versions of this tale have been classified, from Sweden all the way to India. Its first written trace appeared in Apuleius' *Metamorphoses (The Golden Ass)*, in the second century AD.[1]

TARTARUS, THE BLACK PIT OF THE EARTH, THE GOLDEN EAGLE OF THE WORLD

Once upon a time there was a couple who loved each other. There was never a bad word spoken between them. Their neighbours envied them their happiness – especially the women. They tried to cause discord between them. They asked the wife: "What is your husband's name?" But the wife didn't know his name.

So one night she asked him: "What is your name?" He replied, "I must not tell anyone my name. It is a secret." The neighbours kept mocking the poor wife, who started to nag her husband every day to tell her his name, making his head spin. Finally, he had to reveal his name: "My name is Tartarus, I am called the Black Pit of the Earth, the Golden Eagle of the world!" That night they went to bed together, but the next morning he had disappeared; the bed was empty. Poor woman! She got up and set out to look for her husband, still wearing her nightdress.

She wandered on the roads for three whole years; finally, one day, she came to a house where she was hired as a servant. It was the house of Tartarus' mother, who was an ogress. Her son was also in the house. The young woman recognised him, but he didn't seem to know who she was.

The ogress wanted to eat her new servant and was looking for something for which she could blame her. One morning, she told her: "Sweep the

---

DOI: 10.4324/9781032674230-5

whole house and be careful to keep all the dirt." The young woman cried and lamented; her tears filled all of nature with pity. How could she clean the house and leave all the dirt in it at the same time? This is when the ogress's son suggested that she should sweep the house well, and then make little piles of dirt and place them in different corners of the house. When her mistress saw what she had done, she was very impressed. She had no reason to blame her. She said only: "Witch, oh, witch! Either your father is a magician, or your mother is a lamia, or else my son gave you advice. Accursed son, may misfortune follow him!"

"I am not a witch, my father is not a magician, and I had no advice from your blessed son, may good fortune smile upon him," she answered.

The next day the ogress ordered her to cook a lamb in such a way that it be at once raw and cooked. Once again, the ogress's son came to her rescue. He suggested that she place a pot on the fire and suspend the lamb above it, pushing only half of it into the pot so that it cooks, while the other half stays raw. That night, the ogress found that the lamb was both raw and cooked. What could she say? "Witch, oh, witch! Either your father is a magician, or your mother is a lamia, or else my son gave you advice. Accursed son, may misfortune follow him!"

"I am not a witch, my father is not a magician, and I had no advice from your blessed son, may good fortune smile upon him," she answered.

Now, the ogress sent her to see her sister and bring back all her "tumula and mumula". The ogress's sister was going to devour her, of course. The young woman cried and lamented; her tears filled all of nature with pity.

But the son came to her rescue once again. He told her that on her journey she would come across a tied-up dog who for the past seven years had had a pile of hay in front of him to eat; and a little further there would be a donkey with a bowl of bones in front of him, that had been there for seven years. She was to put the bones in front of the dog and the hay in front of the donkey. Then she would meet a woman who put the bread in the kiln with her breasts, burning herself. She was to give the woman her apron, for putting the bread in the kiln. Further along the road, she would see a fig tree full of rotten figs infested with worms. She was to taste the figs and say: "How delicious these figs are! If only my mistress could have some on her table!" Further still, there would be a dirty river; she was to drink from it and say: "How fresh this water tastes!" Finally, she would arrive at the ogress's house, go up the stone stairs that she was to sweep with a broom, because they would be very dirty. Inside the door, she would see the "tumula and mumula". She was to take them and quickly run off, so that the ogress would not be able to catch her and eat her.

The young woman followed this advice faithfully. When she was at the top of the stairs, the ogress greeted her with these words: "Welcome! Come closer and let me bring you a sweet treat!" But, in truth, she went off to sharpen her teeth to better devour her. The young woman quickly picked up the "tumula and mumula" and started running as fast as she could. The ogress cried out instantly: "Stairs, stop this woman! Crush her!" But the stairs, happy to have been swept for the first time in seven years, answered: "You're the one we should crush, you're the one who goes up and down every day without thinking to give us the slightest sweep. This woman only climbed up once and she took care of us."

The ogress, who was running after the young woman, came to the kiln; she shouted: "Baker, kill her!"

— You're the one who should be killed, you're the one who let me put the bread in the oven with my breasts; this woman gave me her apron to do it with.

The ogress came to the river. "River, sweep her away!"

— You're the one who should be swept away; you're the one who said for seven whole years that my water was dirty.

She came to the fig tree: "Fig tree, crush her!"

— You're the one who should be crushed, you're the one who said my figs were rotten. This woman tasted them and wished they were on her mistress's table.

She came to where the donkey was. "Donkey, kick this woman!"

— You're the one who should be kicked, you're the one who let me eat bones for seven years, until this woman gave me hay!

She came to where the dog was. "Dog, devour her!"

— You're the one who should be devoured, you who let me eat hay for seven years, until this woman gave me bones.

This is how the young woman avoided all the pitfalls and was able to return to her mistress.

The ogress wanted her son to marry and she had found him a fiancée. She ordered the poor servant to wash 40 shirts for the bridegroom. She had to take them to the river, wash them, dry them, iron them and bring them back all ready for the wedding day. What was she to do? She cried and she lamented; her tears filled all of nature with pity. But the ogress's son came to her rescue once again: "When you'll be on the riverbank, call out: 'Girls, come! Come quickly because we have to wash the shirts of Tartarus, the black pit of the Earth, the Golden Eagle of the world!' (I have goosebumps as I am telling you this!)

And the girls came. All at once, they were there, they appeared before her. (If this is not divine intervention, I don't know what is.) They washed the shirts, dried them and ironed them. That evening, the young woman brought them to her mistress all ready. The ogress, vexed at being deprived of a pretext to eat her, said: "Witch, oh, witch! Either your father is a magician, or your mother is a lamia, or else my son gave you advice. Accursed son, may misfortune follow him!"

– I am not a witch, my father is not a magician, and I had no advice from your blessed son, may good fortune smile upon him.

She always said "blessed son, may good fortune smile upon him", while his mother called him an "accursed son". Her patience was admirable. Sometimes one has to show great patience to be rewarded in the end. Once again, she escaped the worst.

The wedding day came at last, the day the ogress's son married another young girl. The ogress ordered her servant to hold two burning candlesticks above the couple's bed while they slept. She forbade her to make a sound even if the wax burned her fingers, if not she would eat her. The wax was dripping from the two candles, burning her hands, but she said not a word; tears fell from her eyes in silence.

Seeing this, the husband asked his new wife to hold the flaming candles for a while. The ogress's daughter-in-law took the candlesticks in her hands. The young man moved closer to the servant. The candles burned and the wax dripped, burning the hands of the new bride, who started to scream. The ogress barged into the room, seized the young bride and ate her, as she had warned she would do.

In the morning, when she awoke and realised she had eaten her daughter-in-law, she exploded with rage. And so the husband and wife were reunited.

They lived happily ever after, and we did the same.

Sources

"O Mavro tartaros tis gis, o chrysaetos tou kosmou" [Tartarus, the Black Pit of the Earth, the Golden Eagle of the World].

Origin: Karystos, Euboea.
Collected in 1957 by Angelique Papamichael.

CGMF 425, *The Search for the Lost Husband.*
ATU 425, *The Search for the Lost Husband.*

Subtype A, *Eros and Psyche.*

VRYSSIVOULOS

Once upon a time a mother decided to put a spell on her son, changing him into an earthworm that would sleep by the fountain. And this is what she did. An old woman went to the fountain to fill her jug with cold water; the earthworm fell into the jug. The old woman went home, poured herself a glass of water, and the worm fell into her glass. He said: "My name is Vryssivoulos,[2] and I will stay here with you."

– Very well, answered the old woman.

The young earthworm was growing and changing. As time passed, he started to resemble a beautiful serpent. At that time, the king of the country was waging war against another king. One day, the worm told the old woman: "Go and tell the king to give me one of his daughters for a wife if he doesn't want to lose the war and his kingdom!" (The king had three daughters.)

– I can't tell him such a thing. What makes you think that a king would give you, an earthworm, his own daughter for a wife?

But he insisted: "Go tell the king to give me one of his daughters for a wife if he wants to keep his kingdom!" So the old woman went to the palace and said: "Your Majesty, I have a son who is an earthworm and who is asking for the hand of one of your daughters in marriage. If you agree, he will go to war and save your kingdom!"

The king called his oldest daughter and proposed that she marry the worm. She refused. He made the same offer to his second daughter, but she refused as well. Only the youngest daughter agreed to marry the worm: "I am willing to marry this earthworm, father, so that you don't lose the war."

The day of the marriage arrived. The bride put on 40 dresses for the ceremony. After the wedding, the couple retired to their bedchamber. The young serpent shed his first skin, and the young woman took off her first dress. The groom shed his 40 skins one after the other, and the bride took off her 40 dresses. Then, Vryssivoulos changed into a handsome young man who shone like the sun. The next morning, he took his sword, mounted his steed, went off to war and defeated all the king's enemies. The kingdom was saved. After this, Vryssivoulos went back to the palace and put on his serpent garb again, with its 40 skins.

The princess's older sisters mocked their younger sister: "You are stupid to have married this snake and to stay shut up in the house all day to keep him for a husband! If only you could see the handsome young men who came back from the war!" She remained silent. Her husband had made her promise not to reveal his secret: "If you ever tell them that I turn into a young man, you will lose me and you will need three pairs of shoes made of iron and three iron crutches to find me again."

One day, a race was organised; all the young men in the kingdom were preparing to compete. The serpent changed into a man, donned his handsome uniform, took up his sword and went to the place where the race was to be held, ready to run. His wife came out to watch him, full of admiration. Her sisters told her: "Look at this young man as magnificent as they sun, and you, poor girl, you live shut away!"

– He is my husband, she answered, he is not a serpent!

As soon as she said this, he disappeared. She had three pairs of iron shoes made, and three iron crutches as well, to set out and look for him. She put on the first pair and started her journey, hoping to find Vryssivoulos. When her shoes were worn out, she sat down near a fountain and waited. An ogre arrived, wanting to drink. He asked her: "What are you doing here?"

– I am looking for my lost husband, Vryssivoulos.

Across from the fountain there was a palace where the ogres lived; he took her there. The mother ogress took care to hide the young woman from her sons, who might eat her. That night, when they came back to the palace they said: "It smells like human flesh here! Do you have someone with you?"

– If you swear not to touch my guest, I will let you see her.

The ogres gave their word. They welcomed her warmly, invited her to partake in all the dishes they enjoyed, and then they pointed her in the direction of the next fountain. Across the palace, there was another palace where the cousins of these ogres lived. She thought that she should wait, sitting by the fountain. Someone would surely tell her where her husband was; all these ogres were cousins.

The princess put on the second pair of iron shoes. She walked a great distance before arriving at the next fountain; she sat down close to the water. An ogre arrived, looking for water. He asked: "What brings you to this place?"

– I lost my husband, Vryssivoulos, I am looking for him everywhere.

The ogre took her home and asked his mother to hide her carefully. That night, all her sons came back to the palace and said: "It smells of human flesh around here! Have you hidden someone?"

– If you swear you will not harm my guest, I will let you see her.

The ogres promised. They welcomed her warmly, invited her to partake in all the dishes they enjoyed, and offered her a bed for the night. The next morning, they showed her the direction to follow to continue her journey.

Her second pair of iron shoes was worn out; she put on the third pair. She walked a great distance to the next fountain and sat down near the water. There was a palace across from the fountain. Her husband came to get water from the fountain. He asked her: "What are you doing here?" She had not recognised him and answered: "I lost my husband Vryssivoulos and am looking for him everywhere."

He told her who he was, saying: "I warned you not to reveal my secret! I told you that you would wear out three pairs of iron shoes to find me! He took her home and hid her in a corner. That night, his mother, the ogress, came home and said: "I smell human flesh here! Who have you hidden away?"

– If you swear that you will not touch my guest, I will let you see her.

His mother gave him her word and Vryssivoulos introduced her to his wife. The ogress was fuming with rage. The next morning, she told the young woman: "I am going out now and when I come back tonight I want to see that the house was swept thoroughly and not swept at all.

"How can I sweep and make it look like the house was not swept at all?" the princess asked her husband.

– You will take the broom and pass it over a spot here and a spot there, and then you will leave all the dust on the floor.

That night, the ogress was very surprised at what she had done, and thought that someone had given the young woman good advice. Then she told her: "Tomorrow night I want to see that the house has been mopped thoroughly, and at the same time that it hasn't been mopped!"

"How can I mop the house and leave it looking not mopped at all?" she asked.

Vryssivoulos told her to pass a wet mop here and there, but not everywhere. That night, the ogress was even more surprised than the night before. This time she ordered: "Tomorrow you have to clean the mattresses and fill them with bird feathers!"

Vryssivoulos told her: "You'll go to the river bank with the mattresses, you will beat them and you will shout: "Come birds of all the Earth and sky, come together where I am standing!" The young woman did just as he had told her, and birds from the four corners of the sky gathered beside her and left feathers for the mattresses, which she filled perfectly. Then she took them home.

When the ogress came home that night and saw what the young woman had accomplished, she exploded with rage, and that was the end of her!

From then on, Vryssivoulos and his wife lived happily together, and we even better.

Sources

Elpiniki Stamouli Saranti" Vryssivoulos" ("Apo tin anatoliki Thraki") [Tales from Eastern Thrace], *Thrakika*, 15, 1941, pp. 362–365.

Included in D. Loukatos, Neohellinika Laographika keimena [Neo-Hellenic Folklore], Vassikevivliothiki Aetou, 48, 1957, pp. 85–88.

CGMF 425, *The Search for the Lost Husband*.
ATU 425, *The Search for the Lost Husband*.

Subtype A, *Eros and Psyche*.

ARS-ARSINO RED GRAPE

Once upon a time there was a king who had three daughters. This king decided to wage war against the king of Venice. He made preparations and when he was about to leave, he summoned his three daughters to ask them what gifts they wanted him to bring them when he would return triumphant from Venice. The eldest asked him for a beautiful dress with Venetian landscapes on it. The second daughter asked for a hat with feathers. The youngest asked him to bring her Ars-Arsino Red Grape.

Ars-Arsino was a bewitched prince who lived in the entrails of the Earth, in the muddy soil. His own mother had put a curse on him, and he lived under the Earth, as a crocodile, with a fairy for a companion. The old witch who lived at the palace had told the princess about him and had advised her to ask her father to bring back Ars-Arsino Red Grape, instead of asking for dresses and beautiful hats like her sisters.

So the king set off to war. He defeated the king of Venice and was preparing to return home. He bought the gifts the two older daughters had asked for, and for his youngest he bought red grapes. He embarked on his *caïque* to make the journey, but the vessel was neither advancing nor retreating. So straws were drawn to find out who was responsible for this state of affairs. The short straw was drawn by a priest, who was thrown overboard. But the *caïque* still did not budge; straws were drawn again and this time, the king drew the short straw. He was not thrown in the sea, but was left on land, in a port. He found an old woman and asked her who Ars-Arsino was. She told him that he was a bewitched, accursed prince. "Go and stand before this door and wait for nightfall, when the prince goes to his palace. In the daytime, he lives in the entrails of the Earth."

The king went to stand next to the door the old woman had shown him. At sunset, he saw a crocodile approaching. The king asked him if he was Ars-Arsino Red Grape. The prince answered that he was. He gave the king a ring for his youngest daughter. He said that whenever she wanted to see him all she had to do was squeeze the ring on her finger and he would appear before her, after having filled two fountains, one with honey and one with milk. The king listened carefully so as to remember the prince's instructions, embarked on his vessel and sailed away.

When he arrived at the palace, his daughters were eager to see their presents. The youngest was delighted with the ring. One day, when she was longing to see the prince, she squeezed the ring and he appeared before her. He bathed in the fountain filled with honey, then in the one filled with milk, and was transformed into a handsome young man whose radiance lighted up the little street and the house. They lived together for some time in a separate part of the palace. But one day the princess found herself pregnant. When she told the prince, he asked her to embark on a *caïque* to sail to his country and marry him. When his mother had cursed him, she had said that the spell would be broken if a pregnant woman who loved him was willing to go down into the entrails of the Earth and clean up the child covered in vermin that he had had with the fairy. After saying this, the prince disappeared.

The young woman sailed off on the *caïque* and found him in his workroom. She asked him: "You don't love me anymore, you don't want to be with me?" But he was still bewitched and thought he was conversing with his chandelier. "You are the heart of my heart; so why are you crying, my chandelier?" He repeated this three times, then he rose and left the room. She ran after him and entered the entrails of the Earth. She saw him undress and lie down beside a fairy; lying between them was a child covered in vermin. The princess took the child, washed it, and dressed it in clean clothes. When she finished, the fairy had disappeared. She heard a noise and when she looked, the crocodile had turned into a handsome young man. He told the princess that they could leave and return to her parents' palace to get married, for she had broken the spell that had kept him prisoner.

So they started out on their journey home. They married and had many children, as well as cats and all sorts of other creatures.

Sources

"Ars-Arsino, to Kokkino stafyli" [Ars-Arsino Red Grape]. FS 999, pp. 3–4.

Version from Kastelorizo, Dodecanese.
Collected by Haritomeni Mihalaria.

CGMF 425, *The Search for the Lost Husband*, subtype P.
ATU 425, *The Search for the Lost Husband.*

THE LORD OF THE UNDERWORLD

Once upon a time there was a poor man. One day, he set out to look for wood. He gathered a great bundle of branches and was bringing it back to the village when he was overwhelmed with fatigue. He had to sit down, so he made a seat out of what he could. He let out a big sigh from the bottom of his heart and said: "Woe is me!" Instantly, a black man[3] appeared: "What do you want from me?" he asked. The poor old man, trembling with fright, answered: "I didn't call you; I don't want anything." But the black man insisted.

– Do you have daughters? he asked.
– I have three, the old man answered.
– Bring the eldest here tomorrow morning.

The next morning the old man brought his eldest daughter to that very spot; the black man came up from his world and took the girl into a magnificent garden with giant plane trees. But at noon, when it was time for the midday meal, the black man set the table and offered the young girl a decomposing human foot, eaten by vermin. "If you eat this foot," he told her, "you will marry the Lord of the Underworld; if not, I will take you back to your father." The sight of this dish made the poor girl gag; when the black man left, she threw the foot in the pit of the outhouse. When the black man came back to clear the table, he shouted: "Where are you, little foot?"

— In the pit of the outhouse, where my mistress threw me! the foot answered.
— Come, my girl, let me take you back to your father, for you are not suited to be one of us, the black man told her.

He returned her to the poor old man, saying: "Bring me the second one!" The next day the old man brought his second daughter to the same spot. The black man took her to the Underworld and set the table for her at once. But for her midday meal, he put a human hand before her. To be brief, after thinking for a few moments, she too threw the hand into the pit of the outhouse. The black man came back to clear the table and shouted: "Where are you, little hand?"

— In the pit of the outhouse, where my mistress threw me.

The black man took the girl back to her father, and asked him to bring the youngest sister. The next day, the old man came back with her. The black man took her and offered her a very dirty human belly to eat.

— If you can eat this belly, he told the young girl, you will marry the Lord of the Underworld. If not, you will go back just like your sisters.

But the young girl was very clever: "Yes, I would be glad to, my dear black man, provided you bring me some cloves and some cinnamon to sprinkle on this belly before I eat it." He did as she asked. The young girl prepared the belly to her taste, then she tied it firmly with a wide belt around her waist. When the black man came back to clear the table, he shouted: "Where are you, my little belly?"

"Where my mistress's belly is," was the answer.

The black man was very happy. He treated the young girl with high regard. But the poor girl still saw no trace of her husband, because each night after dinner the black man made her drink coffee laced with a sleeping potion. So that when the Lord of the Underworld appeared, she was asleep and was not aware of what went on. Time passed. But one day, when her sisters saw that the black man was not bringing her back, they decided to go and see what she was doing in the Underworld. They told their father what they planned; he went to the same spot as before and shouted: "Woe is me!" The black man appeared as he had before, and the old man said: "My daughters miss their sister, they would like to see her, if it's possible."

The next day, the old man took his daughters to the same spot, and the black man took them to their sister. She was delighted to see them. They spoke of this and that for a little while. Then one of the sisters told her: "My poor little sister, you think your husband is the black man, but in truth your husband is a magnificent young man you have never seen, because the black man gives you a sleeping potion every night. Tonight, when he will bring you your coffee, throw it away when he is not looking. And when your husband will come, you will see that he has a key attached to his navel. Turn the key and you will see the whole world." This is what her evil sisters told her before they left.

That night, she threw the coffee out and pretended to fall asleep. The black man carried her to her bed; a little later, she saw a handsome young man come into the room and lie down beside her. She waited until he was asleep, turned the key on his navel slowly and gently, and what did she see? Constantinople, Smyrna and the entire world! Then she saw an old woman washing a skein of white thread in the river. The current had carried part of it away, but she hadn't noticed. The poor young girl forgot where she was and cried out: "Be careful, be careful, old woman, the river is carrying off your white thread."

The young man heard these cries in his sleep. He woke up and told her: "Shrew, turn the key! Now I am lost because of you!" Frightened, the young girl turned the key. But the next morning the Lord of the Underworld summoned his servant, the black man: "Take this girl outside; cut off two of her hairs and put them in a basin. Watch them carefully day and night. If ever they should fade, let me know at once. Now go! Give her a piece of bread and send her on her way." The black man did as he was told; the poor girl took her bread and went on her way.

She walked and walked for a long time. Then she saw a shepherd. "Happy man," she said to him, "would you like to exchange your clothes for mine?" "I'll be happy to," he answered. Dressed in shepherd's clothing, the young girl continued on her way. She walked for many days and nights and came to a big country. "I am a good servant, a good servant!" she shouted on the streets. The king heard her shouting. He saw a sturdy young man, neat and clean, and hired him. The king wanted to know his name and he said: "Yannis." Time passed.

It was the queen's misfortune to fall in love with Yannis. One day, the king went hunting with him. Halfway there, he remembered that he had forgotten his watch and asked him: "Can you go back and get my watch? But be careful not to awaken your mistress who is asleep in the room." Yannis went back to the palace and went quietly into the room; the queen was awake in her bed. She tried to seduce him, for she had been thinking about it for a long time. She drew him to her, but Yannis resisted and in the struggle she scratched his face violently, so that his face was covered with blood. He fought her off, took his master's watch and left.

When he saw his bloody face, the king asked: "What happened to you, Yannis?" "I walked through a place full of thorny plants in my haste to get back here, and I got hurt." In the evening they went back to the palace. The queen was furious with Yannis and told the king: "Today, you almost found me dead when you returned, my king, because you sent this scoundrel to my room to get your watch, and he wanted to dishonour me! I was still in bed, a poor weak woman, and I defended myself with my nails; I scratched his face and chased him away!"

Hearing this, the king decided to condemn Yannis to be hanged before all the noblemen of the country. On the day of the hanging, crowds of people were gathered before the palace to see the hanging. But at that moment the black man shouted to the Lord of the Underworld: "Master, hurry, for the hairs in the basin are fading!"

Hearing these words, the Lord of the Underworld mounted his horse and rode to the palace at a gallop, waving his arms to signal that they should wait for him. The queen, who sat in the gallery, asked that they wait, for a man who seemed to be on an urgent errand was hurrying towards them. He arrived and asked: "Why do you want to hang this man?" "It's because he tried to dishonour me," the queen answered quickly, before anyone else could speak.

The Lord of the Underworld asked her: "If we discover that this man is a woman, what should we do with you, my lady?" "I should then be hung in her place!" said the queen. With no further ado, the Lord of the Underworld tore off Yannis' clothes and two breasts were exposed for all to see. "See for yourselves, honourable gentlemen; if you wish, I can tear off the rest of her clothes!" "No," said the king, "that's enough!" And the Lord of the Underworld finally married Yannis. Then the evil queen was hanged.

I was not there to see it, and neither were you, to believe it.

Sources

"To-liero-cheropanaki", FS 1543, 24.

Version collected by Rodanthi Spyropoulou in 1959, in Sidari, Epirus. Collected by Haritomeni Mihalaria.

CGMF 425, *The Search for the Lost Husband*, subtype P.
ATU 425, *The Search for the Lost Husband*.

Subtype R (included in ATU 432, *The Prince as Bird*).

THE PRINCE IN A SWOON

Once upon a time there was a king who had an only daughter. Every day, she sat before her window embroidering. One morning, while she embroidered, a bird landed on her windowsill and sang to her: "What good is embroidering? What good is the gold thread? You are fated to marry a dead man!" She went to her father crying and told him what the bird said. The king answered: "What does a bird know? Let him sing!" But in the days that followed the bird returned and sang the same things to her. Each time, she repeated the bird's words to her father.

Not long afterwards, the princess's friends asked her to go for a stroll with them. In the distance, they saw a castle. They approached, to have a closer look. They found the castle gate wide open. Inside, there was a beautiful garden, flowers and trees in an orchard. They walked together into the garden, talking and laughing; but the princess lagged behind. At last, when they wanted to leave, the young girls went out through the great iron gate, but when the princess tried to leave, the gate suddenly closed before her with a great din, trapping her inside. The young girls started to shout and went to tell the king, who sent soldiers to open the gate. But the gate was so tightly shut that their efforts were in vain. So the king declared a state of national mourning. The palace was draped in black and music was forbidden in the whole kingdom.

Finding herself alone, the young girl decided to visit the interior of the castle. She went through rows of rooms and in the last one she found a deceased young prince, lying on the bed. In his right hand he held a piece of paper with the inscription: "The one who will keep vigil over me for 40 days and nights, if it be a man I shall make him my brother, if it be an old woman she shall be my mother, and if it be a young girl I shall make her my wife."

After she read the note, the young girl sat down beside the dead prince and kept vigil without sleeping for 40 days and nights. On the last day, she saw a maidservant go by below the window. She summoned her and asked her to stay with the young prince "just for two hours" while she slept, and then wake her up.

The servant agreed.

The young girl fell asleep but the servant didn't wake her up; instead, she was left alone with the prince for three hours. When he awoke, he told her: "You are my wife!" The servant answered: "You see this sleeping woman? You should send her to keep the geese." No sooner said than done.

One day, the prince had to go off to war. Before heading, he called his wife and asked her what present she wanted him to bring her when he returned. She wanted a golden dress. Then, he asked the goose keeper: "Is there anything you need?"

— I need the killing knife, the stone of patience and the candle that never melts. You will bring them to me, or else your horse will stay frozen to the spot!" she answered.

The prince went off to war. He defeated his enemies and, when he came back, he brought his wife the golden dress she asked for, but he forgot to bring the things the goose keeper wanted. When he mounted his horse, the horse would not move. He started to think and remembered his promise. He went to the fair to get the three things. He found them in a shop and bought them. The shopkeeper asked who had ordered these things.

— They are for my servant, the king answered.
— Look carefully to see what she will do with them, the shopkeeper advised him.

The king returned home and his wife asked him: "Did you bring my golden dress?" He gave it to her. He gave the goose keeper the killing knife, the patience stone and the candle that never melts. She went into her hut with her three gifts. She put the killing knife on the table; she placed the patience stone on top of it and the candle that never melts beside it. The king had followed her quietly and he heard her say: "Oh, knife of massacre! What are you waiting for? Rise and slit my throat!" The knife rose, but was caught by the stone of patience, one, two, three . . . many times. Each time, the candle went out and was rekindled again. She went on to say: "I was a princess embroidering before her window and one day a bird told me: 'What good is embroidering? What good is the golden thread? You shall marry a dead man!' But I didn't believe it. What are you waiting for, little knife? Rise up!" But once again the knife was caught by the patience stone.

"And one day I was with my friends, we were walking near the castle and I stopped in front of the iron gate. What are you waiting for, little knife? Rise and cut my throat!" But the patience stone caught the knife once again.

"I found myself inside the gate and I visited the rooms in the castle. I went into the room of the prince and I saw him lying dead on his bed. I read the note he was holding in his hand. What are you waiting for, little knife? Rise and cut my throat!" But the patience stone stopped the knife once again.

"I had kept vigil over him for 40 days with no sleep, when a servant – the one he married – went by below my window. I asked her to come in and keep vigil over him for two hours. But she stayed three hours without waking me. When he awakened from his sleep, the prince married her and made me a goose keeper! How can you bear that, little knife, that she became queen after keeping vigil for three hours, while I became a goose keeper after keeping watch for 40 days and nights? What are you waiting for?"

So the knife jumped high in the air, the patience stone could not catch it and the candle went out. In the dark, the prince, who was listening at the door, started to cry. He forced the door open and entered the room. He stopped the knife rushing towards the princess's heart and took her in his arms.

He married her and the other woman became the goose keeper.

Sources

"To machairi tis sfagis, t'akoni tis ypomonis kai to keri t'amalago" [The Killing Knife, the Stone of Patience and the Candle that Never Melts], Jean Pio, *Contes populaires grecs*, 1879, pp. 49–51.

Origin: Epirus.
Included in G. Ioannou, *Paramythia tou laou mas* (Our Folktales), Hermès, 1975, pp. 167–171.

CGMF 425 G, *The Prince in a Swoon.*
ATU 425 A, *The Animal as Bridegroom.* (Includes former subtype 425 G.)

The Tale of Eros and Psyche in the Oral Tradition

Anna Angelopoulos[4]

Most fairy tales end with a marriage. Phrases like: "They were married and had many children", "They lived happily ever after" or "They are still happy to this day" have become standard closing formulas that invite us to leave the magical space of listening in which we were immersed.

When hearing these phrases, each of us is reminded of stories we knew by heart before we could read, before we went to school and could appreciate literature. These stories have happy endings: the triumphant hero marries the princess and they go off to live happily ever after. The hardships with which the story started are forgotten. Indeed, stories begin in different ways but they almost all have the same ending. This is the form in which we generally know them. Marriage is the final accomplishment of the hero after all his trials, after his initiation. Marriage in itself is the continuation of the story. From this point of view, marriage is related to death, which could also have ended the protagonist's adventures. Both marriage and death are endings, Artemidorus wrote in his *Interpretation of Dreams*, suggesting that dreaming of one can lead to encountering the other.

Oral Tale, Written Tale

The story of "Cupid and Psyche" as Apuleius presented it in his *Metamorphoses*[5] in the second century tells the story of a marriage. It is one of the oldest stories put into written form, to become literature. In parallel, this story continues to exist in the oral tradition, in a multitude of versions passed down over the centuries. It is one of the most widely circulated folktales in Europe, and it is found everywhere from Scandinavia to China, including in India. The stories take a countless number of forms, outside the frame of formal literature. This popular myth, which has never stopped being transmitted orally, has been the subject of a great number of studies.

Apuleius' writing has influenced art, philosophy and literature over the centuries, and its fame still exceeds that of current published work on the oral folktale.

A Story that Starts with Marriage

The tale of "Eros and Psyche" (both oral and written) is about marriage and death. Contrary to established tradition, this story starts with a marriage and relates its vicissitudes. It is the story of a couple who come together, separate and find each other again. While they are separated, the husband vanishes into another world, where the devastated heroine must search for him. Only going through this mourning interval can give the soul back its wings; it is a space of narcissistic reconstruction culminating in the recovery of lost love. And this time, the couple are united forever.

This folktale type is exceptional from two points of view: as we have said, it starts with a marriage; moreover, it has many different endings and such diverse plots that even specialists can have trouble recognising certain versions as belonging to the same folktale classification. Swedish folklore specialist Jan Öjvind has established a specific typology based on these different endings of the story.

Let us recall the story of "Eros and Psyche",[6] which is still part of the oral tradition, and which inspired Apuleius' *Metamorphoses (The Golden Ass)*.

A young girl marries a supernatural being or an animal. She must never look at him in the light, or reveal that at night he changes into a handsome young man. Despite her husband's instructions, the heroine tries to see him by the light of a candle, or she reveals his secret. This transgression causes the disappearance of the husband.

The young woman sets out to find him and finds herself in another world, where she accomplishes impossible tasks given to her by a mean fairy (her husband's mother), who keeps her prisoner.

The last trial is one where the heroine must attend the wedding of her husband and another woman, and during the ceremony she must hold two torches intended to light the bridal chamber. The bride complains of the heat, but the heroine tells her that she has gone through many trials without complaining. That is when the bridegroom interrupts the ceremony and takes back his first wife, abandoning the second bride.

Thus, the couple are united twice, at the beginning[7] and at the end of the story.[8] In the introduction, the initiation to love takes the form of a "natural marriage"; at the end of the story, what takes place is a "social marriage", which becomes possible when the protagonists' incestuous problems are resolved.[9]

In this folktale, the marriage is always mixed: a god or a supernatural being marries a mortal woman, whose initiation is narrated. Sometimes the husband is presented in animal form: anything from a reptile (earthworm, crocodile or frog) to the most majestic birds (eagles and other birds of prey). The husband can even belong to the vegetable kingdom: he can be an ornamental plant, for instance.

In this scenario, the young couple are not idealised, since the protagonists – like simple human beings – can procreate, have rivals, separate, lose each other and get back together again. What is idealised, however, is the power of Love as a self-sustaining force.

Here, the couple are transformed after long and difficult trials, during which the young heroine is held captive in another world, "dies" and "is reborn" as part of an initiation process, in order to find her lost beloved.

Apuleius and the Written Version of "Eros and Psyche"

How are archaic mythical patterns – drawn from folklore – reflected[10] in formal literature? In truth, some influences are related to the very nature of oral transmission, which takes place in various ways: in waves, discontinuously, by leaps that carry the tale to far-away lands, etc. But when the tale is set in writing, innovations emerge. For instance, great literary geniuses like Perrault and Apuleius have been able to capture the deepest meaning of the crypted message contained in an oral folktale, transmitted through endless retelling. This message, reformulated and conceptualised by a great writer, is given a place in formal literature, becoming an object of attention and study.

Given the difficulty of identifying the earliest versions of a folktale whose origin is undated, we are forced to make suppositions about the evolution of mythical patterns. Folklorists have often been able to identify and highlight specific factors making it possible to follow with some degree of precision the evolution of mythical sequences belonging to different cultures and eras (for instance, the sequence "loss/wandering/search/reuniting/access to a better situation").

J. O. Swahn's monograph[11] sheds light on Apuleius' contribution to the creation of the literary myth. Swahn shows that the version presented in *Metamorphoses* is only one of the possible forms of the first oral folktale subtype.[12] Numerous popular versions exist and have their own life cycle, largely unknown in the learned sphere. But "Cupid and Psyche" is a very widespread tale that, according to Plotinus, inspired different narratives (*mythoi*) and paintings in his time.

The story told by Apuleius comes from an already modified tradition that the author came to know either through oral transmission or, as is commonly held, through the intermediary of a Greek work.

In either case, the question arises as to what archaic elements in the story seduced Apuleius enough to incite him to write an allegory about the wanderings of the soul on its journey to immortality. Indeed, his allegory was to influence a series of subsequent literary works on the theme of initiation, written by Boccacio,[13] Pedro Calderon,[14] who sees the story of Psyche as illustrative of the three ages of the world (paganism, Judaism and Christianity), and La Fontaine. La Fontaine wrote an amusing fable in parody form, whose meaning also has an allegorical aspect: it refers to the wanderings of the human soul in search of ideal beauty.[15]

Eros and his Stand-Ins

We must keep in mind that in Greek mythology, nine centuries before Apuleius, Eros was, first of all, a primordial deity. In Hesiod's cosmology, Eros guarantees the cohesion of the universe. Hesiod represents him as one of the four primordial beings existing before the universe came into being. "First arose Chaos; then came Gaia, 'the ever-sure foundation of all'; dim Tartarus in the depths of the Earth; and Eros, 'fairest among the deathless gods'".[16] While he himself does not procreate, Eros represents a universal force of attraction necessary for reproduction in the generations after the very first ones, born "without the help of tender love", that is, engendered by one parent.[17]

This first and foremost quality of Eros explains the extent of his power, which extends not only to gods and to humans, but also to elements of nature and to nature itself. However, the evolution of his iconography[18] shows progressive impoverishment and loss of grandeur: after being represented as a winged adolescent, he appears as a flitting cherub. In parallel, his status becomes less exceptional: after being a primordial deity, he will become a godling in Aphrodite's retinue (she is his mother, according to some authors). Eros' stereotyped physical appearance contrasts strangely with the diversity of the moral and philosophical interpretations concerning him.

The Literary Name of the Hero

The physical appearance of the mythical character depicted by Apuleius[19] (known as Cupid) is inevitably linked with the mythological god of Love. Ever since the version of the myth given in *The Golden Ass*, our hero has kept the same name in literature, although the oral tradition designates him by other names as well. This poetic name (or its translations: Cupid, Love, etc.) condenses all the mythical characteristics of the winged adolescent and confines him to a single role-type.

A similar example is that of "Little Red Riding Hood", the folktale heroine known the world over. We know that this name was invented by Perrault, and that the red hood worn by the little girl is an "accessory trait, not a general trait on which to base a symbolic meaning given to the tale".[20]

Yet in the nineteenth century, proponents of myth theory[21] interpreted this "adolescent girl, her brow bathed in morning light", as being the dawn, "making her way to the grandmother, that is, to the dawns of the past" and being "intercepted by the devouring sun in the shape of a wolf".[22] But *this motif is never present in the popular version of the folktale*. It was added by Perrault, who represented the heroine in her inalterable garb (with its definitive identificatory role) for centuries to come.

Similarly, Cupid and Psyche were baptised by Apuleius and since then, their names, and their two entities, are united in a representation symbolising love and eternal marriage.

In addition, psychoanalysis has made Eros one of its key concepts: Eros, the principle of action and of life, is opposed to the death drive,[23] both of which find expression in the libido. "The theory of the instincts is so to say our mythology. Instincts are mythical entities, magnificent in their indefiniteness. In our work we cannot for a moment disregard them, yet we are never sure that we are seeing them clearly," Freud said in the *New Introductory Lectures on Psycho-Analysis* (Lecture XXII).[24]

It is interesting to note that many elements present in the myth of Eros and Psyche are linked with the invention of psychoanalysis: hypnosis (Psyche's lethargic sleep); the prohibition to see the psychoanalyst during the session; the transferential relation between the patient and the analyst (Psyche is in love with someone without knowing anything about him).

Names in the Oral Tradition

Contrary to literary myths, the physical appearance of a folktale character can vary from version to version. The character can have as many as 50 different names and can appear in a multitude of forms.

The supernatural husband is essentially non-human; he is an animal or a god.

The oral tradition has been better able to preserve the hero's intangible, instinctive character. The multiple forms the young man takes – animal,[25] reptile,[26] vegetable,[27] object made by someone[28] or prince of the genies[29] – and his countless mysterious names that make us dream,[30] all designate an intangible psychic force always at work and ever-changing, appearing and disappearing – an unalterable representation of the desire to live.

At the beginning of the story, this hero is not a human. He comes from another world, or rather, from several other worlds. A figure from the beyond or from the animal world,[31] he appears in some strange form when he enters the human realm. At times, he is an enchanted bird,[32] appearing in the sky, the magical space between two worlds.

Apuleius seems to have sensed intuitively, in this hero's nature, the traits of idealised Love. Leaving aside the secular interpretations of the angelic youth shooting his arrows in all directions, Apuleius interpreted the tale as an illustration of the amorous soul of beauty; he condensed the representations of the hero – subject and love object – into a personification of the love drive (always present in folktales).

An Animal for a Husband

One aspect of the oral folktale which is not found in literary works is the hero's animal nature. The hero is born as an animal, but his animal skin disappears at the end of the story thanks to his wife's love. What follows is the general outline of this narrative.[33]

A barren woman wants to have a child, even if it is an animal. Her wish is granted and after nine months she gives birth to an animal. The latter grows up and, one day, he asks to be married. Often, his first two marriages are failures (he kills his young brides during the wedding night), but the third time he marries a young girl who accepts him in his animal form.

During the night he changes into a handsome young man who forbids his wife to tell anyone about his double identity, or else she will lose him forever. But one day the heroine can't resist, and she reveals the truth to her sisters (or she looks at him in the light – which she has been forbidden to do). Now, the animal husband vanishes into another world and the young wife sets out to search for him.

The couple are reunited in this other world, after the heroine goes through terrible trials imposed on her by her husband's mother, her mother-in-law, who keeps her captive. She accomplishes her tasks thanks to the help her husband gives her secretly.

At last, the couple are reunited when the hero is about to marry another woman, whom he abandons to return to his first wife.[34]

Nocturnal Humanisation

The figuration of an animal bridegroom alludes to the distant past when man in his savage state belonged to two worlds. When the husband makes his appearance at night, he changes into a handsome young man. Thus, the hero's humanisation occurs during the night. He sheds his animal skin during the amorous encounter, and dons it again in the daytime, when he will be seen by others. This motif constitutes a surprising inversion of the usual order of nocturnal metamorphoses found in lycanthropic or vampire stories, which illustrate the struggle between diurnal and nocturnal forces, between man and animal, between the natural and supernatural worlds.

It is at night that ghosts and vampires make their appearance, or that Mr. Hyde is able to take possession of Dr. Jekyll. But the dawn and the first rays of sunlight erase the wild or supernatural dimension of all these characters.

However, in this folktale type, the image is inversed. The hero returns to human form at night and is divested of it in the daytime. Here, love plays a role in the humanisation of beings. The hero, who came into the world in animal skin, a child of nature like all of us, meets another person in adolescence. The initiation to love – through the secret of the night inadvertently revealed by the heroine – leads to the definitive rejection of the animal skin, and to complete humanisation.

Thus, this folktale deals with human animality. The word "animality" makes us think of bestiality, the ultimate degradation. But in the myth, the hero's form symbolises the state of all humans at birth. The child in his natural state is different from his mother; it is an animal that, to evade incest, will experience passions that will found his existential reality.

We can consider the animal-child a psyche encased in the maternal envelope,[35] a not-yet-individualized being unaffected by socialisation (which will transform him later through the love relation). While he remains captive in an incestuous relation, the young boy stays hidden in his first skin, with which he came into the world. This is, in fact, the evil spell cast by the witch: "You shall stay a serpent, an earthworm, until a woman loves you as you are." It is also the foolhardy wish of the barren woman, who wants to bear a living being, regardless of what the future holds in store: "If only I could have a child, be it only a frog!" The little human animal can only experience complete humanisation through the miracle of a third person's love.

The hero and heroine's initiation to sexuality is accomplished through the strangeness of human animality and of the magical character of the transformation, illustrated by alternating the human and non-human forms of the hero.

Love Instinct, Death Instinct

Apuleius transformed a version of one of the oral tale subtypes into a great literary myth (which was passed down through the centuries, to finally encounter psychoanalysis). A Platonic philosopher, the author perceived this folktale as a confrontation between love and death. Apuleius turned the hero into a manifestation of Eros, placing the heroine in the only other position possible, on the side of death. The figure of Psyche is suited to this function.

The role of death in this scene of descent into the Underworld (aiming to transform the mortal young woman and elevate her to the status of the god Eros) allows us to see the Eros-Psyche couple as two opposing forces that unite in a continuous exchange that can be interpreted as the inseparable life and death instincts, identified and named as such by psychoanalysis many centuries later.

But Apuleius did not choose the name Psyche (Soul) for his heroine by chance, in the context of his time. The human soul separated from God has fallen to Earth, has experienced a fall, exile and the "loss of its wings". But it seeks to purify itself and be filled with light in order to find God again. Moreover, Apuleius' work has enjoyed such fame that, to this day, Psyche is always pictured as a woman (with or without wings).[36]

Psyche must cross death and pass through the nether regions to finally unite with Eros for all eternity. She is the first mortal woman who returns alive from Hades. Certain heroes of Antiquity, demigods, have made this voyage: Hercules, Orpheus, Theseus, Ulysses and others, but do we know of any heroines?

Does this space of dialectical exchange between Love and Death actually exist in each variant of the oral folktale? I think that it does. We only need to keep in mind that one can change into the other, and even replace it. In addition, in the countless versions of the tale, the place of death is not always attributed to Psyche.

Although the same narrative pattern is present in the oral tradition, the latter includes no philosophical allegory in the literary sense. One thing is certain: given the diversity of versions, there are frequent instances when death can shift position. But both instincts, in their duality, are always present.

We can picture this play between Love and Death in the oral tradition as a formal dance where quadrille dancers change partners, places and groups regularly, based on certain rules. Successive couples of dancers face each other and carry out various dance figures with the melody of the contradance remaining unchanged.

Similarly, the two protagonists' roles change from one variant to another. Love and Death change places regularly. For instance, the heroine's initiatory voyage takes different forms: she undertakes it to save a man who is ill and cures him; or her purpose is to resuscitate a dead prince; she can even create a man from scratch, fashioning him to her liking and giving him life. Thus, Beauty brings about the metamorphosis of the Beast. It should be noted that the young heroine of oral versions is always an ordinary mortal, bearing no special name.

We observe a transformation of the original myth into a constellation of phantasies[37] concerning the feminine. These are, in general, social phantasies: the heroine becomes a saviour, a healer, an initiator, a source of life for the hero. She possesses the amorous character attributed to Eros. She carries out the initiation of her fiancé and is no longer the subject of her own initiatory voyage. Psyche becomes the helper of Eros. In our opinion, these are later developments[38] that modified the original folktale.[39]

Let us take three examples to illustrate. First, an intermediary form between myth and phantasy.[40]

The Tale that Reunites

The couple are about to separate. Before disappearing, the young man tells his wife that she will find him one day *through the story*. The young woman has an inn and a hospital built, where anyone can come and stay or be treated without cost, if he tells a story. One day, her husband arrives, changed into a bird. He takes off his feathers, assumes human form and tells his story. This allows the couple to reunite.

The transformed hero flies away with a flock of migratory birds,[41] but the heroine *stays where she is*. She becomes an innkeeper, a collector of stories. This first mythical displacement from the life events of the protagonists to stories told, from subject to object, paves the way to subsequent transformations of the initial story.

Here, the story within a story, the tale with inserted secondary stories (like the framing narrative of *One Thousand and One Nights*) is used as a magical passage into a-psychic space, where the lost husband will be found. He himself has provided the heroine with the key to this imaginary passage before he left, when he told her: "You will find me in the story." Indeed, when he enters her inn, he enters the world of the tale.

The Dead Prince

The following folktale is very widespread in Greece.[42]

A young girl is fated to marry a dead man. An eagle carries her into his palace, where she learns that if she watches over him for 40 days and 40 nights, he will awaken and marry her. The heroine keeps vigil and cries for the required time. Just a few minutes before the vigil is to end, she asks a young slave girl to replace her, and she falls asleep. The prince awakens and marries the slave girl, for he thinks she is the one who freed him from the spell he was under. The heroine becomes the servant of her servant and lives in misery.

Now the plot takes a turn determined by the young prince who, after his resurrection, becomes the subject of the narration. Returning from a voyage, he brings three magical gifts for the heroine: the stone of patience, the murderous knife and the hanging rope. The young girl tells her story to these enchanted objects, and cries over her sad fate. This is when the prince, who was listening secretly, finds out that he was saved by the heroine. He marries her and banishes the slave girl.

The eschatological aspects[43] of this tale refer to the representation of the woman-saviour, who confers both birth and immortality – a phantasy aiming to make woman the mistress of all life forms. The image of the dead prince, resuscitated or awakened from lethargic sleep, brings Apuleius to mind. When Psyche who descends into Hades falls into a death-like sleep, only Cupid can awaken her, by piercing her with his arrows. He is the one who brings her back to life. But where is Eros in this version?

The Prohibition to See

Of all the prohibitions, the one that forbids seeing Love is the best known. Let us take the example of lovers who live in a world beneath the Earth.[44] The heroine has married a *chthonian*[45] hero and lives with him in his palace.

The name of this supernatural prince is Tartarus, the Black Pit of the Earth. His palace is in the western region of the dark Netherworld. The young girl must not look at him in the light of day. But she disobeys and discovers that a key is attached to his navel. When she turns the key, she sees a strange world hidden in his body: a great market and a clothing factory. She goes in and people tell her that the master of the Underworld is about to marry a mortal woman. In the meantime, Tartarus wakes up, sees his navel open and sends the young woman away. He only takes her back when she gives birth to a boy who, like his father, has a key attached to his navel.

The prohibition to see could be the preliminary stage necessary to the knowledge of sexuality. A certain time is needed for physical contact before the heroine can get used to seeing the body of her beloved, without the risk of destroying her feelings. In addition, seeing and not seeing anymore is the equivalent of having and losing, and at first the players are not very skilled at this game.

The gaze, on its own, holds in it both day and night, presence and absence.

She saw (through his navel) an old woman washing cotton thread in the river. The water had carried part of it away, without the woman noticing. So the young girl – forgetting where she was – the poor creature! – cried out to her: "Granny, granny, the river is carrying your cotton thread away." The prince is awakened by her cries and tells her: "Turn the key, shrew, for now you have lost me." The phallic nature of the look of love – unbearable when thrown by a woman – is presented here in one of the most suggestive representations of the folktale. The young girl opens, literally unlocks, her sleeping lover's body, while he is in a passive state. She even touches the objects she sees inside him, objects and scenes that are part of the dream world.

Such an intrusion is always punished. But, in this folktale, the heroine who confronts the Master of the Underworld, who looks into his belly, always succeeds in defeating him. In this confrontation between – we might say – Persephone and Hades, the tale surprisingly leans in favour of the amorous gaze of Kore, "the maiden" – as Persephone is also called.

Thus, the mythical heroes with countless shapes found in the oral tradition change into conceptual characters in academic texts.

Notes

1 Apuleius, *Metamorphoses (The Golden Ass)*, A. Hanson (Trans.), Harvard University Press, 1989.
2 Name composed of *vryssi* (fountain) and *vouli* (will), expressing the idea of wanting to go to the fountain.
3 The black man lived in the Underworld.
4 A. Angelopoulos, "Le conte d'Eros et Psyché dans la littérature orale", *Topique, Revue Freudienne*, No. 75, 2001, pp. 155–169.
5 Apuleius, *Metamorphoses (The Golden Ass)*, A. Hanson (Trans.), Harvard University Press, 1989.
6 It must be noted that, in the international folkloristic classification, the title of this tale is "The Search for the Lost Husband" and only secondarily "Eros and Psyche". This

title was chosen to refer to the most famous version of the story, written by Apuleius 18 centuries ago. In the folktale-type classification, a number is used after the initials AT (denoting the two editors of the international typology, Aarne and Thompson). In this catalogue, "Eros and Psyche" is designated by the number AT 425.

7 To my knowledge, there is only one other folktale type with the same narrative plot (loss of love object, search, trials, reunion), in which the roles of the two sexes are reversed. This tale is called "The Search for the Lost Wife" (AT 400). Here, it is the man who explores another world in search of his lost enchanted wife. But we will never know which story came first.

8 But there are also tales without marriages, that are exceptions to the rule. In the opinion of specialists like Bengt Holbeck, these tales should not be classified as fairy tales. They tell the story of children who find their way home at the end of their wanderings, without growing up. Among them, we can mention Little Red Riding Hood, Tom Thumb, Hansel and Gretel, . . .

9 Concerning marriage as a social union, in Southeastern Europe and the Near East, stories centring on a heroine, such as Cinderella, Snow White, Sleeping Beauty and many others, always end with the birth of children, because marriage itself is not considered a sufficient accomplishment for a woman, who must always experience motherhood. In these countries, the tale can only culminate in the birth of at least one child.

10 Marc Soriano speaks of the "reflection of primitive structure" (M. Soriano, *Les Contes de Perrault*, Gallimard, 1968). We replaced this expression with "archaic mythical patterns" to take into account not only the structural analysis of the narrative, but also what escapes structural analysis: something completely new, and "irrational", present in each folktale.

11 J. O. Swahn, *The Tale of Cupid and Psyche*, CWK Gleerup, 1954. This typology has been adopted by all national catalogues and by myself, in the analysis of the elements of the "Cupid and Psyche" narrative. See G. A. Megas, A. Angelopoulos, A. Brouskou, M. Kaplanoglou and E. Katrinaki. *Catalogue of Greek Magic Folktales*, FF Communications No. 303, Academia Scientiarum Fennica, 2012, pp. 659–783.

12 Specifically, subtype A in Swahn's typology. Swahn identifies 14 subtypes, based on the resolution of the plot, that is, the circumstances in which the couple are reunited. See P. Delarue and M. L. Tenèze, 2002. *Le conte populaire français*. Maisonneuve & Larose (4 volumes: 1957, 1976, 1985 and 2000), pp. 107–118).

13 G. Boccacio, *Genealogy of the Pagan Gods* (fourteenth century), Harvard University Press, 2011.

14 Pedro Calderon de la Barca, *Psyche and Cupid*, an "auto sacramental" musical play (seventeenth century).

15 Jean de la Fontaine, *The Loves of Cupid and Psyche* (1669), Rare Books Club, 2013.

16 Hesiod, *Hesiod's Theogony*, CreateSpace Publishing, 2010, pp. 116–120.

17 Y. Bonnefoy (Ed.), *Dictionnaire des mythologies*, Flammarion, 1981.

18 E. Panofsky, *Essais d'iconologie*, Gallimard, 1967.

19 "She saw the glorious tresses drenched with ambrosia, on his golden brow, the neatly tied locks straying over his rosy cheeks and milk-white neck, some hanging delicately in front others behind." (Apuleius, *Metamorphoses (The Golden Ass)*, A. Hanson (Trans.), Harvard University Press, 1989, Book V, pp. 22–24, "The Tale of Cupid and Psyche".)

20 C. Perrault, *Perrault's Fairy Tales*, Dover Publications, 1969.

21 In France, Hyacinth Husson is the best-known proponent of this theory.

22 Y. Verdier, *Le Petit Chaperon Rouge dans la Tradition Orale*, Allia, 2024.

23 Despite the parallels our analysis establishes between Psyche and initiation-related death, we must keep in mind that *Thanatos* is a distinct mythical figure connected to another ancient myth, and that the term "Thanatos" is not present in Freud's work. According to Ernest Jones, Freud used it sometimes in conversation (J. Laplanche and

J. B. Pontalis, *The Language of Psychoanalysis*, D. Nicholson-Smith (Trans.), W. W. Norton, 1973).

24   S. Freud (1932–1936), *New Introductory Lectures on Psycho-Analysis*, SE 22, Hogarth

25   He can be a bear, a black dog, a wolf, a wild animal, a clog-shod rooster, a lamb, a turtle, a mule, a black horse, a camel, a frog, a porcupine, a dwarf, a head, a monster, a dead man.

26   He can be a snake, a golden crab, a scorpion, an earthworm, a crocodile, etc.

27   He can be a watermelon, a basil plant, a fragrant flower, a beanstalk, a rod of musk, etc.

28   Unstitched salwar (Indian garment) or stitched cloth.

29   Thus, the hero can take the form of a monster, or a strange being: the son of an ogress, a ghost, a donkey's head, a fez, a giant, the master of the Underworld, the water spirit Drac Philippe, Alexander the Great, Tartarus, the Black Pit of the Earth, Black Sun, the Magician with seven veils, the Rose of Constantinople, the Seven Crown Prince, King Tzertzis, the Mage Aydin, Atys (the golden eagle), the son of patriarch Tzach, King Perzeressis, Master Marketos, the son of the witch, The King of the Sea, Artsibibila-ris, Ars-Arsino Red Grape, The King of Trade, the Golden Green, Thousand-Hairs, the Golden Ruby of the Underworld, Shifting Wind, etc. All these names, especially when considered together, refer to Eros in Ancient Greece.

30   These mysterious names remain secret for the wife, who must neither know them or say them, just as she must never see her lover by the light of day. But in the other world the heroine discovers the secret name of her lost husband, hidden from her during the initial period of their romance.

31   In Antiquity, there were already two figures of the goddess of Love: Aphrodite (according to some, the mother of Eros, according to others, his wife) – thus, a celestial figure and an earthly figure, the characteristics of the latter counting bestiality among them.

32   For instance, Golden Eagle, Golden Flight, the Tjilianos Bird, the wealth-making bird, the Golden-Green bird, the spinning bird, etc.

33   Greek folklorist Georgios Megas wrote a monograph about this folktale, in which he gives 89 versions of this initial form, the oldest of subtype A, according to Swahn, representing one fifth of all Greek versions. See G. Megas, *Das Märchen von Amor und Psyche in der griechischen Volksüberlieferung* (AaTh 425, 428 & 432), Athens, 1967.

34   This summary of the animal husband tale resembles the first summary, that of Cupid, the supernatural husband, in regard to the crucial part of the narrative (both belong to subtype A of folktale type AT 425). This illustrates how closely variants of a folktale can resemble each other just before the final sequence of the story. Indeed, only the start of the story, the prehistory and childhood of the characters, are very different from variant to variant, and often from version to version.

35   On the subject of the maternal envelope, see D. Anzieu, *Psychic Envelopes*, Karnac Books, 1990.

36   On the image of the woman in Greek philosophy, see G. Sissa, *L'Âme est un corps de femme*, Odile Jacob, 2000.

37   J.-P. Valabrega, *Le problème anthropologique du phantasme*, Seuil, 1967.

38   Developments represented by subtypes D, E, G, K, L and P of the folktale-type. However, the initial mythical theme of Cupid and Psyche, as presented by Apuleius, is unchanged in subtypes A, B, C, X and R (AT 432). Here, the heroine enters the netherworld and is subjected to an initiatory trial.

39   We must keep in mind that the names "Cupid" and "Psyche" are not present in oral folktales; they are used here – as is the custom – as a convenient way to designate the protagonists of these tales.

40   Folktales in subtype D.

41 A. Angelopoulos, "L'hirondelle et la Mort", *Ethnologie Française*, 23 (1), 1993, pp. 104–112.
42 It belongs to subtype G.
43 This tale has kept the emphasis on ritual (for instance, respect of the 40 days of Orthodox mourning rites).
44 These folktales belong to subtype L.
45 Related to Underworld deities.

Chapter V

The Realm of Mythical and Psychical Metamorphoses

THE SERPENT PRINCE or THE WOMAN WHO HAD TWO HUSBANDS

Once upon a time there was a king and a queen who had a little girl named Maria. They took good care of her and when she reached the right age, they sent her to school to learn to read and write. At school, her teacher doted on her and was very fond of her, and Maria loved her teacher. One day, the teacher asked her: "Would you like me to be your mother?"

— "But I already have one, so how can I have you for a mother?" But the teacher asked her the same question again and again. After a time, Maria, who liked her very much, said: "Yes, I want you to be my mother!"
— "When you go home, ask your mother to give you some nuts. Insist that she should get them herself from the big marble chest. She will want to send servants to fetch them, but you must insist that you want her to bring them. That way, she will go to get them herself. When she will be bent over the chest, you will slam down the cover on her head to kill her."

After school, on her way home, Maria kept thinking about all this. Because she loved her teacher, she decided to do as she had told her. As soon as she got home, she asked her mother for some nuts; she persuaded her to go and get them from the chest herself.

When she was bent over with her back to Maria, the girl quickly slammed down the cover on her. Her mother let out a loud cry, and before expiring she said: "May God and the Blessed Virgin lead you to the cemetery, to my grave! You'll need my advice after the harm you have done me; you will be in great need of advice in your future suffering!"

The queen was buried with much pomp and ceremony. A few days later, the teacher told Maria to tell her father that she needed a new mother. The little girl went to her father in tears: "I want to have a mother!"

DOI: 10.4324/9781032674230-6

– "But, my child, what woman could love you like your own mother?" Maria did what her teacher had told her to do. She said: "Father, you shall marry my teacher because I want her to be my mother!" And the king finally consented, to make his little girl happy.

For a time, they all lived in harmony. But one day war broke out in a distant country. The king had to go off with his army and Maria was left alone with her teacher. It happened that at that time an old woman who looked after the garden with her husband kept praying and asking God to give her a child. She was barren but she prayed with all her heart: "If only I could have a child, even if it be a serpent!" Her wish was granted, and she found herself pregnant, carrying a serpent. One day when she was in the garden, heavy with her offspring, she lamented: "What will become of me, for soon I will have to give birth, but no midwife will want to help me because they will all be afraid that the serpent will eat them!" The queen, the one who had been the girl's teacher, was on her balcony and said: "Don't worry, when the time comes, I will send you my stepdaughter Maria to help you give birth."

– "No, that's not possible, because the serpent will eat her!"
– "Don't worry, I will give her good advice."

And the teacher ordered her stepdaughter to assist the gardener's wife with the birth. Maria went to her mother's grave: "Mother whom I killed, I beg you to advise me. Help me! For I have to help the neighbour give birth to a serpent! My teacher, who asked me to kill you, wants me to be eaten by the serpent now!" A deep growl rose from the tomb: "My daughter, your trials are not over! Ask the serpent's father to bring you a bowl of milk and another of honey. You must also ask for a closed crate with only one opening through which to slide the serpent inside. At the birth, when you see him come out, you will say: 'Serpent, come and get the milk and the honey!' He will come out, drink the milk and eat the honey, and then go into the box." She followed these instructions. This is how, by following her mother's advice, Maria was able to bring the serpent into the world. From then on, the serpent was fed through the crate opening.

A few years later, the serpent, now a healthy young creature, told his mother: "Mother, I want to learn to read and write!"

– "But who will want to teach you, my child? You will kill them all!"
– "The one who brought me into the world will also teach me to read and write!" the serpent answered.

And so, Maria was asked to do this. Once again, she went to her mother's grave. "Mother whom I killed, give me advice, for I have to teach the serpent to read and write."

— "You will ask his father to make three iron bars, and you will say: 'Alpha, Serpent'; he will answer 'Alpha'. You will continue: 'Beta, Serpent'; he will answer: 'Beta'. Then: 'Gamma, Serpent' and he will answer 'Gamma'. When you will get to Delta, he will want to eat you, but you will hit him on the head with one of the iron bars, so hard that it will break, and you will do the same with the second and the third iron bar. Then the serpent will crawl into the crate and won't come out again to eat you."

Maria followed all her mother's advice closely, and was able to teach the serpent to read and write.

A few years later, the serpent, whose voice was now that of a man, told his mother: "Mother, I want to be married!"

— "Oh, God in Heaven, great is our misfortune! What woman would want to marry a serpent!"
— "The one who brought me into the world, who taught me to write, that one can marry me too! You shall give me Maria for a wife."
— "But how can we let you take Maria for your wife, you, a serpent who will eat her?"
— "No, I will not eat her! But if you don't marry us, I will eat you all! I will come out of my crate and eat you!"

The teacher heard him shout and said: "Maria, we are going to wed you."

— "And to whom?"
— "Your husband will be Serpent; the one you brought into the world, the one you taught to read, is now going to be your husband!"

Once again, Maria visited her mother's grave: "Mother whom I killed, give me your advice, for I must marry Serpent. Help me, my little mother, what am I to do?" A great sigh rose from the tomb: "Heed my words, my daughter, marry him, he will not eat you, but be careful! Ask that a wood stove be built in the bridal chamber and that seven cartloads of wood be brought. On the wedding night, you will be alone with Serpent in the room; you will light the fire to heat the stove seven times, one time for each barrel of wood. You will wear seven dresses and you will take one off each time you light a fire; the serpent will take off one of his seven skins each time, and you will throw them in the fire. When he will have taken off the seventh skin, he will appear naked, in human form. You will bring him men's clothing to wear, and he will be your husband from then on."

Maria married the serpent. After the ceremony, when they were alone together in the bedroom, she took off a dress, he took off a skin, then another and another. Maria burned them one after the other in the hot stove. In the end, the serpent's naked body was that of a handsome young man! His beauty lit up the room! Then he told her: "Be careful, my dear wife, you must not reveal my secret to anyone. I am a prince cursed by a bad fairy whose spell condemned me to be born in the body of a serpent. If you say anything to anyone, you will lose me. You would have to wear out three pairs of iron shoes to find me again. Be warned, tomorrow morning I will turn into a serpent. Not a word to anyone!"

At dawn, he turned into a snake again and curled up in a corner. Her mother came in to see what happened to her. "Did he try to eat you, my daughter?" – "Certainly not, Mother!" For several days the serpent continued to be fed; he was given milk and honey at her request. Members of the family kept questioning Maria to learn more about the young couple, but she made no answer. But one day she gave in to the pressure and told everyone the truth. Instantly, the serpent disappeared and was never seen again. Maria was broken-hearted. She asked her stepmother to order three pairs of iron shoes for her so that she could set off in search of him.

The young woman visited her mother's grave once again, and heard her say: "You shall cross mountains and forests, much suffering still awaits you. Fate has more blows and misfortunes in store for you!" Maria set off with her three pairs of shoes. She crossed mountains and forests, often fell to the ground, was wounded, but picked herself up and went on. Finally, she met an old woman (her destiny) who told her: "You shall go to the end of this road. You shall find a marble slab in the forest; you shall lift it and walk down the stairs. You will find yourself deep underground. You will see astonishing things, but you must not be afraid."

Maria followed the old woman's advice. In the depths of the Earth, she saw a big, luxurious, lit-up house. A young man sat on a chair, looking as if he was glued to it and could not move, paralysed by a magic force. The young man asked her: "Are you a human being or a fairy? Why have you come here, to the Underworld?" Maria answered that she was a human being and asked how he had come to be there, deep in the bowels of the Earth.

He told her: "I am a prince carried off by fairies; my name is Giorgis. They took me from my father's palace and locked me up here; they come every night, I play the violin and they dance. Stay here with me, Maria, and I will turn you into an orange and hide you in my pocket when they arrive. No sooner said than done. The fairies arrived, smelled the air and said: "It smells of human flesh, royal flesh!" The young man answered: "Of course, it is because you have royal origins!" He played the violin and they danced. This went on for many nights.

After a time, Maria, who took human form during the day, became pregnant with Giorgis' baby. A few months later, he told her: "You must leave now, I will send you to my kingdom, where my parents are. You will ask them to let you enter the palace through the small door at the back, which must be covered over with weeds by now, for it has not been opened for a long time. The fairies took me away through that door. You will ask my parents to send me their army; their soldiers must come here and bring me a lot of incense. They have to come and get me."

Maria set off and arrived at Giorgis' palace after walking a long time. The queen mother had instructed the guards to ask all passers-by, whoever they might be, if they had seen or heard of her son, Giorgis. The young woman asked them to let her come in through the small door overrun with weeds. "It might be a good sign," they thought and let her come in. They gave her a room in which to rest. She said: "May you be well and may God bring Giorgis back here, to the palace!" They asked her if she knew him, but she answered that she had only heard of him.

A little while later, her labour pains began. She gave birth to a baby boy. The queen took care of her; she prepared a beautiful cradle and swaddling clothes for the baby. One evening, when the queen was passing by, she heard the young woman sing a lullaby:

> Sleep my little one,
> Sleep my sweet one,
> If your grandmother knew
> That you are the son of Lord Giorgis
> She would make you a golden cradle,
> She would give you golden rattles.

The old queen pricked up her ears. She listened to the lullaby once more. After that, she burst into the room and asked Maria who was the father of her child, and what the words of the lullaby meant. Maria confessed that the baby was her grandchild. The queen gave her the best room at the top of the palace, and also gave her a governess. After that, the whole army set off to rescue Giorgis. They took three big bags of incense with them. When they arrived, they lit the incense, took hold of the young prince and left with him. The fairies wanted to go after them and take Giorgis back, but could not go near them because of the incense. And so they arrived at the palace. The signs of mourning were taken down at once; the black crepe was replaced by brightly coloured cloth. Giorgis married Maria, there was great rejoicing. And they lived happily together.

In the meantime, Serpent, who had become a travelling salesman, learned that Maria had married the son of the king. He went to the palace and asked the servants for a drink of water. He drank from the queen's pitcher and let his ring fall into it; on it, the name "Serpent" was engraved. When she saw the ring, the young woman turned pale, but she said nothing to Giorgis. The next day, Serpent went to see Giorgis and told him: "Your wife, Maria, is my wife."

– "That can't be true!"
– "Yes, it's true. She brought me into the world, she taught me to write, she married me and she is mine."

Neither one of them would give in. So they took their problem to a judge, who said: "You must set out on a long journey all together. Maria will carry her child. Each of the two men will carry a gourd of water. When she will tire, Maria will ask for water. The one she asks is her husband." They set out on the long journey. Maria became tired, was covered in sweat and finally said, exhausted:

For you, Serpent, I disappear,
For you, Giorgi, I am dying,
Serpent, give me water
And let my soul stay with you both.

They gave her water at once, but she died before she could drink. Both of them lost her. Thus, her mother's curse was fulfilled. In the meantime, her father came back from the war. He did not find Maria at the palace. His wife, the teacher, told him she had gone away. But the king learned that it was the teacher who caused poor Maria's misfortunes. He killed her and was left alone, heartbroken, without a wife and without a daughter.

Sources

"O Ofis pou egine vassilopoulo" [The Serpent Changed into a Prince], FS 1871, pp. 2–11.
    Transcribed in 1960 by Maria Chrissalli in Missolonghi.
CGMF 433B, *King Lindorm.*
ATU 433B, *King Lindorm.*
    (CPF, The Prince Changed into a Serpent.)

Mythical and Psychical Metamorphoses

Anna Angelopoulos

I shall let the poet speak first.[1]

> *All may become again as before:*
> *the fingers, the eyes and the lips.*
> *Let us leave behind the old sickness*
> *a shirt shed by snakes yellow*
> *amid green clover.*

Indeed, in Greek the shed skin left behind by the snake has a little-known scientific name meaning "serpent shirt", used here as an image emblematic of mutation or metamorphosis.

Last summer, in my garden, I found in the branches of the wisteria an abandoned bird's nest bearing the traces of broken eggs, and a long serpent skin discarded beside it. It was a powerful image giving rise to a series of associations, a whole range of narratives.

What had happened in my absence to the fledglings, to their mother, to the serpent? The answer remains a mystery.

What came to my mind was the old story about the start of the Trojan War. Before the Greek ships that had gathered at Aulis set sail, and while a sacrifice to Zeus was being prepared, a serpent was seen climbing onto a nearby plane tree; at the top of the tree, there was a nest with eight fledglings. The serpent seized them, seized their mother who was circling around the nest, and swallowed them greedily.

Seeing this, the prophet Calchas declared that the city of Troy would be taken by the Achaeans in the tenth year of the war. Suddenly, the serpent climbing up on the trunk of the plane tree was petrified, becoming a serpent-shaped marble statue.

To begin my discussion, I would like to elucidate a series of metaphors starting with Ovid, continuing with Aeschylus' tragedy *Choephori*, and ending with the folktale "The Serpent Prince". This seems to follow naturally from my reflections on the transitional symbol I found in my garden.

Ovid wrote the *Metamorphoses* in the first century AD. This 15-volume poetic work was comprised of 12,000 verses, describing 250 physical transformations; it was written "to tell of bodies changed into new forms". Ovid's title uses a Greek word describing a world in constant flux, eternally unstable. It is important to note the meaning of "meta",[2] a preposition introducing the *subjective mood* of verbs, which makes it possible to take into account changes of form, the time needed to go on to a new reality, or for characters to reach a different age.

We know that Ovid was influenced by Pythagorian philosophy, and that he drew on sources from Ancient Greece: Homer and the tragedians. He made use of brief tales, a form of writing in vogue in his era. He was considered a worldly man and made visits to the imperial palace.

Moreover, he believed in *transformism*, a major philosophical branch of Pythagoreanism. The legends presented in the *Metamorphoses* establish an uninterrupted chain of species from plant to deity, including all things of a mineral, vegetable and animal nature, human beings and planets, not excluding the belief in the passing of the soul at death into another body, either human or animal. Indeed, Pythagoras himself speaks in the last Book of the poem, providing a key to understanding the whole oeuvre.

Yet Ovid fell into disgrace and died in exile, far from his homeland. The world of the *Metamorphoses* is a world of constant transgression of the rules, of established social and religious order, where the validity of the real and its laws is eroded, rendering the future configuration of beings and things unstable. It is easy to see that this poet threatened the values of young Emperor Augustus (27 BC to 14 AD), who wanted to establish stability after a period of violent civil wars. In 8 AD, Ovid was exiled to Tomis (on the Black Sea, in the Danube Delta) for the rest of his natural life.

I shall use a reading of his poems as an illustration of the subject of metamorphosis. The reader can see the poet's insistence on the moment when each being is transformed, when he is neither man nor animal, but both at once. Ovid brings transformation out in the open. In *The Flood* (Book 1), where all the laws of nature are turned upside down, we can see that he presents a world where nothing is as it should be. Tigers and lions swim in the sea, seals lie on rocky flatlands where goats used to graze, fish frolic on tree branches. And instead of imagining the tragic consequences of such a state of affairs, Ovid portrays its amusing and extravagant aspects.

This being so, is it any wonder that his popularity has been rekindled in the present era, in these times of change, discontinuity and transition? In France, a new translation of the *Metamorphoses* by Marie Cosnay[3] was published in 2020.

Through the mutation of bodies, Ovid discloses the inner workings of the soul and the passions that move us: love, vengeance, hate, envy, etc. But the Ovidian universe also explores human instincts through myths. When looking closely at each metamorphosis, it becomes clear that they make it possible for a destiny to take wing, just when it is in danger of being cut short, as if a resistance to the death of the psyche has been mobilised, taking the form of necessary flight from trauma, to ensure survival. In the Daphne and Apollo myth, for example, it is when Apollo is about to take hold of the young nymph that she begs the God of the river, her father, to take away her beauty, so that she is transformed into a myrrh tree.

These paroxysmal experiences, which one can only escape through a metamorphosis that leads into the plant world, are usually brought about by the unbearable pain of mourning, by unspeakable betrayal, by rape or by incest. In the myth of Myrrha, the mortal maiden who intentionally committed incest with her father without his knowledge is transformed into a myrrh tree. Its bark will give birth to Adonis, the son of incest.

Ovid also reveals some tendencies that have become common in our times, such as transitioning, which brings into question the anatomic sex of an individual, as described in the myth of Tiresias (who experienced being of both the masculine and the feminine sex), or the myth of Hermaphrodite. The fact that this transgender phenomenon has come to characterise our era is no doubt due to the possibility of materialisation – by medical means – of a very old phantasy.

Ovid paints the portrait of a world undergoing a metamorphosis governed by human passions, by the convulsions that agitate gods and men. Ovid's heroes are in a state of rebellion; they disobey the laws of nature and incite the wrath of the gods. Not unlike the hunter Actaeon, who, for unwittingly seeing Artemis naked, was changed into a stag and killed by his own dogs; or the young Tiresias, a symbolic figure associating the serpent with sexuality. The myth of Tiresias can be outlined as follows:

One day when Tiresias was strolling on Mount Cyllene, he came upon a pair of copulating snakes and separated them with his stick by hitting the female. He was instantly transformed into a woman and became a famous priestess of Hera. He lived in a woman's body for seven years. In the eighth year, he saw the same snakes copulating on Mount Cyllene. This time, he hit the male and became a man again.

When Zeus asserted that women take more pleasure in sex than men and his wife Hera contradicted him, they asked Tiresias for his opinion, since he had experienced being each of the sexes. Tiresias confirmed Zeus' opinion. He explained that if the pleasure of the sex act were divided into ten parts, the woman would enjoy nine, while the man would enjoy only one. To punish Tiresias for his judgement, Hera blinded him for eternity. Zeus could not stop her, but compensated Tiresias by bestowing the art of soothsaying upon him, as well as seven generations of life.

Another version of the myth tells the story of Tiresias as a young boy, singing and dancing, and coming upon Athena naked. "The goddess covered his eyes with her hands, and so rendered him sightless."[4]

According to Nicole Loraux,[5] Tiresias saw the unthinkable, the impossible to see for gods and for men, when he saw the naked body of Athena. It was then that he was transformed into a woman.[6]

Heroes often see the unthinkable, the weaknesses of the gods, and are severely punished for it. Exiled by Augustus, Ovid compares himself to Actaeon:

"Why did I see anything?
Why make my eyes guilty?
Why was a mischief, unwittingly, known to me?"

Ovid tells a number of stories about serpent transformations. The one about the Medusa as a lovely maiden is one of the best known. We know that generally serpents symbolise death, poison, disaster. Yet they are also symbols of sexual desire. I shall use this as my starting point, to compare how these images of transition are presented in myths and in folktales.

Let us take as an example the breastfeeding of a snake in Clytemnestra's dream, in Aeschylus' tragedy, *The Choephori*, part of the Oresteia trilogy.[7]

In the play, this motif announces a disaster, foreshadowing the matricide that would follow. Let us remember that Agamemnon sacrificed his daughter (and Clytemnestra's), Iphigenia, so that the wind would fill the sails of the Achaean ship for their journey to Troy. Ten years later, when Agamemnon returned from the war, he was killed in his bath by Clytemnestra and her lover Aegisthus. Orestes, who was then a child, was saved from being killed by his sister, Electra; he was taken out of the country and henceforth lived in exile. Many years later, Orestes returned to Argos in disguise to avenge his father. That night, Clytemnestra, his mother, dreamed that she gave birth to a snake.

This dream is recounted on Agamemnon's tomb by the women's chorus, which reveals its content: the queen gave birth to a snake, wrapped it like a baby and fed it from her breast. But a blood clot came out of her breast with the milk. Terrorised by the dream, the queen asked her daughter, Electra, to go to Agamemnon's grave with the chorus of women, the Choephori, bearing libations to appease the ghost of the murdered king.

The brother and sister recognise each other at their father's grave, and swear to avenge him. Orestes interprets his mother's premonitory dream, identifying with the serpent. He vows to be this dreadful thing (serpent) in the dream, and to kill her himself.

"... the thing of dread she nursed
The death of blood she dies; and I, 'tis I,
In semblance of a serpent, that must slay her."

While the serpent is a key component of the unequivocally tragic and murderous character of the myth, this is not the case in the folktale, where the symbolism of the snake is used to a different purpose. To illustrate, I will discuss the folktale "The Serpent Prince", a variant of "Eros and Psyche". This tale inverts the dynamics of the mythical motif of the nursing of the snake, as well as the ending of the story, to give the plot an optimistic outcome. Thus, this example, like many others, clearly shows that the images in the folktale exert a restorative action on the psyche and impel the characters towards humanisation – always nocturnal and often during a night of love –, in the direction of the life instinct.

But let us look more closely at the plot of "The Serpent Prince".[8]

The Serpent Prince

A barren woman makes a wish to have a child – even if it be a serpent. Her wish comes true nine months later; she gives birth to a serpent and brings him up. When the time comes, the serpent asks for a wife, but he kills all his brides during the wedding night.

No woman will have him, until a young girl (who lives with her evil step-mother) agrees to marry him. Because she risks dying by being poisoned by the snake, the heroine wears seven dresses on top of each other. When they are alone after the festivities on their wedding night, the Serpent Prince asks his wife to undress, but she says she would like him to take off his shirt first. He is wearing seven shirts and she, seven dresses. Each time he takes off one of his shirts, she takes off a dress. When he has taken off his seventh shirt, his last snake skin, the naked Prince changes into a handsome young man. He tells her that she has broken the spell that had transformed him into a serpent. And they lived happily ever after, and we even more so.

This version of the folktale comes from the Scandinavian countries (King Lindorn – type 433B), where it is widespread. In Greece, 23 versions are known to exist; they present a distinct narrative that is also found in Turkey.[9] This version starts with the hero's birth and the circumstances preceding it. Like many oriental fairy tales, these versions reveal the hero's prehistory, in this case, what happened to the heroine and the serpent in their childhood and before birth.

A little girl wants to have her teacher as a mother. To make her father marry her, the girl kills her own mother. But the teacher becomes an evil stepmother once she is married and wants to be rid of the little girl. The stepmother sends the girl to help the queen – who is carrying a snake – give birth. Following advice from her dead mother, the girl places a bowl of warm milk next to the queen's belly, so that the smell of the milk entices the snake to come out.

After that, the stepmother sends the girl to breastfeed the snake, who kills all the wet nurses. She wears a corset made of gold and is able to breastfeed the snake without being harmed. Some years later, she teaches him to read by using an iron bar, and finally she marries him, taking care to wear seven dresses on her wedding night. This is how she fends off the threat of being killed, and how she allows the serpent to recover human form, after removing his seven shirts – his old snake skins.

In my view, in the language of the folktale this image of the snake's moulting symbolises the metamorphosis of adolescence. In adolescence, the boy is replaced by the man, a new being emerging on the wedding night. In fact, the young boy's voice deepens, and sexual characteristics develop. The boy sheds his old appearance like a shirt, just as the snake sheds his skin. Adolescence signals the end of childhood. "The Serpent Prince" describes this transition. In this folktale, we also recognise the stages of sexuality defined by Freud: the young man's passage from the oral to the genital stage.

In the Greek versions of the story the heroine commits matricide (just as Electra would have liked to do in *The Choephori*). In Oedipal terms, we can say that she destroys her mother, her rival, to replace her with another mother, seen as ideal – but who quickly changes into a persecutory stepmother. By contrast, the dead mother remains maternal and supports her.

As soon as persecution by the stepmother begins, the father disappears from the narration. This is regularly the case in folktales about (primary) relations between mothers and daughters.

The Serpent: A Feminine Symbol

But the serpent is not only a phallic symbol, pertaining to young boys. My search for feminine metamorphoses connected to snakes uncovered "The Little Viper", a Judaeo-Spanish folktale from the Balkans.[10] In this story, a young prince finds his future wife by shooting an arrow into a pile of rocks, where it hits a garter snake. The snake would later change into a Beauty of the World once it shed its snake skin, but the Young Man does not know this yet and is disheartened.

"While he sat crying, the viper started to unroll and raised half its body before him. Seeing this, the young man thought: "Never before has she raised herself before me like this!" He was comforted by the way in which the little viper held herself before him, and he thought: "What I see is a good sign." Then the garter snake slid down into her shelter.

The young prince was right to interpret this unrolling of the viper's body as a sign of feminine desire. And what did he do next? He burned the snake sheath so that his betrothed would remain a young woman, the Beauty of the World, and be his wife.

Thus, both the man and the woman reveal their sexual desire through the metaphor of the shirt that is removed, the animal skin that is shed.

To conclude, I will return to Ovid and his treatment of sexual transition in the *Metamorphoses*. I am referring specifically to the myth of the Hermaphrodite (Book 4).

The son of Hermes and Aphrodite, Hermaphroditus was the most handsome young man in the world. A young nymph, Salmacis, who lived in a spring, saw him and desired him. Crazed with passion, she wanted him to take her in the waters of the pool. He resisted and struggled to escape her. But she wound herself around him and held on, like a bird that catches a snake and will not let it go. Salmacis asked the gods to unite them in a single human body. The gods granted her wish. This is how Hermaphroditus became the first two-sexed being. He in turn asked the gods who were his parents that the Salmacis spring be enchanted, so that any person who enters it be transformed in the same way as he was. In Strabo's era (between the first century BC and the first century AD), belief in the feminising powers of the spring was still strong.

Ovid is one of the rare sources of the myth of the Hermaphrodite. He brings us a new human form in which the two sexes coexist in a single body. He also transmits an etiological legend about transgender individuals, which originated in the Orient.

IS IT A BOY? IS IT A GIRL?[11]

Once upon a time there was an old king who only had three daughters, but no male heir. The king was called to war to defend the neighbouring kingdom. But he was getting too old for battle, his strength was leaving him. It was his favourite daughter, the youngest, who offered to wage war in his place. So she put on men's clothing, donning a soldier's uniform, and set off on her magic horse, given to her as a gift for her bravery. As soon as she arrived on the battlefield, she put the enemy to flight. Pleased and grateful, the king of the neighbouring country wished to reward this hero by offering his daughter's hand in marriage. Such an offer could not be refused.

When the wedding night arrived, the two women found themselves in the same bed. The girl soldier took out her sword and placed it between herself and the king's daughter, explaining that she has been promised to a saint and must remain chaste. Time passed and the king's daughter finally complained to her mother that her marriage was still not consummated.

After a while, the king and queen wanted to be rid of this useless son-in-law. They thought up all sorts of impossible schemes to send him to his doom. For instance, bringing back an apple from paradise, collecting taxes in the country of the dragons, stealing a flower guarded by lions. The heroine's horse always helped her to accomplish her impossible tasks, and the girl in boy's clothing always returned successful. Frustrated, the king and queen decided on a truly impossible mission: they asked her to bring back the fire of the Cyclops.

Her horse told her: "This is more than I can do. You have to ask my mother to help." The horse's mother was a very old mare living at the bottom of the ocean. She carried the young girl to the country of the Cyclops, leaving her son at the edge of the water. The heroine stole the sacred fire, and the old mare fought the Cyclops who came after her. The battle was fierce, the mare was wounded but made a great leap forward; she and the young girl crossed the frontier and left the country of the Cyclops. Beyond this frontier, the Cyclops are powerless. Furious, they put their worst curse on the young girl: "If you are a man, become a woman; if you are a woman, become a man!" No sooner said than done. After a few paces, the mare asked the girl:

"Are you a boy or a girl now? Look carefully!" "I am a boy," the young girl answered. And the old mare replied: "I have never had a boy rider. My work is done, I am going to die now. Take me to the edge of the water, where you found me."

There, the horse was waiting for them; the old mare went into the sea to die. The boy who used to be a girl, riding her magic horse, arrived at the palace carrying the Cyclops' fire in her hand. The king could not believe it! The next night, the sword was removed from the young couple's bed. And plans were made for another sumptuous wedding celebration.

Transforming the Unspeakable[12]

Anna Angelopoulos

Before commenting on this tale, I must mention a popular Greek legend called "The Midwife".[13] It tells the story of a midwife who presents a newborn girl to her parents as a boy, by shaping a penis out of wax or soap, to fool them. She does this because the husband has threatened to kill his wife if she has another girl. As a result, since her birth, the heroine has to live under a false identity, since her mother forbids her to reveal the secret, to say that she is a girl.

Folktales and legends bring us face to face with the unspeakable and the unthinkable. What could be more unthinkable than to deny someone's sexual identity from birth, using a piece of soap as a subterfuge? What is more improbable than the fact that the princess's courageous husband is a woman disguised as a man? What is more unspeakable than the revelation of one's true sex, hidden for fear of dire consequences in traditional societies that value male heirs?

In both cases, a metamorphosis provides a way out of the impasse. The metamorphosis is achieved through magic or the use of a trick. In folktales, girls may want to be changed into boys in response to their fathers' desire (in this tale, the need to go to war). In the past, girls could have wished to be men to be free, pursue adventures, be independent. This required taking on masculine appearance to move freely in a society of men, as a vast body of "romantic" literature testifies.

This sleight of hand, this phantasy of becoming a boy is always unidirectional in the folktale: changing a girl into a boy. I have never seen a folktale about a boy wishing to become a girl. Today, women fight for equality with men, for freedom and rights impeded by conventional influences. But this sex shift phantasy also has other manifestations in our time, with questions of gender becoming predominant, no doubt fuelled by ancient dreams. The metamorphosis into one or the other of the sexes, as portrayed in folktales, has become possible through advances in science, leading to an entirely new debate, which we shall leave for another time.

A Serpent Prince on the Couch: Clinical Resonances

Sylvette Gendre-Dusuzeau

"Do you remember my dream with the serpent that came out of a river in the forest?" he asked me one day. Yes, I remembered it very well because when I had heard it, it had reminded me of the two serpents, Cadmus and Harmony, in one of Ovid's *Metamorphoses*,[14] where these two great mythical heroes are transformed into serpents as they are about to die, and slither towards the Elysian Fields represented by the forest.

My patient's question followed upon the discussion of "The Serpent Prince" in our seminar. This clinical story reminded me of the slough, "the shirt", reptiles shed to go through the phases of their animal life. On his wedding night, the Serpent Prince, whose wife is wearing seven dresses, must take off seven shirts one after the other, in other words, moult seven times and be left naked so that his metamorphosis into a handsome young man can take place. Metamorphosis is not a clinical concept; it is a metaphor for effects, such as becoming open to the world and making changes, which result from our psychoanalytic work with the unconscious and with transference. Our patients feel that there is hope for change; at a certain point, we suddenly notice that someone is slimmer, stands up straighter, has a new hair style, meets our gaze more often, no longer looks sad. Other people tell them they have changed: my friend, my sweetheart . . . tells me I've changed. How does this happen?

To describe the "serpent prince" who came to lie on my couch one day, I will focus mainly on two processes: the one that led to the psychical advent of his own birth, and the internal movement connected with his new experience as a father. These processes are depicted in animal metamorphoses present in dreams.

With hindsight, I would say that my patient had unknowingly reached a stage of hindered metamorphosis. He dreamed of large serpents displaying a hole, having a torn shirt that could impede the usual moulting process. He also had a recurrent dream where, as a child, he is chased by a shark with huge teeth under water and even in a swimming pool, as if the predator was watching for signs of the adolescent sex organ that was in no hurry to appear.

The serpent prince on my couch is a young married man living a normal happy life, with a pretty wife and a small son – as well as a demanding mother, to whose requests he does not attend too much. His parents-in-law are easy to get along with. He sees his parents occasionally, he has brothers and sisters who do not especially cause problems, aside from the fact that their mother is not pleased with her two daughters-in-law from Brazil, the wives of the two eldest brothers. She is rigid and authoritarian as a mother-in-law, and my patient remembers that as a mother she was very preoccupied with her work and very demanding at home. He himself had chosen a woman he had met in his neighbourhood, who was the mother of his son, and for whom his mother had the highest regard. She considered her the ideal daughter-in-law. At the time, they were all working in good conditions and had a comfortable life. No strong passions disturbed their tranquillity. Until the day they made a stormy entrance when my patient fell head over heels in love with a colleague who desired him passionately.

He had come to see me to deal with this onslaught of passion. His amorous passion quickly immersed us in the ancestral horrors present in folktales. His lover, who was also from a far-away land, was fiercely determined to have him all to herself, and could not bear not being the most important person in my patient's life. She seemed to embody the stepmother who wants to ignore the child who is already there, and especially that child's mother. But the strong attraction between them made my patient accept all her demands, because the screaming and the blaming were always followed by moments of bliss. His passion remained unchanged for several months. He became aware of his growing desire to change his life, but without imagining that he could do it, as shown by a dream in which he was trying to steer a barge that remains stuck to the bottom of a canal.

As an adolescent, he had been lonely and depressed, and had played the role of chaperone for friends who were more enterprising with girls. He would not have imagined that one day his dream of being passionately desired physically by a woman could come true.

The lovers' passion became even more violent when the woman, who had insisted on exclusivity, revealed her inconsistency when a former admirer of hers appeared on the scene. This intense period marked by despair and jealousy drove him to decide to live alone and to announce to his family that he was leaving for another woman. It was sudden, of course, but he could wait no longer for a life of freedom where no one would tell him what to do.

His wife was crushed, his son was completely bewildered. As for his mother, whose reaction he had feared, she congratulated him for daring to do what she had never allowed herself to do: leave her husband (his father) to be free. He was stunned!

His daring decision, which opened a new channel of communication with his mother, led him to discover certain things about himself. He had been an angry and moody child who always caused a scene because he would not finish the food on his plate. Because her husband lacked authority, his mother would beat the rebellious child, slapping him and hitting his bottom. She had even taken him to a friend of hers who claimed to have healing powers, to make him obey. He had forgotten all this. I had trouble imagining the violent child in this calm, interesting and pleasant adult.

Since his son wanted to see him, he arranged to be alone with him one afternoon a week, on condition that the child not meet the other woman. This is when he noticed that when he was alone with his son he was afraid, felt embarrassed and did not feel like a father.

His dreams provided us with many signs: a large wounded snake, with a large hole again, covered with white blood. It has legs and becomes a lizard. It runs after him, and a ferocious shark appears. Or, he is standing on the edge of a surface where seawater is just beginning to reach, and beside him there is a large snake that is not aggressive, but frightens him.

The period that followed was extremely turbulent and he kept taking blows from all sides. His lover's jealousy reached its peak. She demanded that he cut off all relations with his family for her. To top it all off, his mother announced that she had finally separated from her husband (his father), but she showed no indulgence in her demand that he break off his relationship because she did not want a third foreign woman in the family. She invoked the recurrent argument she used with him, saying: "You don't love, you want to be loved."

His dreams are full of animals. He is standing on a diving board, ready to jump, and below him there is a large dead snake. Then, he is sitting on a rock above a big river; he sees the clear bottom, with some enormous, harmless dark fish. He is looking at them, then looks at a family in the distance.

Then he has the dream I spoke of in the beginning, in which the serpent in the forest had come out of a river. This made him reflect on the relation between water and a woman's sex organs.

In the midst of all this familial and passion-fuelled confusion, he had to answer the questions his son asked when they were together. And since he was able to find the words to answer these questions, his son developed great confidence in his father. He wanted to do everything daddy did, he wanted to go for walks with daddy . . . My patient grew stronger in his paternal feelings but continued to be afraid.

His son entered his dreams, where he was pictured in the act of bringing up out of the water, with difficulty, a lobster pot containing a dead, large, green and orange tropical fish. There are two adults beside him.

My patient does not like the colour orange, his mother's favourite colour. He realises that all his life he has been looking for someone maternal. He is torn between his love for his mistress and his love for his son, whom she rejects.

As the sessions go on, we examine together the traumatic family relations in his past, and the ones in his lover's past, which are quite similar. In a dream, he sees himself falling out of a boat. From the deep, an enormous stingray with a shark's mouth comes towards him. A large bluish crab comes from the beach, takes hold of the stingray's mouth, drags it out of the water and injures it so badly that it is no longer a threat. I ask myself what place I hold in the transference, in this battle with the aggressors.

His mistress becomes pregnant. They are living together. He will be a father once again. In a dream, he explains to her how to give birth. After this, the serpent never appears again. He shows the mother of his unborn child that the head of the baby comes out of the mouth of a cat lying on the ground, saying: "It is a serpent that spits out and swallows."

We were able to discuss this fantasy about birth, in which the baby pushes his head out and the serpent takes it back, like in a double movement of spitting and swallowing down, which makes it impossible to come into the world. Covered over by the previous images of hindered metamorphoses, his birth was what his mother was preventing, in a continuous movement of spitting him out and swallowing him down again. He felt himself to be not yet born, not separated from his mother, who could take him back at any moment. Thus, he kept piling up his moulting skins without becoming free of them, until analysis made this possible.

Notes

1 G. Seferis (1932), "The Cistern", A. Anagnostopoulos (Trans.), Belknap Press, 1975.
2 This self-referential meaning is absent from the Latin "trans", which indicates direction.
3 Ovid, Les Métamorphoses, M. Cosnay (Trans.), Le Livre de poche, 2020.
4 Apollodorus, The Library, Book 3, J. G. Frazer (Trans.), Harvard University Press, 1921.
5 N. Loraux, The Experiences of Tiresias, P. Wissing (Trans.), Princeton University Press, 1995.
6 N. Loraux, The Experiences of Tiresias, P. Wissing (Trans.), Princeton University Press, 1995.
7 Aeschylus, The Choephori, Clarendon Press, 1999.
8 AT 433, G. F. Straparola, Fourth Night, Second Fable, "The Trial of the Serpent", W. G. Waters (Trans.), Nights of Straparola, Vol. I, Pook Press, 2018.
9 AT, Eberhard-Boratov Index of Turkish Folk Tales, Nos. 101, 106, 1961.

10 C. Crews, *Judeo-Spanish Folktales in the Balkans*, 1935; Textos judeo-españoles de Salonica y Sarajevo, 1979; in A. Angelopoulos, *Contes judéo-espagnols des Balkans*, José Corti, 2009.

11 The folktale "Is It a Boy? Is It a Girl?" bears the number 514 in the ATU international classification. The folktale is very widespread in the Mediterranean region. It tells the story of a young girl who goes off in search of adventure on her magic horse. At the end of the tale she finds herself transformed into a boy.

12 "Transforming the Unspeakable" was presented in Algiers in April 2023, at the Conference "Metamorphosis of hostile places into places of encounter and sharing", under the auspices of the Amine de Bab el Qued Association, the Ben Aknoun Equitherapy Association, the Psyche Group and the Fédération des Ateliers de Psychanalyse. Éditions FAP, 2024.

13 N. Politis, *Paradoseis*, S. Laografia, 1915–1916, p. 206.

14 Ovid, *Metamorphoses*, Book 4, Oxford World's Classics, 2008.

From Myth to Folktale

While the myth relates imaginary events based on a set of beliefs intended to explain a certain order of the world, the oral folktale, "paramythi" in Greek, suggests a degree of proximity to mythical materials. This collective narrative sometimes contains elements taken from major myths, presented at the human scale of everyday life. Folktale characters can change shape, just like mythical characters, but they often do this in response to a subjective impasse.

THE BAYBERRY CHILD

Once upon a time there was a king and a queen who had no children. The queen prayed to God for a child every day. "Dear God, grant me a child, even if he be no bigger than a bayberry seed," she begged. At long last her prayers were answered, and she gave birth to a tiny bayberry seed. The palace was filled with joy. But on the third day, when they went to the river to wash the baby's swaddling clothes, the tiny bayberry child fell into the water and was gone. No one could find him. At the palace there was only grief, lamentation and sorrow. One and all were inconsolable.

In the meantime, the bayberry seed was carried down the river and came to a far-away land where another king reigned. It took root next to the palace and grew to be a tall, beautiful bayberry bush covered with flowers. The king's son was a handsome, vigorous young man. He had been brought up with the greatest of care; every night, a servant brought him a glass of syrup. But for some time now, a ravishing young woman had come out of the bayberry bush at night, had quickly drunk the syrup and gone back to hide in her bush. This went on for some time, until the prince asked the young servant: "Why don't you bring me my syrup anymore?" But she had no answer. So he decided to keep watch all night to see who came to drink his syrup.

DOI: 10.4324/9781032674230-7

The next night, he stayed awake and kept watch. At midnight, a young girl appeared and was about to drink the syrup. But the prince caught her quickly, kissed her and squeezed her. They stayed together for a long time, and he finally let her go. The young girl went back to the bayberry bush and shouted: "Mother bayberry, open your branches and let me in!" But the bayberry bush would not let her in: "If to be kissed and squeezed you tarry, seek not shelter in the bayberry."

What was she to do? The poor girl started to cry. She went back to the king's son. "What will become of me?" she lamented. You squeezed me, you kissed me and now my mother has sent me away!" She cried and moaned. The prince knew not what to do. He kept her near him. But, alas, he was already engaged, and his parents wanted him to marry quickly. The prince loved the young girl, but what could he do?

One evening, while she slept, the prince gathered roses and basil to make a crown and placed it on her head. Then he rode off on his horse to the place where his marriage was to be celebrated. When she woke up in the morning, the young girl saw that he was not there. Gone without a trace! She wept and moaned, crying out: "Oh, roses; oh, flowers; oh, basil; why did you lull me to sleep and let my beautiful bird fly away?" She set off to look for him at once.

On her journey, she met a monk. She stopped him and asked: "How much do you want for giving me your clothes and taking mine?" They came to an agreement. The young woman was impossible to recognise in the monk's clothes. She continued on her way. She came upon the young prince on his black horse, but he did not recognise her and, thinking the traveller was really a monk, he asked: "Have you seen anything on the road?"

"Yes," said the monk. I saw a young girl who was crying and lamenting, saying: "Oh, roses; oh, flowers; oh, basil; why did you lull me to sleep and let my beautiful bird fly away?"

Distressed, the prince asked the monk to mount his horse. "Sit behind me." She accepted at once. As they rode, the young man kept asking: "Did you see anything on the road?" And she kept repeating the same thing, and her words tore at his heart and filled him with sorrow. But what could he do?

At last, they came to the spot where the marriage was to take place. The prince declared that he would not enter the church without the young monk. They went in together, under the great arch, between the rows of candles. During the ceremony, the prince continued to ask the monk the same questions. But when he saw tears in his eyes, he suddenly recognised the young girl. His heart was pounding, but he was careful not to show his joy.

But, a little later, when everyone was asleep, he went to look for her. He and the bayberry girl went away together, very far away.

They lived a long and happy life together, and we did even better.

Sources

"To daphnou koutsaki [The Little Bayberry Seed], FS 1622, pp. 1–4.

> Origin: Kambos, Chios.
> Transcribed by Ioulia Tetteri, as told by woman age 60.

CGMF 407, *The Bayberry Child.*
ATU 407, *The Bayberry Child.*

The Folktale, Child of Myth

Anna Angelopoulos

Ever since man acquired speech, he felt the need to tell stories, be it through his dreams, his thoughts, his suffering. Unlike written stories signed by their authors, the oral folktale is a collective creation transmitted in the telling since time immemorial. It is addressed to everyone and has always been passed on orally in traditional societies. It draws its vitality from the fundamental human experiences it portrays – birth, death, falling in love, wealth and poverty, envy and rivalry, the apprenticeship of life, the mystery of the origins.

All these elements are present in the myth as well. By comparing the myth with the fairy tale, we will shed light on the specificity of the latter: that it is built on a collective popular fiction – on a lie. All its characters and narrative elements are fictitious. In fact, in traditional societies the storyteller sometimes interrupted his narrative to say: "I am not paid to tell the truth." Stories were often told at evening gatherings where people were finishing collective tasks such as weaving or distilling home-made alcohol. Stories were told to help keep the workers awake, just like in military barracks or on ships, where sailors listened to stories on night watch.

These examples clearly show that the story is closely tied to the sphere of somnolence, an intermediary state between day and night, the space of waking dreams and night dreams. The three main functions of the fairy tale are to entertain, to lie and to come to our aid.

How does the fairy tale help us? By providing consolation. In fact, the Greek word "paramythia" means consolation. Thus, the folktale is a narrative used since ancient times on the occasion of funeral orations or other events requiring consolation. Moreover, as we know, fairy tales usually have a happy ending, contributing to their consoling character in the midst of family or social conflict.

I shall now turn to Vladimir Propp, the great Russian scholar and folklorist, who published his work *Morphology of the Folktale*[1] at the age of 33. Translated into many languages, this work changed the frame of reference of folklorists and greatly influenced research in the field. Propp maintained that fairy tales or magic tales must be distinguished from everything else, since they are, strictly speaking, tales. His definition of the fairy tale is close to that of the myth. He states that there are traditions, legends and tales whose structure resembles that of the myths they came from. Analysing them is not easy; they are myths in miniature, as Claude Lévi-Strauss put it.[2] Propp analysed the structure of mythical tales and fairy tales and identified 31 functions of the fairy tale. Some are compulsory for the tale to exist, such as the *departure* of the hero and *a lack* of some kind. There can be no tale without departure, Propp starts out by saying. The hero must necessarily depart, since he suffers from a lack, from psychic distress. If he does not suffer, the storyteller must invent a lack that will force him to leave home (as in "Tom Thumb" or "Thumbelina").

These functions are encountered in all mythical and magic tales, so much so that it is easy to imagine that the genre originated from a single source. For example, in the nineteenth century, the prevalent idea was that all fairy tales came from India and spread throughout the entire world. Propp considers the single source to be of a psychological nature; this would account for the similarity of form among fairy tales.

> A way of life and religion die out, while their contents turn into tales. [. . .] tales contain such obvious traces of religious notions [. . .]. The [Russian] tale evidences three basic forms of Ivan's bearers through the air. These are the flying steed, the bird, and the flying boat. But [. . .] these forms represent bearers of the souls of the departed, with the horse predominating among agricultural and herding peoples, the eagle prevailing among hunters, and the boat predominant among inhabitants of the sea coast. The tale has still been studied very little on the plane of its parallel with religion and [. . .] the cultural [. . .] aspects of daily living.[3]

These important concepts, developed by Propp, brought a new perspective to the study of the folktale, making it possible to illustrate the relation between myths and folktales through concrete examples. Mythical thought is transformed in a crypted manner to create the folktale, using language made up of images, metaphors and inversions, such as the ones found in dreams. To clarify, I will discuss two folktales that stem from a transformation of ancient myths: "The Bayberry Child" and "Muskamber".

I will start with "The Bayberry Child", which, strange to say, I did not include in my first book *Paramythokores*.[4] Recently I asked myself why, since it had been one of the first folktales I read as an adolescent, along with "Born of His Mother's Tears", "Muskamber" and "Cinderella". Encountering these characters was a very moving and decisive experience, and inwardly I promised them to bring them out into the world and make them known in other countries. I knew by heart all the little poems that were part of the dialogue between the bayberry girl disguised as a monk and the prince.

Later, when I studied the oral tradition and its rules, I agreed with researchers who considered nursery rhymes and dialogues in verse as archaic manifestations, indicating the folkloric origin of a tale. Therefore, "The Bayberry Child" assembled all the criteria needed to be part of my first collection, making it altogether suitable to being presented among the tales and heroines of the para-myth. Why, then, had I not included it?

Now, the time has come to elucidate this form of narration, since I perceive more clearly its mythical origin, and am better able to write about its creation. I will make reference to Hellenist Françoise Frontisci-Ducroux's wonderful book *Filles arbres, garçons fleurs*,[5] in which she analyses the myth of Daphne (bayberry) and Apollo. Her analysis reveals – not for the first time – the surprising inversion of a Greek myth in a Greek folktale.

Let us look at this tale. The Greek catalogue contains 41 attested versions of it.

A poor and childless young girl asks God to give her a child, be it no more than a bayberry seed. Her wish is granted and nine months later she gives birth to a bayberry seed. She is very happy, but the baby is so small that while she is doing the washing in the river, he slips out of his swaddling clothes and into the water. She has lost him and is stricken with grief. After a while, a tall bayberry bush springs up on the riverside; every night a beautiful young girl comes out of the bush and strolls in the moonlight. At dawn, she goes back to the bayberry and calls out: "Mother bayberry, open your branches and let me in." And the bayberry takes her in. And so it is each night. One night, the king's son happened to pass by. He was on his way to the castle to get married. He fell in love with the young girl and they stayed together all night. At dawn, he rode off on his horse and left her asleep. The young girl went to the bayberry bush and called out: "Mother bayberry, open your branches and let me in." But the bayberry wanted nothing to do with her, saying only: "If to be kissed and squeezed you tarry, seek not shelter in the bayberry." She had now lost her mother, as well as her lover. Heartbroken and forlorn, she set off in search of her lover.

On the road, she met a monk. She stopped him and asked "How much do you want for giving me your clothes and taking mine?" They came to an agreement. The young woman was impossible to recognise in the monk's clothing. She continued on her way. After a while, she came upon the young prince on his horse. He did not recognise her. He asked her: "Did you see anything on the road?" "Yes," said the monk. "I saw a young girl crying and lamenting, saying 'Oh, roses; oh, flowers; oh, basil; why did you lull me to sleep and let my sweet love fly away?'."

Distressed, the prince asked the monk to mount his horse. "Sit behind me," he said. She accepted at once. While they continued on their long and exhausting journey, the young prince kept asking: "Did you see anything on the road?" And she kept repeating the same lament: "Oh, roses; oh, flowers; oh, basil; why did you lull me to sleep and let my sweet love fly away?" Her words tore at his heart and filled him with sorrow. But what could he do? At last, they came to the spot where the marriage was to take place. The prince declared that he would not enter the church without the young monk. They both went in, under the great arch, between the rows of candles. During the ceremony, the prince continued to ask the monk the same question. But when he saw her eyes filled with tears, he suddenly recognised the young girl. His heart was pounding, but he was careful not to show his joy. But later, when everyone was asleep, he went to look for her. He and the bayberry girl went away together, very far way.

They lived a long and happy life together, and we did even better.

This version of the tale comes from the Island of Chios and is called "The Little Bayberry Seed". But before its happy ending, the young girl has to go through difficult trials after her encounter with the prince (which causes her to be rejected by her mother, the bayberry bush). This unexpected situation forces her to confront the harsh reality of life, as is the case with other unusual heroines of the fairy tale, like the Daughter of the Sun or the water nymph Ondine who married a shepherd. Thus, the Bayberry girl joins the sad procession of young girls seduced and abandoned. She bears with great fortitude the trials the storyteller imposes on her.

In this tale, the heroine is able to win back the lost love of the prince. Only 3 of the 41 versions have a tragic ending where the girl kills herself or both young people end their lives, unable to face the harsh social reality standing in their way, since the prince has been promised to another. It is interesting to look at the Mytilene version, where the name of the heroine is Daphne, but can also be Vaghia or Myrsina.

Mirsina branches are used on Palm Sunday in rituals opening the way for Jesus' descent into the world of the dead, during the Holy Week. In the version from Mytilene, the young girl stabs herself with a dagger, after which the prince kills himself with his sword. These tragic versions contrast with the idealisation of the couple in love, able to overcome all social obstacles in order to marry.

In most attested versions, at the moment when the young girl is recognised by the prince, she shines like gold in the great palace hall. As we know, there are several fairy tales in which the young heroine shines like the sun ("The Magic Donkey", "Cinderella", etc.). It occurred to me that in this folktale the bayberry girl shines in Apollo's golden light. The idea came to me when I read the myth of Daphne and Apollo, as set forth in Ovid[6] and Parthenius.[7]

Apollo, the most handsome of the gods, was unlucky in love, hard as that is to believe. He did better with the muses, Zeus' immortal daughters. He himself was Zeus' son; he had children with the muses, whom he inspired. But things were different with mortal women. Daphne was his first love, as well as his first heartbreak.

One day, when Apollo was mocking little Eros, the god with the arrows, Eros shot two arrows to avenge himself: one of gold and the other of lead, the first to awaken love, the second prevent it. The arrows hit Daphne and Apollo. The god fell in love with the beautiful young girl who drove all her suitors away, wishing only to remain a virgin and live peacefully with her mother, Artemis. Apollo tries to speak to her, but she runs away. He chases her, but when she is about to be caught Daphne begs the gods to deliver her of her alluring body. She then turns into a bayberry tree. Apollo still loves her and when he places his hand on the bark of the tree, he can still feel her heartbeat. He says: "Since you cannot be my wife, you shall be my own bayberry tree!" Since then, the bayberry has always been used in celebrations of Apollo. Daphne, who refused her feminine condition, lost human status forever and remained a plant. The success of this myth is demonstrated by the countless works of art it inspired: Greek and Roman mosaics, Pompeian canvases, and other European paintings. Undoubtedly, Berni-ni's sculpture of Apollo and Daphne at the Villa Borghese in Rome is the most remarkable of these.

This folktale was collected by Giambattista Basile, a seventeenth-century Nea-politan author. His version speaks of a branch of bayberry; the mother asks God for a child, be it only a branch of bayberry. The girl lives in the bayberry pot. The prince buys the plant and falls in love with the girl who comes out of it every night in his room. When he is not there, the girl-flower is attacked by her jealous rivals. But the gardener waters her in secret, reviving her, so that she is thriving when the prince returns.

The magical birth motif predominant in the oriental versions of this folktale since the second century portrays the girl as a flower, not as a tree. Moreover, a version by the Brothers Grimm takes up the motif of the girl-flower, delivered of the spell by the prince, who gives her back her human form. The theme of the girl-flower exists in the Baltic region, in Germany, in Scandinavia, as well as in Southeast Europe, in Turkey and in India. In the Balkans and in the Mediterranean region, several plants engender young girls – among them, myrtle, basil and carnations, as well as several berries such as blueberries and blackberries. But we must point out that it is only in Greek folktales that the young girl is born from a bayberry tree, which grew from a bayberry seed lost by a barren woman.

Looking more closely at the bayberry seed, we see that in the 41 Greek versions the seed is mistreated or subject to a misfortune. Sometimes it falls into the river with the baby's swaddling clothes, sometimes it is blown away by the wind or even taken by the Devil. In other versions, the angry mother throws it in the river, or in the garden of a witch who finds it and plants it. In any case, the seed lives a perilous life, and is always threatened with death. The human world does not welcome it warmly. Obviously, the only shelter from which it can emerge is the womb of the Earth; the barren woman cannot carry it. We see her ambivalence about a child, expressed in the words: "be it only a seed". This woman seems to desire the maternal status more than a child of her own. The analysis of this tale reveals that what it describes is not hate of the child, as some have said, but rather a failing, an ambivalence in the woman's desire for children. This is how the bayberry tree is born, and then gives birth to the young girl, the heroine of the tale, who is humanised through the double rejection she has to bear: that of her mother and that of her lover.

What is to be learned from the evolution of this folktale? That in the Greek myth of Apollo, the beautiful nymph Daphne wanted no child and no man, and that she achieved her desire by giving up her woman's body and turning into a tree. In the Greek folktale, in the para-myth (which, contrary to the folktales of neighbouring countries, kept the identity of the tree that gave birth to Daphne), the situation is reversed: the girl-tree becomes human and experiences everything that Daphne, the mythical heroine, wanted to avoid.

As to my initial question about why the seed planted by this heroine did not develop at first – and was even forgotten –, it is undoubtedly because unconsciously (since all forgetting is unconscious) I found that this heroine had to bear too much rejection, thus disturbing my idealisation. I had not yet noticed the extraordinary reversal of the myth that the folktale had operated.

Muskamber, Son of Incest[8]

Anna Angelopoulos

The folktale type bearing the number AT425 in the Aarne-Thompson international classification, better known as the story of Eros and Psyche,[9] is one of the folktales most analysed in recent generations. The theme of the marriage of a girl to a super-natural being, who could even be a monster, has been the object of several studies.[10] The analysis of the Greek versions of this folktale type focuses on identifying the elements proposed by Jan-Ojvind Swahn in his monograph,[11] which comprises about 1,100 versions collected throughout Europe.

G. A. Megas catalogue only includes the Greek versions.[12] But well before Swahn defined folktale subtypes, the tale of Muskamber had given rise to a series of interpretations, comments and speculations about its origins. Speculation concerning the origins of the magic couple has differed depending on particular schools of thought: natural phenomenon, totemic animal, remembrance of ancient rites or symbols; in the over 400 Greek versions, after Eros and Psyche unite, Eros disappears into another world through which Psyche must journey to find him, so that they can live out their lives together. The best-known version of the story, very strongly rooted in the oral tradition – especially in Western Europe – is the one below.

A monster is born as a result of the ill-advised wish of his barren parents; often, he is a man during the night and an animal during the day. In some versions, a bad witch has cast a spell on a man who refused to marry her. When the man marries, the couple live together in harmony until the heroine breaks a taboo that was the condition on which their happiness depended: she looks at her husband in the light, she throws his animal skin in the fire, or she tells those around her that at night he is a handsome young man. He then vanishes into another world. She sets out to look for him.

The story of her journey and of their reunion constitutes the basis on which researchers classify this folktale into subtypes.[13]

According to Greek storytellers, the husband has more than one appearance. The circumstances of his birth – often involving a spell – vary depending on the mythical tradition in which the theme is rooted. Swahn identified a group of folktales belonging to subtype B,[14] coming from three Eastern Mediterranean countries: Greece, Italy and Turkey. In the different versions of this subtype, the supernatural husband is a living puppet, an artificial man made by the heroine, often from culinary ingredients, just as she would bake a cake. Among the many names of the hero[15] in these three countries, the name "Muskamber"[16] was chosen for the analysis of the Greek versions. The hero is a magic husband fashioned by a princess who finds no one to her taste among the suitors her father brings her.

The version below was collected by A. Karanikola-Christofi on the island of Symi. It was published in 1974.[17]

MUSKAMBER

Once upon a time, there was a king and a queen. They had a daughter of marriageable age and often asked her to choose a husband among her suitors, but she rejected them all. Then, one day, tired of her parents' insistence, she told her father, her sovereign:

"My sovereign, my king, since you want me to marry no matter what, please order that these things be brought to me: buy me twenty okas of flour, one oka of musk (about 1,300 grams), one oka of amber and a kneading trough. I want all these things brought to my room with a jug of water. And no one is to enter my room for forty days; you will let no one come in, not even a bird flying in the sky. Only the slave will be allowed to enter once a day, to bring me a cup of coffee."

When everything had been bought, she locked herself in her chambers; she took the flour, mixed the spices into it, poured the water in and started to knead the dough. She kneaded for a long time, over and over, until the dough resembled no other in the world. She then placed the dough on the baking board and shaped it into the figure of a man – but what a man – tall and handsome! But she found him too tall, so she destroyed the figure. She started over, shaped another, and then another, until, after many attempts, she had a man exactly as she wished him to be. Then she started to pray, on her knees, day and night; she was praying to God to make her hand-made man talk.

After forty days, the man sat up on the edge of the board and spoke. He said: "My sleep was so heavy and I woke feeling so light!"

The princess opened the doors and shouted: "Christians, come and see! God heard my prayers and granted speech to my dough man."

The king ran to see for himself; as soon as he saw him and heard him speak, he ordered that his daughter's dough man be dressed royally and taken into the great hall of the palace.

– And now, what shall we call him? the king asked.
– Muskamber, the princess answered.

But Muskamber only spoke a little. So the king suggested that he stand before the palace to see people coming and going, and to learn to speak by listening to them.

A few days later, another princess was walking by the palace. She saw Muskamber and lost her head; she could think of nothing else, and she ordered that he be brought to her. Two ships arrived and four men came ashore. The king asked his son-in-law to visit them. The men took him with them and left.

The princess cried inconsolably. She blamed her father; then she asked him for four pairs of iron shoes and set off to look for her husband. On her journey, she exchanged her clothes for a monk's habit. She walked until her iron shoes wore out; then, she kept walking barefoot. She came to a palace where the servants took pity on her; they shook the tablecloth near her, so she could catch some crumbs. While she ate, she saw Muskamber sitting on a balcony across from her. She was troubled but, without saying a word, she took a silkworm cocoon from her monk's habit, opened it and started to weave the silk. The servants told their mistress what she was doing. "How much will she sell it for?" the queen asked. – "I am not selling it for money, but for a night with Muskamber," the princess answered.

The queen ordered Muskamber to be put to sleep with a sleeping potion, and then taken to the girl. When the princess was alone with him, she said: "Muskamber, Muskamber, at first I made you too tall and I didn't like that; then I made you too short and I didn't like that either. Then I shaped you just the way I wanted and they came and took you away." She repeated this a few times, while he snored peacefully. At dawn, he was taken away.

On the second day, the monk opened the second cocoon. The same thing happened again. When she was alone with Muskamber, the princess talked to him and kept crying, for she talked in vain. He was still asleep at dawn when he was taken away.

Near the monk's room there was a tailor who heard everything that went on during the night. The next day, the tailor asked Muskamber who was asking him questions during the night. Muskamber didn't answer, but the next night he only pretended to be sleeping. He was taken to the monk's room; the princess cried again as she kept saying: "Muskamber, Muskamber . . ." He did not let her go on. He took her by the hand, and they went out through the small back door that led to a path in the wild. They walked for three days and three nights, until they came to Michaïli, where they met a priest.

– Go and tell the king to rejoice, for his daughter is coming back with Muskamber.

When he heard this, the king sent twelve musicians to welcome them. The whole city came out to meet them. They were married and had so many children that they filled the whole neighbourhood.
   But I wasn't there, and neither were you, to believe it.

Before discussing the theme presenting this type of magical birth, let us remember the characteristics of the group of folktales we are looking at: according to Megas and Swahn, they always end with the motif – specific to subtype B – of three nights bought by the heroine (with her valuable objects) to spend in a room alone with her husband. This makes it possible for the spouses to recognise each other. The same two authors also assert that the introductory motif of these folktales is, in most cases, the fashioning of the artificial husband by the heroine. Thus, the best-known element of "Eros and Psyche", the negative condition (prohibition to see the husband) associated with the young girl's marriage to the mysterious bridegroom, is absent from this fairy tale cycle. The couple is separated when Muskamber is carried off, not when a taboo is violated.
   As for magical birth, it is an initial myth, no doubt borrowed from an old myth of creation. A woman fashions a man to her liking; she imagines him as she would like him to be and undertakes unhesitatingly to create him. Therefore, she alone sets out on an initiatory journey, a long journey through another world, when she is separated from her beloved. Once she has borne the trial of loss at great cost to herself, the tale enables her to find her creation and claim it for the second time. To do this, she must discard her feminine attributes and her power of seduction, as well as her other possessions, including valuable objects given to her during her journey. She uses these magic gifts, rather than her own charm as she once did, to be reunited with her beloved. But the man she finds at the end of her journey has changed. Separation, the loss of the love object she herself had created, transforms not only the heroine – so much so that her husband does not recognise her[18] –, but also the man she loves, who expresses for the first time his desire to start a new life with her. Only when her search is over does the princess hear her artificial husband speak to her. He speaks to the woman who "made him too tall . . . too short . . . as she wanted him to be", and who then had to separate from "the sweet image she created in her inner world", as Max Lüthi says.[19] While he journeyed through the

other world, separation completed her creation: it was a different being that the princess, transformed by her apprenticeship, encountered in the world beyond. He has become someone she must win over and make her own again, someone existing in reality just as she does.

This explains the fact that the separation of the couple in this group of folktales is not caused by the violation of a taboo: here, the separation motif does not function as a sanction,[20] but as a preliminary step in the narrative, preparing the episode of creation. Indeed, in this type of tale, each time the heroine creates a human being, their separation is inevitable; it is the necessary event allowing two different beings to recognise each other in another world. For instance, in a version from Thrace,[21] the angel who descends from the heavens to bring Muskamber to life, foresees his subsequent disappearance: he gives the heroine three nuts to help her find him in case she ever loses him. Thus, the loss of the bridegroom is clearly an integral part of the narrative of his creation.

Most researchers point out that, in the folktales belonging to this subtype, there are similarities between the myth of Pygmalion who created Galatea and the story of our princess who created Muskamber.[22] This myth is alluded to in a work written three centuries ago (Basile's *Pentamerone*) and cited by every folklore specialist. Indeed, in Basile's *Pentamerone*, it is easy to find the reference to Pygmalion; in the oldest version of our folktale, called *Pinto Smalto*,[23] the princess, "when she finished, having heard of another statue which came to lifelong ago to answer the prayers of a king named Cyprus (Pygmalion), [. . .] implored the Goddess of Love so fervently that her statue opened his eyes, then spoke and finally moved his limbs and walked."

In addition, Sophia Gedeon, the only Greek researcher to have attempted an analysis of the motif of the creation of an artificial husband, notes in her comments on the Symi version of the tale:[24] "The materials used by a woman in her daily tasks in the kitchen – dough, sugar, flour, spices (musk and amber) – are only ready for use when they are mixed with water; they are easy to handle; she can shape them into any form she wants. Her creation is intended to have some of the characteristics of these materials. Thus, the wish expressed in the tale is: may the man be malleable, like the dough, in the woman's hands! [. . .] Could this be an imaginary compensation in response to the man's dominant role?"

These remarks allow us to perceive a major difference between the myth of Pygmalion, who sculpts an ivory statue, and the story of our heroine who, after all, is only baking Easter buns. The myth presents a man working alone with a hard material, difficult to fashion, to achieve his creation; there is no hint of the relationship he will have with this creation. By contrast, in the story, a young girl benefiting from the active participation of her father, constructs a dough figure she plans to marry. The storyteller comments that "she did not like men", and this was the reason she could only like what she created with her own hands.

"All the people, starting with children only seven, prayed to God for the princess; the king left her alone in the church with her bread kneaded seven times; he gave the key to the monk so that no one, 'not a living soul', could enter.

The princess kneaded the dough seven times; with the spices and her tears, she fashioned a figure like a baby and asked God to give it a soul. And so, an angel came down and gave it a soul. For forty days, the king believed that his daughter would die, and he was very sad. People gathered and when forty days had passed they found the king's daughter with a seven-year-old son, *who smelled so good* that they were dazzled. The king went off with his daughter and the boy, and the festivities began."

This version creates the impression that the object of the princess's desire is the son begotten through covert incest. Indeed, the story portrays a double incest; the princess comes together with two men: with her father to create Muskamber, and with Muskamber, the son of the father. This should not come as a surprise, since her father is involved at every stage of the process that will produce Muskamber: he is always the one who brings the ingredients his daughter requests for making the dough. Often, he brings them on his return from a long trip to a distant country. Moreover, in the version from Symi, when the father sees Muskamber for the first time, he asks his daughter a strangely out of place question: "And now, what should we call him?"[25] The ingredients the heroine uses define precisely enough her sphere of action, that is, the feminine interior space transformed by the fragrant substances associated with desire.

In addition, the locked enclosure of the church or of the young girl's room, off limits to visitors for the length of time required for the transformation of the dough into a man, can also be seen as a metaphor representing the female body, the place of gestation of a new life. As Sophia Gedeon remarked, the materials used by the heroine are amorphous; but mixing them does more than render them useful: after lengthy kneading and at the end of forty days, inert matter changes into living matter. This process of preparation and then baking of the ingredients can surely be viewed symbolically as a metaphor for a baby being formed in the womb.

It should be pointed out that all versions of the tale agree on Muskamber's infantile character: he cannot speak,[26] he follows his abductors without protest,[27] he has no will of his own in grown-up affairs, and willingly submits to the instructions given by his father-in-law and his wife. Docile and malleable, like the dough, in the narration he holds the place of a silent object of desire, until the resolution of the plot. As we said earlier, the artificial child or husband can only start to live in a far-off country, when his mother or his wife, after a long search that has completely changed her, summons him, tries to wake him and, as she laments, names the substances that went into the making of the hero, thus alluding to her desire and Muskamber's covert incestuous origin.

Another difference between the story of Muskamber and the myth of Pygmalion becomes apparent when we consider the materials used by the woman who creates the hero, and the role of each participant in making the dough. Indeed, we note that in order to create the magical child or husband, the folktale presents a coherent set of signs with a symbolic function; therefore, we will look more closely at the Greek versions, to try to understand the meaning of the ritual accompanying the birth of Muskamber.

Muskamber, the magical child, fills the air around him with a singular aroma: "When they took him out of the oven, the girls couldn't stay close to him because of the dizzying scent that emanated from his body."[28] These girls are the princess's servants, who sometimes help to prepare the dough. In a version from Patmos, they accompany her to her country house:

Six of them were sifting flour and the other six were crushing the spices; then they all worked on the dough table together, kneaded the dough together, sprinkled it with rose water so it would be perfect and fragrant [. . .]. But the princess shaped the man all by herself, as she wanted him to be [. . .]. As soon as he came out of the oven, all the girls lost their heads, dazzled by his beauty; they called him Muskamber. The king rubbed his eyes at the sight of this astonishing spectacle.[29]

Muskamber's name itself refers to the fact that he is created from two rare, precious substances: musk and amber. They often come from far away and are valuable objects of trade. The name of the artificial husband can also be Baked Musk, Pressed Musk, Pressed Sugar and, less frequently, "Master Semolina".[30]

Let us compare the different recipes suggested by the storyteller, for the use of lovelorn princesses:

- "She asked her father for an oka of cinnamon, an oka of cloves, an oka of all spices and aromas in the world."[31]
- "She asked her father for all the spices and all the aromatics from Istanbul.[32] [. . .]. She kneaded him with rose water and sugar."
- "She asked her father, who was going on a journey, to bring back ten okas of nutmeg, ten okas of cloves, ten okas of cinnamon, ten okas of incense, a three-wick lamp, a double-edged knife and a patience stone [. . .]. She crushed the nutmeg, the cinnamon and the cloves, kneaded them together and fashioned a dough man. She burned incense and kept watch over him."[33]
- "She bought all the aromas in the world; for forty days she sifted the wheat, for forty days she shaped the man to make him as she wanted."

Forty days and nights of prayer and incantations – this is usually how long the young princess must keep watch over her creation. In most recipes, the storyteller only names the spices that the princess crushes and mixes; sometimes it is a dry mix; sometimes, the princess pours rose water, fragrant water or tears over the mixture, so that she can knead the dough. Sometimes, the ingredients include wheat, semolina, sugar and almonds, but these are present less often than the aromatics.[34] In the Greek corpus compiled by Megas, the artificial husband is made of aromatics and spices; the storyteller often leaves out the grains, but he rarely forgets the spices.

Before discussing the narrative role of the making of this unique spice dough, let us note that its recipe is given twice in each version: in the initial sequence by the storyteller, and at the end of the narrative by the heroine, who tells the story of his creation to her sleeping bridegroom not only so that he will recognise her and make it possible to recover her lost happiness, but also to perfect her act of creation. We must also point out that the princess's fragrant bridegroom is abducted by a rival living in a distant kingdom, at the other end of the Earth. This rival loves Muskamber and wants to live with him; in the version from Thrace, she arrives disguised as a "foreign king with forty daughters disguised as sailors."[35]

Two constitutive elements of the mythical theme of Muskamber are unfailingly present in all the versions of the fairy tale: the princess's father's contribution to the making of the magic dough, and the major characteristic of the artificial man – his aroma.

Interestingly, the narrative thread that emerges brings to mind the Greek myth of the "irresistible seducer [. . .], superficial, unsubstantial, immature", who in ancient times was venerated as a deity; the myth of Adonis, son of Myrrha and her father Theias, king of Syria, also starts with a magic birth. Let us look at the best-known form of this myth:

The king of Syria, Theias, had a daughter named Myrrha who roused Aphrodite's anger because she refused to marry; to punish her, the goddess caused her to wish for incest with her father. She was able to trick him, and she slept with him for twelve nights. But on the last night Theias became aware of his daughter's ruse and chased her, knife in hand, intending to kill her. Myrrha implored the protection of the gods; they transformed her into a myrrh tree. Ten months later, her bark raised up and burst, and a child emerged; he was named Adonis. Aphrodite was enchanted by the infant's beauty, took him and entrusted him secretly to Persephone's care. But the goddess of the Underworld became very fond of the child and refused to give him back to Aphrodite. Zeus was asked to pronounce judgement in the conflict between the two goddesses. It was decided that Adonis would live a third of the year with Aphrodite, a third with Persephone and a third wherever he wanted. Adonis always chose to spend two-thirds of the year with Aphrodite and one-third with Persephone.

According to Marcel Detienne,[36] the Greek mythological tradition emphasises two of Adonis' attributes:[37] his seductive character and his relation to aromatics. As for Myrrha, she is changed into a tree (particularly fragrant) after committing incest with her father. The magic birth of Adonis serves as a screen for the incestuous act that preceded it.

"Some god listened to her prayer: [her] request found its way to the heavens. [. . .] her bones strengthened, [. . .]; her skin [became] solid bark. [. . .] she still weeps. [. . .] There is merit, also, in the tears: and the myrrh that drips from the bark keeps its mistress' name, and, about it, no age will be silent.

The child, conceived in sin, had grown within the tree trunk. [. . .] the tree bends, like one straining, and groans constantly, and is wet with falling tears. [. . .] At this the tree split open, and, from the torn bark, gave up its living burden, and the child cried. The naiads laid him on the soft grass and anointed him with his mother's tears. Even Envy would praise his beauty . . ."[38]

These two instances of magic birth – the creation of Muskamber by the princess and Myrrha's change into a fragrant tree from which Adonis emerges – show that the hero's essential trait (his scent) was carefully preserved in the oral tradition of the Eastern Mediterranean region. The name of Adonis' mother, who becomes a sweet scent in the myth, disappears from the folktale, to be replaced by the name of the artificial son. He retains a relation with rare and precious aromatics, although their "positive function as incense and their negative function as perfumes"[39] is no longer perceivable because the ancient Greeks' religious system is no longer in effect. The storyteller has been able to preserve Muskamber's major mythical attributes, while covering over his incestuous origin with the narration of his extraordinary creation by a beautiful princess longing for love. We must admit that the storyteller often warns us that he could be telling lies, as he does at the end of the version from Symi, saying: "I was not there to see it and neither were you, to believe it." This closing formula is one of many examples of a type of discourse which stays deliberately ambiguous about its deeper meaning, and which sometimes openly preaches lying.

"There was once – or rather, there was not, a king . . ."[40] Usually, this introductory formula is followed, as the narration progresses, by other comments the storyteller makes to warn the audience of the fallacious nature of his words: they must not believe him, must keep in mind that the one who speaks is a liar, and that he must keep the tale enigmatic, especially since the portion of truth it contains might threaten the system of religious or moral values of the audience. The storyteller's art consists of displaying in all their splendour the representations that have always been present in the myth, while hiding its irrational elements, called magical, which nevertheless oppose the morality of a Christian audience. His audience must not believe that young girls have incestuous desires, or that daughters can eat their mothers, that there are gods of Hell, or that parents can curse adolescents, condemning them to live in animal skins. The storyteller must knowingly employ symbolic language, indecipherable most of the time, and use all the means at his disposal to transmit a number of mythical themes preserved in the collective memory, masking or inverting them.[41] Hence, the subgroup of the "Eros and Psyche" folktales transforms or inverts the sequences of the myth of Adonis. The only difference is that in the myth there is only one incest: Myrrha disappears from the narrative as soon as Adonis is born.

The folktale: "Muskamber"	The myth: "Adonis"
A young princess refuses to marry.	A young princess refuses to marry.
She decides to fashion an artificial husband (son) with her father's help.	She is condemned by Aphroditis to fall in love with her father and seduces him.
Servants help her joyfully.	
Her father acquiesces to her desire.	Ashamed, she is helped by her maidservant.
She creates her husband (son) alone.	
He changes into a fragrant bridegroom.	Her father does not know they committed incest.

She keeps him in the palace.
Another woman abducts him and takes him to a distant kingdom.
She sets off to look for him and finds help in the distant kingdom.
She finds him and they return together to her kingdom forever.

She gives birth to her son alone.
She changes into a myrrh tree.
She delivers the baby outdoors, in nature.
Aphrodite is smitten with the baby; he is entrusted to Persephone, who keeps him for herself in another world.
Aphrodite asks Zeus to intercede; he is impartial.
Adonis lives with Aphrodite most of the time.
He is killed by a boa.

Let us try to find the thread which could have guided the storyteller of "Moskambaris" through the wider narrative network of the "living doll" folktales. In other words, we shall try to answer the questions: "What problem does this type of magic birth raise?" "In the imaginary realm, what becomes of the incestuous girl and her deeds?" "What is the resolution found in the folktale?"

These folktales are about relations between members of the same family, prohibited in reality but tolerated in the imaginary realm. Through the metaphor of the dough made of spices, the tale expresses the incestuous desire of a young girl who does not like men of her own age. Because the folktale, unlike the myth or the ritual, is outside the sphere of the sacred and is told "to pass the time pleasantly", it can more easily examine questions of great importance by translating them into a language of its own: contradictory attitudes to family structures, different modes of filiation, taboos, rites of passage, . . .

The element-by-element comparison of the mythical sequence about Adonis and the folktale about Moskambaris reveals that in the folktale there are two types of inversions. The first aims to cover up the violation of the incest taboo: instead of seducing her father, the princess asks him for the ingredients she needs to make the dough out of which she fashions an artificial being, alone in her chambers. Thus, the tale replaces the father with a son, condensing two sequences of the myth into one. The other inversions aim at changing family law, or social and religious laws: in the folktale, the father acknowledges his daughter's desire and helps her to create a bridegroom; the servants work alongside her, the entire nation prays for her, including the priest. Even God contributes to her plans by sending an angel to breathe life into Moskambaris. The princess alters cosmic laws with impunity, since she can decide to create her beloved "as she wants him to be", while in the myth, Myrrha, who scorns young men, is condemned by the goddess of Love to love her father, and she pays for her crime dearly. Thus, these inversions bring about maximalism in the folktale, and in the imaginary sphere.

To what extent do these tales recognise incestuous desire? Can we assume that what we see here is an optimistic and amoral elaboration on the old theme of

Adonis, and that the storyteller is expressing a wish for the everlasting union of a mother with a son brought into being with her father?

The answer is in the narrative development itself. In all the versions of Eros and Psyche, what is recounted is the painful trial of the loss of the love object, and the transformation of the protagonists by what they experience in the other world. After their separation, when they reunite, they have both become different. The only condition imposed for allowing them to recognise each other is that each of them be changed. In this way, the storyteller can respect the rules of his society in a story whose hidden theme is, nevertheless, transgression. He tells his listeners: you must separate from those you love if you want to find them changed when you are reunited.

In our role as psychoanalysts, we are often presented with requests for psychic transition and metamorphosis. We witness a deep desire for the "throwing off of the serpent shirt", and the need of a new life for the subject. As in the fairy tale, the impetus for psychoanalytic therapy is always provided by the life instinct. In contrast to the tragic character of the myth, the fairy tale, as we have stated earlier, becomes an aesthetic therapeutic tool.

TZITZINAINA

Once upon a time there was an old woman whose three daughters all worked to make a living. But a shortage of oil forced the king to issue an ordinance forbidding the lighting of lamps in the evening. Hearing this, the old woman's daughters said: "What will we do? When the days are short in the winter, we won't be able to work at night. How will we make a living?"

So they covered up all the openings (the cracks in the doors and windows) to stop the light from showing through, and they continued to work. After working hard late into the night, they were hungry and the eldest said: "If I had the king's pastry chef for a husband, I would eat warm cake just out of the oven."

– Oh, poor girl, you only want the king's pastry chef! If I had the royal cook for a husband, I would eat all the royal dishes, the middle daughter said.
– My poor sisters! the youngest said. Is that all you want? I would like the king himself and then I would have all the treasures of the kingdom. And I would give him three golden children: Sun, Moon and Star.

That night, the king was riding through the kingdom in disguise, to see who lighted their lamps and who did not. He happened to be in front of the young girls' door when they had this conversation. He heard them and left without saying a word. But the next day he summoned them to the palace and asked each one what she had said the night before. First, he asked the eldest: "What did you say last night while you were working?"

- We were not saying anything, Your Majesty, the poor girl replied.
- No, you must tell me exactly what you said.
- Well, Your Royal Highness, we worked late into the night and I said: "If I had the king's pastry chef for a husband, I would eat warm cake just out of the oven." We had been working for a long time and I was hungry.
- Very well, the king said and sent her home, telling her she would marry his pastry chef.

He then spoke to the second sister and asked her: "What were you doing last night?"

- We sat and talked together while we worked, Your Majesty.
- Tell me exactly what you said.
- What can I tell you, Your Highness? I was saying that if I had the royal cook for a husband, I could taste all the royal dishes.

The king sent her home and ordered his cook to marry her. Finally, he summoned the youngest girl and asked her: "What did you say last night while you all sat working?"

- Your Majesty, here is your sword and here is my head to chop off. I cannot repeat what I was saying.
- No, I will not cut off your head. But I want to know what you said. You will not lose your head.
- Your Majesty, what can I say? My sisters said, each one in turn, that they wished to marry the royal pastry chef and the royal cook. And I said: "My poor sisters! Is that all you want? I would like to marry the king himself and then I would have all the treasures of the kingdom. And I would give the king three children: Sun, Moon and Star."
- Can you really give birth to such children?
- Yes, Your Majesty, she replied.

So the king married her and made her his queen. But once she was the king's wife, she was hated by her mother-in-law. Still, her son had married her, so what could she do? But she never stopped being hostile. While the queen was pregnant with her first child, the king had to go off to fight a war. He went to his mother and made this request: "Mother, I have to go to war.

While I am gone, take great care of my wife, especially since she is about to give birth."

– Rest easy, my son. See to your duties and be sure that I shall take good care of your wife.

When the queen was ready to give birth, the king's mother summoned the midwife and conspired with her to make the child disappear, promising her a generous reward. They had a chest made, put the queen's baby in it and threw it in the sea. Then they put a puppy in the queen's bed.

When the king returned from war, he asked his mother: "What kind of child did my wife give me?"

– A dog, my son.

The king said nothing. After a time, the queen found herself with child again. And again, while she was pregnant, the king had to go off to war. As before, he asked his mother to take care of his wife, who was about to give birth. She gave him the same assurances as she had the first time. But when he was gone, she plotted with the midwife to replace the baby with a kitten. They had a chest made, threw the baby into the sea and put a cat in its place.

The king came back and asked: "What kind of child did my wife give me?"

– A cat, my son, his mother replied.

The king said nothing, and their life followed its course. When the queen was pregnant again, the king learned that he had to go off to war. Again, he entrusted the queen to his mother's care. As before, his mother plotted with the midwife. They threw the baby into the sea and put a serpent in its place.

The king came back from war and asked: "What kind of child did my wife give me?"

– A serpent to strangle you, my son. What a shame! To have such a wife and keep her in the palace, instead of sending her to live in an old shack!

So the king told his wife: "You promised you would give me three children: Sun, Moon and Star. But instead, you gave birth to a dog, a cat and a serpent. Go away, I don't want you here anymore." He took the poor woman and shut her up under the palace drain.

But what happened, in the meantime, to the children who were cast away? Each time a chest was thrown into the sea, it floated directly to a small mountain with a monastery at its summit. The monk who lived there went to the seaside each day and caught a fish for his supper. One day, he caught two fish and turned to God, asking: "Why, Lord, are you sending me two fish? I did not ask for so much food!"

When he returned to his hut, he found the chest with a child in it. "Oh, he said, God gave me the other fish so that I can feed the child he sent me." So he kept the child for a whole year and nourished it with the fish. At the end of that year, he went to the seashore and caught three fish. Again, he asked God to hear his prayer. When he returned home, he found a chest. He opened it and found a child inside. "Oh," he said, "this is why God has sent me the other fish." One year later, he caught four fish and he found the third child.

The monk kept the children with him, in his hut. He would go out and come back bringing them food, and he raised them. When they were grown up, he told the eldest: "My children, you can't stay here on the mountain. Take your brother and sister (for Star was a girl) and go to the city to discover the world, because here there is nothing to learn."

So they went to the city, rented a house with the money the monk had given them, and got busy learning the ways and customs of the world. One day, the eldest went to the marketplace, where a Jew who had a chest to sell was saying for all to hear: "Whosoever buys this chest will regret it, and whosoever does not buy it will regret it as well."

The prince (for the young man was indeed a prince) thought: "Whosoever buys the chest will regret it, as will whosoever does not buy it. So I better buy it! He took the chest and went home. There, he found his sister sitting and crying. He asked her: "Why are you crying, little sister?"

- I am crying, she answered, because you left me here without anything to play with.
- And what would you like to play with?
- An old woman came by and told me that I am beautiful (the old woman was the midwife, but the children did not know her; she had learned that they were alive and wanted to kill them, because the queen's mother-in-law had paid her again to do this) but if I had the golden apple which is in a garden guarded by forty dragons, I would be lovelier still.

Her brother said: "I have to open this chest, for I was told that whosoever takes it will regret it, as will whosoever does not take it." He opened the chest and found a wingèd green steed inside. "Oh, this horse is just what I need to go and get the apple my sister wants." He mounted the horse and set off.

Once on the road, the horse spoke these words: "Good day, master; where shall I take you?"

– We are going to bring my sister the golden apple guarded by forty dragons, the young man replied.
– Oh, unhappy man! the horse said. Your task is very difficult. But I will make a bolt of lightning and a clap of thunder and we will land in the garden. If you can steal the apple, all will be well. Or else, we will both be lost if the dragons catch us.

So they continued on their way. When they were close to the garden, in the space of a flash of lightning and a clap of thunder, they seized the golden apple. They took it back to the young girl, who amused herself with it.

One day, the same old woman came by again and told her: "How lovely you are, my girl! You have the golden apple to play with, but if you also had the golden branch on which all the birds in the world gather to sing, you would be lovelier still!" When her brother came home, he found her in tears again.

– What is troubling you, dear sister?
– The old woman came by again and told me that if I had the golden branch on which all the birds in the world gather to sing, my beauty would be even greater.
– I will go and bring it to you, he replied.

He went to get his horse and they set out. The horse said: "Good day, master. Where shall I take you?"

– We are going to bring my sister the golden branch where all the birds in the world gather to sing.
– Oh, unhappy man! We succeeded with the golden apple, but trying this . . . Still, let us go, I will make a lightning bolt and a clap of thunder. You must bring an axe to cut the tree branch.

They continued on. In the space of a flash of lightning and a clap of thunder, the young man cut the tree branch and they rode away. He took the branch to his sister. All the birds in the world gathered on it to sing, and it was a heavenly joy!

The old woman came by a third time. "Oh, how lovely you are! You have the golden apple and the golden branch where all the birds in the world gather to sing. But if you had Tzitzinaina to tell you what the birds are saying – because she speaks their language –, you would be lovelier still!"

When her brother came home, she told him: "The old woman came by again and said that if I had Tzitzinaina to tell me what the birds are saying – because she speaks their language –, I would be even more beautiful.

"I will bring her to you," he said. He mounted his horse once again and set out. As before, his horse spoke these words: "Good day, master; where shall I take you?"

- We are going to find Tzitzinaina who speaks the language of birds, so she can tell my sister what they say.
- We escaped the other dangers, the horse said, but we won't get away from Tzitzinaina because she will turn us to stone.
- Let her do what she might! Let us go and may God help us!

They travelled a long way and stopped before Tzitzinaina's house. The horse said: "Now you must call out her name."

The young man shouted: "Tzitzinaina!" She shouted back: "Marble!" And he turned to stone up to his knees. He shouted again: "Tzitzinaina." She cried out: "Marble", and he turned to stone up to his thighs. He shouted once again: "Tzitzinaina." She shouted: "Marble!" And he turned to stone up to his waist. So he stopped to think. The horse asked: "What are you waiting for? Shout again and let us be petrified altogether, for now we can neither advance nor retreat. We can't get away from here!"

That is when the young man remembered that before they left each other, the monk gave him a few hairs from his beard, saying: "When you will need me, burn these hairs and I will come to your aid." So he made a lighter and set fire to a few hairs from the monk's beard. The monk appeared before him at once and asked: "What is your wish, my child?"

"This is the situation I find myself in. So I thought that you could help me." And he told the monk the whole story. When he finished, the monk shouted: "Tzitzinaina!"

- What is your wish, master?
- Come quickly to help my children!
- Right away, master.

Tzitzinaina came out, bearing a bottle of water that confers immortality. She sprinkled some on the young man and the horse and their petrified legs came back to life. Then the monk told her: "Deliver all those you have turned to stone here." (She had petrified many people.) So she delivered them all, and among them was the other prince, the brother they had lost. So they set out on their journey back, and the monk told Tzitzinaina: "Now that you are accompanying my children, take care to be like a mother to them, like a madonna." So Tzitzinaina left on the journey with them. Along the way, she taught them the language of all birds, as well as all things in the world, for she knew everything. One day, the children wanted to go strolling through the kingdom. Tzitzinaina said: "Today you will cross paths with the king. He will look at you, will come close to you and will invite you to dine at the palace tomorrow. Tell him that you will go."

The children set out and they really encountered the king, who said: "It's strange how much these children look like the children my wife promised to give me!" He came close to them and said: "It's strange how much I love you although I have never seen you before! I would like you to dine with me tomorrow. Will you come?" The children answered: "We shall come." Then they went home. Tzitzinaina asked them what had happened. She said: "Tomorrow, take a little dog with you and when you will be dining, throw him a spoonful of your food."

So the next day they took the little dog with them. They threw him a spoonful of food and when he ate it he died. The children said: "Your majesty, we have not come here to be poisoned. You see this dog? He died as soon as he ate the food. But if you wish, come to our home to dine with us tomorrow night."

The king was very fond of the children and accepted the invitation. "I shall come," he said. The children told Tzitzinaina that they had invited the king, as she had advised them to do. They also told her to prepare a sumptuous meal, for he would come the next day. "Don't worry," she told them.

The next day, the king arrived. The children were waiting for Tzitzinaina to prepare the meal. But they saw no dishes, no table set for a meal, nor anything else. So they said: "Tzitzinaina, look, the king is here and you haven't set the table or prepared the food." She asked: "What time is it, my children?" They answered: "Only a quarter of an hour before dinner." Indeed, while the king sat on the sofa talking to Tzitzinaina, she clapped her hands three times and a royal feast appeared before the king – almost too magnificent to imagine.

The king was astonished to see such a splendidly laden table suddenly appear. He tried every dish and was extremely pleased. When the feast was over, he asked: "My children, what favour would you like to ask of me? I am so happy to see you that I will grant you anything you ask."

The children said that the only thing they wanted was that the woman shut away under the drain be taken out. The king sent the order to free her at once. She was bathed, dressed and made ready, and she was brought before the king. Tzitzinaina took her by the hand and told the king: "Do you want to know what kind of children this woman gave you? She is your wife, and these are your children."

Then Tzitzinaina told him the whole story, including what his mother and the midwife had done. "These are your children: Sun, Moon and Star. Take them." The king took them in his arms, and they covered each other with kisses. Then, he went back to the palace with his wife. There, the king's mother and the midwife were tied to four horses and dragged through the streets of the city. Everyone learned of their evil deeds. Then the horses were whipped until they galloped and tore them to pieces.

Sources

CGMF 707, *The Three Golden Children.*
ATU 707, *The Three Golden Children.*

Gorgo and the Bird of Truth: An Altered Petrifying Deity

Anna Angelopoulos

In his book *Myth and Tragedy in Ancient Greece*, Jean-Pierre Vernant[42] dedicates a chapter to Gorgo's mask, Medusa, the only one of the three Gorgon Sisters (Stheno and Euryale are the other two) who is mortal. We shall never know why she is mortal, while her sisters are not, according to sources such as Hesiod, in *The Theogony*, and other authors.[43] The Gorgon Sisters are the daughters of Phorcys and Ceto (born of the union of Pontus and Gaia, the primordial gods of the Sea and the Earth – pre-Olympian deities said to have existed even before death). Pontus and Gaia are also the parents of the three Graeae, the sisters of the Gorgons, who live beyond the frontiers of this world. Medusa (the word means "that which stuns, makes fleeing impossible") and her sisters live far from the gods and from mortal men, beyond the ocean, at the frontier of the night, guarding access to forbidden spheres. The Gorgons' hair is made of living snakes, they have sharp fangs like those of boars, brass claws and golden wings. Their bright gaze can turn men and gods to stone.

Poseidon seduces Medusa in a meadow. When Perseus cuts off her head, from her neck springs the wingèd horse Pegasus, as if from a vulva.

As we know, Vernant is not the only author who draws a parallel between the Gorgon's face and the image of female genitals; this monstrosity, which is at once laughable and terrifying, has given rise to several interpretations related to the fear of castration, specifically those elaborated by Freud and Sandor Ferenczi. But Vernant offers a different interpretation.

The image of a face transformed into female genitals has been compared to Baubo, or the old woman Iambe, depicted as a torso constituted of a vulva but transformed into a face – a grimace (see Georges Devereux, *Baubo, la vulve mythique*, and Salomon Reinach, *Cults, Myths and Religions*[44]). Baubo, a servant to King Celeus of Eleusis, received Demeter as a guest while the goddess was mourning the loss of her daughter, Persephone, who had been abducted by Hades. The crone lifted her skirts and exhibited her secret parts to the goddess (a ritual gesture called "anasyma"). This made Demeter laugh, and she put an end to her fasting as a result.

Aside from Freud's notion of fear of castration, it is important to recognise, as Vernant says, that the question discussed here is a more radical monstrosity. Gorgo's mask presents a frontal view. Gorgo, who turns onlookers to stone, is always shown full face, she is a *terrifying power* out of the ordinary: she is pure terror. She belongs to a supernatural category whose classification remains nebulous: she is a disturbing mix of men, gods and animals. This stand-alone head is alterity itself, for it mixes together, indiscriminately, all the usual frameworks: masculine and feminine, young and old, beautiful and ugly, heavenly and hellish, high and low (Gorgo gives birth through her neck – to Pegasus –, like weasels described in medieval texts as giving birth through the mouth; she reverses the roles of the vaginal and buccal cavities).

Jean-Pierre Vernant considers that the figure of Gorgo's mask is established in a sphere of the supernatural that brings into question the rigorous distinction between gods, men and beasts, as well as between cosmic levels and elements.

We can also think of the supernatural space and of alterity from the perspective of Marcel Détienne,[45] who defines the space "between animals and gods" as delimiting the space of the human. On the other hand, the captivating space of Medusa is found elsewhere, at the bottom of the ocean, in the sphere of night, of Hades. Thus, Medusa belongs to an entirely different category, that of the radical alterity of the otherness of death in the human.

As Pascal Quignard[46] says, each time a human being is brought into the world through a reproductive act, a part of animality and a part of death are both present. The sex act, which reproduces animality in the fitting together of the masculine and feminine bodies, takes place in parallel with death, which makes a selection as well, specifically in the genealogical lineage. This part of death is unforeseeable in the genealogy of human beings. "We are always absent from the primal scene, we come from a scene in which we were not present. [. . .] Man is the being who is missing an image." Perseus grants an image to Medusa's mask, as we shall see.

Perseus was the hero who dared to confront the danger of Medusa's mortal gaze. The Etruscan Phersu, a man wearing a death mask, has often been likened to the Greek Perseus, whose story can be resumed as follows.

Acrisius, the king of Argos, had a daughter, Danae. The oracle announced that if she had a son, he would kill his grandfather. Acrisius locks up Danae in an underground chamber with brass walls. But Zeus comes to the young girl in the form of golden rain, which streams down into her womb. When her child, Perseus, is born, his cries alert Acrisius. He puts Danae and the baby in a wooden chest that he casts into the sea. The waves push the chest ashore on the island of Seriphos, where a fisherman, Dictys, the brother of the king, catches it in his net. He then raises Perseus to manhood. The king of Seriphos, Polydectes, desires Danae, but Perseus watches over her. One day, King Polydectes invites all the young warriors and nobles of Seriphos to a great feast – an *eranos* –, where each guest is asked what would be the best gift for a king. While all the others say it would be a horse, Perseus boasts that he can bring the king the head of a Gorgon. Polydectes takes him at his word and commands him to do what he promised.

Perseus has a truly "heroic" trajectory: a magical birth, a voyage of discovery, drifting on the infinite expanse of the sea, survival and return to the world of men after a trial that would be fatal for an ordinary being.

How does he kill the Gorgon? He must not look at her, nor she at him. He needs magical help: talismans, the helmet of invisibility made of dog skin – *kyneê* – (worn by Hades), which overlays his living face with the mask of death, while at the same time protecting him from the forces of Death; wingèd sandals, the magic knapsack (*kibisis*) and Hermes' sickle (the *harpe* used by Cronos to castrate Uranus).

The three Graeae, the Gorgons' sisters, have only one tooth and one eye to share between them. Perseus steals them when they are being passed from one sister to another, coming close to them without being seen, thanks to the helmet of invisibility. To get back the tooth and the eye, the three Graeae tell Perseus how to find the secret road to the Nymphs, who then give him the other talismans.

Jean-Pierre Vernant points out that the theme of seeing and being seen is present throughout the narrative about Perseus, as illustrated by the theft of the eye and the tooth of the Graeae. This theme is consolidated starting with fifth-century versions of the myth, which introduce *a mirror*, making it possible to see the reflection of Medusa without meeting the gaze that turns men to stone. Perseus only sees her faint reflection on his polished shield. The shield sends the reflection of Medusa's face back to her, terrifying her and turning her to stone. Perseus cuts off her head, puts it in his knapsack and takes it to Athena, who places a representation of it in the centre of her breastplate.

Later in the narrative, the myth alludes again to the reflection of a hero in a mirror: when Perseus saves Andromeda, the sea monster does not attack him directly while they fight, but attacks his shadow instead. However, the monster encounters only the smooth surface of the ocean instead of his adversary.

In fact, some versions of the myth alternate beauty with ugliness in their description of Medusa. In the writings of Apollodorus and Ovid, Medusa is a beautiful woman whose loveliness competes with that of the goddesses, and who is transformed for this reason. The myth places greater and greater emphasis on the mirror and on reflection (Ovid): front view of Perseus looking straight ahead, his eyes fixed on the spectator, with Medusa standing at his side; or Perseus with his head turned, looking in the opposite direction, or looking at the face of the monster reflected in a mirror, in the shine of a shield or on the surface of the water.

The Odyssey, Book II:[47] The site of battle is now the Underworld. When Odysseus descends into Hades, the throngs of clamouring "shades" fill him with "pale fear" at the thought that Persephone might send him "a horrific monster, the Gorgon's head". He leaves the depths and makes his way back to his ship. Gorgo dwells at the bottom of Hades. Her mask conveys the radical alterity of the world of the dead, not accessible to any living being.

The face of Gorgo is a *mask*. The face of Gorgo is one's double. "It is a strange response to your own face, like an image in the mirror (in which the Greeks could only see themselves frontally and in the form of a disembodied head), but at the same time, it is an image that is both less and more than yourself." Vernant goes on to say that the Gorgon "specifically conveys extreme alterity, the terrifying horror of what is absolutely other [. . .]: for man, the confrontation with death to which Gorgo's eye subjects those who meet her gaze. [. . .] when I stare into Gorgo's eyes, I see myself [. . .]. The face of the Gorgo is one's double, the double in the world beyond."[48]

Among the categories established by Vernant, let us note the ones that concern the *polarity* of these terrifying goddesses, like the river goddess Styx, for instance. The river Styx drops down from a cliff, but her "down-flowing waters" are associated with "the broad Heaven above" in the oath of deities, for swearing by her waters is the most solemn oath of the gods. It is as if the goddess represents two extremes: the lowest point (Hades) and the highest point (Heaven). This polarity also applies to the Graeae, who bring together youth and old age (their milky skin is wrinkled); to the Gorgons, who combine mortality with immortality; and to Demeter of Thelpusa, with the vengeful face of an Erinys, and the peaceful face of Louisia, the "bathed Demeter", once her anger is washed away.

What is of note here is the polarity between the power of a Fury, which causes a fit of delirium, and the power of appeasement, which brings serenity and the return to a normal state. This polarity is also embodied by Black Demeter (Melaina). These goddesses have a double function: causing madness or killing on the one hand, and healing on the other.

This is an essential fact to keep in mind before discussing a folktale that is widely known "throughout Europe, in Asia, as far as Mongolia, in India, Africa and the American continent,[49] . . . one of the eight or ten best-known narratives in the world." This tale centres around the terrifying figure of "*the bird of truth*", which lives on a glass mountain and turns to stone all those who come near.

But at the end of the story this terrifying figure looks after the heroes of the tale, reveals the secrets of their family history to them, and helps them to find their father and to be inscribed in the lineage. "The bird of truth", also known as "Tzitzinaina" in Greece (an onomatopoeia), plays a crucial role in the story of these three abandoned children who do not know their origins. I have always been astonished by the two extremely contradictory roles played by "the bird of truth" in this story, which effects a stunning redirection of paralysing destructive forces towards the life instinct, in a manner specific to fairy tales.

But let us look at the story more closely.

Galland's version of the *Arabian Nights* presents the tale (night 756) under the title "The Two Sisters Who Envied Their Cadette". But the oldest known version is that of Straparola,[50] "Ancilotto, King of Provino".

One of the most famous versions of the story is Alexander Pushkin's adaptation in *The Tale of Tsar Saltan*.[51] It should also be noted that according to the editors of the French catalogue, Mme d'Aulnoy's version of the story ("Princess Belle-Etoile"), which was widely popularised by street vendors, as well as Galland's, greatly influenced oral tradition, which drew its inspiration from it. The Brothers Grimm called this tale "The Three Little Birds". It was Paul Delarue[52] who gave the title "The Bird of Truth" to this tale type, because this phantasmatic creature bears this name in most French versions.

Three young girls who are sisters are talking as they work through the night in their humble home, while the king and his men ride by in disguise and hear them. The oldest sister says she wishes to marry the king's baker so she can eat fresh bread every day; the second sister wants to marry the chief cook, to eat delicious dishes; but the youngest wants to marry the king himself and give him *three golden children*. This formulation speaks of dream children, imaginary children. It is used as the title of the fairy tale in the international classification "The Three Golden Children". The young woman wishes the oldest boy to have the sun on his forehead, the second the moon, and the youngest – a girl – to have a star on her forehead. These miraculous children are also known as Sun, Moon and Starry Sky in other versions of the tale.

The king marries the youngest sister and has his baker and chief cook marry the other two. But each time his wife is about to give birth, the king is away at war. His mother and the midwife, jealous of the heroine, take advantage of the situation. They take away her beautiful children, throw them in a well, and replace them with a puppy, a kitten and a piece of wood.

A compassionate hermit finds the newborns and raises them. The king, who feels betrayed, disavows his wife and imposes a horrible punishment on her. He has her shut away under the sewage drain, or else boxed up somewhere far from the city, at a crossroads where passers-by spit on her. Or she is left in a far-off pond with wild beasts.

In the *Arabian Nights*, her punishment is described as follows:

"Let a box be built for her at the door of the principal mosque, and let the window of the box be always open. There she shall sit, in the coarsest clothes, and every Mussulman who enters the mosque shall spit in her face in passing. Anyone that refuses to obey shall be exposed to the same punishment himself. You, Vizier, will see that my orders are carried out."

A few years later the king meets the miraculous children in the forest by chance; he is enchanted with them, sees them every day and invites them to dine at the palace. When she realises that they are still alive, the evil stepmother decides to kill them, afraid that the truth will be revealed. She sends the midwife to see the young girl to tell her that she would be happier and more beautiful if she had the bird of truth. In the many different versions of the story, the malevolent midwife incites the children to seek various magic objects: the white blackbird, yellow water and singing wood, for instance, in Guiana; in the *Arabian Nights*, the story refers to the speaking bird, the singing tree and the golden water.

In Straparola's version, one of the two enchanted objects to acquire is the "singing apple", guarded by an ogre. Here we find the noteworthy motif of the "mirror dress", which must be worn by one of the brothers; the ogre turns to stone at once, when it sees itself in the mirror. The second object is the "beautiful green bird that twitters day and night". The two brothers set out in search of the bird. At the top of the mountain where it lives, they make three attempts to catch it. They are helped by a wise old man but are turned to stone at their third attempt because strange music made them turn around.

In the Greek versions, the coveted object is the speaking bird, the bird of truth or Tzitzinaina.

After her two brothers, it is the sister's turn to go in search of the bird of truth. At the foot of the mountain, she is helped by the same wise old man, and is able to catch the bird, for he is its master. She does not turn around and the old man orders the bird to accompany her down the mountain. And so the young girl returns with the bird that reverses the spell put on all the petrified people they see along the way, including her two brothers, who come back to life. The old man asks the bird to take care of the three golden children, to watch over them like a mother from then on.

We now come to the end of the fairy tale. The king invites the three children and the bird of truth to the palace. After dinner, the king asks the bird to tell a story. But the bird answers that someone is missing from this distinguished gathering and demands that the woman shut away under the drain for all those years be brought to them. She is freed and brought before them, bathed and dressed in royal garb, and just as beautiful as before. Now, the bird of truth asks that all the doors be locked so that no one can leave the palace, and tells the story of the three golden children, from start to finish. The parents recognise their children, to everyone's great joy. Thus ends the happy story inserted in the fairy tale. The bird of truth has brought everyone together again. As for the stepmother and the midwife, they meet their end by being drawn and quartered.

Truth is terrifying, no one can look it in the face – a monstrous face, like Gorgo's mask, whose gaze turns any onlooker to stone by revealing its radical alterity, that of death, of the non-human part of the human.

In this fairy tale, the heroine has to confront the bird of truth, to learn "where she comes from". When she reaches the bird's dwelling place, without having looked back on the way, the bird goes with her willingly as the old man tells it to do. Instead of turning the youngest of the golden children to stone, the bird of truth leaves its mountain top and walks down with her, to help the three children take their places in the family genealogy, not in the frontal, absolute truth of a deadly gaze – an element of the story inherited from the myth. The folktale turns this archaic phantasy of radical alterity leading to death into a life force.

This is achieved by the revelation of the children's family story, which had remained concealed until then. The tale "The Speaking Bird", as it is called in many of its versions, recounts to those concerned, when they are gathered together, the hidden drama that preceded the birth of the three golden children. Imaginary, dream children, animal children and finally real children reunited with their parents.

Thus, the bird heals all the characters through narration, by revealing the truth about the cruel punishment of the mother and the attempt to kill the children. This makes it possible for them to be reunited with their lost father.

By bringing order to the prevailing chaos without imposing an absolute truth, the mythical bird helps the young heroes of the tale to discover their subjective reality. This story centres on the polarity of the bird of truth – the theme of meta-morphosis in myths, presented in the style of the folktale.

Notes

1 See Vladimir Propp, *Morphology of the Folktale*, Martino Fine Books, 2015.
2 Claude Lévi-Strauss, *Structural Anthropology*, Basic Books, 1974.
3 V. Propp, *Morphology of the Folktale*, University of Texas Press, 1968, pp. 106–107.
4 A. Angelopoulos, *Paramythokores*, Hestia, 1991.
5 F. Frontisci-Ducroux, *Arbres filles et garçons fleurs*, Seuil, 2017.
6 Ovid, *Metamorphoses*, Oxford Paperbacks, 2008.
7 A mythography of Nicaea (first century BC) tells the myth of Daphne and Apollo dif-ferently. Apollo's rival Leucipos disguises himself as a young girl in order to approach Daphne. Apollo manipulates the situation so that the girl discovers while bathing in the river that he is a man and kills him. This is where the myth of Daphne and Apollo as we know it begins.
8 "Muscambre fils de l'inceste" in *L'Homme*, 28 (105), pp. 49–63, journal published by EHESS School for Advanced Studies in the Social Sciences.
9 The best-known version of the story of Eros and Psyche, after which the folktale type is named, is related by Apuleius in his *Metamorphoses* or *The Golden Ass*, a novel from the second century AD. I refer to the annotated work by Louis C. Purser, *Apuleius, the Story of Cupid and Psyche*, Aristide Caratzas Publisher, 1983.
10 E. Togethoff (1922), *Studienzum Märchentypus von Amor und Psyche*, Generic Pub-lisher, 2019. For the work of researchers such as E. Cosquin, A. Lang, C. Kawczynski, A. Wesselski, and others, see J.-O. Swahn, *The Tale of Cupid and Psyche*, CWK Gleerup, 1954, pp. 395–418.
11 J.-O. Swahn, *The Tale of Cupid and Psyche*, CWK Gleerup, 1954, pp. 24–26.
12 G. A. Megas, *Das Märchen von Amor und Psyche in der Griechischen Volksüberlief-erung*, Collection Academy of Athens, 1971.
13 The motif of the couple's reunion was used by Swahn to classify the folktale type into subtypes; see Swahn, *The Tale of Cupid and Psyche*, CWK Gleerup, 1954, pp. 24–36. The same breakdown into elements is applied to French folktales in Delarue's critical catalogue. See P. Delarue and M.-L. Tenèze, *Le Conte populaire français*, Maisonneuve & Larose, 1963. For the Greek versions, Megas also used Swahn's

typology (G. A. Megas, *Das Märchen von Amor und Psyche in der Griechischen Volksüberlieferung*, Collection Academy of Athens, 1971, pp. 100 ff.).

14 J.-O. Swahn, *The Tale of Cupid and Psyche*, CWK Gleerup, 1954, pp. 222, 279, 293–294.

15 The name of the artificial husband is Candiozymomenos (pressed sugar, 5 times), Zacharoplasmenos (pressed sugar, 1 time), Margaritarenios (man of pearls, 1 time), Moustokarydos (made of musk and nuts, 1 time), Moschocanellatos (made of musk and cinnamon, 2 times), Canellatos (made of musk, 1 time), Moshovassileas (the musk king, 1 time), Moshoplasmenos (pressed musk, 1 time), Sekerbeim (sweet gentleman – in Turkish –, 1 time), Simigdalenios (the cornmeal man, 3 times), Moscaberis (Moskambris, 4 times), Moscozaphirou (musk and sapphires, 1 time), Dyosmosakratos (made of pure mint, 1 time), Moshocambanos (wrapped in musk, 1 time).

16 Megas cites 27 versions of the tale we shall call *Muskamber*. Also see J.-O. Swahn, *The Tale of Cupid and Psyche*, CWK Gleerup, 1954, p. 27.

17 A. Karanikola-Christofi, *Symaïka*, Vol. II, 1974, pp. 259–262.

18 "Is it really you? And how did you change so much? – It is because I lost you and searched for you all this time." G. A. Riga, "Simigdalenious" (Mr. Simigdali), Culture populaire de Skiathos, *Hellinika*, 1962, Vol. II: 5. Origin: Skiathos.

19 M. Lüthi, *Once Upon a Time*, Indiana University Press, 1976, p. 92.

20 J.-O. Swahn, *The Tale of Cupid and Psyche*, CWK Gleerup, 1954, pp. 27–28.

21 E. Stamouli-Saranti, "Moshoplasmenos" (Pressed Musk), *Thrakika*, 1941, pp. 341–345. Origin: Silymvria.

22 G. A. Megas, *Das Märchen von Amor und Psyche in der Griechischen Volksüberlieferung*, Collection Academy of Athens, 1971, pp. 135 ff.; J.-O. Swahn, *The Tale of Cupid and Psyche*, CWK Gleerup, 1954, p. 294.

23 G. Basile, *The Pentamerone*, Franklin Classics, 2018, p. 481.

24 S. Gedeon, *L'Homme*, 105, XXVIII (1), Jan.–Mar. 1988, pp. 49–63.

25 S. Gedeon, *Symaïka*, Athens, 1974, p. 264.

26 S. Gedeon, *Symaïka*, Athens, 1974, p. 264.

27 S. Gedeon, *Symaïka*, Athens, 1974, p. 264.

28 P. Kritikos, *"Moscambaris"*, in "Contes de Patmos", *Laografia*, 16, 1957, p. 399.

29 P. Kritikos, *"Moscambaris"*, in "Contes de Patmos", *Laografia*, 16, 1957, p. 399.

30 A. Karanikola-Christofi, in *Symaïka*, II. 1974, pp. 259–262.

31 P. Kritikos, "Moscambaris", in "Contes de Patmos", *Laografia*, 16, 1957, p. 178.

32 E. Stamouli-Saranti, "Moshoplasmenos" (Pressed Musk), *Thrakika*, 1941, p. 341.

33 P. Kritikos, "Moscambaris", in "Contes de Patmos", *Laografia*, 16, 1957, p. 399.

34 M. Lüthi, *Once Upon a Time*, Indiana University Press, 1976, pp. 84–86. The author discusses the theme of the "living doll", comparing an Alpine legend to the Greek folktale. But he makes no distinction between the different materials used in each case: cream-covered thrash, fabric, wood, cheese, sugar.

35 E. Stamouli-Saranti, "Moshoplasmenos" (Pressed Musk), *Thrakika*, 1941, p. 341.

36 M. Detienne, "Adonis et les Adonies", in *Dictionnaire des mythologies et des religions des sociétés traditionnelles et du monde antique*, Flammarion, 1981, Chapter I, p. 2.

37 P. Grimal, *Dictionnaire de la mythologie grecque et romaine*, PUF, 1969, p. 11.

38 Ovid, *The Metamorphoses*, Book 10, A. S. Kleine (Trans.), CreateSpace Publishing, 2014.

39 J.-P. Vernant, *Les jardins d'Adonis*, Gallimard, 1977, ch. XXXIV.

40 E. Athanassoula, *There was . . . There Was Not . . .*, Academy of Athens, 1929. The introductory formula: "There was . . . there was not" is the title of the collection of stories. This version of Muskamber is taken from the folklore archives of the Academy of Athens; it was collected in Euboia in 1914, and was included in G. A. Megas, *Folktales*

of Greece, Hestia, 1971. It was translated by Irene Naumann Mavrogordato, *Es war einmal, Neugriechische Volksärchen*, Istanbul, 1942, pp. 5–9.

41 N. Belmont, "Orphée dans le miroir du conte merveilleux" ("Orpheus through the Looking Glass of the Fairy Tale)", *L'Homme*, 93, 25 (1), 1985, pp. 59–82.

42 Jean-Pierre Vernant, *Myth and Tragedy in Ancient Greece*, Zone Books, 1990.

43 Hesiod, *The Theogeny*, SMK Books, 2012.

44 Georges Devereux, *Baubo, la vulve mythique*, Payot, 2021. Salomon Reinach, *Cults, Myths and Religions*, Ulan Press, 2012.

45 M. Détienne, "Entre bêtes et dieux", *Nouvelle Revue de Psychanalyse*, No. 6, 1972.

46 P. Quignard, *Sex and Terror*, C. Turner (Trans.), Seagull Books, 2011.

47 Homer, *The Odyssey*, Book II, W. W. Norton, 2018.

48 J.-P. Vernant, *The Universe, the Gods, and Mortals*, Profile Books, 2001.

49 S. Thompson, *The Folktale*, University of California Press, 1977.

50 Anonymous, *Les Mille et Une Nuits*, A. Galland (Trans.), Flammarion, 2004. Jack Zipes, *The Great Fairy Tale Tradition: From Straparola and Basile to the Brothers Grimm*, W. W. Norton, 2001.

51 A. Pushkin, *The Tale of Tsar Saltan*, Methuen Publishing, 1974.

52 P. Delarue and M.-L. Tenèze, *Le Conte populaire français*. Maisonneuve & Larose, 2002.

Chapter VII

The Representation of the Unthinkable

Aside from folktales in the Cinderella category, other types of oral tales cover over blank zones and unthinkable episodes by creating a toned-down version that tells a less unexpected and more reassuring story. This, in fact, resembles what happens in an analysis, where the emergence of unconscious thoughts often causes one story to be covered over by another.

THE FISH HEAD

Once upon a time there was a poor woman who had a daughter. The woman went begging from house to house so she could feed her daughter, and she succeeded well enough. What she most desired was to eat a mackerel head with warm bread. When she knocked on doors, she was sometimes given a mackerel head, but she didn't have the warm bread. At other times, someone gave her warm bread, but no mackerel head. Her torment went on for years, because she never had the warm bread and the mackerel at the same time.

One day, the people in one of the houses wanted to give her all sorts of good things to eat. But she told them: "Instead of all these dishes, give me what my heart most desires: a mackerel head with warm bread!" The mistress of the house sent her servant to look in the pantry for what the old woman wanted. The servant came back with warm bread and a mackerel head, and gave them both to the old woman. Filled with joy, the woman blessed her, saying: "May God protect you, my child." And she hurried home. "I brought food for us, come quickly!" she called to her daughter. It's a mackerel head with warm bread." But her daughter answered that she was not hungry. So the mother decided to wait for her to get hungry. She left the warm bread and the fish head on the table and went out. But a cat came by and devoured everything.

- Where has all the food gone? the mother exclaimed.
- It was sitting there, the daughter answered. Maybe the cat ate it.
- What did you say? the mother shouted. The cat? The cat ate everything?

DOI: 10.4324/9781032674230-8

She took hold of her daughter and gave her a terrible beating. When she stopped, the girl was half dead. "Go away! All these years I struggled to have mackerel and warm bread one day, and you let the cat eat them! I don't want to see you anymore! Leave! Be gone!" The girl begged her mother not to send her away, but in vain. The mother put her out and locked the door.

The girl found herself on the road, not knowing where to go. Her mother had told her to disappear: "If I see you in the village, I will kill you." So she started out on a path, not knowing where it led. She just continued on, straight ahead. Finally, she came to a garden and at the back of it she saw a palace. She reached the door of the palace and knocked. The servants opened the door and asked her: "What brings you here?" Night was falling, so the young girl asked: "Can you let me spend the night here, for I am a stranger?"

— We must ask the king.
— Your Majesty, they said, a girl is sitting outside the palace; she asked us to let her come in for the night. She told us she would leave tomorrow at dawn.
— Let her come in, the king ordered.

The young girl was taken to a room and food was brought to her. Then the king's son came to see her. The prince did not have a fiancée. He found the beautiful young girl to his liking. "Since you happened to find your way here, he said, you must not ever leave. I shall marry you!" So the young girl stayed at the palace. Preparations were made for their wedding and two days later she became queen.

The girl's mother was still roaming the roads in search of a mackerel head and warm bread. She came and went tirelessly, never giving a thought to her daughter. Her wanderings led her to the palace one day. She knocked on the door over and over, and when the door was opened her daughter caught a glimpse of her from inside. At the sight of her mother, the young woman felt great sadness and great joy at the same time. She thought: "I will give her a lot of money, so she does not have to beg anymore." She ordered her servants to welcome the old woman, and asked that her mother be brought before her. The servants took the old woman by the hand and brought her before the queen.

— Welcome, my little mother. How did you find me? How did you know I was here?
— Oh, it's you! Now give me the mackerel head and the warm bread. Give them back to me!

Her daughter had prepared a magnificent platter with all kinds of delicious dishes.

– Let us have something to eat first. We can talk about everything else later.
– No, her mother replied. First, give me back the mackerel head the cat stole!

The daughter gave her mother a bag filled with marvelous things, and another one full of gold coins.

– Take these, mother, she said, so you will never be in need again.
– Go to the Devil with your gold coins! the mother answered. What I want is my mackerel head!

And she kept making the same demand from morning to night, as she wandered from one end of the palace to the other.

– My Lord, the daughter thought, what grief she is causing me! Go home, mother, she finally told her. I will find the mackerel head and send it to you!
– No, her mother insisted. I want it right now!
– Very well, then, the daughter agreed. Come with me and I will give it to you now.

They went to the staircase and started to walk down; the mother, who was walking ahead, said: "If you don't give me my mackerel head, I will kill you." She walked down two or three steps. The daughter had the idea of pushing her, so that the fall would kill her. She gave her a push and the old woman died. The queen took the body to the servants and told them to dig a pit near the door and bury her there. "Thank God, I am rid of this pest! I was offering her all the money in the world, and she kept shaming me. I did the right thing!"

About twenty days later, a lemon tree started to grow near the door. "Take good care of it," the queen told the servants. "Look after it well!" Every day, the little lemon tree was watered, and it kept growing. Three months later, the lemon tree had grown so big that it could cover the whole world. The king sought refuge under its branches: he brought his pillow and his mosquito net and settled down. One day, when he was lying under the tree, he called the queen: "Come and delouse me!" But the queen refused. "Stay where you are", she said, "I'm not moving." She was sad, thinking of her mother. But the king insisted, and she had to go to join him under the lemon tree. He put his head on her knees and she started to delouse him. But as she did this, a branch of the tree bent down and stung her with its thorns.

The queen pulled away from the branch, but it stretched to reach her; she pulled farther away, but the branch followed her. She suspected that her mother wanted to hurt her and tried to stay as far away as she could. She told the king that she wanted to get away from the branch, but he would not let her. "Where do you want to go?" he asked. A thorn pricked her, and she moved away; the thorn pricked her again, and again she moved away. She did not have a moment's peace. She started to laugh and cry at the same time. The king woke up and asked her: "What is troubling you?"

- It's just a thought I had, she replied.
- Tell me what it was at once! he ordered her.

The queen was alarmed and answered on the spot: "I remembered the broom in our bathroom. It is fuller than your beard!"

- Get up at once and come with me, her husband answered. Show me this bathroom and this broom! If it looks better than my beard, so be it; but if it doesn't, I will have your head cut off!

What now? Where could she take the king? Cry, young queen, you have only yourself to blame!

- Keep going! the king shouted.
- But I don't remember which way to go.
- I will have your head cut off!

She walked ahead of him. She turned right, she turned left, she went this way and that. Which way should she go? She didn't know where she was going but pretended to be showing the king the way. In the end, she took the path along the seashore. Suddenly, she saw a creature emerge from the waves. It was a giant crab, as big as a sea monster. He came close to her. "Why are you crying?" he asked. "Tell me, talk to me, I am your good fortune." So the queen told him her story. The crab held out a set of keys to her: "Here, take these keys and walk down this road. Soon you will see a magnificent palace. It has forty-one rooms, and the forty-first is the bathroom. You can show it to the king. You can stay in the palace for forty days. But after the forty days you have to bring me back the keys. If you don't, I will come and eat you."

The queen felt reassured and took the keys. "Hurry," she told her husband, "so we can get there before nightfall." They walked on for a few hours, until they saw the palace at last. The king himself had never seen such splendour. His wife must know what she was saying, and he was anxious to see the broom that resembled his beard. They both went into the palace gardens. And what magnificent gardens! And what a palace! The walls were studded with diamonds. The king ran from room to room. "Quick, bring a boat!" he shouted, dazzled. He went up and came down the stairs, again and again, going into each of the forty rooms. Then they came to the forty-first room. When they went in, they saw a small broom, but the king's beard paled in comparison with it.

- This is the broom, the queen said.
- You were right to say what you did, the king admitted. Now, we will stay here, we will live in this palace. The servants can keep our old palace!

The queen bit her lips. The king couldn't have been happier, but the queen was unhappy again. She took to her bed. She refused to eat or drink.

- What is wrong? the king asked, concerned.
- I am lost, she answered, no matter what happens, I am lost!
- But why?
- It is because of my good fortune.

These were the only words she spoke for forty days. On the forty-first morning, she told the king: "Today, the giant crab will come and eat me. You shall remarry, but this is my final hour. You can stay here, or you can leave, as you wish." The clock struck noon. The queen kept asking her husband to leave the room. He finally agreed and went for a walk in the garden. She was left sitting alone in the upstairs room. That is when the crab arrived. Sharpening his teeth, he walked towards her. A great quantity of carded cotton had been placed at the palace entrance. It was left there while it waited to be spun. The crab's claw got caught in it and he could no longer advance.

- Don't I have enough troubles already? he scolded the cotton. Did you have to get in my way too?
- Tut-tut! the carded cotton answered, what are these troubles you complain of, dear crab? Look at me: I must put up with being carded, spun, woven, and made to suffer in so many other ways. But you? What could make you suffer?

No sooner had these words been spoken than the crab fell to the ground, dead. The queen, who had heard everything, came down to make sure the crab was really dead. And this is how she stayed queen of the palace forever.
They rejoiced, they ate, they drank, but we were not invited to the feast.

Sources

"I Psarokephali" [The Fish Head].
Version collected in Rhodes by Ch. Papachristodoulou.
CGMF 545A*, *The Fish Head.*
ATU 545A, *The Magic Castle.*

The Folktale and the Representation of the Unthinkable[1]

Anna Angelopoulos

Transmission is what the oral tale aims to achieve. It is a folklore genre recreated and reshaped at each telling. This form of collective, anonymous transmission is thousands of years old. The folktale has no author. Its origin is unknown. It is time-less, since we know that mankind started to tell stories as soon as language was acquired. In similar fashion, the spoken word is what lies at the heart of psycho-analytic practice.

Contrary to written tales with their fixed content, like Grimm's or Perrault's fairy tales, the oral folktale is created while the storyteller tells it. Its transmission is largely responsible for its poetic attributes. This form of oral literature is constantly recreated across generations, languages and countries. Oral literature, a tireless independent traveller, borrows motifs, narrative passages and even whole stories from the regions through which it passes. It transforms or rejects this borrowed content at its next stop, to take into account the expectations of its new audience. But each time it keeps intact the narrative thread to be transmitted. And when the listeners tell the tale in their turn, they reshape it according to the most popular story form in their community, unwittingly excluding from transmission any nar-rative contribution that differs from their shared lore. It is as if, unconsciously, the tales corrected themselves in the transmission. As time goes by, this process brings into being a collective object in which each person can find something of his own self, as well as a shared piece of fiction.

Human memory is fallible. When he tells a tale, the storyteller sometimes forgets a narrative motif; this doesn't prevent him from continuing, but it changes the meaning of the story.

For instance, the desire of a pregnant princess to steal strawberries in a forbid-den garden does not have the same implications as a desire to steal parsley, which is an abortifacient plant.

Sometimes, the storyteller may forget one or two episodes entirely, as if he had an unconscious blank. In that case, he transmits a fragmented story, like a dreamer who only remembers a part of his dream.

This fragmented aspect of the folktale is the first thing one notices while conduct-ing research in folklore archives. It is what I myself experienced for several years.

In the nineteenth century, before there were audio archives, folktales were transcribed by hand, by a teacher, an educated local resident, a poet . . . These transcriptions are often elliptical, and one sometimes has to read up to 300 versions of the story to have a complete idea of a folktale type. We are faced here with the fragile nature of human memory, always fragmentary, a fabric full of holes transmitted just as it is, and around which each storyteller weaves a new version.

The folktale does not emerge from the individual unconscious, but from a transgenerational unconscious, which relies on symbolic reference points embedded in the culture. In this sense, the folktale and the dream are subjected to the same mechanisms of figuration, condensation, displacement and secondary elaboration. This last lends its established form to the genre. But it is primarily through figuration that the unconscious thoughts of the story are translated into images, and that archaic phantasies are acted out, so that the unconscious of the listeners recognises them and elaborates on them.

At times an unlikely image emerges, an image with no apparent function in the story. This type of image has been called a "blind motif" by Max Lüthi, one of the twentieth century's most eminent analysts of the folktale. These motifs or blind spots allude to the background of the tale, from which archaic traces of the common foundation of humanity can surface in the narration. The following illustrates this.

In one of the versions of a Judaeo-Spanish folktale from Istanbul, an old woman working in a *hammam* receives *bimuelos* as a gratuity from a rich lady; *bimuelos* are honey doughnuts eaten at Easter. The old woman's granddaughter gives the doughnuts to the cat instead of eating them. Her grandmother says: "Don't worry, I will make you some more." The child keeps asking for honey doughnuts; she eats some, gives some to the cat, gives them to beggars and asks for more. The grandmother is happy to make them for her. Throughout the granddaughter's life, her grandmother continues to make *bimuelos* to mark all important occasions: the granddaughter's marriage, her husband's departure for war, his return, etc.

There seems to be no reason for the incongruous repetition and excessive presence of this *bimuelos* motif. But its meaning emerges when we remember the Greek versions of the tale "The Fish Head". In the same traditional context, in Greece it is the custom to eat fish on the day of Annunciation. On that day, a beggar-woman is given a fish head that she takes home, very happy at the thought of sharing it with her daughter. But her daughter gives it to the cat. Enraged, her mother gives her a beating. This causes a break between mother and daughter, eventually leading to the murder of the mother, who keeps demanding the fish head from her daughter even from beyond the grave.

In light of the Greek fairy tale, we understand that the Jewish storyteller from Istanbul has simply *forgotten* the murder and the eating-related frustration between mother and daughter. But in fact, the hidden meaning behind the blind motif of the *bimuelos*, revealed by the Greek versions, is most likely this matricide. Thanks to this oversight, after skipping a generation, the Jewish storyteller erased the mother's murder by the daughter and replaced the protagonists of the conflict with a grandmother and granddaughter who love each other and who experience no oral frustration. Thus, in this elliptic scenario, the break caused by the rejection of food in the transmission of the feminine is displaced, covered over.

Three Spinners on the Edge of a Chasm

I spoke earlier of the elliptic transmission of folktales, and the omission of entire episodes, sometimes due to geographic and cultural displacement. There is one story whose founding motif relies on an enormous gap, a veritable chasm. Paradoxically, everyone has always known this folktale, because it is universal. The story is "Cinderella". We all remember the cinder-covered girl persecuted by her stepmother, her two cruel stepsisters, the prince and the glass slipper.

The Greek version of the tale starts with a scene where a mother and her three daughters are weaving on the edge of a chasm. They are poor and have to keep working at night. To stay alert, they play a game: they will eat the one whose thread breaks or whose spindle falls into the chasm. The mother is the one who loses and who is eaten, either right away or after being transformed into a cow by her two oldest daughters; only Cinderella, the youngest, refuses to eat the maternal flesh. She gathers up her dead mother's bones and buries them in the garden, where a tree starts to grow. In other versions of the story, she buries the bones in the ashes of the hearth. After that, she cries, she waters the young tree, and observes mourning rites. During her mourning she stays in the hearth, among the ashes. This is the reason for her nickname, Cinderella (in Greek, to be precise, her nickname is *Stachtopouta*, from *stachti*, "ashes" and *poutti*, "female genitals"). Later in the narrative, among her mother's bones the heroine finds the beautiful dresses and marvellous slippers that allow her to meet the prince.

What the Greek fairy tale adds to the incomplete Western versions is the initial episode of the terrifying chasm at the origin of the feminine, where the thread and the spindle are teetering on the edge. This chasm represents archaic fears and lets unspeakable phantasies emerge from the primal sphere. We have all had the dream of falling endlessly into a void. Psychoanalysis is well acquainted with psychic chasms, be it that of mourning, of trauma, of psychosis, Winnicott's "breakdown", or the void left by sudden maternal withdrawal in autism.

While the folktale creates a collective object that, like a mask, is constructed by successive layers intended to counter the chasms of fear and death; metaphorically speaking, psychoanalysis does its work by weaving thread by thread, around the void, to reinforce the edges, sometimes back and forth from one margin to the other, trying to recreate psychic tissue in the transference between two people or in institutional transference. This image of a gaping hole standing for the unthinkable, around which the Cinderella folktales are built, gives rise to the powerful unconscious image of weaving around the void, a collective reaction of weaving as a way to keep death at bay – a central image in myths.

Here, it is not the father who is killed, but the mother. While the older sisters partake in a cannibalistic feast, *incorporating* the mother, to use Maria Torok's concept, the youngest refuses this nourishment. She mourns her murdered mother's death, observing the proper rituals. In my view, the process of *introjecting* the mother is the means by which the feminine is transmitted in this myth. To kill the mother in phantasy is an enactment of the inevitable and necessary psychic separation we often work on with our patients in their analyses.

But sometimes the folktale kills its own heroes, as in some unusual versions with tragic endings. Although in general these popular tales always have a happy ending – "they lived happily ever after and we did even better", as the Greek tales say –, there are exceptions. Indeed, in some cases, instead of growing up and marrying the prince, the heroine dies, defeated by the torments of her fate. For instance, a Greek oral version of Cinderella depicts a little girl whose mother is transformed into a cow, which is then killed. The tree that sprung up where her bones were buried is cut down, and its fruit, intended for the prince in most versions, is devoured by animals. Little Cinderella, left without her mother-cow-nursemaid, dies of hunger.

The unexpected happy ending of the folktale turns into its opposite, as if the founding archaic phantasy, "an orphan is left to die of hunger", has come true. These minimal, fragmented forms produce what I call "counter-tales" in which the unconscious emerges, uncovering the bare phantasy, a figure of the unthinkable. Thus, the narration never comes to an end, because, for his own reasons, the storyteller does not provide shareable symbolic reference points. Cinderella never grows up.

Over time, through oral transmission, the folktale generates recurring archaic images – devouring monsters, chasms, sorcerers. In truth, these are images that combat death and unthinkable primitive fears. Fairy tales and myths have always served to mask states associated with atavistic fears of wolves, ogres, predators – primitive fears against which the collective narration constructs a seemingly innocent protective image, such as the seven little baby goats dancing around the well in which the wolf drowned.

The "lessons" learned from folktales show us that these fears always take centre stage, as if the tale absorbs the dread of the unknown. Thus, the folktale enables us to withstand a timeless fear, while at the same time endlessly reawakening it intensely and in a unique manner at each retelling, in each of its versions. Wolves, witches, ogres and giants are transitional objects offered by the folktale, to accompany us for a time and then be left behind. From this point of view, the folktale itself can be experienced as a transitional space, since it depicts imaginary rites of passage serving to accompany certain crucial transformations.

I still remember the transitional dream of a young girl on the brink of puberty. Looking out of the window of her room, she saw a visitor leave the house, walking down the stairs very slowly. It was a wolf, wearing a jacket and tie. His face, which bore a very sad expression and a bitter smile, was turned towards her as if to say: "Alas, young lady, I have to leave you, there is nothing more for me to do here." It was her way of bidding farewell to her childhood.

The particular manner in which the folktale achieves the transmission of the unthinkable through motifs of separation and abandonment in the narrative is reminiscent of certain turning points occurring in our clinical practice.

A patient – a beautiful young woman – came to see me in a state of pervasive despondency. After a while, it became clear that after being abandoned by her mother at the age of three, she had tried in vain to win the love of her stepmother. The stepmother gave preference to her half-brothers and half-sisters. After being abruptly separated from her older sister, who was sent to boarding school very early, my patient had lived in fear, thinking that she too could be sent away from her father's home.

Her mother had gone back to her far-away native land, had remarried and stopped sending any news. An initial portion of analysis had incited my patient to re-establish contact with her birth mother. While I felt this was probably a good thing, I was aghast every time the gaping wound of the abandonment resurfaced in the sessions.

A few years later, when she was settling down with the man she loved, she wanted to invite her mother and her eldest sister to Paris, to spend Christmas with them. Finally, she would spend the holidays with family. It was then, when her relationship with her mother was being reinforced, that everything blew up.

When her mother was about to approach the territory my patient had so painstakingly carved out for herself, she suddenly started to scream in our sessions that this woman, her mother, was a selfish monster incapable of love, that she didn't want to see her, and that her father had been right to complain about her. I was shaken by the intensity of the sudden hatred directed at this mother who, until then, had been idealised in her absence.

In truth, the gaping wound of abandonment existing between the two of them had been negated up to that point. The analytic work my patient was pursuing with me brought into question the meaning of her family relations and made it necessary for the stepmother or any other maternal substitute to be given a place in the overall picture. One day I told my patient that in Greece, after a powerful earthquake, rebuilding is never done in the seismic gap, but always next to it. She had inherited a void and, in the analysis, we had to weave around it, to allow her to internalise the fact that she would have to, and could, live without a mother from then on.

To conclude, let us look more closely at the comparison between the orally transmitted folktale and the written tale. Andersen's "The Little Match Girl"[2] is a literary fairy tale, a completed work signed by an author. This poor little girl is beaten by her father if she does not sell her boxes of matches. On Christmas Eve, while everyone is merry, she shivers with cold on a street corner. Out of desperation, she lights her matches one by one to warm herself, until she sees in the flame her deceased beloved grandmother holding out her arms to her. And the little girl dies. This literary text is set in writing in definitive form by its author, Andersen. "The Little Match Girl" becomes a counter-tale when it takes the form of the popular version of Cinderella mentioned earlier, where the heroine dies of hunger. The "counter-tale" brings into focus deadly elements and instinctive diffusion. When the tale is given a definitive written form, as is the case with Andersen's story, it must be taken as it is; no changes to the text are possible. Of course, life is always seen with the possibility of death as its counterpoint. All fairy tales illustrate this reality. But the particularity of the oral folktale is that it is not set once and for all, and can evolve as it is transmitted, depending on the storyteller, the languages and the countries involved. It often starts with the worst archaic fears, as illustrated by the version of Cinderella I mentioned; but, version after version, as the tale continues to be told, the heroine is given symbolic references in various ways, allowing her to live her own life and be happy. Indeed, in most oral folktales there is a happy ending for the hero and heroine.

In conclusion, what distinguishes the folktale is that it remains alive; it is constantly shaped and recreated through a process of collective transmission that includes both the storyteller and the audience, so that the life drive may triumph in the end.

With – and despite – all its cruelty, the oral folktale, a genre constructed by a multitude of past contributors, carries and transmits across centuries the strength to see us through the darkest night and into the dawn. Its representations of the unthinkable act against fear and against the repetition compulsion tormenting its heroes. A product of fragmentary memory, the folktale tirelessly weaves the collective fabric of human memory.

Interference of Narratives Created in the Transferential Relation[3]

Sylvette Gendre-Dusuzeau

Long, long ago, in a house by the sea, a widowed and very poor mother who was about to drop in on her neighbour asked her daughter to keep an eye on three magnificent fish heads, a rare and delicious delicacy. The girl had to make sure the cat wouldn't eat them. But when her mother returned, no more fish heads! Where had they gone? The cat had eaten them, but where was the cat? Gone! The mother screamed and hit her daughter, demanding that she give her back her fish heads on the spot – the very ones that had disappeared.

This is nothing like the story of Little Red Riding Hood, where the lost object reappears when the wolf's belly is laid open, to everyone's great joy. Here, on the contrary, there is an unacceptable, impossible loss – that of an object not yet enjoyed, an irreplaceable object. The episode ends with a matricide – a very unhappy ending.

This tale drew my attention to an idea that I translated into words, like in analysis: "How can one forego what one hasn't had?" It is easier to lose what one has possessed. The tale tells a mother-daughter story that cannot leave anyone indifferent, since so many of us have experienced, in analysis, the difficulty of giving up phantasised ideal parents and the love we would have liked but did not receive.

Love for the mother often becomes the object of a complaint likely to be endless, since the complaint maintains the tie with the missing lost object.

At the time when I heard it, this folktale resonated with the ongoing analysis of a young woman, not yet 30 years of age, whose complaint was: "My mother never loved me." This caused her real suffering, inconsolable grief. Compassion only helped a little, and I hoped that we could produce a real effect on her complaint, which was kept alive by maternal failings. The actual circumstances of her life had been difficult; my patient's mother had regularly left her with other people, either people she knew or strangers. But what my patient most blamed her for was not her lack of affection, but her lack of interest in her through the years, lasting unchanged to the present day.

What I wish to discuss here, in the context of this analytic treatment and its narration, is how we were able to alter her grievance to avoid breakdown. Her various ways of going through her suffering again solicited my transferential contribution.

She was missing whole segments of her childhood, and this past she was exploring both interested her and was hard to face. This is when she lost her watch, and the past moved into the present; she would come to her sessions more or less near the appointed time, disorganising my schedule. I was irritated but aware that she was subjecting me to the absence of stability she had known all her life. Things went on like this for about a year. Then, one day, she arrived very happy, with a new watch that was a perfect replacement for the old one. I thought that lost time was starting to find its place.

Another time, she disappeared for two weeks, and did not answer my messages. When she returned, when I told her I had been worried, she feigned indifference, surprised not to be chastised. The following month, on a stormy day, she came to the session sick, with a sore throat (as a child, I was terrified of throat infections). I gave her an umbrella, even though she had not asked for it. This led to some provocative behaviour. She came to the following sessions with another umbrella, setting it down next to her. When I commented that she had found shelter, she said: "Oh, yes, your umbrella, I lost it in the subway, but I found one. They all look alike." In her place, I would have dried and closed my analyst's umbrella properly and brought it back promptly, I thought, somewhat derisively. I realised she was making fun of me, like the child who didn't take her mother's fish heads seriously.

One day she brought me a cartoon in which a psychotherapist kept making mistakes and had to be treated by his patients. It occurred to me that she was trying to treat her mother through me. "Ah, yes, we always want to treat our parents," I said, making her laugh. And she went on about her mother's foolish behaviour.

Since she couldn't ask her mother directly whether she loved her, because she was afraid of the answer, she explained that the previous weekend she had talked to her "in code", to see what she could find out. "Coded" language was her invention. She had said: "You don't pay attention to Pierre [her half-brother, but through Pierre she was speaking of herself], because when people have problems, they are aggressive." Her mother did not answer, of course; she had no idea what her daughter was trying to say. Later, when she came back from a short vacation, my patient told me that she had discussed with a friend the fact that they did not miss their sessions with the analyst during their holidays. Since I thought that she meant just the opposite, I said: "That's perfect coded language!" And we laughed together.

In her everyday life, she tried to get her mother's attention but was irritated that their plans never came to anything: cancelled dates, unkept promises. Finally, she was able to admit that her mother was not maternal.

In the transference, her silent question: "Do you love me, do you miss me?" triggered her fear of rejection and, of course, a positive answer on my part would not have healed the serious narcissistic wound of her childhood. As Pierre Delaunay[4] would say, she did not have an "underlying ego". Therefore, we had to have recourse to roundabout means, such as the shifting around of lost objects and the invention of a "camouflage" language. Being her analyst required that I restore her missing under-structure, to recreate "the other" impossible to find within it.

I will now elaborate on another fish story related to the fundamental rule of psychoanalysis. Although Anna O. is a well-known term of reference, we often forget that Von N. was the person who introduced the passage from narration to free association in analysis. She asked Freud not to always interrupt her to ask where such and such a thing came from, but to let her tell him what she had to say.[5] After this, Freud imposed the paradoxical rule of free association, using a rather heavy-handed formulation to assert his authority: "We pledge [the patient] to obey the fundamental rule for analysis, which is henceforward to govern his behaviour towards us."[6]

In my practice, I prefer to state this rule in my own way, at some point, because it is a rule specific to psychoanalysis and acts as a third element. Often, new patients say: "All right, I'll try." Sometimes, in moments of silence, I might say: "What are you telling yourself now?" I remember that my first analyst told me: "Say whatever comes into your mind, without necessarily analysing it." And that was a lot!

As we remember it happening to us, once the fundamental rule is stated, the analysand strives to put his thoughts in order, to relate the facts of his everyday life, which he wants to change. It is the transferential exchanges that produce a psychic event that, given sufficient time, enables the deconstruction needed to put things into words. But, in any case, once the rule has been stated, even with all due care, there is no way to predict what its effects will be.

The following clinical case will serve as an illustration. A man comes to see me after spending several years on the couch with another analyst; he now prefers to sit facing me. Our work together starts; he is very prompt to talk about his life, about what happened in the previous analysis, what his analyst told him . . . But soon a leitmotif makes its appearance: the analyst "wants him to talk, wants to pull something out of him" that the man does not want to give him; because without knowing what it is, my patient knows that, if he complies and gives up this thing, he would risk losing his mind. He "always felt this" with his analysts.

Struck by his vision of a predatory analyst, I ask him: "And is it the same thing with me?" The question is stupid, and he answers: "Yes, it's the same thing; you want me to tell you everything too." Suddenly, all his frustration comes spilling out: "Since I started analysis, long ago, I tried to do what I was asked, to say everything that came into my head, but I am fed up with this rule for beginners that infantilises us, demands that we speak like children, in a disconnected way. I am tired of it. And you want me to do the same thing!" I feel I must explain the rule, using gestures. I tell him that Freud's rule has to do with the unconscious, with what we don't know about ourselves, which is not easy to get hold of. I make gestures while I continue to explain: "You start to talk (I draw a straight line with my finger in the air), and you say to yourself: 'This is not important.' I draw a bubble and continue: 'This is silly, I won't say it.' I draw another bubble and I go on: 'This is not interesting', followed by another bubble. You see, Freud thought that it was in these little, unimportant spaces, in the bubbles, that there is something that can move the analysis forward."

He answers: "Oh, yes, it's as if there are little fish and big fish, and you only give away the small ones. But I am afraid that a big fish will slip out." In the next session, he says: "I understand that I will not lose my mind if I myself give you the little fish. I can give away many small ones, but I wouldn't want everything in the net to fall out at once." Thus, he became active in the process of speaking and escaped the phantasy of being a potential victim of a predator/killer-other who wants to empty his being against his will. But in addition to the threat of predation suggested by the fundamental rule which initiates the analysis, I sense the danger of coming close to a devastatingly traumatic zone in him too soon.

This short story about the fundamental rule, which shows that telling is equivalent to conceding a part of the body, reveals that, paradoxically, what is done to facilitate free association can in fact hinder it greatly without anyone noticing. Here, I would like to draw. attention to the care with which Pierre Delaunay treats the fundamental rule, which he considers a guiding principle to accompany the analysand on his journey, and which he reformulates every time to make it fit and constitute veritable support for the patient.[7]

There are many other forms of speech when the spoken word is inadequate, as I described in the first case I presented. When this happens, writing can prove useful. For example, a young woman patient I saw had trouble putting things into words. She would start, stop, then say: "How can I put it?" One day, she came with her notebook; she wrote at home and she brought me her writings, which included her interpretations of our exchanges. In her family, where everyone spoke out freely, telling her what to do and what was best, she took refuge in writing. She was asking me to listen and, sometimes, to say what I thought, sharing the intimate world of her diary with me. At other times she left the diary at home; we would then venture to work without a net, like she did on the trapeze, which was her passion.

At times, patients bring us letters, as proof of how the other talks to them, how mean and toxic the other is. "Here, this is from my mother," my patient says in a commanding tone. She is trembling. I don't feel like saying, as I was taught to do: "Tell me what it says." Instead, I put on my glasses, read to myself and repeat the content out loud. Who am I in the transference just then? The positive superego, an agency that cancels the toxic effect of the parent? I serve as an intermediary in this shared transferential zone, for the purpose of countering the persecutory internal object.

Given the contributions of modern technology, I am sometimes presented with sheets and sheets of printed messages to read. It's practical, because there are several exchanges, several short letters, on the same page. But the quintessence of high-tech is the cellular phone: "So, I sent him a text." The phone is seized quickly, the fingers slide on the screen and my patient reads aloud the text she sent. "And then he answered . . ." And so on. It's impressive. I see it as dialogue with ping-pong balls. Ultimately, only the bottom line counts: does he love me or not? Just as it would if the exchange took place face to face. I wait for the phone to be put away before I ask: "How do you feel about what you just read me?" Now, something can begin to be said.

In these scenes that involve written material, the analyst's attitude is crucial. The emergence of true speech depends on our reaction to a great extent. To say: "Tell me about your letter" or "Read me your letter" compels premature separation, diverting the attempt to reach the analyst, to bring him into the patient's world, to awaken his interest on a personal level. These new means of communication replace speech. If we ask the patient to speak with his own voice before he finds it, if we don't respect this non-verbal communication, we will have narrative, but we will not generate articulate insight. In this regard, patients know surprisingly well what is not done in an analysis. When they first come, the superego is manifest: "I would like to bring a photograph, a letter, a drawing . . ., but I know it's not done."

To conclude, I would like to say something about what I call unbearable talk, opinions or suggestions that exasperate us. For instance, a man who had pushed his previous analyst to the limit. From the first session, I felt like sending him to someone else. But something held me back: he looked a lot like my brother. The same height, the same body build. Almost the same face, and if I squinted, which I could not help doing stealthily, it was really him. The resemblance was stunning! I was confronted with the familiar in a total stranger. All at once I had the bizarre impression that I did not dislike having my brother in analysis. I thought it would be good for him, and for me to be his analyst was very amusing. This is how I accepted this man as a patient. We might think that starting the work on such a basis is reason enough to fear the worst. But in fact, this is not what happened. The resemblance helped me to continue to treat him, although there were unbearable moments when I could not help voicing my disagreement and threatening to stop the analysis. So we continued. The difficulty of the situation forced me to invent, to imagine, to try to change the worst. I used gems of inventiveness to reduce the unbearable. I think I never said so much in analysis.

After a number of quite difficult years, but rewarding once we started working on the immense distress of the child he had been, one day he announced: "I think I have finished my analysis." "Oh, really?" "Yes, I did everything to make you reject me and find me despicable, like my parents who didn't understand me and hated me when I was a child. They made me crazy. I don't blame them anymore. But you, you didn't fall for my tricks. You kept me and I believe you don't even hate me." What I thought was: "The power of transference is incredible!" And all the while I believed we were making progress thanks to my clever interpretations. But in truth, while we were talking, the transference did its work on its own, without our knowledge.

Often, what was said in an analysis, and all the complexity of the process, can be summed up in a few words. For my patient, it could be: "I am not as hateful as I was made to believe."

There are myths, epic tales, stories, all kinds of narratives that can move us deeply, that tell us about ourselves and can even produce changes in us, but only the practice of psychoanalysis has the particularity of deconstructing the narrative in the in-between space of the transference, to let emerge speech that most closely reflects subjective truth, because, where the unconscious is concerned, a story always hides another story.

THE DANCED OUT SHOES

Once upon a time, in a great castle, there lived a mighty king and his only daughter. He was a happy man, but he worried about his daughter who, night after night, was changed into a she-devil and wore out a pair of shoes. The king could not imagine what she was up to. Near the palace dwelt a shepherd who took his sheep to pasture every evening and often saw the princess go off in the distance with a stranger: they went down the hill together and disappeared into the darkness.

The shepherd told other people what he saw and, through word of mouth, the king finally heard about it. "Bring this shepherd to me at once," he ordered his servants, who brought the shepherd to the palace. The king gave him three days to discover what the princess was doing every night, where she went and how she wore out her shoes. The shepherd went home very worried. He was a pious man and implored God, from the bottom of his heart, to help him. That night, he had a dream in which he saw the Virgin, who told him: "Take this cap, it will make you invisible. You will be able to follow the princess without being seen. She will go off with the demon, she will drink from three glasses and you will drink from them too; you will also eat out of her plate. She will dance on razors and, after that, she will nurse her baby. You must take the baby away from her." The shepherd did everything as he was told.

When he was called before the king again, the princess was with him. The shepherd told the king what had happened during the past three nights, and how the princess danced on razors. When he showed the king what the princess had eaten and drunk, she started to scream at him and insult him. But when he showed the baby to the king, she fell to the ground, lifeless. The shepherd said: "Now you know, my King, why the princess tore her shoes every night!" The princess's body was placed in a casket and taken to a chapel, where the palace guards were left to watch over it until morning. But in the morning they were all found dead, without a drop of blood left in their bodies. Each night, the dead woman sucked the blood out of the guards who kept watch over her. But one night, the son of a priest was among them. His mother asked the Blessed Virgin to protect her child, and her prayers were heard. The Virgin appeared to the young man and told him to sit under the altar, where the Devil could not harm him.

From where he sat under the altar, the young man saw the princess come out of her coffin and shout: "My father, today you did not feed me. Why?" She kept shouting for a while, then she stopped; exhausted, she sat down under the icon of the Virgin. The young man went and sat beside the princess, and they were both turned into marble. The next day they were found, turned into a statue. Crowds of people ran to the church to see the miracle. But when the priest started to sing, they came back to life. This is how the princess was disenchanted. Grateful, she thanked the icon of the Blessed Virgin. Filled with joy, the king gave the two young people a big wedding.

They lived happily ever after, and we did the same.

Sources

"O Geronikolis" [Old Nikolis], FS 516, pp. 9–11.
 Version collected in 1959 by Konstantina Kapari in Hiliomondi, Corin-
 thia, as told by Despina Mezini, age 79.
CCG, 3A, 143–144.
CGMF 306, *The Danced Out Shoes.*
ATU 306, *The Danced Out Shoes.*
GFT, No. 9, *The Twelve Dancing Princesses.*

The Typical Dream and the Fairy Tale[8]

Anna Angelopoulos

Paradise itself is no more than a group phantasy of the childhood of the individual [. . .].
But we can regain this Paradise every night in our dreams.
(S. Freud, *The Interpretation of Dreams*[9])

In *The Interpretation of Dreams*, Freud distinguishes between the individual dream, the particular creation of a single, unique author, and the "typical dream", a symbol-generating, repetitive creation, whose meaning is shared by the collectivity.[10] Every one of us has dreamed, at least once, that we are falling from a height, that we are flying, or that we failed an exam. Freud considers these dreams typical.

Even if each dream seems different than the others, even if a repetitive dream seems different each time it recurs, we must admit that at least one part always stays unchanged. This is characteristic of the typical dream: the recurrent sensation and/or dream image shared by everyone (falling, flying, failing, being naked in public), regardless of the dreamer's incidental ideas.

Freud considered that these common characteristics of the dream have a supra-individual source, and that the same interpretation[11] applies to everyone.

At first, Freud established dream symbolism, to be used like a "key to dreams". But he hastened to add: ". . . this symbolism is not peculiar to dreams, but is characteristic of unconscious ideation, in particular among the people, and it is to be found in folklore, and in popular myths, legends, linguistic idioms [. . .], to a more complete extent than in dreams."[12]

Throughout his work on dreams, Freud stressed that, in his opinion, the sources of typical dreams are common to everyone. He looked for them in poetry and in stories, whose frequent connections with our typical dreams, he asserted, "are neither few nor accidental". He also looked for these sources in "the deepest and eternal nature of man [that] lies in those impulses of the mind which have their roots in a childhood that has since become prehistoric". A good example is the dream of nudity, which turns into a nightmare.[13]

The same thing can be said about fairy tales: that they are rooted in the deepest and most enduring essence of humanity, and that they belong to all humankind. This is why folktales the world over are so similar. And this is why they must be classified into types. Today, there is an international classification of folktales, *The Types of Folktales*.[14] Moreover, one of the authors of that catalogue, S. Thompson, has drawn up an inventory of motifs as part of his monumental oeuvre, the *Motif-Index of Folk Literature* (Thompson, 1975).[15]

I shall try to draw a parallel between the concept of "motif" in folklore and "typical dreams" in the unconscious (which is thus rendered collective). Motifs are stereotypical formations constituting a set of figurative elements recognisable in folklore. This is a creation of specialists in the oral domain who, in order to understand how orally transmitted folktales are constituted, have to rely on the distinction between what is stable (invariable) and what is variable (original, created at each telling, depending on the context).

Thus, motif is a tool that is surprisingly well designed. Consisting of a gripping, condensed image, this stereotypical cliché is pervasive both in the narrative content of the tale and in the semantic form, because the motif has a double nature.[16] In addition, the use of a motif in a narration makes it easier to remember. Let us look at the motif of the rose in "Beauty and the Beast".

A father who is about to set off on a voyage asks his three daughters what they would like him to bring them upon his return. The two older sisters ask for expensive dresses and jewels, while the youngest asks only for a rose. But it is precisely this rose that will turn out to be a threat to the father's life, and will bring about the encounter of the heroine and the Beast.

As in embroidery, the motif is a small figurative element, made up of fixed purely decorative or functional forms. The motif can recur regularly in the overall picture, as a reminder of the theme of the embroidery. In the folktale, the motif is stereotyped and accompanies the plot,[17] just as the typical dream is present alongside the dreamer's incidental ideas. The image suggested by the motif always stands out, like the images and feelings in the typical dream.

Let us look at an example taken from a dream, as well as from a folktale. It concerns a conflictual situation based on enmity between brothers and sisters from earliest childhood. One of Freud's patients recounted a dream she had when she was four years old, and which she had often dreamed since: "A whole crowd of children – all her brothers, sisters and cousins [. . .] – were romping in a field. Suddenly they all grew wings, flew away and disappeared."[18]

Folktale lovers will have no trouble recognising this image as one often appearing in the story of the young girl looking for her brothers.[19]

A man and his wife who have many sons finally become the parents of a girl. The sons leave when their sisters is born, or before, because they fear her arrival in the household, and because their parents often carelessly promised them to the Devil in exchange for a girl. They disappear, changed into birds, and fly far away. One day, their sister hears of their existence and sets off to look for them. After the heroine is put through many trials, her brothers recover their human form.

The motif of the brother-birds clearly plays a narrative role in the story of the young girl in search of her brothers, but it also plays a semantic role in what is traditionally called imagery. The fact that, since ancient times, birds have been considered "psychopomps" (beings who accompany souls in their voyage to the beyond) makes it easier to accept the unusual image of brothers who disappear into the sky, transformed into birds.

. . . it is not hard to recognize that in its original form it had been a dream of the death of all her brothers and sisters, and had been only slightly influenced by the censorship. I may venture to suggest the following analysis. On the occasion of the death of one of this crowd of children [. . .] the dreamer, not yet four years old at the time, must have asked some wise grown-up person *what became of children when they were dead?* The reply must have been: 'They grow wings and turn into little angels.' In the dream which followed upon this piece of information all the dreamer's brothers and sisters had wings like angels and – which is the main point – flew away. Our little *baby-killer* was left alone, strange to say: the only survivor of the whole crowd!"[20]

Classifying typical dreams is important for the elaboration of a dream symbol system. Their stereotypical scenarios can be interpreted based on their fundamental characteristics, overlooking the specific incidental ideas of the dreamer.

If Freud had read Stith Thompson's Motif Index, would he have been able to explain – to his own satisfaction – the formation of typical dreams? To compensate to some extent for the lacks to which Freud refers – "My material has left me in the lurch precisely at this point"[21] –, I shall remind you of a folktale dear to children in the days of my childhood: "The Danced Out Shoes" (AT 306). It is the story of a princess who flies off into the sky every night, to dance with fairies in the moonlight, until dawn. A dream of flying, the image of amorous pleasure, as well as an activity invariably associated with the immortality of the soul when it leaves the body, finally free to fly away to the other world.

This is the freedom of the dreamer. Indeed, certain folktales resemble dreams, because they have adopted representations and motifs found in typical dreams. The Greek version[22] of folktale AT 306 is a clear illustration of this.

A king has a beautiful daughter who refuses to marry. Each night, the king places a pair of satin slippers under the princess's pillow, and each morning the slippers are found worn out. The king is mystified; he declares that whoever solves this mystery shall have his daughter's hand in marriage. Princes from far and wide arrive at the palace, but none of them can find an explanation to the puzzle. At last, a handsome young prince wants to try his luck as well, much to his parents' dismay. On his way to the palace, he is very kind to an old woman he encounters; wanting to help him, she gives him a cap that can make him invisible and tells him that the princess has dealings with "princesses from the outer world", *Exoticas*. She also tells him what to do to carry out his task successfully. Then she disappears, after telling him she is his Destiny.

Following the instructions he was given, the prince does not drink a drop of the wine the princess offers him, but lets it flow into a sponge he has placed under his chin; he then pretends to fall into a deep sleep. He is laid on a bed, from which he observes the princess donning magnificent attire, putting on her satin slippers and walking to the door with two golden rods in her hand. The prince follows her, wearing the cap that renders him invisible. She opens the palace gates with a golden rod, and he walks behind her into the dark night. After some time, they come to a brightly lit palace. There the heroine is greeted by three lovely princesses, the *Exoticas*. Three years earlier, they had seen the young girl dance and became fond of her.

This is why the princess refuses to marry, preferring to come and amuse herself with the fairies. The next day, the prince who followed her recounts her adventures at the court and, as proof, he shows the king objects taken from the palace of the fairies. Upset and angry, the king wants to kill his daughter. But the prince says that he will marry her on condition that she burn her "demonic" books and the two golden rods. The princess agrees and they are married.

In this example, the dream leaves traces in the day that follows. The heroine can be seen as a sleepwalker. Her psychical activity during sleep shows her flying off into the sky. Just as in puberty a dream can lead to ejaculation, the princess's nocturnal dancing with the fairies causes her to leave a pair of torn slippers on her threshold, providing a trace of the nightly ball. The worn-out slippers are a mystery indicating to the king his daughter's crossing into the space of dreams. Each day she asks for a new pair of slippers, only to bring them back torn the next day. According to Emmanuel Cosquin, the *hypnotised* princess was acting innocently, since she was put in this state by fairies, not by some masculine character who would not be at all innocent, a son of the gods, an evil Pari, demon or dragon.[23]

According to Freud, this questionable innocence often hides erotic dreams. What, then, are the images that hide guilt? How does the tale reconcile the princess's amorous flights with her ordinary life? An Indian version might give us the answer. In India, the princess dances with a thousand Paris[24] before Indra, the king of the skies. She flies through the air all the way "to the Milky Way"; she does not walk to the world of the fairies, as in Greece.[25] The more explicit Indian version of the tale depicts the bed, sleep and the dream.

The Perfumer's Daughter[26]

A young prince marries a perfumer's daughter, who is really a Pari, and who agrees to marry him on two conditions: that he never lift any of her seven veils, and that she return each night to her father's house.

A fakir gives the prince a ring that renders him invisible and allows him to follow the princess into her father's house one night. There, he sees her take off her seven veils and start to adorn herself as if she was going to meet a lover. She then sits down on a bed, and the invisible prince seats himself next to her. She begins to sing and the bed rises and flies in the air. First, it sets itself down on a stream to let a fairy embark, and later another fairy who rises from a well joins them on the bed. To both of them the princess says: "Come quickly, for the night passes and the king awaits us."

The first fairy brought fruit, and the second cakes, but they all quickly disappeared, eaten by the invisible prince. The princess explained this to herself as best she could. As she sang, the bed rose higher and higher, all the way to the Milky Way, until it arrived at a great palace. In a great hall, on his throne of jewels, sat Raja Indra, the king of the skies. When the princess entered, he scolded her for arriving late, addressing her as "Fairy of the diamonds". The princess and her companions took their places among the thousand fairies gathered there to dance before King Indra. When the dancing ceased, the flying bed, with the three Paris and the invisible prince took them back down to the Earth.

The next day, when the princess arrived at the palace having come from the perfumer's house, she found the prince lying on a sofa, asleep. She

> *awoke him and he scolded her for having interrupted a charming dream. She insisted on knowing what the pleasant dream had been. He then recounted everything he had seen the previous night, as if it had been his dream. As he was telling the story, the princess removed another and another of her veils, until only one was left. Finally, the prince was heedless enough to talk about the ring the fakir had given him, although he had promised not to reveal this. And when the princess removed her last veil, as the prince asked, she rose up in the air and flew away.*

Here, the heroine never closes off the passage to the supernatural space of fairies while she lives in the world of humans. She does not give up the mysterious side of her nature, despite her marriage to the prince. Indeed, she returns to sleep in her father's house every night, and in her sleep she recovers her psychical roots and the strength to fly away to join her exotic sisters.

This brings to mind certain neuroses described by Freud, which take us back to earlier phases of affective and functional life (Freud, 1915, *Thoughts for the Times on War and Death)*: "Since we have learnt to interpret even absurd and confused dreams, we know that whenever we go to sleep we throw off our hard-won morality like a garment, and put it on again next morning."[27]

In the story presented above, the fairies take on a different role when they change their attire: as soon as they remove their veils they are transformed into exotic women or dutiful spouses. When the princess falls asleep in her magical bed, she can rise into the sky or descend into hell (in some versions of the tale, her demonic tendencies are revealed when she falls in love with crafty demons who kill all her suitors).

The prince is required to cure her of her "illness", to kill these demons and to rid her body of the serpents dwelling in it. But she prefers to remain free, until the prince awakens her by killing her lover and revealing her secret to the king and the whole of society. She then gives in to him and, after promising to give up her double nature and forget the dream space she visited every night, she marries him.

Awakening is painful; the dream, the fulfilment of unconscious desire, cannot be shared with another – it belongs solely to the dreamer. In other words, it belongs to one who needs no magic wand, no invisibility cap or enchanted rod to enter the imaginary space of the other. In the Indian version of the tale, the heroine is ready to recognise the hero as part of her dream, and to fall in love with him. But she leaves him as soon as she learns that he followed her into the skies thanks to a magic ring. She removes her last veil and disappears into the air, free to obey her exotic nature unfettered.

Of course, other interpretations of the tale are possible. But the poetic image of the young girl flying off into the sky to join in the amorous dance of the fairies remains an archaic dream image that the folktale has captured.

The fairy tale with its sleeping heroine might not have a great deal in common with the fairy tale in its relation to the dream, except for the supra-individual sources of these typical images originating in the deepest and most enduring essence of humanity.

In the Afterword of his book *The Paradox of Sleep: The Story of Dreaming*, neurophysicist Michel Jouvet, who studied paradoxical sleep (the stage when dreaming occurs[28]), describes a dream scene drawn in the Lascaux caves about 18,000 years ago: a sleeping man with an erection is shown beside a bird taking flight, a broken spear and a wounded bison.[29]

> This rock drawing [. . .] associates [. . .] a man lying on his back, in erection, [. . .] with a bird. [. . .] 20,000 years ago, our ancestors must have noticed this physical manifestation during the dream [. . .] (the erection of the penis is present during the dream phase of sleep). How can we explain the marvelous and illogical imagery in a dream of flying or levitation without invoking the concept of spirit or soul? They leave the body like a bird to travel through time and space: either in the past – (by means of recollections of the previous day), or in the future (by means of premonitory dreams).

Notes

1 A. Angelopoulos, "Conte oral et représentation de l'impensable", in P. Chemla (Ed.), *Transmettre*, Érès, 2016, pp. 219–226.
2 H. C. Andersen, *The Little Match Girl*, Dial Books, 2002.
3 Symposium of *Ateliers de Psychanalyse*, "Play and the Role of the Narrative in Psychoanalysis – Literary Fiction and Works of Art", December, 3 and 4, 2011.
4 P. Delaunay, *Les quatre transferts*, Fédération des Ateliers de Psychanalyse, 2012.
5 S. Freud and J. Breuer, *Studies on Hysteria*, Penguin Books, 2004.
6 S. Freud, *An Outline of Psycho-Analysis* (1940), Penguin Classics, 2003.
7 P. Delaunay, *Les quatre transferts*, Fédération des Ateliers de Psychanalyse, 2012.
8 A. Angelopoulos, "Le Rêve typique et le conte", *Cahiers de littérature orale*, 51, 2002.
9 S. Freud, (1900–1901) *The Interpretation of Dreams*, SE 4–5, Hogarth.
10 S. Freud (1900–1901), *The Interpretation of Dreams*, SE 4–5, Hogarth.
11 As was the case for symbolic interpretation in classical antiquity.
12 S. Freud (1900–1901), *The Interpretation of Dreams*, SE 4–5, Hogarth, pp. 364–365.
13 "It is only in our childhood that we are seen in inadequate clothing both by members of our family and by strangers [. . .]; and it is only then that we feel no shame at our nakedness. [. . .] When we look back at this unashamed period of childhood it seems to us a Paradise; and Paradise itself is no more than a group phantasy of the childhood of the individual. [. . .] But we can regain this Paradise every night in our dreams." S. Freud (1900–1901), *The Interpretation of Dreams*, SE 4–5, Hogarth, pp. 262–263.
14 A. Aarne and S. Thompson, *The Types of Folktales. A Classification and Bibliography*, FF Communications, No. 184, Academia Scientiarum Fennica, 1961.
15 S. Thompson, *Motif-Index of Folk Literature: A Classification of Narrative Elements in Folktales, Ballads, Myths, Fables, Medieval Romances, Exempla, Fabliaux, Jest-Books and Local Legends* (6 volumes), Indiana University Press, 1975.
16 N. Belmont, "L'enfant cuit", in "Le Motif en sciences humaines", *Ethnologie Française*, Vol. 25, Armand Colin, 1995, pp. 180–186.

17 Similarly, an identical motif can be found in different folktales, myths or rumours.
18 S. Freud (1900–1901), *The Interpretation of Dreams*, SE 4–5, Hogarth, p. 271.
19 In the international classification, this tale, *The Maiden Who Seeks Her Brothers*, is number AT 451.
20 S. Freud (1900–1901), *The Interpretation of Dreams*, SE 4–5, Hogarth, p. 271.
21 S. Freud (1900–1901), *The Interpretation of Dreams*, SE 4–5, Hogarth, p. 290.
22 Version published in Greek by A. Kambouroglou in A. Angelopoulos and A. Brouskou, *Descriptive Catalogue of Greek Fairy Tales: Types and Versions*, AT 300–499, I.A.E.N., F.N.R.S. (in Greek), 1999, pp. 142–153. Also used by Emmanuel Cosquin in, *Les Contes indiens et l'Occident*, Edouard Champion, 1922, pp. 381–391.
23 E. Cosquin, *Les Contes indiens et l'Occident*, Edouard Champion, 1922, p. 388.
24 The word Pari or Peri (of Persian origin) refers to a spirit or fairy in many Oriental myths and tales.
25 A. Angelopoulos and A. Brouskou, *Descriptive Catalogue of Greek Fairy Tales: Types and Versions*, AT 300–499, I.A.E.N., F.N.R.S. (in Greek), 1999, pp. 142–153.
26 M. Thornhill, *Indian Fairy Tales*, Forgotten Books, 2018.
27 S. Freud (1915), *Thoughts for the Times on War and Death*, SE 14, Hogarth, p. 286.
28 Also called "rapid eye movement" or REM sleep.
29 M. Jouvet, *The Paradox of Sleep: The Story of Dreaming*, MIT Press, 2001, Figure, p. 33.

Chapter VIII

The Riddle Tale

The riddle tales that follow portray different types of interactions between the characters. There can be either three characters, one of whom is supernatural and often religious, charged with answering questions of a metaphysical nature ("Master Chickpea"); or two characters for whom the riddle can provide a crucial means of allowing love to triumph, protecting it from destructive forces (*Turandot*, "The Lazy Man and the Riddle", "Out-riddling the Judge").

MASTER CHICKPEA

Once upon a time there was a widow who had a son. They were so poor that they had nothing but the water in their jug. The widow worked as a servant to raise her son. When he grew up, he tried to think of an occupation that would allow him to provide for their needs. One day, when he was lost in thought, sad that he had not found work, as he sat looking at the ground, he spotted a chickpea. He picked it up and asked his mother: "Mother, if I plant this chickpea, how many will I harvest?"

- A handful, my son.
- And if I plant that handful, how many will I harvest?
- A pailful, my son.
- And if I plant that pailful, how many will I harvest?
- Twenty pailfuls, my son.
- And if I plant those twenty pailfuls, how many will I harvest?
- Two hundred pailfuls, my son.

They went on like this until they arrived at a million okas of chickpeas. The son was awake all night, undecided and lost in thought. He held the chickpea tightly in his hand. He was asking himself where he might find a good place to store all those millions of chickpeas he would harvest.

DOI: 10.4324/9781032674230-9

At dawn, he decided he must first choose the best storage shed, and plant the chickpea afterwards. This thought quieted his mind and he fell asleep.

The next day he woke early and told his mother that he had something to do in the city and that she must not worry, for he might be gone a whole month taking care of this matter. His mother gave him her blessing and he set off. In the city, he asked the town crier to make this announcement: "Let anyone who has a large storage shed, big enough to store a million okas of chickpeas, make himself known." But he found no such person and went to another city; he asked the town crier to make the same announcement, but he had no better luck. No storage shed was big enough. He went to a distant city, and on to several others, farther and farther away. He came to be known in the entire region and people gave him the nickname Master Chickpea.

Finally, he arrived in a city where the town crier made the same announcement and where, when the king heard of it, he invited the young man to come to the palace. The king wanted to meet him and speak to him about the storage shed. Master Chickpea went to the palace, his heart beating wildly, for he feared that the king would discover his secret: that all he had was one chickpea. He was given a splendid reception. He found himself at table with the king's council of twelve wise men. They had been asked to help the esteemed guest, wealthy Master Chickpea, to find what he needed. The twelve wise men concluded that several sheds in a row had to be built, because it was impossible to find a building big enough to store such a great quantity of peas. Master Chickpea was invited to stay at the palace and supervise the progression of the work. When the twelve wise men left, the king ordered his servants to prepare a bed of feathers and silky cotton for his guest, so that he may sleep in the greatest comfort, as he was no doubt used to doing.

The servants did the best they could. But during the night, the chickpea fell out of the Master's hand several times. So he kept tossing and turning, afraid that he would lose it. He fell asleep and woke up constantly to make sure he had the chickpea in his hand. The king was keeping an eye on all this from afar. He was displeased, for he saw that his guest was not sleeping comfortably. The next morning, he scolded the servants, who placed more mattresses on the bed the next night. Now, the chickpea was firmly held in place between the two mattresses. Each time Master Chickpea woke up, he found it at once and fell asleep again, reassured. The king was satisfied.

A few days later, the king, who held his guest in great esteem, offered him the hand of his daughter in marriage. This was unexpected. Master Chickpea did not want to offend the king or his daughter. He answered with great deference: "May the will of God be done." At the same time, he never let the chickpea out of his sight, for what would happen if he were to lose it? What would be stored in the warehouses that were being built in such great haste?

Months passed and one day the king asked Master Chickpea to show him his plantations and to take him to meet his mother. This would also be an opportunity for his son-in-law to inspect his fields and the work of his labourers.

When he heard this, he was truck with terror. But he could not refuse. Therefore, he told the king to prepare for the journey, so that they could set out at the right time. The king organised a great expedition and, at last, the day of their departure arrived. They set out, accompanied by soldiers of the royal army, musicians, knights and all of the princess's attendants. Master Chickpea said that he must ride ahead of them, for he wanted to arrive first to check on the state of his crops.

They had covered a great distance advancing this way, Master Chickpea ahead, with the king and his army following behind, when they came to a great prairie full of grazing cattle – thousands of oxen and calves. Arriving before all the others, Master Chickpea shouted, speaking to the cowherds: "Do you see this procession coming towards you?"

- Yes.
- It is the king and his attendants. If he asks you who owns these animals, you must answer: "Master Chickpea", if you want to keep your heads.
- Praise the Lord for sending you to warn us! How could we have thought of such an answer? We would have died and been scattered about, like the garments of a dead man.

The king's convoy was approaching. The king asked the cowherds who owned the cattle. "Master Chickpea", they answered. Happy to see for himself what a wealthy man his daughter was marrying, the king ordered his musicians to play merrily.

Master Chickpea was still ahead of the procession when he came to a great prairie full of sheep as far as the eye could see. He shouted to the shepherds:

- Do you see this army coming towards you? It's the king and his attendants. If he asks you who these sheep belong to, you must answer: "to Master Chickpea", if you want to keep your heads.
- May the Lord bless you and keep you. May He keep you out of harm's way, as you have just done for us!

Soon, the king arrived. He admired the beauty of the plump sheep. He asked the shepherds who they belonged to. "To Master Chickpea, Your Majesty." Very happy to hear this, the king asked for more music, songs and rejoicing.

Master Chickpea stayed ahead of the procession as they went on, until he came to another prairie full of fowl – hens, ducks and geese – thousands of fowl of all sorts. He shouted to the chicken herders: "Do you see the army coming down the hill? It's the king and his attendants. If he asks you who owns these fowl, you must answer: 'Master Chickpea', if you want to keep your heads." And this is what they did.

They went on and saw lush fields and valleys of cotton, wheat and green beans. Each time, the young man warned the farm labourers to tell the king that Master Chickpea owned all these bountiful croplands.

Finally, they came to a huge palace, where the young man ordered the servants to say that the palace was his. He ordered them to take great care of His Majesty and all the royal company. The servants told him that the palace belonged to an ogre, who also owned all the fields and livestock he had seen on his way there. The ogre was a stone-hearted monster who devoured his servants on a whim. He would then bring other servants to the palace, perpetrate his cruel acts on them and then replace them with yet more servants.

– Pray the Lord to help us, for we are all in danger of being eaten, along with the procession that will be here soon, through no fault of our own!

Soon, the king arrived at the palace. The servants who greeted him said that they were all in the service of Master Chickpea. Delighted, the king and his attendants savoured the dishes set before them and the rejoicing began. As for Master Chickpea, he set out alone on the road that he was told the ogre took to come to the palace. He waited on the roadside to confront him.

At nightfall, the ogre appeared; he was ten feet tall. Master Chickpea rose, stood before him and told him his whole story: how he found the chickpea, how, without wanting to, he had led all these people to disaster, how he dreaded the fate that awaited them, and many other things.

The ogre said: "Go to the palace and manage my affairs in your own name. At midnight, go out and sit down there, by the chimney hood. You will then hear me speak thirteen words; if you give the right reply to each one, everything I possess will be yours." The ogre left, taking a side path. He did not go to the palace that night. Master Chickpea went inside and joined in the festivities. The king kept asking him: "My dear son-in-law, how is it that you were able to stay with me so long, when you had to see to the management of all your domains?"

At midnight, he left the others and went to sit under the chimney hood to wait for the ogre who would ask him to solve his riddles. But he was so sad and so tired that he fell asleep.

Soon, the ogre arrived and shouted: "Master Chickpea, do you hear me?"
But instead of Master Chickpea, it was an old man[1] who answered:
"I hear you."

- One, said the ogre.
- The Lord is one, the old man answered.
- Two, said the ogre.
- The ox has two horns and the Lord is one, the old man answered.
- Three, said the ogre.
- The Holy Trinity is composed of three hypostases, the ox has two horns and the Lord is one, the old man answered.
- Four, said the ogre.
- The olive tree has four roots, the Holy Trinity is composed of three hypostases, the ox has two horns and the Lord is one, the old man answered.
- Five, said the ogre.
- The hand has five fingers, the olive tree has four roots, the Holy Trinity is made up of three hypostases, the ox has two horns and the Lord is one, the old man replied.
- Six, said the ogre.
- There are six Pleiades we can see, the hand has five fingers, the olive tree has four roots, the Holy Trinity is composed of three hypostases, the ox has two horns and the Lord is one, the old man answered.
- Seven, said the ogre.
- Seven virgins dance in heaven, there are six Pleiades, the hand has five fingers, the olive tree has four roots, the Holy Trinity is composed of three hypostases, the ox has two horns and the Lord is one, the old man answered.
- Eight, said the ogre.
- The octopus has eight tentacles, seven virgins dance in heaven, there are six Pleiades, the hand has five fingers, the olive tree has four roots, the Holy Trinity is composed of three hypostases, the ox has two horns and the Lord is one, the old man replied.
- Nine, said the ogre.
- Nine months for a baby, eight tentacles of the octopus, seven virgins who dance in heaven, the six Pleiades, five fingers of the hand, the four roots of the olive tree, the Holy Trinity composed of three hypostases, the two horns of the ox and the Lord is one, the old man answered.
- Ten, said the ogre.
- The sow has ten teats, nine months for the baby to be born, eight tentacles of the octopus, seven virgins who dance in heaven, the six Pleiades, five fingers of the hand, the four roots of the olive tree, the Holy Trinity with three hypostases, the two horns of the ox and the Lord is one, the old man replied.
- Eleven, said the ogre.

– Eleven months for the colt to be born, the ten teats of the sow, nine months for a baby, the eight tentacles of the octopus, seven virgins who dance in heaven, six Pleiades, five fingers of the hand, the four roots of the olive tree, the Holy Trinity with three hypostases, the two horns of the ox and the Lord is one, the old man answered.
– Twelve, said the ogre.
– The year has twelve months, the colt is born in eleven months, the sow has ten teats, nine months for a baby to be born, eight tentacles of the octopus, seven virgins dance in heaven, there are six Pleiades, the hand has five fingers, four roots has the olive tree, the Holy Trinity has three hypostases, the ox has two horns and the Lord is one, the old man replied.
– Thirteen, said the ogre.
– The year has thirteen moons, it has twelve months, the colt is born in eleven months, the sow has ten teats, the baby is born in nine months, the octopus has eight tentacles, seven virgins dance in heaven, there are six Pleiades, the hand has five fingers, the olive tree has four roots, the Holy Trinity has three hypostases, the ox has two horns and the Lord is one, the old man answered.

And the ogre turned into a lump of salt.

Master Chickpea was still slumped over on the chair, and stayed asleep all night. The light of dawn woke him, and he thought: "My goodness, what have I done? I fell asleep and the ogre must have eaten half of these poor people I brought with me to the palace!"

He came out of the chimney and, to his great surprise, he heard music, singing and dancing still going on. He asked the servants what happened while he was gone. He was told that he had answered all the questions perfectly and that they – the servants – could see the ogre from afar foaming at the mouth after each right answer.

Master Chickpea realised that someone else had given the right answers to the riddles. He crossed himself and told the servants that while he slept an old man had saved him.

Master Chickpea became the sovereign ruler of the ogre's domains.

They all lived happily ever after, and we did even better.

Sources

"Polyrevithas", folktale well-known in Greece, especially the versions containing riddles.

   Version collected in Archanes, Crete.

CGMF 545D*, *Polyrevithas* [The Chick-pea King].

ATU 545D*, *The Pea King*.

ATU 812, *The Devil's Riddle*.

THE LAZY MAN AND THE RIDDLE

Once upon a time there was a woman who had a very lazy son. She turned him out of the house, saying: "Go out and earn a living!" She gave him a pita with a fish in it, for the road. She also gave him a little dog named Morfula to keep him company.

The boy set off on his journey. After a time, he stopped to eat at the side of the road. He opened his food pack, cut a slice of pita and was about to swallow it. But it was God's will that he gave a bite of it to his little dog first. As soon as she swallowed it, she died. Seeing this, the young man understood that this was the fate his mother had intended for him.

Just then, an eagle appeared overhead. It swept down to devour the dead dog. The boy shot arrows at it to chase it away. But the eagle flew away with its prey; the arrows had hit a cow grazing in a prairie. The boy wanted to eat the cow, for he was very hungry. He approached the dead cow to cut it up, but he saw a little calf spring from its belly and start to saunter gaily on the grass. The boy cut the cow into pieces and carved out cutlets for his meal. Since he had no fire on which to roast them, he looked around and saw a little church. Inside, he found books, which he burned to make a fire and cook the cutlets. After he ate, he wanted to drink. But there was no fountain in sight. He took the holy-water stoup and drank from it.

After that, he continued on his way. On the road, he came across a herd of goats coming down the mountain. But just as they were crossing a bridge, the river below turned into a raging torrent that swept them all away and destroyed the bridge.

The young man continued on. After a while, he came to the palace. Earlier, the king had announced to his people: "The man who asks me a riddle that I cannot solve, and that is not taken from a book, shall marry my daughter. But if he found the riddle in a book, he shall have his head cut off."

The lazy young man went to the palace dressed in rags and barefoot.

– What do you want?
– I want to ask the king a riddle.

Everyone at the palace burst out laughing. But the king heard what was said and ordered his servants to bring the stranger in. The young man recited his riddle, which was in fact the story of the journey that had brought him there:

The pita killed Morfula
A bird came and snatched Morfula!
I aimed at what I saw and hit what I didn't see.
I killed a being born
And freed a being unborn!
I ate meat roasted on the scriptures.

I drank water
Not from the Earth or the sky.
The frail one that moves prevails over the sturdy one that stays in place.

Lo and behold, the riddle did not come from a book! Everyone praised the young man. The king gave him his daughter for a wife, and this is how our story ends.

Sources

"O oknos kai to ainigma" [The Lazy Man's Riddle], D. S. Loukatos, 1957. Version originating in Adramyti, Asia Minor. Collected in 1940 in Mytilène by D. S. Loukatos.
Source: A refugee.
ATU 851, *The Princess Who Cannot Solve the Riddle*.

The Figuration of the Enigma[2]

Anna Angelopoulos

Let us imagine a child ready to go to sleep at night. Starting to drift off dreamily, he asks to be held and to hear a story. He is already held captive in the zone of slumber that has taken over the entire space. He lets himself be lulled by strange images and sounds impossible to define – voices of adults talking and laughing in the next room, noises coming from the neighbours, from outside, or the call of birds gathering on tree branches at dusk.

The child feels himself sinking into sleep – the half-brother of death[3] – and asks to be rocked, comforted. He fears separation, he fears being swallowed up in the void of the unknown. But, at the same time, this is also the sphere of dreams. The story and the lullaby reside there as well, as an antidote to fear. I believe that this is the true connection between dream and folktale, woven on the rim of this well, on the threshold of sleep.

Geza Roheim calls this sphere of drowsiness a "maternal well of sleep".[4] The designation is poetic and optimistic, if we hear it as vouching for salutary maternal protection in the face of these two inseparable and menacing brothers, Hypnos and Thanatos. Roheim also thinks that the first fairy tales were individual dreams, told, retold and passed on collectively, becoming a common good. Despite their different origins,[5] the dream and the story are connected through the enigmatic images they harvest from the raw material of the psyche. These are nocturnal creations. To deal with the unimaginable depth of the well of sleep, with what primal repression has submerged, figurations are created: enigmatic images so strange that they are sometimes unfathomable. They lead into another dimension of sense, into an imaginary play space not unlike popular children's games such as riddles, puzzles, guessing games or charades. In truth, behind the veil of mystery on which these language and image games rely in their quest for meaning, we also find the cryptic words of ancient oracles and sanctuaries.

But how can we describe the riddle common to all these types of creations? Does the riddle have a shape of its own? The Greek word αίνιγμα (enigma) contains "aïnos", meaning "fable", "insinuation" or "oral tale" – hard to understand and predict.

Let us not forget that Freud loved enigmas. His greatest contribution in "The Psychopathology of Everyday Life"[6] was to replace *metaphysics* (mystery, prophecies, superstition) with his *metapsychology*, which allowed him to theorise about the functioning of the psychic apparatus rooted in the unconscious. His key concept was "the riddle", which only the psychoanalytic method can solve, through transference. Years later, in 1923,[7] speaking of his treatment of Dora, when he failed[8] to grasp the importance of the young girl's feelings of love for a woman, Freud noted: "I ought to have attacked this riddle and looked for the motive of such an extraordinary piece of repression."[9]

Was it Freud's passion for riddles that prompted him to place Oedipus at the centre of his theory of neurosis? Oedipus found the answer to the riddle of the Sphinx to save Thebes from the plague. It was before he knew anything about his fate. But the riddle was essential. And it was intended for him. How did he find the answer? In fact, he heard the answer in his own name, for *oida* in *Oedipus* means "I know" in Greek. A Greek speaker also hears *oedi* (oedema) and *pous* (foot) in Oedipous,[10] a reference to the swollen, wounded and bound feet of the infant left exposed on a hilltop. Therefore, when the Sphinx poses his riddle, with its numeration of feet, as J.-P. Vernant[11] points out: "tetrapous" (four feet) in the morning, "dipous" (two feet) at noon, and "tripous" (three feet) at night, Oedipus hears his own description, recognises his own feet, and names himself *Anthropos*. It is the right answer.

Oedi-pous not only solves the riddle, but he puts together the image of his fragmented body, creating a whole entity, "man". He is the key to solving the riddle. But his own riddle is not solved, for the first enigma conceals a second. He lives in a universe of confusion, chaos and incompatibility, he does not know who he is or what tragic destiny awaits him. Indeed, this notion of incompatibility is part of Aristotle's definition of the riddle, in his *Politics*,[12] where he says that the riddle uses "ornamental" words, and has the power "to bring together strange, contradictory elements" by metaphorical means.

Because its concealed content awaits liberation, the riddle always introduces a third element, a contest between two adversaries, a life-and-death struggle. The call to take part in the sacred game of crucial questions and answers draws its power from the folkloric roots of human life. As is the case with Oedipus, in oral folktales the answer to the riddle often reveals the name of the one who asks or the one who answers.

Some classic authors consider the Sphinx *a weaver of riddles* who makes picture puzzles on a loom, rather than a prophet delivering obscure pronouncements. Whether expressed in symbolic language or prophetic words, the riddle always speaks in metaphors. A good example would be the Sphinx's second, less famous riddle, about two sisters: one gives birth to the other who, in turn, gives birth to the first. The answer is day and night.

The riddle expressed in words reminds me of a patient who had been looking for a foreign psychoanalyst who was certain not to speak her mother tongue. It was the condition she needed to be able to talk to someone. Her mother tongue was not a rare language, so she had been referred to a number of possible analysts, but she had eliminated them one by one. She said she felt outraged at the idea of "being understood by someone because he speaks the same language, outraged about such an assumption". So the analysis was conducted in our common adopted language, French. I had never spoken her mother tongue, but since I was a "foreigner", I could create another space between us, a space of closeness and distance at the same time, a common space of reverie and possible divination, where her inaccessible unconscious desire could be heard. I was reminded of Tosquelles, who said that it benefitted the transference for patients to make an effort to understand the Catalan language[13] he spoke. As for my patient, I understood that, for her, the riddle was in the language, and that the language had to remain a riddle.

This way of working together led us back to childhood, to a time when we were learning the language of adults by imitating them, without understanding what they said; we were exerting a magical power of divination on the speech of the other, an enterprise necessary for psychic survival. This childhood period also abounds with comical misunderstandings, particularly when it comes to words with a double meaning.

Thus, children can shock adults by using obscene expressions they don't understand, such as the question of a little boy to his mother, when he refused to go to bed: "Are you going to break my balls?" For the child, this adult expression referring to male genitals had only to do with a threat to his toys. When we were children, it took us time to learn to guess, in the adults' conversation, the double meaning of certain "dirty" words, so as to avoid being scolded.

In my work, the magic of divination was also confirmed by a ten-year-old patient. He was a handsome boy with a sharp and penetrating gaze, whose speech was incomprehensible – a "special language", I called it, to make him laugh, as he strung words in a row, mumbling with a serious air but granting me a smile. One day, he told me: "My dream is to invent a language that I am the only one to speak! No one else would understand it, I would share it with no one!" I told him: "It might be possible, it could be invented . . . and it would really be very original!" We liked each other. I had agreed not to understand his confusing words, and just play with him. "And what good is talking? It makes you unhappy, like my parents are, because they don't understand each other. I, at least, won't take the risk. Whoever loves me will understand me!" I accepted his argument.

Our alliance was sealed the day he asked me: "Do you want me to invent a language for the two of us? But we won't tell anyone. Only the two of us will know." The transference had been established and there could have been no better metaphorical expression of his "concrete utopia". He wanted us to create together a secret language for two, a transferential riddle. I was hearing this boy from an imaginary position in my past, a time when being a stranger was valuable to me in my attempt to examine human relations.

The Infantile and Love

My young patient had said "Whoever loves me will understand me", to cover over his disappointment at not being loved and understood as he would have wished. We all know that this disappointment is at the root of many unceasing complaints, on the couch and elsewhere – complaints about not being loved as one would wish.

In certain folktales, a cruel princess asks her suitors riddles that are impossible to solve, in order to marry the one who will finally understand her. It is in this expectation, hidden in the riddle to be solved, that the one poorly loved in infancy places his hopes when the romantic encounter takes place.

Now let us look at a minor hero of the folktale, who would have been considered psychotic today. This story belongs to the wide category of "Foolish John" folktales, whose hero is a young simpleton mocked by the narrator for his foolishness. See the story "The Lazy Man and the Riddle",[14] at the beginning of this chapter.

The hero's riddle went as follows:

The pita killed Morfula
A bird came and snatched Morfula!
I aimed at what I saw and hit what I didn't see.
I killed a being born
And freed a being unborn!
I ate meat roasted on the scriptures.
I drank water
Not from the Earth or the sky.
The frail one that moves prevails over the sturdy one that stays in place.

What becomes clear is that the formulation of the riddle occurs far from the maternal sphere, as the fate of the hero unfolds – an unknown fate discovered little by little. This formulation takes its place in the tradition of ancient riddle tales, which spoke of travel adventures.

But what is enigmatic in these adventures, and why are these stories so popular? They describe extreme situations, on the edges of death and madness.

Indeed, our hero experienced one catastrophe after another: his mother tried to kill him; his little dog was poisoned, saving him; he himself killed something without intending to; he saw an unborn creature emerge from a corpse; he was famished and had to violate the sacred space of the church; he survived the collapse of the bridge that was the border of the world known to him, so that turning back became impossible. He composed his riddle as a survivor of extreme situations. He is now a man, no longer a foolish boy, since his life has been shaped into a riddle. Gisela Pankow[15] would have called it "dynamic structuration".

It is obvious that in this folktale the riddle is not there to be solved, but to become an endowment of the hero. Like all stories about survivors of extreme catastrophes, the tale is unbelievable, it seems mad and incomprehensible, even delusional. Of course, no one can solve the riddle with its sacred quality, since its content is unimaginable.

The Princess

But what about the princess? In stories where marriage is connected to a riddle, the princess is always silent and solemn, resembling a figure of death.[16] The young hero who wants to approach her is often asked to open a great armoured door, to reach such a *femme fatale*. The princess is described as being proud, intelligent and convinced that she possesses the fatal riddle, like the Sphinx. Her virginal body serves as a shield, akin to that of certain goddesses of Antiquity such as Athena or Artemis the huntress (whose Roman name is Diana). These princesses are out of men's reach, and if any man chances to see them naked, he is severely punished. This is what happened to Actaeon, the son of Apollo, who was turned into a deer by Artemis, and torn to pieces by his own dogs. The folktale has clearly kept the trace of this unthinkable deified virginal body, forever closed, illustrated by the metaphor of the riddle, when in fact the key to the solution is access to the princess and her body.

In these folktales, the riddle brings about change. It acts as the door that opens onto unspoken sexuality, indicated by the metonymy of marriage. The riddle opens the way towards the other, even as it blocks his access. It is a merciless struggle, to the death.

But what has turned the princess to stone? It could be an old trauma resembling the tale Puccini invented in his opera *Turandot*, which has become a general designation for stories about cruel princesses. Turandot is the princess who beheads her suitors. She surrounds the palace with stakes holding the heads of those who failed to solve her riddles. Prince Calaf solves the riddles because he hears her tell of a trauma in her lineage: her ancestor, the empress, had been captured and raped.

Another source of the princess's cruelty could lie in incestuous phantasy. In some versions, the father does not want his daughter to marry. Or the girl's attachment to her father stops her from leaving him. Incestuous phantasy is at work in the plot of numerous popular tales about princesses who never married or were forced to marry.

Let me illustrate with a folktale from the Menton region.

Once upon a time, there was a king who fell in love with his daughter. So they went to a distant country where it was possible for them to marry. The young woman became pregnant, but she died before giving birth to the child, who was brought into the world by cutting her belly open. She was buried under the palace in a copper chest. When the child grew up, he looked for his mother's body and found it. He removed the skin from the hands and used it to make gloves. Then he found a horse born in circumstances resembling his own birth, and he set off on his adventures.

He arrived in a foreign country, introduced himself at the Court and challenged one and all to solve this riddle: "I was not born, and neither was my horse; I am the son of my father's daughter and I wear my mother's hands." The princess at the palace promised to give him the answer the next day. She disguised herself as a man and followed the stranger to his inn. There, she

> befriended him and he told her his story without suspecting anything. They went to bed, putting their shirts under the pillow. She woke at dawn and left but forgot her shirt. When he awoke and wanted to put on his shirt, he found a woman's shirt as well as his own, and he understood he had been tricked. He went to the palace and, when the princess pretended that she had solved the riddle, he showed all those present her shirt, revealing her deception. She was forced to consent to marry him.[17]

But it must be noted that in other versions of the story the young girl is able to escape from her suitor forever.

In this story, the hero desiring to marry the princess constructs his riddle based on the incestuous trauma suffered by his dead mother. Being a son of incest allows him to win the showdown with the princess, and to take her away from her father.

The riddle of the "lazy man" brings us face to face with the unimaginable catastrophe suffered by the hero, whereas in the riddle involving incest, what stands out is the monstrous element.

The riddle's blind spot consists of our resistance to accept the inhuman and the monstrous as part of the human. What, then, defines the Anthropos? "If This Is a Man": Primo Levi's question remains open.[18]

And What of Institutions?

An interesting aspect of riddle stories concerns collectivities and institutions. Are we not accustomed to saying "the institution of marriage"? The traditional societies in which these stories are set are built around the authority of the father, about whom Émile Benveniste[19] says that he disposes of his daughter as he does of his other goods. There is no room in this for individual freedom and desire. Marriage, truly an institution, consecrates the heroes' successes in their endeavours and promotes an image of ideal love, of eternal and enduring happiness. This phantasy is still alive and well, as we have seen recently, when the royal wedding in England, 2018, kept the eyes of millions of people glued to their screens.

The riddle about marriage introduces a subjective element in the institution, modelled on the "whoever loves me will understand me" we formulated earlier. The riddle brings flexibility to the established social order and has greater power than one would suspect. It is a creation of the imagination, a knot tied in the fabric of language, and has a subversive dimension. I would even venture to say that the riddle disturbs the symbolic aspect of the institution of marriage.

Even the institution of justice can be shaken by an enigma, because a man sentenced to death can obtain a pardon if the judge cannot solve the riddle this man composes. For instance, a husband with the rope around his neck saw his pregnant wife approaching the scaffold on a pregnant donkey. He composed this riddle: *On this road I see approaching the sad, weeping woman with four heads, 48 nails and a rose on each cheek!* Mystified, the judge had to grant him a pardon.

How does this miracle come about? The man condemned to be hanged is merely describing his present situation, which the judge doesn't understand, because real life extends beyond legal matters. Thus, the judge is helpless and has no choice but to free the man. For a little while, the hero is triumphant: through the power of metaphor, he creates a reversal of the situation, opening a space of freedom. The judge is temporarily at his mercy. In other stories, the figure of authority is the king, the bishop or the chief of the army. The hero uses the power of imagination and language to overturn the effects of the power that holds him captive, as Castoriadis[20] reminds us: "Our mobility within language is limitless and allows us to question everything."

Returning to Freud and Oedipus, we can see the similarity between the device used in analytic treatment and the device of the riddle, in which two entities engage in a verbal confrontation that is sometimes an avowed life-and-death struggle: "I can't bear my life anymore." Is it not the case that transference advances from one riddle to another in search of unconscious desire?

What, then, can we conclude about the riddle? After considering Aristotle's definition, which asserts that the riddle makes use of ornaments and can bring together contradictory, we looked at several levels of its figuration and arrived at its blind spot, its unfathomable depth. The "ornamental elements" contribute to the pleasure of play, to the elucidation of the imaginary through the use of language. As for the contradictory elements, I see them as referring to the fundamental question of the human: where does it begin and where does it end?

The Riddle Tale in the Transference

Anna Angelopoulos

The patients who come to see us often hope to find some portion of themselves of which they are unaware, which escapes them. They trust us because we have made the journey before them. To quote Freud: "Nor, indeed, do we understand what the dreamer was trying to say to us, and he himself is equally in the dark."[21] The patient's utterances in analysis, produced and elaborated within the prescribed framework, are interspersed with silences, which include the unspoken and memory traces – in short, material originating in the primary process, whether or not it has been metabolised in the secondary process. What the patient puts into words can and at times must remain enigmatic and obscure for a long time – even indefinitely –, to allow for elaboration in the transference.

The enigmatic is present from the beginning, as Piera Aulagnier points out when speaking of the originary process (in *The Violence of Interpretation*), creating an effect of anticipation. "The mother's words and deeds always anticipate what the infant may know of them, if the offer precedes demand, if the breast is given before the mouth knows that it is up to it to respond, this gap is even more evident and more total in the register of meaning. The mother's flow of words is the bearer and creator of meaning, but that meaning only anticipates the infant's capacity to understand it and to act on it."[22] Thus, the initial creation of meaning remains enigmatic for the infant. The enigma is tied to the originary process, and this explains why, in the major myths on which psychoanalysis is founded, its resolution is a crucial question of life and death. We might remember that the Sphinx dies when Oedipus solves the riddle.

Here, I would like to recount an analysis in which meaning was created from a series of repeated enigmatic dreams a young woman had been having for years. Over time, they gradually changed in the transference, until they were finally resolved when I was able to associate in response to her distress, and most importantly, when I changed places with her in the transferential relation. Initially, we did not know what path to take in this analysis; we groped our way through incoherence until the highly suggestive figurations in these dreams formed a small enigmatic phrase, a fragment of narrative that found a resonance in me.

This young patient came to see me after she had almost died of a rare disease two years earlier. An insect sting had caused an immune system reaction, a serious and unexpected illness that weakened her considerably. She was hospitalised in intensive care and she was able to recover. Her convalescence lasted several months and, little by little, she regained her strength.

In the aftermath, she realised that she wanted to understand. In our first session, she told me that she liked the word "psychoanalysis" and often murmured it to herself.

When I first saw her, a pretty 28-year-old woman, I found she looked young for her age, so childlike that her appearance made me think: "She hasn't left the egg." In Greek, not yet born can be said in one word, the equivalent of "unborn". I sensed her unease, nothing was right for her – not her studies, or her love life, the country she came from, or the country she lived in.

Her dreams were filled with strong images, striking displays that were very different from the description of her orderly daily life. At first, the dreams portrayed all kinds of bathrooms: in her home, at school, in all the schools she ever attended. Sophie dreamed of vomit in the toilet bowls; she described everything in detail: her disgust, how she flushed the vomit down the toilet, vomit on the floor, dying young girls vomiting in the bathtub and leaving stains on it.

There was vomit where she did not expect it, and when she wore a pretty dress, drops of vomit splashed on it. She scrubbed them off as hard as she could, but the vomit reappeared in the next dream.

In another dream, she was going on a short trip with her parents and her aunt in a new car; riding through beautiful scenery, she was holding a large bag of vomit outside the open window, calmly, without letting it drop. She was thinking: "I have to be careful with the bag when I leave the car, so that my aunt doesn't notice that it's my mother's vomit."

Her mother had had several miscarriages before and after her birth. She had one every year, until she was forbidden by physicians to risk another pregnancy. Sophie was born by Caesarean section after nine months of uninterrupted bed rest, since the mother was forbidden to move. But she admitted that she had "caused their loss" because she was not careful, she moved around all the time, she did household chores. As a result, she lost several babies – especially a boy who haunted Sophie's dreams. In her adolescence, Sophie often addressed him in her daytime reveries. Being an only child, she had spent years in the company of this phantasy brother.

In Greek there is a very grim expression designating aborted babies or babies lost in a miscarriage. They are called "toilet babies" (flushed down the toilet). One day I told my patient that the cumbersome, shameful vomit she was disposing of in the toilet could be an image of her mother's miscarriages. She agreed at once, saying: "In that case, it's all over me, even when I don't think about it!" I started to understand more clearly the picture I had had of her when she first arrived and I saw her as a little one who "hasn't left the egg", who was unborn. I was better able to see the difficulty she had to be born, to have her own psychic space (in both senses of the term) at this stage of analysis.

Since she had been born, my patient had shared a room with her handicapped and feeble-minded grandmother, who was almost insensible. For years, the mother had spoon-fed them both, calling them jokingly her "two babies". Sophie also joked when she spoon-fed the grandmother. Once, when she must have been fed up, she purposely let her grandmother fall out of her wheelchair. Clearly, it was not the place of a child to feed the grandmother. The analysis progressed very slowly, but little by little, in the transference, the vomit-filled dream was replaced with an account of dreams about the blue sea, great expanses of blue sea she saw from afar with the man she loved. Indeed, in the meantime she had met a young man who was different from the destructive men she had known before. They were in love. They went to San Francisco together. When they returned, Sophie recounted a dream that was a little different. She was in a skyscraper with her beloved, looking at the blue sea, and she decided to go out. She tried to go down but there were no stairs and she kept slipping. She looked down and saw cement; the sea was stormy. She could not go back up because there were no stairs. She feared that she would drown trying to leave the building. Then she told herself: "Never mind! It's only a dream and my sweetheart is coming with me."

This sliding down towards the stormy sea, because of the absence of stairs, made me think that in this dream she was coming to life in the transference and in her actual life. I told her this and she asked: "Are the vomit dreams over now?" We are often asked this kind of question about the trustworthiness of therapeutic interpretation.

Soon afterwards, Sophie planned to get married. It would be a rebirth for her, the start of a new life, her own life. But once again her mother interfered. She announced that she had an important secret to reveal to Sophie, but only after her wedding.

This mystery created anxiety on the eve of Sophie's new life. What could it be? She started to have anxiety attacks; the vomit dreams returned insidiously. This time, she saw me wading in vomit. She constantly fought with her lover and had hysterics. Her mother's announcement of a revelation, she feared, was endangering her fragile coming into the world.

In my view, this foretold threat can be seen as a vital enigma, like those often found in myths and tales.

To come back to Sophie – for some reason, I did not share her fear. I did not imagine a possible crime or suicide – which had already occurred in her family –, nor did I anticipate the revelation of an adoption. Strangely, I felt I was on familiar ground. But I was affected by her regression, which reduced her to a helpless little creature again. I asked myself if the fact that she was born by Caesarean section after all those miscarriages, that is, without "travelling" from the uterus into the outside world, made her more vulnerable on the threshold of her marriage, which was propelling her into the world.

For the first time in our work together, I identified with the little being who is trying to be born. I felt the threat hovering over the birth – hers and mine – that we have brought about together. Inwardly, I protested against the omnipotence of the maternal hold, against the danger of the announced parental revelation, that caused Sophie to regress as she did. She had been seeing me for seven years and my counter-transference let me foresee the harmful effect of the enigmatic announcement.

Matters related to miscarriage are familiar to me from my childhood, when women changed their age on paper, especially after the war, because being younger gave them a better chance to find work or a husband, at a time when the official registers had been destroyed. In 1922, immigrants from Asia Minor – Sophie's family among them – arrived in Greece without papers, declared fictitious names and changed their ages. It was a common practice. It occurred to me that miscarriages are rare at 30 years old, but can happen more frequently after the age of 40. What if the secret was this, it was the mother's age that had prevented her from carrying her pregnancies to term? I thought this likely and told Sophie what I believed. And it proved to be right. What exactly was it, in the transference, that motivated my intervention intended to protect her? I believe it was my desire to prevent the return of the inseparable pairing of the psychic apparatus of the mother and that of the daughter, which had only recently been separated.

The analysis took a different course after this, because the ten extra years in age changed the perception of the tragic events constituting the transgenerational story of the family. For instance, the violent death of Sophie's maternal grandfather occurred when Sophie's mother was age twelve, not two. And the grandmother became a widow at a much older age. "Everything has to be done over," Sophie said.

In the end, I placed myself in the role of the older and wiser person who can speak of the feminine condition from experience. I took it upon myself to solve the maternal enigma, which I felt threatened Sophie's psychic life. This enigma was related to the elements in my counter-transference connected to what we could share regarding maternal miscarriages.

During the sessions, I often used free association to speak of riddle tales, and especially of one folktale whose enigma is built around the birth and the "non-birth" of a small animal brought into the world by Caesarean section. As any art form can, this folktale, "Out-riddling the Judge", provided images for my reverie throughout this delicate phase of Sophie's analysis. The tale follows here.

234 Greek Folktales and Psychoanalysis

OUT-RIDDLING THE JUDGE

Once upon a time there was a king who had an older brother. This brother had a daughter as lovely as an angel, intelligent and ingenious. One day, the devil took hold of the king's thoughts and made him believe that his brother wanted to kill him and take his place on the throne. Tormented by this idea, the king had his brother arrested. He told his soldiers: "Throw him into a dark cell, with no food or drink, no bread and no water. Let him starve." These were the king's orders, and this is what was done: the poor man was thrown into a dungeon so dark that he could not see his hand before him.

His daughter, seeing her father imprisoned without reason, suspected her uncle's bad intentions at once. She did all she could to learn more, and finally learned that the king had decided to let his brother starve to death in a dungeon. She ran to see her uncle, the king, fell at his feet and begged him to allow her to visit her father twice a day. The king granted her request, since it would not interfere with his plans. He warned his soldiers that they would have to search the girl carefully to make sure that she is not bringing food to her father. And he also ordered them to make a hole in the dungeon wall so that father and daughter could speak through the opening.

The young girl understood that she was the only one who could save her father's life. She went to the bath house, bathed and felt milk coming into her breasts. Then she went to the jail where her father was imprisoned. She placed her breast in the opening that had been made and asked her father to suckle. He did, and he continued to do this every day when she came to visit him. In this way, he did not need any other nourishment.

But the king started to wonder how his brother could survive for so long without food. He suspected his niece of performing some magic feat. So he ordered his soldiers not to allow the girl to visit her father under any circumstances.

Not knowing what to do, lost in thought, the young girl walked aimlessly, not caring where she went, until she found herself far from the city. She came upon a blacksmith struggling to cut open the corpse of a mare. "Good day, friend," she greeted him. "What is it you are doing?" "Woe is me, my pretty one. I am trying to pull out the colt that my poor mare was carrying in her womb. I am very poor, you see, so I will try to sell the hide of this mare and to save the colt she was about to have. And then I might be able to buy another horse."

— Will the colt survive? she asked in a concerned tone.
— Yes! Do you see that young horse frolicking on the prairie? Four years ago, when his mother died just before giving birth, I took him out of her entrails just like this.

These words filled the girl with joy. Bright as she was, she thought of another way to save her father. For a hundred gold coins, she bought from the blacksmith the colt pulled out of his mother's womb, as well as the hide of the dead mare. She went to see the king and gave him the young colt to mount and the mare's hide to lie on. And she asked to be allowed to see her father again. The king granted her wish because he was very pleased with the little colt.

One day, while the king was riding his new horse, he came face to face with the young girl. She pulled in the reins of her horse to stop it and said: "You are sitting on a creature not born and you rest on its mother!"

Not understanding the meaning of these words, he asked her to explain. She answered: "I will explain this enigma if you give me back my son, my mother's husband! Then he can be my father. But he will remain my son if you don't give him back to me." The king was perplexed; he could not solve the enigma on his own. So he said that she could have anything she asked for if she gave him the solution to the riddle. The young girl asked that her father be freed from the prison where he had been locked up all this time. The king freed his brother, and the girl explained each word of the riddle, one by one.

The king was impressed with his niece's intelligence and realised that his suspicions concerning his brother's intentions were unfounded. He had been told lies; it had all been malicious gossip.

And so they all lived happily together, and we even better.

Sources

N. G. Politis, 1870. "I kori pou thilaze ton patera tis" [The Girl Who Breast-fed Her Father].
   Origin: Peloponnese.
ATU 927, *Out-riddling the Judge.*

The transgenerational confusion of place and function manifest in the heroine's enigma shows us that the riddle can encapsulate a situation so extreme that it touches on the unfathomable. Are we not, in fact, an enigma to ourselves? In these tales, either the enigma fascinates by upholding the subjective reality of another, or its resolution brings an answer to the initial difficulty. It is through the sheer strength of its formulation that the riddle holds life-and-death power over those who risk relying on its formulation, as we shall see next in the story of Princess Turandot.

"Turandot"

Sylvette Gendre-Dusuzeau

"Turandot" is a popular story often staged as an opera. Composer Giacomo Puccini was the one who made "Turandot" famous the world over.[23] The question posed in the riddle is presented as if it were the secret code on which the life or death of the psyche depends. The libretto is based on a folktale – a riddle tale.[24]

The common theme shared by all stories about the princess Turandot can be summarised as follows. In China, in ancient times, an emperor's only daughter refuses to marry. To solve the problem, the emperor agrees to his daughter's strange demand to make it known that her suitors will have to solve three riddles she will pose to them, at the risk of being decapitated if they fail.

Many were those who lost their heads. The people lamented this decadent ending to China's reign and wished that the princess would soon find love so that the terror brought by the executions might cease.

Turandot is very beautiful, cruel and proud, a princess who inflicts death, who is frigid and castrating, who makes heads roll. She is portrayed as a cruel and prideful sphinx. Mysterious and inscrutable, she fascinates the hero, Calaf, for whom she is herself a riddle. To solve Turandot's riddle would mean discovering the feminine, which she embodies.

Turandot is unmoved by the repeated pleas of the crowd to pardon the latest suitor who failed the test, and whose head would soon be added to those already displayed on the stakes surrounding the palace. This is when Calaf appears, rings the gong and announces that he has come to seek the princess's hand in marriage, a feat that had cost former suitors their lives.

Calaf answers the three riddles perfectly, as follows.

First riddle: What is born each night and dies each dawn? The answer is: hope.

Second riddle: What flares warm like a flame, yet it is no flame? The answer is: the blood.

Third riddle: The ice that gives you fire, what can it be? – You are the ice that gives me fire: Turandot.

"Turandot", "the blood", "hope". The solution to the riddle reveals that princess Turandot herself is the riddle. Her strongest emotion is hope. Her cold blood seeks warmth, her icy body seeks a flame. The presence of the other, of the stranger, reveals an ambivalence in the content of the riddle. The pairs of opposites: cold/hot, ice/flame, supported by hope, indicate that Turandot's psychic flow is impeded, divided between life instinct and death instinct.

Now that Calaf has triumphed by solving the riddle, will he marry the princess?

In fact, his victory is in vain, because despite the sacred promise about the riddles, Turandot refuses marriage, saying that she herself is sacred as the daughter of the emperor, and that if she married the stranger, she would become a slave and die of shame. "Do not profane me, stand back! No one will ever possess me, touch me not, it is a sacrilege, I'm lost."

Now that Turandot is unmasked, the question of the riddle becomes moot, and the death drive becomes predominant.

This is when Calaf sets in motion the arrested psychic flow by proposing a riddle himself: his own name. If Turandot can tell him what it is, he will accept being put to death.

If we listen very carefully, we understand that, from the start, Turandot reveals the trauma at the root of her murderous acts. A great misfortune has befallen China since the king of the Tartars invaded and conquered the country, centuries ago, when they raped and enslaved the empress who was Turandot's ancestor.

By refusing to marry, is Turandot avenging her ancestor, as she claims?

There can be no doubt, but her narration also reveals the double trauma, historical and transgenerational, inflicted by her ancestor, which causes her deathly suffering. Turandot is the psychical container of this trauma inflicted on the imperial family, a trauma that places the mark of terror on any representation of love relations or desire. This is the drama envisaged psychically when Turandot is expected to marry.[25] Since physical relations are terrifying for her, she makes herself impenetrable by using the three riddles which hide her symptom of being unable to experience desire as a woman, and which are, at the same time, an appeal for help.

Calaf answers this appeal by initiating a process we could call therapeutic, since it acts on the symptom which stands in the way of Turandot's desire.

He sets the process in motion by presenting Turandot with an enigma concerning his own name. In his opera, Puccini introduces two characters at this point: Timur, Calaf's blind father, accompanied by Liu, his slave, who is secretly in love with Calaf. Dethroned and exiled, hunted by the Tartars, they are hiding in the city. Hence, investigating Calaf's name puts him in danger of being found and killed. This enigma could prove to be deadly for him.

It is through Liu that the enigma concerning Calaf's name will be solved, in a rather brutal way. When she is seen with Calaf, Liu is arrested by Turandot's guards. Despite being tortured, she does not reveal Calaf's name. Thus, Liu, through her sacrifice, shows Turandot that a powerful force called "love", exists. Turandot's acceptance of love comes about in a context of cruelty, trauma and the refusal of sacrifice.

The word "love", which emerged from the violence done to a woman, names the feeling Turandot is looking for without knowing it. The second stage of the therapeutic process prompted by Calaf's desire for love consists of putting into words the sensual feelings he has for her. Deeply touched, Turandot breaks out in tears, letting the ice inside her melt. Calaf, driven by his desire, is able to make the life instinct triumph over the deadly repetition of the trauma. Turandot, delivered from her fears, announces that she has been able to find the name her suitor defied her to discover, and that name is "Love".

In conclusion, the riddle takes place between two protagonists. One guesses, the other dies. The life of one depends on the death of the other. This fluctuation between life and death is very well expressed in the verbal duel between Turandot and Calaf: "The enigmas are three, but death is one!" the princess says. "The enigmas are three, Life is one!" her suitor replies.

Here, the question of the riddle seems to indicate a point of connection with the intimate, the secret code that makes the psyche waver between the life instinct and the death instinct. This oscillation is reactivated in different ways by fables and riddle tales, with their variants. Turandot is a prime example of the psychical elements at stake in a riddle.

Notes

1 In the Christianised versions, the old man is Jesus Christ.
2 A. Angelopoulos, "Figurations de l'énigme", in P. Chemla (Ed.), *L'imaginaire dans la clinique, psychiatrie, psychanalyse, psychothérapie institutionnelle*, Erès, 2020, pp. 9–20.
3 Hypnos (sleep) and Thanatos are brothers.
4 G. Roheim, *The Gates of the Dream*, International Universities Press, 1969.
5 One is a creation of the unconscious, while the other is a literary creation.
6 S. Freud (1901), *Psychopathology of Everyday Life*, SE 6, Hogarth.
7 "The longer the [. . .] time that separates me from the end of this analysis, the more probable it seems to me that the fault in my technique lay in this omission: I failed to discover in time and to inform the patient that her homosexual (gynaecophilic) love for Frau K. was the strongest unconscious current in her mental life. I ought to have guessed . . ." S. Freud (1901–1905), *A Case of Hysteria*, SE 7, Hogarth, p. 102, note 1.
8 In *Clefs pour l'imaginaire*, Octave Mannoni drew attention to Freud's decisive passage from the theory of transference to dream theory and its uses in the treatment. Referring to what has been called "the failure" of the Dora case, Mannoni states that Freud supposes Dora's attention to have been caught by some detail in his person (an unknown quantity, an x factor) that concealed something analogous about Herr K. Freud was looking for a "misalliance", a displacement – that is, a metonymy. Indeed, this is how displacement takes place in dreams, in the sphere of unconscious desire. Starting with this simple association, the study of the elements of transference and that of dream elements can reinforce each other. This also confirms the connection between transference and the notion of the riddle, a connection made through displacement. See O. Mannoni, *Clefs pour l'imaginaire,* Seuil, 2016.
9 S. Freud (1901–1905), *A Case of Hysteria*, SE 7, Hogarth, p. 120.
10 The name Oedipus means "swollen feet": a Greek speaker hears "foot" in *pous*, and "two feet, three feet, four feet" in *dipous, tripous* and *tetrapous*.
11 J.-P. Vernant and P. Vidal-Naquet, "Ambiguity and Reversal", *Tragedy and Myth in Ancient Greece*, Zone Books, 1990, pp. 113–140.
12 *The Poetics of Aristotle*, S. H. Butcher (Trans.), Section 3, Part XXII, Macmillan, 1922: "For the essence of a riddle is to express true facts under impossible combinations. Now this cannot be done by any arrangement of ordinary words, but by the use of metaphor it can."
13 *François Tosquelles*, film, directors J.-C. Polack, F. Pain and D. Sivadon, 1989.
14 "The Lazy Man and the Riddle", folktale collected in Asia Minor by D. Loukatos in 1959.
15 G. Pankow, *L'homme et sa psychose* (Man and His Psychosis), Flammarion, 1993.
16 Vladimir Propp's analysis invokes Nesmejana (Marzanna), the goddess of death, in his study "Ritual Laughter in Folklore", in *Theory and History of Folklore*, University of Minnesota Press, 1984, pp. 124–146. The princess could be in mourning, if we consider Propp's statement: ". . . interdiction of laughter [occurs] while the hero is inside the beast, combined with the command to laugh at the moment he comes out of it" (symbolic birth in ritual), p. 132.
17 J. B. Andrews, *The Folk-Lore Record*, Vol. X (1881), pp. 244–245.
18 P. Levi, *If This Is a Man*, Everyman's Library, 1999.

19 E. Beneviste, *Indo-European Language and Society*, University of Miami Press, 1973.

20 C. Castoriadis, *The Imaginary Institution of Society*, MIT Press, 1998.

21 S. Freud (1932–1936), *New Introductory Lectures on Psycho-Analysis*, SE 22, Hogarth.

22 P. Aulagnier, *The Violence of Interpretation*, A. Sheridan (Trans.), The New Library of Psychoanalysis, 2001.

23 *Turandot* was staged a year and a half after Puccini's death. The opera is based on a libretto by Giuseppe Adami and Renato Simoni, who drew inspiration from a Central Asian legend by Carlo Gozzi, staged in Venice in 1762.

24 The earliest illustration of the theme is that of the great Persian epic poet Nizami, in the twelfth of One Thousand and One Nights (*The Arabian Nights*) to date – a collection of Middle Eastern and South Asian stories and folk tales. At the start of the seventeenth century in France, Pétis de La Croix published *Les Mille et un jours*, containing the tale of Turandocte. Carlo Gozzi's play Turandot followed. After the Enlightenment and the revolution, Friedrich Schiller portrayed her as a knowledgeable princess in line with the 1701 *Declaration of the Rights of Woman* made by Olympe de Gouges. In 1967, Bertolt Brecht wrote the comedy *Turandot or The Whitewashers' Congress,* which presented a nymphomaniac heroine in the context of a political satire. Thus, from the twelfth to the twentieth centuries, in the Orient as well as the Occident, the character of Turandot has evolved from a mystical, spiritual and political concept, to the humanisation of a conflict of emotions.

25 Nicolas Abraham and Maria Torok's theoretical contributions on ghosts are useful here. The "ghost" is the work pursued in the unconscious by the guilty secret of another, whose manifestation, "the haunting", returns through strange actions; in *The Shell and the Kernel*, University of Chicago Press, 1994.

Chapter IX

Therapeutic Languages in Folktales

"The Language of Animals", "The Three Languages", "The Language of Frogs"

The riddles presented so far are formulated and solved using words in an intelligible form of language. In Sophocles' tragedy enacting the myth of Oedipus, we encounter the Sphinx who poses riddles. She is also described as a singer who enchants and bewitches her victims with her songs.[1]

The song carries a primaeval mystery that cannot be reduced to its lyrics, to words. If we consider only the verbal message of the riddle, the originary dimension related to the musical register is overlooked, together with the sensations and affects it carries. When Freud used Sophocles' tragedy to create the founding myth of psychoanalysis, he presented an intelligent hero who finds the words to solve the riddle. Thus, Freud gives precedence to understanding over feeling. He sets aside the original dimension present in the rhythm of the riddle, in favour of a logical formulation suitable to a verbal resolution.[2] In psychoanalytic treatment, the riddle of the symptom seeks resolution in the transference.

The folktales below present riddles that question the symptom and try to resolve it without recourse to verbal expression, by using other means of expression, such as symbols, non-verbal language, and in particular the language of animals.

Portrayal of Therapy in Folktales

Anna Angelopoulos

We all remember fairy tales in which a young prince is wasting away from a mysterious illness that none of the countless doctors called to his bedside by the king are able to cure.[3] The illness worsens dangerously until, when there is nothing left to lose, a beggar-woman or a shepherd who claim to have healing powers are allowed to enter the palace. After this strange visitor brings him a message from his beloved, such as a cake with her ring hidden in it, or even the beloved herself in disguise, the prince miraculously recovers his health. Curing love sickness is the best-known therapy in fairy tales.

But fairy tales also describe other therapies that are less obvious. They are associated with the relationship between the hero, the heroine and various animals. These stories take us back to a primaeval era when men and animals conversed with each other. This mythical idea has always been present in the folktale.

DOI: 10.4324/9781032674230-10

Not all stories start with the opening phrase "Once upon a time". Many folktales have opening phrases such as "In ancient times, when men and animals talked together . . .". In the internal space of the tale, it is natural for the characters to ask other species for help, since they communicate with them in the course of their daily lives. Indeed, the heroes and heroines of the folktale consider animals, birds, plants and insects not only travelling companions, but also advisers about human destiny. These beings all communicate easily with each other. But in what language?

The question of human knowledge of the language of animals is very ancient. Apollodorus,[4] an eleventh-century mythographer, recounts the myth of Melampus, called the black-footed seer because when he was born his mother placed him in the shade, but carelessly left his feet in the burning sun. He had received the gift of divination after giving two dead snakes funeral rites by burning them on a woodpile; to show their gratitude, their children licked his ears, endowing him with knowledge of the language of birds and animals. He also knew the properties of magical and medicinal herbs. His divinatory abilities enabled him to treat the sick successfully, as well as to prevent catastrophes threatening to befall him. For instance, while in prison, he heard two woodworms talking about the delight they took in having eaten through the main beam, so he knew it was urgent for him to be transferred to another prison. Later, thanks to his medical skills, he was able to cure a number of sick people, including the daughters of the king of Argos, who had been struck by collective madness.

Communication between men and animals has always been present in folktales and legends. Three folktales on the theme of the language of animals constitute a mythical nucleus, or rather a cluster of stories on this subject; in them, a man is endowed by magic with the ability to understand the language of animals, or he makes a great effort to learn it.

These stories form three folktale types in the international classification and have been the object of ample commentary by experts on oral tradition.[5] They are "The Language of Animals" (ATU 670), "The Three Languages" (ATU 671) and "The Language of Frogs" (ATU 671*).

"The Language of Animals"

The first folktale, "The Language of Animals", is widely known in Eastern Europe and Asia; certain written versions originated in the Middle Ages. Its hero is a man who was endowed with the ability to understand all the languages of animals and birds, on condition that he never tell anyone, at the risk of his life.

This man saves his herd from wolves by listening to a conversation between dogs. Another time, he hears his donkey complaining and decides to let his ox be laden instead. One day, he hears ants whispering in an erotic language. As he listens to their jesting, he bursts out laughing. His jealous wife wants to know what is so amusing. She insists so much that he is ready to reveal his secret and risk his life, until the rooster intervenes, advising him to beat his wife to make her obey, like he does with his hens. The man takes his advice and saves his life as a result. Gentler, less misogynous versions of the tale talk about shaking out his wife's fleas.

"The Three Languages"

The second folktale, "The Three Languages" (ATU 671), undoubtedly originates in a literary work, *Seven Wise Masters*, a cycle of stories of Sanskrit origin, very famous in the Western world between the twelfth and the sixteenth centuries.[6] Their hero is a boy described as simple-minded, whom the animals reward for saving them or sparing them by granting him the knowledge of three languages: the languages of dogs, of birds and of frogs. The boy is in conflict with his parents. They fight and they chastise him for his pride; he tells them, "You'll see, one day you will wash my hands."

Indeed, one day the birds come to reveal his future greatness to him. Two doves tell him that he will become Pope. He decides to leave home and travel to Rome. While he is there, the prediction comes true. He becomes Pope Innocent. His parents, who had wanted to kill him because of his pride, now have to serve him.

This folktale makes reference to the sanctity of the cretin,[7] confirmed by the prediction in the Scriptures: "Blessed are the poor in spirit, for theirs is the kingdom of heaven."

And now, let us look at the third folktale, "The Language of Frogs".

"The Language of Frogs"

This tale is well-known in Greece and in the Balkan countries. Its hero is a young boy, a foolish simpleton. The storyteller calls him "a little crazy". The foolish boy is set on learning the language of frogs. The refrain "ki, ki ki . . . ba-ka-ka-kia" runs all through the story. "Ba-ka-ka-kia!"

His brother goes off to foreign lands to study and explore the world, leaving him alone in the forest, near a river full of frogs where he sits with his feet in the water, listening to their croaking, determined to learn their language. He stays there a year, two years, the time that it takes to accomplish his task.

One day, his brother comes back and wants to take him home. – But how did you survive here all this time? – Some days one way, other days another, the foolish boy replies. Go away, I want to stay here with the frogs! Ba-ka-ka-kia! And his brother leaves.

Sometime later, the foolish brother leaves the river and the forest to return to his native city. On the way there, he finds himself in a foreign city where he hears that the king's daughter is very ill. Doctors can do nothing more for her. Something is *squirming in her belly*. She hears voices coming out of her body and no one can cure her.

The boy hurries to the palace at once to cure the princess. The guards want to stop him from entering, but the king intercedes in his favour. When he finds himself alone with the sick princess, he asks her where she feels pain. "What can I tell you?" she asks. "I have something inside me that doesn't let me breathe; something squirms and what I hear sounds like the croaking of frogs!"

He goes nearer and introduces himself to the frogs in their language: – *Ki, ki ki . . . ba-ka-kia . . .* What are you doing in there? – We're doing very well, my twelve children and I, the mother frog answers. It's a very good place, it's warm and the food is good! – Quick, make some aioli,[8] the fool tells the palace cook. And the princess must eat two or three spoonfuls!

A little later, the mother frog confides to "the doctor": "I don't know what happened, the food was bad and I lost half my children!"

Hearing this, he gives the princess more aioli to kill the rest of the frogs. Then he prescribes a laxative to cleanse the intestines. And the princess is cured.

Grateful, the king gave the boy all the gold he could ever want. Now that he was rich, he set out for his own country.

The king, the princess and the fool lived happily ever after, and we even happier.

Reflections on the Tale

What do we learn from this strange therapy centred on a belly, a crowded womb?

"Frogs in the belly" brings to mind a child's world. Do we not tell children: "Don't drink too much water or you'll have frogs in your belly"?

As for the world of folklore, in fairy tales belonging to "the persecuted heroine" genre, eliminating a rival is often accomplished by making her drink water full of tadpoles. This causes her belly to swell, she soon appears to be pregnant out of wedlock, and is therefore taken for a woman of easy virtue who deserves nothing better than to be abandoned in the forest.

Naturally, this tale reminds us of Freud's young "hysteria" patient – with an illness in the womb –, like the one treated by the strange therapist in the tale.

Géza Roheim,[9] familiar with Freud's teaching, studied this category of folktales about the language of animals, interpreting it as a phantasmatic world centred on the primal scene and infantile sexuality theories, but his focus was not on the strange illness of the princess.

What exactly has been ailing the princess all this time? All interpretations are possible to explain this disquiet in the belly: intestinal troubles, the mysteries of conception, of pregnancy, of childbirth. But also constant painful sensations originating in unknown sexual abuse, not understood and not named.

The only thing we know for sure is that the young therapist cured the princess by speaking the language of frogs, which he learned patiently and with great determination, taking all the time he needed. In other words, he understood and spoke the language of his patient's illness. Is this not what we do in our analyses: learn to speak the language of our patients?

Once the princess is cured of her illness and each of the heroes is free to follow his destiny, why should it be the case that revealing the secret of knowing the language of animals can lead to a death sentence?

Over the centuries, the representations of man's connection to animals have fluctuated. In the Middle Ages, man and animal were very close. Since Descartes, because animals do not reason but act by instinct, they are considered inferior to humans.

Let us remember that in the first Book of Genesis, in the story of creation, which establishes the relations between the species, God says: "Let Us make man in Our image, according to Our likeness: and let them have domination over the fish of the sea and over the birds of the heavens and over the livestock and all the wild animals, and over all the creatures that crawl along the ground."[10]

In stories, legends and myths, men and animals speak to each other, and this mixing of species that communicate is natural. We note that the hero is often presented as simple-minded, a nitwit or a fool, in other words, not responsible. In human societies where reason prevails, is there not a perceived danger in a possible linguistic contact between humans and other species, if they were to speak a common language? Perhaps these tales contain a warning not to ignore the ancestral prohibition governing our relations with the other species. Could it be that this warning concerns the unimaginable consequences of an intelligible exchange between species, which would overturn the established dominance hierarchy?

Clinical Illustration: "The Language of Frogs"

Anna Angelopoulos

"I don't want squirming inside me!" my patient said the other day. What she said set me thinking, trying to imagine what she could have meant. What was it that she didn't want? Was it the living child? Was it the pregnancy, feeling another inside her? "Anything but that!" she was crying out.

Traumatised by repeated incest in her childhood, just as her mother had been, she later became a successful actress. One day she asked me if I didn't have a story she could put on the stage and act in. She was certain that I could find her a plot that suited her, since she thought of me as a sort of story repertoire – I could just pull them out of my sleeve.

I had been neglecting the imaginary world of stories for a while. I had almost given it up altogether in that post-Covidian era when my patients showed little desire to phantasise, to dream, to live.

But this patient's traumas were all too real. Her emotional life was locked in an impasse: I want/I don't want, I can/I can't. Tyrannised by this dual attitude, the young woman had constant nightmares, persecutory dreams: she kept seeing evil people running after her, catching her, finding her where she was hiding, raping her. Her dreams showed an absence of sublimation; persecutory scenes were repeated endlessly. Yet this was the patient who was asking me to bring her a story that could make her dream.[11]

As we prepared our folktale seminar, we were thinking about ways to counteract this generalised discouragement among our patients, and to resist the melancholic mood that had insidiously kept us captive for the past two years. This despondency caused a loss of interest in interactions with others, a withdrawal of each individual "in his own bubble". But who was the other, the one outside the bubble? How did we think of him, the one who threatened, for example, to "squirm" inside my patient? Who was the other animal, the other god, like in fairy tales?

These questions led me to go back to treating my patients as before, replenishing their supply of metaphors, and mine. I remembered the folktale "The Language of Frogs" – the one I just told above – and with it, we continued our work.

Two clinical illustrations follow, involving subjective relations to animals: "Non-verbal Communication in the Session" and "On Horseback".

Non-verbal Communication in the Session

Sylvette Gendre-Dusuzeau

The folktale "The Language of Frogs" made me reflect on a clinical case involving the adjustment of language in the course of an analysis, a question at the heart of the transferential relation. Certain psychic events directly related to this question arose in our work together; I shall describe them here.

For about six years I saw a patient in his fifties. He had already been in analysis, which he interrupted for lack of time, difficulty getting to the analyst's office and disappointment about communication in the sessions, which was not what he expected. He had thought that working with a psychoanalyst meant that the latter would quickly guess the causes of his unhappiness and tell him what they were, alleviating his suffering. Therefore, his most urgent question in the first session was: "Are you going to speak to me?" Would I tell him why he feels unwell? I explained the nature of psychoanalytic work, what setting it required, and I asked whether he wanted to make a change in himself. I also said that I may not have something important to tell him about himself in each session, but that I would keep his concern in mind.

His complaint had to do with difficulty communicating, although he had no difficulty speaking, especially to women, whose company he sought, but who did not sufficiently awaken his desire. There was something about this he did not understand, a puzzle he could not solve. During this first session I felt he nurtured great hope, a hope as great as the passivity and fear revealed in what he was saying.

In the sessions that followed, I noticed that this man spoke easily but with great care, telling me things without saying them, alluding to them, or launching into what could be a revelation, and then erasing it immediately as one would a blackboard, with a sideways hand movement, saying: "I'm talking nonsense." At one point, I told him I had the impression he was afraid of my reactions. Yes, he admitted. "There are things I never said in my previous analysis for fear of being judged. I am afraid of being judged."

In the weeks that followed I gradually got to know his internal world and I reacted freely to his distress and to his questions whenever possible.

He was an only child and had felt very alone. He had a particularly vivid memory of the day his mother lost him in a department store. She was shopping for bargains with a friend and forgot about him. For ten minutes, he was in acute distress in the middle of a crowd of noisy, agitated women. His mother had forgotten him like that several times in public places. It also happened that she promised to tuck him in when he went to bed at night and then forgot her promise. He understood very early that calling her was useless, that she would not come. What's more, she would leave him with a cousin he disliked when she went out.

He remembered his mother as being cold. He felt alone in her company. He had a psychosomatic theory about his asthma which, he believed, was replacing the tears he didn't shed. At night, he dreamed of tall sand dunes where he was walking alone, as well as of a cat stuck in a jar, folded over like a foetus. At times, he had childish reactions – or at least, that is what he was told by those around him – when he acted inappropriately, suddenly becoming very provocative, with anyone, even at work with his superior. He had great confidence in thinking and numbers, but mistrusted feelings greatly. He was fascinated by knowledge and had always dreamed of using it to gain control. As a child, he spent many hours alone performing calculations. They reassured him. He loved abstractions. Being a computer programmer suited him well. But he felt something was not right with him. By coming to see me, he hoped to change everything, to reshape the mould from which he originated.

One day, in the session, he asked me a question that had long been on his mind. His appointment was always at one o'clock and he wondered when I ate lunch. When I told him that I ate before that, he was reassured because for him this meant that I was human, and took into consideration the time of his appointment. I asked myself about the possibility of an archaic fear of being devoured.

Sometimes, he grew bolder and asked me what I thought when he revealed his fears. I responded in ways intended to contain his distress and his worries. Little by little, his body seemed to relax. He had a dream in which, in the middle of a field full of flowers, someone was "quartering" sheep covered with soft wool. He meant to say "caressing", but the sudden slip of the tongue revealed the quartering (processing) of animal carcasses. The two signifiers bumped into each other. In the expressions he used and in other dreams, strong terms often surfaced, terms such as "relegation, rejection, exclusion". He thought that his problem was that he did not speak the same language as other people, and therefore felt marginalised. He suddenly connected this with his previous attempt at analysis, saying "It didn't work because I did not speak the language of the analyst."

One day he ran into an acquaintance involved in the use of assistive technology with autistic persons. He was very impressed and was able to take part in a session. Now he understood: he was autistic, he had a milder form, most likely Asperger's syndrome. Personally, I did not at all agree with his supposition, but this new identity provided reassuring reasons for his difficulty to communicate.

The analysis continued. One day, he proudly brought me the text of a report he had been asked to write at work. As he was handing it to me, he described the reverie into which he had fallen while he walked along my street towards my office. He was seeing himself in the subway and then everything stopped, and everyone got out because a woman was giving birth. He saw the baby, the blood. He took the baby, wrapped it in his jacket and brought it to my office. His analysis was: "It's me as a child, the one who was abandoned at birth." All at once, a part of his early life was revealed to him. At the end of the session, he insisted that I keep his report as a gift. I told him: "I will keep this baby then, but I am also keeping the baby from the subway, to take care of him."

After this, he did not come to his next session. When he came back the following week, he explained that he was too deeply moved to come to the session, and that he had shed bitter tears over his dead father and wept sorrowfully for his mother. This was a very moving moment of insight that brought forth critical transgenerational elements that preceded his birth. Our sessions continued.

One day, when I returned from vacation, he brought me a tape he had recorded on a BBC channel. It was a fascinating documentary about the way animals communicate.[12] He was enthusiastic and wanted me to see it. He said that while I watched it, I should mentally replace "the animals" with "autistic people", to understand clearly that, in both, thoughts take the form of images. He presented the tape as a great discovery he had made about autism, in which he was passionately interested.

When I watched the tape, I discovered a world that was new to me, the world of animal communicators and interpreters of animal language. They were therapists who communicated with animals through images or through intuition. There were several videotaped consultations with cats, dogs and horses. The communicator perceived the mental images transmitted by these animals and deciphered them. I remember the consultation with the horse. The reason for it was that the instructor was concerned to see one of his best racehorses showing signs of extreme fatigue after a month of rest spent at the horse ranch of a friend. The horse communicated images to the interpreter, who decoded them and was able to tell the trainer that not only had the horse been made to run every day, but that he had been beaten. The horse ranch had abused the horse, a fact its amazed owner was able to confirm.

What attracted my attention was that my patient had once again brought me something intended to help me to help him, to guess his underlying desires. But we were thinking very different things. What I saw was that he was showing me his dream method, a way to understand this preverbal, or even infra-verbal, language where his suffering was lodged passively, so that I could cure it without asking him to make the painful effort of expressing himself – like a wounded animal counting on his trainer, like a baby searching for a *Nebenmensch*.[13] I felt that in his phantasy I played the role of an omnipotent good mother, and that he was passively waiting for me to rescue him.

My patient spoke with great passion about the unusual experiment conducted by this therapist with exceptional powers. How wonderful it would be if things unfolded the same way in his analysis, if I could guess without him saying anything! His dream of passivity in the analysis was reaching its peak. Yes, it would be wonderful. But I had to tell him that although this communication experiment was fascinating, I did not have the unusual gift this therapist had developed and therefore we would have to continue with the more usual human possibilities we had. In his next session he recounted a dream he found stupid and which he thought made no sense at all. In the dream there was an electrical circuit in which the current had to be redirected.

I refrained from giving an interpretation, thinking to myself that perhaps he was giving up his magical wish to succeed in seeing the light through someone else's efforts.

On Horseback[14]

Sylvette Gendre-Dusuzeau

After a year during which she had not remembered any of her dreams, my patient, whom I shall call Chloe, suddenly recounted the following nightmare.

"A sick mare she loved had died. Beside it stood a cousin of hers whose seven-year-old child had died several years ago from the sequels of a fall from a horse. His wife was also standing beside him in silence."

This dream was related to real events we had talked about, yet it had the effect of a nightmare. A missing element in the dream was the fact that her sister-in-law had had a serious fall while skiing but had recovered. Silence was present in the dream. Chloe's associations were based on what occurred in reality. It was as if, in her dream, she had brought together traumatic events she had experienced, and added the element of silence. What silence? I was thinking that silence was at the heart of the relation with a beloved animal, a transitional object, between inside and outside, which restores the hope of being listened to without being judged. Chloe herself was not very talkative; she had sought therapy because of her lack of confidence, her fear of being wrong, of having nothing to say, and her guilt about having no reason not to be happy. Chloe was a beautiful young woman, intelligent and physically sturdy.

Her mother had had Chloe take dance lessons, learn to play the flute, and learn to ride a pony during her vacations. But one day she told me: "My mother couldn't imagine that I might want to pursue horseback riding." "Really?" "Yes, she didn't think it was an intellectually stimulating activity, only a leisure pastime. And she is always afraid that I will fall. That's why my parents never come to see me jump hurdles."

Chloe was gentle and sensitive with the horses, although they had their temperament and were not always easy to handle. I was very interested in what she said about her relationship with the horses, because I myself am a rather mediocre rider. She wanted to gain professional status in horse riding and was an active member of an equestrian centre, while pursuing her profession in the restoration of works of art.

In the sessions, she often described her disagreements with her instructors, two in particular who were the opposite of each other. Let us call them Bob and Jack. Bob, who was very demanding and outspoken, criticised her technical faults and was hard on the young horses he trained. He complained that she was too slow and was wasting his time. Jack, who was more understanding, used criticism sparingly but often took refuge in silence, shrouding himself in mystery, insensitive in his own way. She was infatuated with him, but he showed no sign of a similar interest. Chloe practised diligently, clearly wanting to succeed but, it seems to me, leaving little room for the simple pleasure of riding.

Little by little, behind the contrasting figures of Jack and Bob and the painful experience of always being admonished for her incompetence, other figures from other scenes started to emerge. Bob was demanding like her mother, who expected good results, good grades at school, success in intellectual endeavours. Indeed, her mother still treated her like a child unable to protect herself from the weather or eat nutritious food. When she visited her parents in the weekend, they only talked about her work, not about horseback riding. Chloe felt that both her parents expected her to conform to a model impossible to question. Nothing must change. She did not even dare to tell them that she wasn't well.

That is when something happened in our sessions. I had had to make a change in our usual schedule, and she came at the wrong time. She was very apologetic. She said: "I am making you waste *my time*." "Your time?" Her slip of the tongue astounded her. Did she really have time that was "hers", time of her own? In fact, recently she had talked about giving all her free time to the equestrian centre, taking care of the horses, making herself useful and tacitly helping Jack. Yet Jack had criticised her for not knowing when to stop, for working all the time and never leaving the horses alone. He was saying that she can never let go. She was jolted into this awareness. "He hurt me but he was not wrong. When I work, when I make myself useful, I am running away. It's my way of avoiding speaking."

I understood that Chloe had given up speaking long ago. And I thought of asking her if her mother ever talked about herself. This set our work on a new path.

Chloe had learned, from seeing family photographs, that her mother had suffered from a serious illness in her youth, during which she had been separated from her parents. She took refuge in reading and then started her studies, until she married. I was struck by the contrast between her fragile mother and Chloe, in splendid health as a child and as a young woman, in complete contrast with the limitations of her mother's health. How could her mother bear this physical strength that drove her daughter to gallop, to jump, to live in her body, and even to desire? How does such vitality dare to exist impudently, without risking death? No doubt, envy and frustration clashed in her mother's emotional reactions. How could they have communicated without violence? Communication had to be excluded to avoid conflict. No one must be disturbed. So no one talked about themselves. Silence covered over what was painful. Silence! It was back again, as Chloe realised. Silence that served to hide maternal pain never voiced, something unspeakable.

In the period when we were discussing these things, a close friend advised Chloe to leave the equestrian centre before becoming convinced that she was a hopelessly incompetent rider. She agreed in principle, but she had to take the risk of confronting Bob and Jack. She had the courage to do this with them and an unexpectedly lively discussion about teaching methods ensued. Technique was not everything.

Chloe insisted on the need for a certain complicity with the horse, requiring sensitivity. She understood that she had relied too heavily on the trainers.

The weekend following our discussion of these matters so dear to her, she went to the equestrian centre again. After grooming the horses, she mounted a mare she was fond of, ambled and galloped. "I was enjoying myself," she said. I felt sure that our work had taken off at a trot!

VOURDALO[15]

Once upon a time there was a sheep breeder called Costas. He and his wife had a daughter they both cherished greatly. Costas, who owned several herds of sheep, hired a young shepherd to take them out to pasture.

One day, while the shepherd sat among his sheep, he saw a dried-out tree in flames. He went closer and heard a hissing voice say: "Shepherd, my good shepherd, could you put your cane here, on the tree trunk, so I can slide along it and escape the flames?" Surprised, the shepherd went around the tree and saw a strange sight that made him laugh: a poor little snake was trapped on the trunk of the flaming tree. And the snake kept begging him to prop his cane against the tree so that he could glide down it and escape the flames. "Help me and I will do anything you want in exchange!"

– But what can you do for me, my poor friend, except to bite me and cause my death?

The snake kept insisting; he begged the shepherd so piteously that the young man finally placed his cane on the tree trunk. The snake slid all the way down and escaped from the fire. Then he asked the shepherd what he wanted in exchange and the man said: "I would like you to give me the power of making everything stick together whenever I say 'Vourdalo'! And then, when I say 'xe-Vourdalo', all these things will come apart again!" The snake gave the shepherd a pearl, which came out of his mouth. "Take this, but don't tell anyone!" he said.

And so they agreed. The shepherd was a hardy fellow and one day his master offered him his daughter for a wife. He was happy to accept and they were engaged. But a while later the girl's father changed his mind; he broke the engagement, choosing for a son-in-law a young man much wealthier than the poor shepherd. The couple's engagement was celebrated, in anticipation of the marriage.

On their wedding day, a sad day for the shepherd, he went to the church with everyone else. The guests gathered around the young couple. Then, when the priest blessed the married couple and invited them to walk around the altar three times, at the precise moment when the priest was leading the couple in the Dance of Isaiah, the young shepherd mumbled: "Vourdalo" and all those present found themselves stuck together. Distraught, the guests fought to set themselves free, trying to pull away from each other, but this only made them stick together more. The marriage was turning into a disaster. The sheep breeder ordered the shepherd to go and fetch the witch in the next village, to break the spell placed on those present at the wedding.

The young shepherd went to look for the witch. He crossed a river, came to her house and explained that the people in his village needed her craft. They went back together to the church where the married couple, the crowd and the priest were waiting. When they were crossing the river, the witch lifted her skirt to avoid getting wet; the young shepherd mumbled "Vourdalo" again, and the woman's skirt became stuck to her belly. The lower part of her body and her buttocks were bare for all to see. They continued on like this until they came to the village entrance. There, a young man was roasting mutton on a spit. When he saw the half-naked witch, he flung a "kokoretsi" (roasted sheep intestines) straight at her buttocks. The shepherd mumbled "Vourdalo" again and the section of intestine stuck to her, its length dragging on the ground. A little dog approached, attracted by the smell of roasted meat. The shepherd said "Vourdalo" again and the dog too became stuck.

The procession arrived at the church, with the shepherd following the little dog stuck to the piece of grilled meat, which stuck to the bare buttocks of the witch. She tried to break the spell holding all those present captive, but her efforts were in vain. No matter what she did, they stayed stuck together.

The young shepherd watched all this from a little distance for a while. Finally, he shouted: "Master, do you agree to give me your daughter's hand in marriage as well as all your sheep? If you do, I will break the spell!" "I agree," his master answered. The good shepherd mumbled "xe-Vourdalo", they all became unstuck and quickly ran off in all directions.

And the shepherd went home with the girl and the sheep.

Sources

"Vourdalo-Xevourdalo", FS 715 B.
    Origin: Argithea, Karditsa, in Thessaly.
    Collected in 1957 by Angelique Papamichael.
CGMF 571, *All Stick Together*.
ATU 571, *All Stick Together*.
CGMF 425, *The Search for the Lost Husband*.
ATU 425, *The Search for the Lost Husband*.
    Subtype A, *Eros and Psyche*.

ALL STICK TOGETHER[16]

Long ago, a king had an ailing daughter whom no one was able to cure. Her state declined from day to day, going from bad to worse; never smiling, always gloomy, she seemed to teeter on the edge of her grave.

Not knowing what else to do, the king announced that he would give his daughter's hand in marriage to anyone who enticed her to laugh. Three brothers lived in a miserable hut somewhere in the kingdom. They heard about the king's promise and decided to see if in some way or other they could not bring a smile to the ailing princess's lips.

The eldest fills a basket with red apples and sets off. On the road, he sees an old woman in a sorcerer's den where she has fallen, struggling in vain to get out. She starts to holler, asking him for help. But the young man barely glances at her and continues on his way. He enters the king's palace and is taken to the princess's chamber. The sick maiden looks at the beautiful apples and pushes them away with both hands, while her countenance grows darker than ever. The second brother gathers the prettiest flowers to take to the palace. On his way, he sees the same old woman in the sorcerer's den, but he pays her no more attention than his brother did and continues on. At the palace, he holds out the beautiful flowers to the sick princess, but she pushes them away at once, without so much as a glance. Then, the youngest brother sets out for the palace taking nothing with him. He sees the old woman calling out for help from the sorcerer's den, and he pulls her out without delay. Happy to be free, the witch says: "How can I reward you for what you have done? Are you seeking your fortune? Do you want to be rich?" "Am I seeking my fortune? That is precisely why I left home, to try to make the king's daughter laugh so that I can marry her." "Then take this black lamb. Take him with you and always keep him close. No matter what happens, never let him out of your arms."

The young man goes off carrying the lamb in his arms. In the evening, arriving at an inn in the capital, he asks for a bed for the night. But he is told that there is no room and that he must go and see the priest, who will provide everything he needs. He hurries straight away to the priest's house where, as he has been told, the housekeeper makes him welcome. She offers to take the lamb to the stable and to give the young man a room. But he refuses, saying he wants the lamb to stay with him. The good Father is surprised, but the young man will not change his mind.

However, towards morning, the priest cannot contain his curiosity anymore; he must find out about the mysterious lamb. Very softly, not making a sound, he enters the room where the young man is sleeping soundly with the lamb in his arms. The priest takes hold of the lamb by one of its ears. The animal starts to bleat. The young man awakens, frightening the priest, who wants to run away. "Ah! By my word!" He finds it impossible to let go of the lamb's ear. He starts to holler and scream: "Help, help!" Awakened by his screams, the housekeeper, dishevelled, with a big tear in the middle of the ragged robe she has hastily thrown on to hurry to her master's rescue, comes running. She grabs the lamb by its other ear and finds that she also cannot let go of it. As the young man is pulling the lamb, while the priest and the housekeeper are pulling it in a different direction, the three of them find themselves outside, heaped into a most disorderly pile. While they cross the garden, to cover her shame, the housekeeper pulls off a huge cabbage leaf and sticks it on her behind to hide the tear in her clothing. And they continue on together, crossing the village in the direction of the palace. But three huge goats standing by the side of the road see the cabbage and want it for themselves. As soon as they touch it, they remain stuck to it. They start to run madly, with the housekeeper, the priest, the lamb and the young man. On their way, they come cross the baker, who is already awake. They shout: "Come, for pity's sake, come and separate us!" The baker reaches them and is soon stuck himself. He sees a blacksmith working in his shop and cries out to ask for his help. The blacksmith runs towards them, touches them and stays stuck. A little further, two women holding brooms are chatting before their door. They hit the long chain of people and animals with their brooms . . . "Ah, yes!" But the brooms stay stuck after the first blow, and the women are stuck to their brooms. At a turn in the road, a blind man is following a dog tied to him. When the mad chain brushes against him, the dog starts to bark and gets hold of one of the housewives by her apron. He becomes stuck at once, and the blind man with him. They all go twirling by, getting closer to the royal palace.

Awake because she has not been able to sleep, sadder than ever, the poor princess is in the palace, reclining near a large window. When she sees coming nearer, attached to each other in an unbelievable chain, . . . the young man, the lamb, the priest, the housekeeper, the cabbage leaf, the goats, the baker, the blacksmith, the two women, the dog and the blind man, the poor princess bursts out laughing wildly. She can't stop laughing; she just can't, she keeps hooting with laughter like a mad woman. Suddenly, the young man stops; all those running behind him fall on top of each other, hitting themselves. But they have been separated, loosened free. The young man shouts at the princess: "That's enough now!" The lamb starts to bleat and the young queen's mad laughter ceases on the spot.

Cured once and for all, the princess became as charming as can be. The king kept his promise, and his daughter married the young man before that month was up. They lived happily and had many children.

Sources

Origin: Basque.
    Barbier collection.

"All Stick Together": Clinical Resonances[17]

S. Gendre-Dusuzeau

This folktale could be called "How to Make a Melancholy Girl Laugh". A king is looking for a "suitor-therapist" to bring his daughter out of her melancholy state, whose cause is a total mystery; sick as she is, she is not fit to marry. She seems barely alive. The king's offer is intended to kill two birds with one stone: his daughter will be cured by the therapist who can make her laugh, and the therapist will be given her hand in marriage. The form the cure shall take is announced in advance: laughter. Here, the absence of laughter is a symptom, as enigmatic as symptoms always are.

The tale begins with three brothers who decide to try their luck with being granted a princess's hand in marriage. The two elder brothers, hurrying to bring her apples and flowers, ignore an old woman who asks them to help her free herself from the sorcerers' den into which she has fallen. Of course, the old woman is a fairy. To thank the youngest brother, who frees her on his way to seek the princess's hand, she gives him a magic object in the form of an animal, a black lamb, accompanied by the admonition that he must never let it go, that they must never separate.

Starting from the moment when the priest, curious, comes to see for himself the lamb from which the young man refuses to part, and suddenly finds his hand stuck to the lamb's ear when he touches it, a series of unexpected adhesions magically follow, culminating in an unbelievable procession arriving before the palace, offering the princess the ludicrous sight of the villagers all stuck together in an obscene jumble of human and animal body parts, which sends her into a wild fit of laughter.

This folktale is constructed around a magical object, the black lamb. The boy keeps it close, like a transitional object[18] accompanying his passage from childhood to adolescence and adulthood, when he suddenly desires to seek the princess's hand in marriage. The presence of the lamb plays an important part in the princess's recovery. Indeed, in some versions of the tale, the young man keeps the lamb with him at the palace after his marriage.

A young girl's fear of reaching marriageable age could very possibly take the form of dreading to lose one's childhood with all its familiar habits, and be forced to enter a completely unknown world. We can imagine that the princess's royal father has started to mention marriage to her. But suddenly, the young shepherd with his magic lamb shows her an upside-down world where adults – even those in important symbolic positions –, have kept some element of a child's world. The sight of bare buttocks is an evident aspect of that world, one that always amuses children. This sudden collapse of the idealisation of serious adults associated with symbolic values reassures the princess, allowing her tension to ease and bringing on a fit of laughter. The shepherd, never letting his lamb out of his arms, also shows her that even a grown-up can hold on to his childhood. Growing up is not a brutal break that makes one a stranger to oneself; it is the entering of a world where one's childhood still has a place. When she is relieved of her anxiety about the changes awaiting her, the princess's life-saving laughter bursts on the scene in a flash.

This psychoanalytic fiction resonates with transferences in our practice, which involve the comical, humour, the *Witz* and laughter, for indeed, we do laugh with our patients.

I think it interesting to take this opportunity to look more closely at this phenomenon and its consequences.

Using humour, laughter and even play in analysis requires trust between patient and analyst, and solidly established transference, without which transferential guilt and aggressivity could become too intense. I would say that the use of humour requires good enough emotional security. Not all our patients can deal with humour, if they are not sufficiently at ease in the secondary spheres of the psyche where humour dwells. If there was trauma or abandonment in their past, humour is experienced as persecutory violence that threatens to destroy the therapeutic alliance. To use humour, to play, requires first of all liking to do this, as well as sufficient separation from the other – a difference –, and the ability to set aside affects and emotions likely to cause narcissistic wounding. Sometimes our patients acquire a sense of humour during the analytic process, and this is one of the best things we can hope for.

But even without using humour directly, there are situations involving slips of the tongue and wordplay in a context of encouragement offered by the analyst, or childlike games, which produce surprising effects.

"Laughter makes men human," Rabelais said, taking up Aristotle's thought. Laughter can also lead to a "fit of laughter", as we have seen. In common parlance, some situations are said to make one "die of laughter". These expressions clearly show that laughter, closely linked with life and death, is deeply part of the human.

But while humour is part of psychoanalytic work, laughter is its effect, a vital supplement. This is what our tale shows, that laughter and healing go together. Freud noted that "laughter produced by jokes signals the release of repression", even the end of the analysis.[19]

When I was a child, people used to say: "A good laugh is worth a thick steak." This sentiment inscribed laughter in the domain of the body, made it nourishment for survival. In addition, the gestures of the body, which indicate a presupposed context, can provoke laughter, with no need for words. This is what brought about the healing of the princess. The startling image spoke wordlessly to her psyche, which used it as nourishment. Laughter displaces, dislodges, and this distancing is effective.

Laughter, closely tied to crying, undoubtedly has archaic ties with the psyche; one has only to think of the age-old success of the clown, generation after generation.

Laughing in Analysis

My patient was a woman in her late fifties, but I felt her to be a little girl of six or seven, very anxious, tragically distressed by the need to take the slightest initiative, and whose unexpressed revolt was as tenacious as the submission of which she had never freed herself. Repeated displays of her infantile powerlessness connected to the fact that "she had not cut the umbilical cord", as she said, prompted me to overcome my own powerlessness, making use of my counter-transference in a very specific way. She forced me to become very inventive in creating word images that ridiculed the reality dictated by the superego, which made her suffer. She complained endlessly about her superior. One day, she was furious as she told me that this woman was bragging to people at the office about eating lobsters on the beach with her husband. This little incident fuelled her complaint: "She couldn't care less about us. We're there working and it's not with a salary like ours that we could do what she did!" At that moment, a picture came to my mind of these two people of retirement age, sitting on the sand with a lobster, the blue horizon ahead, a kind of surrealist painting, and I described it to her straight away. I said: "So you imagine her on the beach, in her bathing suit, with her retired husband beside her, and the lobster high up in her hand", and she burst out laughing. She laughed several times at the mere mention of the lobster.

Another time, a new colleague was taking liberties my patient would never have dared to take. This person invited the whole department to have tea in his office, and my patient had to prepare everything. She brought in the teapot, put it down and then disappeared for a quarter of an hour, but felt bad about it retrospectively: I said, "I see, that sounds just like an invention of yours, like in 'Alice in Wonderland'. 'I am letting the teapot serve everyone and make conversation with people, while I disappear for a while.'" This caused joyous laughter which put an end to anguish for the rest of the session. Another time, when a friend visiting from England created a mess in her apartment, upsetting her greatly, I said: "Ah, these, young people who act so cool, leaving their socks on the floor, throwing their pullover on top of a lamp, leaving a sandwich on the corner of the television and teacups all over the place!" This provoked the same cathartic laughter that kept aggressivity at bay.

Each time, laughter showed that a fragment of the unknown had surfaced.

The emergence of the images of mockery I put into words for my patient seem to me to have been a defensive reaction in the counter-transference. In those dark moments when she was engulfed in depression, I led her to make a sideways move by conjuring up images at the limit of impropriety, which made her laugh. Laughter had entered the analysis as a space in which we could have a dialogue.

You can see why the folktale "All Stick Together" had no trouble winning me over.

Notes

1 Quoted from Hellenist Marie Delcourt's book *Oedipus, The Legend of a Conqueror*, Michigan State University Press, 2020.
2 N. Zaltzman, "Le point aveugle de l'énigme", *Topique*, 3 (84), 2003, pp. 201–206.
3 For instance, the hero in "The Bayberry Child", in which the heroine cures the prince of his love sickness.
4 Apollodorus, *The Library*, Books 1–3.9, Loeb Classical Library, 1921.

5 A. Aarne, *The Trilingual Man and His Curious Wife*, FFC No. 15, Hamina, 1914. Here, the author of the international classification notes that a few folktales can be traced back to an ancient Indian origin, as is the case with this one.

6 L. De Lincy, *Seven Wise Masters*, after A. L. Deslongchamps, *Essay on Indian Fables and Their Introduction in Europe*, Techener, 1838.

7 Etymology: from Swiss French "crestin", meaning Christian.

8 Mediterranean sauce made with garlic and olive oil.

9 G. Roheim, "The Language of Birds", in *Fire in the Dragon and Other Psychoanalytic Essays on Folklore*, Princeton University Press, 1992.

10 Bible, English Standard Version, Genesis 1:26.

11 The analyst's entrance into the scene of the trauma is described by Radmila Zygouris in the chapter "Sortilèges de la scène traumatique" (The Spell Cast by the Traumatic Scene), in *L'amour paradoxal ou une promesse de séparation*, Éditions des Crépuscules, 2023.

12 Samantha Kury, *I Talk to Animals*, April 2017, shown on PBS and BBC. Anna Evans, a veterinarian in California, invented the concept of intuitive communication in the 1980s. It is based on the basic principle that we have a natural capacity to sense what an animal feels, since human beings also have an animal nature allowing them to perceive, beyond concrete sounds and gestures, more subtle manifestations. These are intuitive telepathic communications that can take the form of visual flashes or various sensations that have to be skilfully retranslated. Kury has opened a school for the methodical teaching of this communication, beyond its intuitive understanding.

13 S. Freud (1886–1889), *Project for a Scientific Psychology*, SE 1, Hogarth. The *Nebenmensch*, "fellow human-being", the helpful person who is sufficiently aware that the infant is in a state of distress (*Hilflosigkeit*) and helplessness.

14 "On Horseback" was presented in Algiers in April 2023, at the Conference "Metamorphosis of hostile places into places of encounter and sharing", under the auspices of the Amine de Bab el Qued Association, the Ben Aknoun Equitherapy Association, the Psyche Group and the Fédération des Ateliers de Psychanalyse. It was published in 2024, Éditions FAP.

15 Based on the version of the tale in P. Delarue and M.-L. Tenèze, *Le Conte populaire français*, Maisonneuve & Larose, 1978.

16 Version in P. Delarue and M.-L. Tenèze, *Le Conte populaire français*, Maisonneuve & Larose, 1978, pp. 467–470.

17 Based on the Basque version in P. Delarue and M.-L. Tenèze, *Le Conte populaire français*, Maisonneuve & Larose, 1978.

18 D. Winnicott, *Playing and Reality*, Routledge, 2005.

19 S. Freud (1905), *Jokes and Their Relation to the Unconscious*, SE 8, Hogarth.

Chapter X

Lying and Popular Fiction

The Lying Contest: An Old Collective Response to Hard Times

Anna Angelopoulos

Our journey through the world of the folktale is drawing to a close. We are about to leave the sphere of fiction, of diversion, and put an end for the moment to the beneficial psychical stirrings they produced in us. The closing formulas of traditional folktales, usually harsher than those of the fairy tale, are often phrases such as "They lived happily ever after and we even happier." These formulas remind us very bluntly of reality, of the condition of the audience. The storyteller ends his narration with the words: "I was not there to see it, and neither were you, to believe it." Often, after the wedding at the palace, the storyteller addresses the audience: "They married and, if they are not dead, they are still living there," or else: "The celebrations lasted forty days; I was there too and they gave me gold coins, but when I opened the bag all there was in it was coal." Another common closing phrase is: "They ate and they drank, but gave us not a crumb," which became a Greek saying.

The traditional folktale is consoling, therapeutic and entertaining. And it lies, of course, since it takes us into an imaginary world where everything is possible, for reality is transformed to create fiction. The lie generates tales. But it is surprising to see how well the tale can, in turn, weave into its progression the question of the lie, and treat it as an integral part of itself, as would become obvious in "lying contests".

It is an old dream of humankind to be able to turn established values on their head. Misleading by nature, the folktale is an ideal vector. The Brothers Grimm revived a short tale in High German from the fourteenth century called "So istdiz von lügenen" ("This Is How the Lies Go"), which they renamed "Schlauraffenland", meaning "the upside-down world", and published under the title "The Story of Schlauraffen Land".[1] Here it is:

DOI: 10.4324/9781032674230-11

The Story of Schlauraffen Land

In the time of the Schlauraffen I went forth and saw Rome and the Lateran [Cathedral] hanging by a small silken thread, a man with no feet who won a race against a swift horse, and a keen sharp sword slicing through a bridge. I saw a young ass with a silver nose, which pursued two fast hares, and a huge linden tree on which hot cakes were growing. I saw a lean old goat, which carried at least a hundred cartloads of lard and sixty cartloads of salt. Have I told enough lies? I saw a cart ploughing without a horse or an ox, and a one-year-old child throwing four millstones from Ratisbonne to Trêves, then from Trêves to Strasburg. A hawk swam over the Rhine, and everyone found it natural. I heard fish making such a disturbance bickering with each other that it resounded as far as Heaven, and sweet honey flowed like water from a deep valley to the top of a high mountain, and these were strange things. There were two crows mowing a meadow, and I saw two gnats building a bridge, two doves tore a wolf to pieces, two children brought forth two [goat] kids, and two frogs threshed grain together. I saw two mice consecrating a bishop, and two cats scratching out a bear's tongue. A snail came running up and killed two furious lions. A barber was standing there shaving a woman's beard off, and two toddlers bade their mother to hold her tongue. There I saw two greyhounds which brought a mill out of the water, and a broken-down old horse beside it was telling them it was right. In the yard there were four horses threshing wheat with all their might, and two goats who were heating the stove, and a red cow pushed loaves of bread into the oven. Then a rooster crowed: "Cock-a-doodle-doo. The story is all told, cock-a-doodle-doo!"[2]

This tale does not invent one particular scenario; rather, it presents a dream of complete inversion. In this subversive animal fable that casts doubt on ecclesiastic power and parental power, the weak become strong, slow animals become swift, the obligation to work is lifted. What's more, the tale exaggerates all things, especially the abundance of food, contrasting with the severity of all too frequent scarcity existing at the time. "Have I told enough lies?", the storyteller asks the audience, thus drawing a clear line between telling a subversive tale and being a mythomaniac.

Considered a sin and condemned by morality, the lie opens a royal road to invention in fiction. We know that the lie can serve different purposes: to protect oneself, to be polite, to protect others. One can also lie by omission. These little acts of hypocrisy allow us to get along together, as long as they don't cross the line into mythomania.

Freud revealed the psychical aspect of lies, related to unconscious content. In his "Two Lies Told by Children",[3] he gives the example of two patients, young women whose analyses revealed that in their childhood one of them stole a few coins to buy paint for her Easter eggs and lied to cover it up, while the other lied and boasted inordinately at school. They were punished and reprimanded. The analytic work would reveal that, for unconscious reasons, they had both been, unknowingly, motivated by Oedipal passion. The first experienced the punishment imposed by her father as a refusal of affection; the second wanted to be worthy of a strongly idealised father. Lying is always addressed to someone and presupposes an emotion, as we can see in these two examples.

Without referring to the unconscious directly, it is its intimate sphere that the child most often protects by creating this subjective reality of the lie, by carving out a space of freedom when the pleasure principle is threatened, and punishment is imminent. Usually, the lie is a conscious construction, as a little girl explained when she was caught red-handed: "What I'm telling you is a little changed, but it's the beginning of the truth." This short tale reveals the close relation between the lie and subjective reality, and how the invention of the lie differs from fiction.

This aspect of the lie, the invention of another reality, makes it suited to play. By playing with the truth, the lie opens a creative space filled with pleasure and jubilation, a *transitional space*,[4] as we see in the particular tales that constitute the "lying contest". Here, the aim is not to reveal truth or to misuse a commonly held belief, but rather to confront the collective to the subjective.

The art of lying was a highly respected skill among traditional storytellers, and greatly admired by their listeners. Contests were held to let the most unbelievable lying tales compete, and it was an honour to be considered a great liar.

Thus, lying tournaments could be held during evening gatherings. Each participant had to tell the most enormous lies in the most unbelievable way possible, and so slyly as to cause his to cry "It's not true, it's a lie!" thereby eliminating him from the contest. Losing a match could cost a sack of wheat, paying for a round or paying a penalty. The three tales that follow provide fine examples of such tales, taken from a lying contest.

The Miller and the Boy

Once upon a time, there was a very old and very sick man who had a son. Feeling that his death was near, the old man called him to his bedside and said: "My son, when you will have grain to grind, never take it to a bald and beardless miller."

Soon afterwards, the old man died, leaving his son alone in the world. One day, the boy himself with grain to grind. He went to a miller and saw that he was bald and beardless.

Seeing that he was a young boy, no doubt naïve and innocent, the miller said: "I will make a deal with you. We will have a lying contest. If you win, I will grind your grain and won't take any payment, but if you lose, I will keep your grain and you will have nothing!" The child agreed, saying: "In that case, you go first."

This is the story told by the miller.

The Miller's Story[5]

When I was a child, I had the pleasure of witnessing my grandfather's baptism ceremony. I was in a corner of the room. The ceremony was magnificent. But all at once, the priest realised that he didn't have the oil for anointing the infant.

Everyone starts to look for sacramental oil high and low, but no oil is to be found. Then, the priest suddenly says: "But of course, the oil is in heaven, with the Lord." So I decide to go and bring it back. I leave the house and look around in the street, but I see no high branch or staircase – nothing, in fact – that I could use to reach Heaven. Suddenly, I see an enormous squash whose stalk rises into the sky. So I grab hold of the stalk and, leaf by leaf, I climb all the way to the clouds. And there, in the sky, I notice that I forgot my bottle. I must go down again.

And what do I see? That the stalk has disappeared. A donkey came by and ate it. What am I to do? What can I do? I look and look all around me; there is no way down. Suddenly, I hit upon the idea of pulling on a thread that hangs from my clothes, and I kept on pulling and dropping down the thread to see if it reaches the Earth. But the thread is too short. I double the length of it and try again, but it is still too short. Finally, I triple its length and, that time, it goes all the way down to Earth.

So I start to glide down; I come all the way down and there I realise that my bottle has been stolen; I don't have it anymore. What can I do? What can I try? That's when I feel something on my neck. I take it between my fingers, and I see that it's a flea. And I think: "This is my answer!" I kill the flea and I slit it open. I take its skin and blow into it to make it swell; I blow and blow until I've made a bag. I go up into the sky with my bag and I fill it with oil, then I come down and I return to the place of the baptism. I give the oil to the priest and the ceremony continues. It was a magnificent ceremony and I stayed in a corner of the room to watch it until the end.

"This is my story," said the miller. "Now it's your turn."

The Boy's Story

When the Devil died, far away in China, there was a cabbage so huge that no pot big enough could be found in which to boil it. All the blacksmiths and all the gypsies in the world went there to try to make a big enough pot. I said to myself: "Why don't I try my luck too?" I mounted my horse and started out. But after a while my horse refused to continue on. I climbed down from the saddle; I looked him over and I saw that he had a wound on his back that surely made him suffer. As I looked around me, I saw a huge walnut tree laden with nuts; below it, a crowd of people were throwing stones and clods of earth up in the tree, to make the walnuts fall on the ground. I took a walnut leaf and placed it on my horse's wound; he was healed instantly, and we continued on, on our way to China. Now I'll make it short. When we arrived in China, the Devil helped me. We built a huge pot. We cooked the cabbage in it and there was a great feast. Everyone ate cabbage and then we left.

On the way back, I passed the walnut tree we saw on our way there. And what did I see? At the top of the tree, on the branches, there were huge fields, and in the fields men with oxen were planting, ploughing, harvesting and threshing grain, on the tree top.

"What had happened?" the miller asked.

"I didn't understand right then," said the boy, "but thinking about it later I came to suppose that all those stones and clods of earth the mob threw into the tree to make the nuts fall ended up forming fields at the top of the tree, those very fields that were now being ploughed. I continued on my way until I had to stop to quench my thirst. I finally found a fountain, but I had neither flask nor bottle to fill. But since I was really very thirsty, I decided to take a part of my skull and use it as a container from which to drink. Thus, I drank the water, quenched my thirst and continued on my way. Then, after a while, I scratched my head and realised that I was touching my brain. And I said to myself: "My God! I forgot a piece of my skull at the fountain, I have to go back. So I turned back. I went to the fountain and just as I got there, I saw a fox running off with the piece of my skull that I had left there. "Well," I said to myself: "that's too bad then; first, I have to go and have the grain ground, and after that I'll take care of the fox."

– But how will you find the fox? the miller asked. He must be very far by now, with that piece of your skull.

– Oh, so you believed me! You've lost. Give me the flour and don't worry about the fox.

The miller had to admit he lost. He gave the boy his flour so he could take it home.

The King and His Sister[6]

Once upon a time there was a king who had a daughter he adored. The king was a great liar and for that reason he wanted to marry his daughter to the greatest liar in the world. Men came from all over the world to try to win his daughter's hand in marriage. But none of them was able to outdo the king at lying.

One day, a peasant came to the palace. He was young and very intelligent. This is the story he told.

My father was two hundred years old and I was only three hundred when I went to get wreaths of flowers for his wedding. On the way, I accidentally stepped on a turtle. She flew away, carrying me off on her back, all the way to the sky. Once we got there, she left me. I looked around me, I paddled in the clouds, I saw the angels coming up and going down as they pleased, but there was no way for me to go back down. After a while, I thought of taking a thread of my clothing and attaching it securely to a corner of heaven; hanging from the thread, I started my descent. While I was sliding down, it started to rain hard. To protect myself, I tied a knot in the thread and hid under it. Thanks to this clever scheme, not a drop of rain fell on me. Once the rain stopped, I continued to climb down and arrived on the ground. And there, what do I see? The turtle! I rush to get a hold of it. I hear "pom, pom" and I see a piece of paper come out of her backside. And then she disappears once again.

I take the piece of paper, unfold it and what do I read, Your Highness? "The king's sister cheats with the scales at her store."

"What!" exclaimed the king. "You dare to call my sister a cheat? You're the one who is a dirty liar!"

– Yes, the peasant said, I am a dirty liar, but you believed me and you lost. So you have to grant me your daughter's hand in marriage.

The peasant married the princess and they lived happily ever after, and we happier still.

\What magic trick allowed the eruption of reality into the lying tale told to the miller and the king? The losers were seized by an unexpected emotion connected to a subjective reality.

In the case of the miller, he is confronted with the "brainless" boy whose desire to grind his grain makes him risk losing his skull; this confronts the miller with the unbearable representation of a missing skull, lost forever. This vision, castrating in the wider sense of the word, indicates above all an element of psychic fragility specific to the miller, since he is presented as bald and beardless, and therefore as prohibited by the father – a prohibition the child successfully defies.

Given the accent placed on the skull in this tale, we should mention that folklorists consider bald and beardless characters as having a demonic dimension.

In the case of the king, who wants to marry his daughter to an even greater liar than himself, the attack on his sister's honesty diverts him from his plan by suddenly plunging him in the infantile. Indeed, this accusation is made in the little note that comes out of the turtle's backside with a little fart. It is the sister of the king's childhood who is being attacked, and he feels duty bound to defend her. This affect emerging from the region of the infantile pulls him out of the sphere of lying fiction.

Lying contests always take place in a context of hard daily reality, of work done together at evening gatherings. The contests are each a collective creative act that calls upon the subjective in a unique manner. These fictitious creations are, in a manner of speaking, an art of the poor, *arte povera*, practised in traditional communities.

Here, dear reader, ends our journey into the world of folktale and fabulation, with its meanders that never lead you astray.

Notes

1 The Brothers Grimm, "The Story of Schlauraffen Land", in M. Hunt (Trans.), *Grimm's Fairy Tales*, Maplewood Books, 2013.
2 This tale has enjoyed great popularity since antiquity. In the Middle Ages, one of the most detailed descriptions of this imaginary land was given in the thirteenth century, in the "Fable of Plenty", in which people are paid – but not to work – to sleep, and houses are made of fish, of lard, of sausages and so on . . .
3 S. Freud (1911–1912), "Two Lies Told by Children", in *The Case of Schreber*, SE 12, Hogarth, pp. 303–310.
4 Space between internal and external reality, shared by two people.
5 Told by Dimitrios Evangelidis, "Symikta (Mixtures)", *Laografia*, Vol. 2, 1910–1911, pp. 475–477. Origin: Epirus. The narrative duplicates, word for word, a truncated twelfth-century Byzantine chant from the Saint Dionysios monastery on Mount Athos, codex 301. The tale was published by A. Papadopoulos-Kerameas, *Laografia*, Vol. 2, 1909, pp. 567–572. This lying contest with a prize is classified in the ATU international index as ATU 1920, "Contest in Lying".
6 In *Laografia*, 1909, p. 57 and following, Georges Megas points out a Byzantine tale similar to this, classified as type AT 852 in the international index.

Bibliography

Aarne, A. and Thompson, S., *The Types of Folktales: A Classification and Bibliography*, 2nd edition, revised, FF Communications, No. 184. Academia Scientiarum Fennica, 1961. [AT]

Aarne, A., *The Trilingual Man and His Curious Wife*, FFC No. 15, Hamina, 1914.

Abraham, N. and Torok, M. *The Shell and the Kernel*, University of Chicago Press, 1994.

Andersen, H. C., *The Little Match Girl*, Dial Books, 2002.

Andrews, J. B., *The Folk-Lore Record*, Vol. X 1881.

Angélopoulos, A., "Blanche-Neige ou l'enfant- ancêtre", *Revue des études néo-hélléniques*, 2, Daedalus, 1992, pp. 170–188.

Angelopoulos, A., "Conte oral et représentation de l'impensable", in P. Chemla (Ed.), *Transmettre*, Érès, 2016.

Angelopoulos, A., "Figurations de l'énigme", in P. Chemla (Ed.), *L'imaginaire dans la clinique, psychiatrie, psychanalyse, psychothérapie institutionnelle*, Erès, 2020.

Angelopoulos, A., "Fuseau des cendres" (Ash Spindle), in "Cendrillons" (Cinderellas), *Cahiers de Littérature Orale*, No. 25, 1989, pp. 71–95.

Angelopoulos, A., "L'hirondelle et la Mort", *Ethnologie Française*, 23 (1), 1993, pp. 104–112.

Angelopoulos, A., "Le conte d'Eros et Psyché dans la littérature orale", *Topique, Revue Freudienne*, No. 75, 2001, pp. 155–169.

Angelopoulos, A., "Le Rêve typique et le conte", *Cahiers de littérature orale*, 51, 2002.

Angelopoulos, A., "Un Homme nu le couteau à la main", *Cahiers de littérature orale*, 46, *Le mort reconnaissant*, INALCO, 2000.

Angelopoulos, A., *Contes de la nuit grecque*, José Corti, 2013.

Angelopoulos, A., *Paramythokores*, Hestia, 1991.

Angelopoulos, A. and Brouskou, A., *Descriptive Catalogue of Greek Fairy Tales: Types and Versions*, I.A.E.N., F.N.R.S. (in Greek), 1999.

Anonymous, *Les Mille et Une Nuits*, A. Galland (Trans.), Flammarion, 2004.

Anzieu, D., *Psychic Envelopes*, Karnac Books, 1990.

Apollodorus, *The Library*, Book 3, J. G. Frazer (Trans.), Harvard University Press, 1921.

Apollodorus, *The Library*, Books 1–3.9, Loeb Classical Library, 1921.

Apuleius, *Metamorphoses (The Golden Ass)*, A. Hanson (Trans.), Harvard University Press, 1989.

Aristotle, *Poetics*, Book XVI.

Aristotle, *The Poetics of Aristotle*, S. H. Butcher (Trans.), Macmillan, 1922.

Athanassoula, E., *There was . . . There Was Not . . .*, Academy of Athens, 1929.

Aulagnier, P., *The Violence of Interpretation*, A. Sheridan (Trans.), The New Library of Psychoanalysis, 2001.

Basile, G., *The Pentamerone*, Franklin Classics, 2018.

Belmont, N., "L'enfant cuit", in "Le Motif en sciences humaines", *Ethnologie Française*, Vol. 25, Armand Colin, 1995.

Belmont, N., "Orphée dans le miroir du conte merveilleux" (Orpheus through the Looking Glass of the Fairy Tale), *L'Homme*, 25 (93), 1985, pp. 59–82.

Beneviste, E., *Indo-European Language and Society*, University of Miami Press, 1973.

Bettelheim, B., "Individual and Mass Behavior in Extreme Situations", *The Journal of Abnormal and Social Psychology*, 38 (4), 417–452, 1943.

Bettelheim, B., *The Uses of Enchantment: The Meaning and Importance of Fairy Tales*, Vintage, 2010.

Boccacio, G., *Genealogy of the Pagan Gods* (fourteenth century), Harvard University Press, 2011.

Bonnefoy, Y. (Ed.), *Dictionnaire des mythologies*, Flammarion, 1981.

Bottingheimer, R., "Luckless, Witless and Filthy-Foote: A Sociological Study and Publishing History Analysis of the Lazy Boy", *Journal of American Folklore*, 106 (421), 1993, pp. 259–284.

Brothers Grimm, "The Story of Schlauraffen Land", in M. Hunt (Trans.), *Grimm's Fairy Tales*, Maplewood Books, 2013.

Calame-Griaule, G., *Contes cruels, contes tendres du Sahel nigérien. Le langage du conte*, Gallimard, 2002.

Calderon de la Barca, P., *Psyche and Cupid*, an "auto sacramental" musical play (seventeenth century).

Castoriadis, C., *The Imaginary Institution of Society*, MIT Press, 1998.

Chamoiseau, P., *La matière de l'absence*, Paris: Seuil, 2016.

Chamoiseau, P., *Le conteur, la nuit et le panier*, Seuil: 2021.

Chamoiseau, P., *Le vent du nord dans les fougères glacées*, Seuil, 2022.

Chardenet, V., *Destins de garçons en marge du symbolique: Jean Le Sot et ses avatars*, José Corti, 2010.

Cosquin, E., *Les Contes indiens et l'Occident*, Edouard Champion, 1922.

Crews, C., *Judeo-Spanish Folktales in the Balkans*, 1935; Textos judeo-españoles de Salonica y Sarajevo, 1979; in A. Angelopoulos, *Contes judéo-espagnols des Balkans*, José Corti, 2009.

Dawkins, R. M., *Modern Greek in Asia Minor*, Cambridge University Press, 1916.

de la Fontaine, J., *The Loves of Cupid and Psyche* (1669), Rare Books Club, 2013.

De Lincy, L., *Seven Wise Masters*, after A. L. Deslongchamps, *Essay on Indian Fables and Their Introduction in Europe*, Techener, 1838.

De Macedo, H., *De l'amour à la pensée*, L'Harmattan, 1994.

Delarue, P., *Le conte populaire français*, PU MIDI, 2017.

Delarue, P. and Tenèze, M. L., 2002. *Le conte populaire français*. Maisonneuve & Larose, 4 volumes: 1957, 1976, 1985 and 2000. [CPF]

Delaunay, P., *Les quatre transferts*, Fédération des Ateliers de Psychanalyse, 2012.

Delcourt, M., *Oedipus, The Legend of a Conqueror*, Michigan State University Press, 2020.

Detienne, M., "Adonis et les Adonies", in *Dictionnaire des mythologies et des religions des sociétés traditionnelles et du monde antique*, Flammarion, 1981.

Détienne, M., *Apollon, le couteau à la main. Une approche expérimentale du polythéisme grec*, Gallimard, 1998.

Détienne, M., "Entre bêtes et dieux", *Nouvelle Revue de Psychanalyse*, No. 6, 1972.

Devereux, G., *Baubo, la vulve mythique*, Payot, 2021.

Dimakopoulou, A., *Pâle Rossignol*, Apolis, 2009.

Djéribi, M., "Oeil d'amour, oeil d'envie" ("Eye of Love, Eye of Envy"), *Nouvelle Revue de Psychanalyse*, 38, Gallimard, 1988, pp. 99–110.

Dolto, F., *Paroles pour adolescents ou Le complexe du homard*, Gallimard Folio, 2007.

Evangelidis, D., "Symikta (Mixtures)", *Laografia*, Vol. 2, 1910–1911, pp. 475–477.

Ferenczi, S., "The Principle of Relaxation and Neocatharsis" (1929) *Final Contributions to the Problems and Methods of Psycho-Analysis*, Routledge, 2018.

Folklore Studies, Hellenic Folklore Research Centre, Academy of Athens. [FS]

Freud, S., *The Standard Edition of the Complete Psychological Works of Sigmund Freud*, Hogarth, 1953–1974.

Freud, S. (1886–1899), *Project for a Scientific Psychology*, SE 1, Hogarth.

Freud, S. (1900–1901), *The Interpretation of Dreams*, SE 4–5, Hogarth.

Freud, S. (1901), *Psychopathology of Everyday Life*, SE 6, Hogarth.

Freud, S. (1901–1905), *A Case of Hysteria*, SE 7, Hogarth.

Freud, S. (1905), *Jokes and Their Relation to the Unconscious*, SE 8, Hogarth.

Freud, S. (1911–1912), "Two Lies Told by Children", in *The Case of Schreber*, SE 12, Hogarth.

Freud, S. (1915), "Thoughts for the Times on War and Death", *On the History of the Psycho-Analytic Movement* (1914–1916), SE 14, Hogarth.

Freud, S. (1918), *The Taboo of Virginity*, SE 11, Hogarth.

Freud, S. (1931), *Female Sexuality*, SE 21, Hogarth.

Freud, S. (1932–1936), *New Introductory Lectures on Psycho-Analysis*, SE 22, Hogarth.

Freud, S. (1940), *An Outline of Psycho-Analysis*, Penguin Classics, 2003.

Freud, S. and Breuer, J., *Studies on Hysteria*, Penguin Books, 2004.

Frontisci-Ducroux, F., *Arbres filles et garçons fleurs*, Seuil, 2017.

Gail, H., *The Road to Rembetika*, Denise Harvey, 1973.

Gedeon, S., *L'Homme*, 105, XXVIII (1), Jan.–Mar. 1988, pp. 49–63.

Gedeon, S., *Symaïka*, Athens, 1974.

GEM, "In Search of the Normal Man"] published as "Health and Life", *Le Coq Héron*, 2018/3, No. 234, Erès, pp. 11–16.

GEM La Locomotive, *À la recherche de l'homme normal*, Éditions D'une, 2021.

Gendre-Dusuzeau, S., "Le miroir de l'envie" (C. Guy), *Le Coq-Héron*, No. 228, Érès, March 2017.

Gow, A. S. F. and Page, D. L., *The Greek Anthology: Hellenistic Epigraphs, The Garland of Philip*, Vol. II, Cambridge University Press, 1968.

Grimal, P., *Dictionnaire de la mythologie grecque et romaine*, PUF, 1969.

Grimm, J. and Grimm, W., *Grimm's Fairy Tales*, Calla Editions, 2010. [GFT]

Hassoun, P., "L'envie et le désir: les faux frères", *Autrement*, 1998. p. 19.

Hesiod, *Hesiod's Theogony*, CreateSpace Publishing, 2010.

Hesiod, *The Theogeny*, SMK Books, 2012.

Homer, *The Odyssey*, Book II, W. W. Norton, 2018.

Jouvet, M., *The Paradox of Sleep: The Story of Dreaming*, MIT Press, 2001.

Kaës, R., *Contes et divans*, Dunod, 2022.

Kambouroglou, A. in A. Angelopoulos and A. Brouskou, *Descriptive Catalogue of Greek Fairy Tales: Types and Versions*, I.A.E.N., F.N.R.S. (in Greek), 1999.

Karanikola-Christofi, A., *Symaïka*, Vol. II, Athens, 1974.

Kentro Erevnis tis Ellinikis Laographias tis Akadimias Athinon [Folklore Archive of the Hellenic Folklore Research Centre, Academy of Athens]. [KEEL]

Klein, M., *Envy and Gratitude*, M. R. Khan (Ed.), Random House, 1997.

Kritikos, P., "Moscambaris", in "Contes de Patmos", *Laografia*, 16, 1957.

Kury, S., *I Talk to Animals*, TV programme, April 2017.

Lacan, J., *The Seminar of Jacques Lacan: Four Fundamental Concepts of Psychoanalysis*, Book XI, W. W. Norton, 1998.

Lacan, J., Didier-Weill, A. and Hassoun, P., "Envy and Desire, a False Alliance", *Autrement*, 24, Special Issue, 1998.

Laplanche, J. and Pontalis, J. B., *The Language of Psychoanalysis*, D. Nicholson-Smith (Trans.), W. W. Norton, 1973).
Le petit Robert dictionary.
Lessana, M. M., *Entre mère et fille: un ravage*, Hachette, Pluriel Psychanalyse, 2009.
Lévi-Strauss, C., *Structural Anthropology*, Basic Books, 1974.
Loraux, N., *The Experiences of Tiresias*, P. Wissing (Trans.), Princeton University Press, 1995.
Loukatos, D., *Aetiological Tales of Modern Greek Proverbs*, Ermis, 1972.
Lüthi, M., *Once Upon a Time*, Indiana University Press, 1976.
Mannoni, O., *Clefs pour l'imaginaire*, Seuil, 2016.
Megas, G. A., *Das Märchen von Amor und Psyche in der Griechischen Volksüberlieferung*, Collection Academy of Athens, 1971.
Megas, G. A., *Folktales of Greece*, Hestia, 1971.
Megas, G. A., Angelopoulos, A., Brouskou, A., Kaplanoglou, M. and Katrinaki, E., *Catalogue of Greek Magic Folktales*, FF Communications, No. 303. Academia Scientiarum Fennica, 2012. [CGMF]
"Muscambre fils de l'inceste" in *L'Homme*, 28 (105), pp. 49–63.
Naumann Mavrogordato, I., *Es war einmal, Neugriechische Volksärchen*, Istanbul, 1942.
O'Dwyer De Macedo, H., *Letters to a Young Psychoanalyst*, Routledge, 2017.
Ovid, *Les Métamorphoses*, M. Cosnay (Trans.), Le Livre de poche, 2020.
Ovid, *Metamorphoses*, Oxford Paperbacks, 2008.
Ovid, *Metamorphoses*, Book 4, Oxford World's Classics, 2008.
Ovid, *The Metamorphoses*, Book 10, A. S. Kleine (Trans.), CreateSpace Publishing, 2014.
Pankow, G., *L'Homme et sa psychose* (*Man and His Psychosis*), Aubier Montaigne, 1977.
Pankow, G., *L'homme et sa psychose* (*Man and His Psychosis*), Flammarion, 1993.
Panofsky, E., *Essais d'iconologie*, Gallimard, 1967.
Papadopoulos-Kerameas, A., *Laografia*, Vol. 2, 1909, pp. 567–572.
Perrault, C., *Perrault's Fairy Tales*, Dover Publications, 1969.
Plato, *Theaetetus*, The Liberal Arts Press, 1955.
Polack, J.-C., Pain, F. and Sivadon, D. (directors), *François Tosquelles*, film, 1989.
Politis, N., *Paradoseis*, S. Laografia, 1915–1916.
Propp, V., *Historical Roots of the Fairy Tale*, Western Washington University, 1997.
Propp, V., *Morphology of the Folktale*, University of Texas Press, 1968
Propp, V., *Morphology of the Folk Tale*, Martino Fine Books, 2015.
Propp, V., "Ritual Laughter in Folklore", in *Theory and History of Folklore*, University of Minnesota Press, 1984.
Purser, L. C., *Apuleius, the Story of Cupid and Psyche*, Aristide Caratzas Publisher, 1983.
Pushkin, A., *The Tale of Tsar Saltan*, Methuen Publishing, 1974.
Quignard, P., *Sex and Terror*, C. Turner (Trans.), Seagull Books, 2011.
Reinach, S., *Cults, Myths and Religions*, Ulan Press, 2012.
Riga, G. A., "Simigdalenious" (Mr. Simigdali), Culture populaire de Skiathos, *Hellinika*, 1962, Vol. II: 5.
Roheim, G., "The Language of Birds", *Fire in the Dragon and Other Psychoanalytic Essays on Folklore*, Princeton University Press, 1992.
Roheim, G., *The Gates of the Dream*, International Universities Press, 1969.
Seferis, G., "The Cistern" (1932), A. Anagnostopoulos (Trans.), Belknap Press, 1975.
Seferis, G., "Last Stop" (October 5, 1944), E. Keeley and P. Sherrard (Trans.), *Collected Poems*, Princeton University Press, 1967.
Sissa, G., *L'Âme est un corps de femme*, Odile Jacob, 2000.
Soriano, M., *Les Contes de Perrault*, Gallimard, 1968.
Stamouli-Saranti, E., "Moshoplasmenos" (Pressed Musk), *Thrakika*, 1941.
Straparola, G. F., *Le piacevoli notti* (*The Facetious Nights*), Salerno, 2000.

Straparola, G. F., "The Trial of the Serpent" (Fourth Night, Second Fable), W. G. Waters (Trans.), *Nights of Straparola*, Vol. I, Pook Press, 2018.

Swahn, J.-O., *The Tale of Cupid and Psyche*, CWK Gleerup, 1954.

Syllogi Mathiton (Collected from schoolchildren, archived at the KEEL). [SM]

Thompson, S., *Motif-Index of Folk Literature: A Classification of Narrative Elements in Folktales, Ballads, Myths, Fables, Medieval Romances, Exempla, Fabliaux, Jest-Books and Local Legends* (6 volumes), Indiana University Press, 1975.

Thompson, S., *The Folktale*, University of California Press, 1977.

Thornhill, M., *Indian Fairy Tales*, Forgotten Books, 2018.

Togethoff, E. (1922), *Studienzum Märchentypus von Amor und Psyche*, Generic Publisher, 2019.

Uther, H. J., *The Types of International Folktales*, Academia Scientiarum Fennica, 2004. [ATU]

Valabrega, J.-P., *Le problème anthropologique du phantasme*, Seuil, 1967.

Verdier, Y., *Le Petit Chaperon Rouge dans la Tradition Orale*, Allia, 2024.

Vernant, J.-P., *Les jardins d'Adonis*, Gallimard, 1977.

Vernant, J.-P., *Myth and Tragedy in Ancient Greece*, Zone Books, 1990.

Vernant, J.-P., *The Universe, the Gods, and Mortals*, Profile Books, 2001.

Vernant, J.-P. and Vidal-Naquet, P., "Ambiguity and Reversal", *Tragedy and Myth in Ancient Greece*, Zone Books, 1990.

Winnicott, D., *Playing and Reality*, Routledge, 2005.

Zaltzman, N., "Le point aveugle de l'énigme", *Topique*, 3 (84), 2003, pp. 201–206.

Zipes, J., *The Great Fairy Tale Tradition: From Straparola and Basile to the Brothers Grimm*, W. W. Norton, 2001.

Zygouris, R., "Sortilèges de la scène traumatique" ("The Spell Cast by the Traumatic Scene"), in *L'amour paradoxal ou une promesse de separation*, Éditions des Crépuscules, 2023.

Index

For Product Safety Concerns and Information please contact our EU
representative GPSR@taylorandfrancis.com
Taylor & Francis Verlag GmbH, Kaufingerstraße 24, 80331 München, Germany

* 9 7 8 1 0 3 2 6 7 4 1 7 9 *